The Ultimate Keto Instant Pot Cookbook

The Ultimate Keto Instant Pot Cookbook

1000 Easy and Foolproof Keto Diet Recipes for Your Instant Pot Electric Pressure Cooker on a Budget | 21-Day Meal Plan to Help You Manage Your Figure

Lawrence V. Stevens

CONTENT

Introduction

The keto diet has become very popular recently because of its many benefits. The keto diet restricts carbohydrates and emphasizes eating plenty of fats.

The Instant Pot is a modern electric pressure cooker that allows you to cook a variety of dishes in no time at all. As a busy professional, learning how to use the Instant Pot can help you save time, money, and effort in the kitchen.

The Ultimate Keto Instant Pot Cookbook includes more than 1000 delicious keto recipes that will guide you through the process of using the Instant Pot.

In this book, you'll discover how to cook your favorite keto dishes at home and much more. Take advantage of the latest kitchen gadget and cook delicious meals for you and your family!

This book will give you a number of keto recipes that are not only easy to follow, but also provide you with instructions on how to prepare these dishes in the Instant Pot. All of the recipes are also low carb, and you will not need to add any carbs to them. For people who want to lose weight, these dishes are great options as they will not pile on your body more calories than it can handle. You can find a number of keto diet recipes online, but why waste time on searching when you can have them all in this book?

Some of the things you will learn in this cookbook include:

- What is Keto Diet?
- Benefits of the Keto Diet
- Foods to Eat and Avoid on Keto Diet
- Tips for Keto Success
- What is an Instant Pot?
- Benefits of Using the Instant Pot

- Functions of the Instant Pot
- The Procedure of Using the Instant Pot
- Cleaning the Instant Pot
- Troubleshooting and Cooking Guide
- Instant Pot FAQs
- Recipes

With this cookbook, they have everything they need to get started as soon as possible.

Happy cooking!

Chapter 1: Keto Basics

What is Keto Diet?

It is a low-carb, high-fat, and moderate-protein diet. It's a way of eating that helps you get to your ideal body weight.

The Keto diet aims to force the body into a state of metabolism called as ketosis. Ketosis occurs when the body produces energy by burning fat instead of carbs.

How Does the Keto Diet Work?

The most fundamental principle of the ketogenic diet is that it mimics starvation. Our bodies are designed to store carbohydrates in our muscles and liver. When we limit the amount of carbohydrates we eat, our bodies start to use up these stores, releasing free fatty acids into the bloodstream. The keto forces the body ketosis state of metabolism.

But how does this happen? You have to eat a lot of fat and very few carbs. The ratio should be about 75% fat, 20% protein, and 5% carbohydrates. This will force your body to generate ketones in the liver and burn fatty acids for energy.

Benefits of the Keto Diet

Weight loss–The biggest benefit that comes when you start using keto is that your weight gets reduced drastically. This is because this diet does not involve anything sweet or less healthy. This is made for people who want to lose weight. When you start this diet, you will find that the rate of fat burning is high and you don't get hungry in a short time.

Visible results–The other good thing about the keto diet is that it provides visible results in no time. You don't have to wait for weeks or months to start seeing some changes in your body because these changes happen within few days. You will find yourself getting slimmer and your health will improve too.

Reset your body–When you regularly use this diet plan, you will notice that your body gets re-set in a good way. This is because keto works to flush out the bad and replace it with good in the form of nutrients. Most people who go for keto diet find that they are healthier than before and their body's immune system also improves significantly.

Prevents acne–Many people have not found any solution to their problem of acne until they started the keto diet. This is because this diet does not allow you to eat or drink anything that can cause acne in the body. When you give up processed food, your body will get rid of all the bad and start producing good skin cells.

The solution to your diabetes problem– You don't have to worry about your diabetes when you are using this diet because it improves the level of insulin in the body. This makes it easy for you to regulate sugar in your blood and thus keeps all other complications at bay.

The solution to your heart problems– When you use this diet, you will notice that the risk of having a heart attack or stroke will decrease significantly. This is because this diet helps the body get rid of cholesterol and thus prevents heart ailments.

Feel full and energetic–If you are using keto, you will find that you don't feel hungry at all. This is because this diet makes it easy for the body to work efficiently and burn fat quickly. When the body is able to do this, it feels energized and you don't get tired quickly.

The solution to your bad complexion–If you are having a bad complexion and don't know why, the answer is very simple. It is because of the food you eat. You need to stop eating so many processed foods and eliminate carbs from your diet. This will allow your body to get rid of toxins and make sure that your complexion stays good.

The solution to your hormonal problem– If you have been suffering from hormonal imbalance, you need to use this diet because it resolves this problem in no time. This is because you eat good and beneficial foods when you are on keto, and this makes sure that your hormones are well regulated.

The solution to your immune system– If you want to improve your immunity, you should try this diet because it makes sure that the body gets all the nutrients it requires for a strong immune system. This diet flushes out toxins quickly and allows for better absorption of nutrients in the body.

Your mental health will also improve– When you use keto, your mental health will also improve significantly. This is because this diet makes sure that your body gets all the nutrients it needs to make you feel good. If you have had trouble concentrating because of poor mental health, this diet will solve that problem for you.

The solution to your various digestion problems–If you are suffering from constipation and other digestion problems, you should try using keto. This diet makes sure that the absorption rate in your body improves and thus allows for easy digestion and prevents constipation and other issues related to it.

The best thing about this diet is that it allows you to eat all kinds of food but with less carbs. This works well for almost anyone who wants to lose weight or improve their health in any possible way.

Foods to Eat

Non-Starchy Vegetables

- Radishes
- Cucumber
- Endive
- Celery stalk
- Zucchini
- Asparagus
- Lettuce
- Bamboo shoots
- Spinach
- Kale
- Chives

Healthy Fats

- Monounsaturated (olive, macadamia and avocado oil)
- Polyunsaturated Omega-3 (seafood and fatty fish)
- Saturated (goose fat, tallow, clarified butter/ ghee, coconut oil, duck fat, lard, butter, and chicken fat)

Dressings

- Creamy Caesar
- Ranch
- Blue cheese
- Balsamic vinegar
- Apple cider vinegar

Fruits, e.g. Avocado, berries

Protein

Meat: Goat, beef, lamb, and other wild game

Fish: Cod, halibut, tuna, salmon, trout, flounder, mackerel, snapper, and catfish.

Poultry: Chicken meat, duck meat, and quail meat

Shellfish: Squid, clams, scallops, lobster, mussels, crab, and oysters

Sausage and bacon

Whole Eggs

Peanut butter

Pork products

Spices

- Black pepper
- Cayenne pepper
- Oregano
- Sage
- Thyme
- Rosemary
- Sea salt
- Basil
- Parsley
- Cumin

Dairy Products

- Heavy whipping cream
- Whole milk yogurt (unsweetened)
- Cream cheese

Nuts and Seeds

Macadamia nuts, pine nuts, walnuts, sunflower seeds, sesame seeds, hemp seeds, pumpkin seeds, pecans, hazelnuts, and almonds

Beverages

- Water
- Unsweetened herbal tea
- Unsweetened coconut milk
- Decaf coffee
- Unsweetened soy milk
- Unsweetened herbal tea
- Unsweetened almond milk

Foods to Avoid

- All grains, pastas, and breads
- Beans, lentils, and other legumes
- Corn
- Potatoes
- Most fresh and dried fruits
- Juice and soda
- Milk
- Pastries
- Pizza
- Maple syrup, honey, agave, and table sugar

Tips for Keto Success

Limit Carbohydrates

Since the keto diet is a low-carb diet, obviously, you need to reduce your consumption of carbohydrates. This is the key that will help you achieve ketosis.

This can be a big challenge at first, especially if you are used to including carbs in your daily diet.

Calculate Calories Consumption

This is very important while on the keto diet. Carbs are almost everywhere out there, and you need to keep track of all that you eat. The way to determine how much you should eat is by considering your basal metabolic rate. This is the number of calories you would burn by doing nothing at all on a regular day.

Track Progress

If you are not sure whether you have reached ketosis or not, you should make use of a ketone meter, which can be purchased in drugstores. Some testers measure ketones in the breath, urine, and blood. The one that measures ketones in the blood is the most accurate, but also the most expensive.

Manage Electrolytes

Electrolytes are of great essence on the keto diet as they are removed from the body system.

Ensure that that you take enough potassium, magnesium, and sodium to curb excessive hunger, cramps, water retention, headaches, and cravings.

Drink Water

Among the common keto diet side effects, is dehydration. Dehydration can often lead to symptoms such as headaches and muscle aches. To keep yourself in the best health, drink up loads of water and replenish your electrolytes. You should, therefore, drink lots of water to keep your body hydrated.

Eat Only When Hungry

When on a keto diet, you should only eat when hungry. Eating any time, especially when not hungry, or for fun, slows down weight loss and reduces ketosis.

Increase Physical Activity

Anyone using the ketogenic diet should know that just like with any other weight loss diet program, diet is not effective on its own. You also need to get moving and to engage in regular exercise. If you are more active, it will be easier for your body to reach ketosis.

Enough Sleep and Rest

The stress level in a person is also a factor in losing weight. When you are more stressed, the level of cortisol increases, which in turn causes weight gain or retention.

Rest is also another very important factor. Most people require seven to nine hours of sleep for proper rest of the body each night.

Be Determined and Consistent

As with any other diet program, you need to have both determination and consistency to achieve your goals with the ketogenic diet program. You cannot reach your weight loss objectives if you are not determined to succeed and if you are not consistent in following the diet's strict rules.

Chapter 2: Instant Pot Unmasked

What is an Instant Pot?

The Instant Pot is a modern electric pressure cooker that allows you to cook a variety of dishes in no time at all. It features a simple and intuitive control panel with digital timer and temperature settings. The Instant Pot is easy to use and clean, the lid features a small and removable pot-in-pot that can be used as a steam tray. The Instant Pot can cook meals that require long cooking times at high pressure, while bringing the ingredients to temperature faster than on stovetop. The device also has a sauté setting that lets you brown foods such as onions or garlic before pressure cooking without dirtying another dish.

Benefits of Using the Instant Pot

Multifunctional

The Instant Pot can be used be used for many cooking functions. It can be used as a pressure cooker, slow cooker, warming pot and rice cooker. It is also used to bake and also make yogurt. This makes it an all-in-one appliance which saves you the need to buy other appliances.

No Mess, Easy Clean

You have almost no mess to clean and wash after you are done with cooking because you have only used one pot for everything, which gets clean in no time.

Instant Pot comes with a removable stainless-steel inner cooking basket. Just simply remove it and place in the dishwasher or rinse with soapy water. A simple wipe-down with a cloth on the outside and that's it. It spares you from heavy cleaning of your pots and pans.

Energy Efficient & Safe

Instant Pot is capable of cooking your foods fast using high-pressure steam and generating a high temperature; it can save up to 70% of electric consumption by taking less time to cook. It has been designed to concentrate energy only on cooking the added ingredients to prevent energy waste.

Perfectly Cooked Meals

With the Instant Pot, you can make all types of perfectly cooked foods like pot roast in one pot. You can then "Keep Warm" using the 24-hour programmable timer. It spares you from using a skillet to brown your meat and sears in the juices. You won't need to be home to turn it to "Keep Warm" setting after the cooking process is over, as the device will do that by itself. You can come home to perfectly cooked pot roast that is tender and succulent without falling apart into smithereens.

Food Retains More Nutrients

When pressure cooking, heat is distributed more evenly, and less water is used in the processing, so nutrients are not leached away. Not only does food retain its nutrients, but it also retains its colour. Green beans stay green instead of turning gray. And the texture is much more appealing; no more soggy, mushy vegetables!

Space Saving

If you are always fighting for the space in your kitchen, then Instant Pot is for you. Since you can pressure cook, slow cook, sauté, and brown along with multiple cooking setting mentioned earlier, you don't need to purchase multiple utensils as owning Instant Pot only is just enough. Its compact design takes less space and you can easily store it in your kitchen cabinet or countertop.

Functions of the Instant Pot

The great thing about an Instant Pot is that it is precisely designed with buttons for specific functions that will help cook your food better. The sensors associated with the buttons know exactly how hot a specific food should be and will help to prevent the food from overcooking or burning- but you still control the time, so don't leave it all to the Instant Pot.

Some of the wonderful cooking and safety features that you need to understand to make cooking with the pot easy for you include the following:

Keep Warm/Cancel

This cancels any program that has been previously set, putting the cooker in standby. When the cooker is in this standby mode, pressing this key will set forth the keep warm program, which can last as long as 100 hours.

Soup

This setting is used to make a variety of broths and soups. The default is set at 30 minutes of high pressure, although this can be adjusted using the ADJUST or plus and minus buttons.

Porridge

This is for making oatmeal or porridge with various types of grains. The default here is high pressure for 20 minutes. Make sure you don't use quick release for this setting, as it will result in a major mess.

Note: Only use this setting with the pressure valve set to SEALING.

Rice

This is the setting which turns your Instant Pot into a rice cooker. It's an amazing program for cooking either parboiled or regular rice. For excellent results, use the provided water measurements inside the pot and the rice measuring cup.

The default for this setting is automatic and cooks rice at low pressure.

For instance, the manual indicates that the cooking duration for the rice changes automatically depending on the food content. Cooking 2 cups of rice will take approximately 12 minutes, and more cups will take more time accordingly.

When working pressure is reached, the pressure keeping time will be shown, but the total cooking time is not displayed. On this setting, the 'ADJUST' key has no effect whatsoever.

Multigrain

This setting is used to cook a mixture of grains such as brown rice, mung beans, wild rice, etc. The set default for this setting is 40 minutes of high pressure while the 'LESS' setting is 20 minutes of cooking time while the 'MORE' setting involves 45 minutes of just warm water soaking, which is followed by 60 minutes of cooking time on high pressure.

Steam

This setting is used for steaming veggies, or reheating foods. You should not NPR on this setting as you will be likely to overcook your food. The default here is 10 minutes of high-pressure cooking. You will require about 1 to 2 cups for steaming and make sure you use a basket or a steamer rack as this setting can burn food, which is in direct contact with the pot.

Manual

This button allows you to manually set your own pressure and cooking time (the maximum time is 240 minutes). This button is best used when you have a recipe indicating that you should cook on high pressure for a specified number of minutes.

Sauté

This setting is for open lid browning, sautéing, or simmering.

For regular browning: 'Normal'- 160 degrees C (320 degrees F); For darker browning: 'More'- 170 degrees C (338 degrees F); For light browning: 'Less'- 105 degrees C (221 degrees F).

Slow Cook

This setting converts your Instant Pot into a slow cooker, which can run to up to 40 hours- but the default is Normal heat for 4 hours of cook time.

Yogurt

There are 3 programs on this setting: make yogurt, Jiu Niang (fermented rice), and pasteurizing milk. The default of this setting is 8 hours of incubation.

To pasteurize milk, adjust to 'More' and to ferment rice or proof bread, adjust to 'Less.'

Timer (For Delayed Cooking)

Usually, many people confuse this setting with an actual cooking timer, which crushes their expectations regarding the cooker.

To use this setting the right way:

Start off by selecting your cooking program (e.g., 'Steam' or any other function except the 'Yogurt' and 'Sauté') and then press on the timer button. Use the '+' and '-' for setting the delayed hours. Press on the timer setting again to change the minutes.

The time that you have set is the delayed time before the program begins. This is where you can set the pot to start cooking a few hours before you get home or wake up so that you find freshly cooked dinner, lunch, or breakfast. You should allow for both sufficient cooking time and cooking down time before serving.

With that understanding of the basics, i.e., an understanding of the functions and abbreviations, we will now move on to getting rid of any confusion that you might have while using the Instant Pot and how to avoid it the common mistakes and pitfalls of owning this helpful device.

The Procedure of Using the Instant Pot

With the Instant Pot, cooking is done automatically so you don't need to press so many buttons in order to be able to start cooking. It is important to take note that different Instant Pot settings and functionalities require a certain amount of modification of the steps, but this section will discuss the basic things and steps to do when using the Instant Pot for its pressure cooker function.

Place all ingredients in the Instant Pot and give a good stir. Make sure that there is enough liquid (about a cup) to create steam that will, in turn, generate the pressure needed to cook the food faster.

Close the lid and make sure that it is in the sealed position. If not, the Instant Pot will not turn on or an audible sound can be heard indicating that something is not done properly.

Press the appropriate button and adjust the cooking time. The best thing about the Instant Pot is that it removes the guesswork involved in cooking your food. So, if you are cooking stew, press the Meat/Stew button or the Poultry button if you are cooking chicken.

As soon as you press the button, the clock will not immediately begin to count down but don't worry. The thing is that the Instant Pot needs to first build pressure, and it takes between 5 to 10 minutes depending on the amount of ingredients placed inside the inner pot. Once it is able to build enough pressure, it will start the countdown to cooking your food.

When the cooking time is up, the Instant Pot will automatically change to the Keep Warm function and it will begin to lose pressure slowly. You have the option to allow it to naturally release the pressure or do quick pressure release. You don't have to do anything with the natural pressure release. If the recipe calls for a quick pressure release, turn the steam valve into the venting position and the pressure will be released within a minute. When doing this step, make sure that you are away from the valve because the steam released is very hot and might scald you.

Cleaning the Instant Pot

As every electrical appliance needs constant care and maintenance, so does the instant pot pressure cooker. To ensure your personal safety, check all of its components at least once in a week. Regular maintenance will add up to the life of your cooker and will regulate its functionality.

It is recommended that the product should be cleaned after each use. As instant pot consists of several different units, each part should be cleaned with extreme care.

1. Never clean the instant pot immediately after cooking. Unplug the appliance first, let it cool for 30 minutes, and then start the cleaning process.

2. The black inner housing rim has to be wiped using a piece of cloth. Avoid washing, as it can cause rusting of the exterior pot rim.

3. **To clean the inner pot:** First, remove the lid and take the pot out. Now wash it with any detergent or soap then rinse with clear water. Use a soft cloth to wipe dry the inner pot from inside out.

4. Wash the lid along with the sealing ring, anti-block shield, and exhaust valve with clear water. Wipe them dry using a soft cloth.

5. While washing the lid, make sure to leave the steam release pipe intact and do not remove it from the lid.

6. **To clean the base unit:** Remember not to immerse it completely in water. Use a wet cloth to wipe all the dirt out of it. Make sure that the device is completely unplugged while you are cleaning its pot.

7. **To clean the power plug and the cord:** Always use a dry brush to remove the dirt or dust from the surface.

Troubleshooting and Cooking Guide

The pressure cooker is convenient and easy, but there are still some possible issues you can come up with:

Problem While Reaching Pressure

If the cooker isn't coming to pressure, make sure that the gasket ring is secure on the lid. Check for food or cracks that might have built up as it can prevent the lid from sealing properly.

Lid and Stuck

Even after opening the steam valve and allowing the pressure out from the cooker, the lid sometimes gets stuck. It happens as there's probably still pressure trapped in there. In such cases, take off the pressure valve and turn on the cooker again to build the heat. The heat building will push the leftover pressure out, and your lid will be open.

We have learned a lot about pressure cooker functions and its versatile use. The power pressure cooker is easy to use and energy-efficient: It saves your effort, money and most importantly, along with delivering better-tasting, nutritious food. It's just that simple!

Undercooked Foods

If the food isn't cooked in the time mentioned in the recipe, you might have poured too much water. Also, there is a thick sauce or liquid in the recipe, or you've simply added too much food.

Double-check the quantity of liquid used and always measure. It's easy to add ½ cup of more water, and it can make a big difference.

Overcooked Food

Power pressure cookers are powerful, and it's common for first time used to overcook or even burn their recipes. Many people add a few minutes to cooking time "just to be sure," but with a pressure cooker, it may overcook your food. So never add time to the recipe and only set time that is mentioned in the recipe.

Steam/Water Leaking Out of the Cooker

Water leaking is a pretty common thing, and it usually means that your food is building up in the vent pipe. Clean out all valves and vent pipe after cooking every 2 to 3 times, and the problem should go away. Steam leakage can also mean the gasket isn't placed securely enough, so check on that and secure properly.

Instant Pot FAQs

What can I cook in the Instant Pot?

Pretty much anything! The foods that are named on the buttons on the front area useful primer, but they're by no means an exclusive list of all the recipes you can rejuvenate with a spin in the Instant Pot. Just take a look at the 100 recipes in this book to get a sense of how incredibly versatile the Instant Pot can be.

Can I cook frozen food in the Instant Pot?

Yes! You can cook food directly from frozen in the Instant Pot without first defrosting it in the refrigerator or microwave. Just increase the cooking time for a few minutes to account for the thawing time.

Do I have to soak beans before cooking them in the Instant Pot?

Nope! Using the pressure cooking function, you can cook dry beans in less time than it would take to soak the using conventional cooking methods. Use the "Bean/Chili" button to take advantage of this feature.

Why does the pressure valve release steam?

This is a safety feature - if all the steam stayed inside the pressure cooker, the pressure would eventually become so great that the machine would explode. Not good! This feature ensures that the Instant Pot is safe to use for everyone.

Is the Instant Pot dishwasher safe?

The inner pot and steam rack are dishwasher safe, but the rest of the unit is not. The lid should be hand-washed and the housing unit should be wiped clean with a damp cloth.

Where can I buy an Instant Pot?

You can buy any of the three existing models of the Instant Pot off Amazon or directly from the Instant Pot website at Instant Pot.com.

Chaptr 3 Basics Recipe

Rosemary-Dijon Mayo

**Prep time: 5 minutes | Cook time: 5 minutes
Serves 7 to 8**

1 teaspoon vinegar
¾ cup extra-virgin olive
oil
1 teaspoon Dijon
mustard

1 egg
1 tablespoon lemon
juice
½ teaspoon rosemary,
ground

1. Preheat the Instant Pot by turning on Sauté
   mode.
2. Add the vinegar to the Instant Pot, then pour
   in olive oil, mustard, egg, lemon juice, and
   rosemary.
3. Whisk continuously, until an even texture is
   obtained. For a smoother sauce, briefly blend
   using an immersion blender.
4. Hit Cancel and pour the mayo into a storage
   container. Refrigerate for at least 1 hour, until
   ready for use.

Per Serving
calories: 171 | fat: 20g | protein: 1g | carbs: 0g
net carbs: 0g | fiber: 0g

Healing Bone Broth

**Prep time: 12 minutes | Cook time: 30 minutes
Makes 4 quarts**

3½ pounds (1.6 kg)
beef, chicken, ham, or
fish bones
2 stalks celery, chopped
1 medium onion,
chopped
7 cloves garlic, whacked
with the side of a knife
and peeled

2 bay leaves
2 teaspoons fine sea
salt
¼ cup apple cider
vinegar or coconut
vinegar
¼ cup fresh herbs of
choice, or 1 teaspoon
dried herbs (optional)

1. Place the bones, celery, onion, garlic, bay
   leaves, salt, and vinegar in an 8-quart Instant
   Pot, then add enough cold filtered water to
   cover everything. Add the herbs, if using.
2. Seal the lid, press Manual, choose Low
   Pressure, and set the timer for 30 minutes.
   (Cooking on Low Pressure allows more gelatin
   and minerals to be extracted from the bones.)
   Once finished, let the pressure release
   naturally.
3. Pour the broth through a strainer and discard
   the solids.

Per Serving
calories: 21 | fat: 1g | protein: 2g | carbs: 1g
net carbs: 1g | fiber: 0g

Hotter Than Hot Sauce

**Prep time: 5 minutes | Cook time: 5 minutes
Serves 40**

½ cup white vinegar
2 poblano peppers,
finely chopped
2 cloves garlic, minced
½ pound (227 g)
cayenne peppers, finely

chopped
1 habanero pepper,
finely chopped
½ teaspoon freshly
ground black pepper

1. Preheat the Instant Pot by turning on Sauté
   mode.
2. Add the vinegar to the Instant Pot, then
   add in the poblano peppers, garlic, cayenne
   peppers, habanero pepper, and black pepper.
3. Whisk continuously until an even texture is
   obtained. For a smoother sauce, briefly blend
   using an immersion blender.
4. Hit Cancel and pour the hot sauce into a
   storage container. Refrigerate until ready for
   use.

Per Serving
calories: 9 | fat: 0g | protein: 0g | carbs: 2g
net carbs: 1g | fiber: 1g

Ketchup

**Prep time: 5 minutes | Cook time: 5 minutes
Serves 20**

1 (14-ounce / 397-g)
can sugar-free or low-
sugar tomato purée
1 teaspoon garlic,
minced
½ teaspoon cloves,
ground
½ teaspoon kosher salt

½ teaspoon freshly
ground pepper
¼ (4-ounce / 113-
g) small onion, thinly
sliced
⅓ cup Swerve,
confectioners (or more,
to taste)

1. Preheat the Instant Pot by turning on Sauté
   mode.
2. Add the tomato purée to the Instant Pot,
   then add in garlic, cloves, salt, black pepper,
   onion, and Swerve.
3. Stir continuously, until an even texture is
   obtained. Blend with an immersion blender
   until smooth (about 20 seconds).
4. Hit Cancel and pour the ketchup into a
   storage container. Refrigerate until ready for
   use.

Per Serving
calories: 9 | fat: 0g | protein: 0g | carbs: 2g
net carbs: 1g | fiber: 1g

10-Minute Bacon Spinach Dip

Prep time: 5 minutes | Cook time: 5 minutes
Serves 5

½ cup full-fat cream cheese, softened
6 slices no-sugar-added bacon, crumbled and cooked
½ cup sour cream, at room temperature

½ cup spinach, chopped
½ teaspoon turmeric, ground
¼ (4-ounce / 113-g) small onion, thinly sliced
¼ cup garlic, minced

1. Preheat the Instant Pot by turning on Sauté mode.
2. Add the cream cheese to the Instant Pot, then add in the bacon, sour cream, spinach, turmeric, onion, and garlic.
3. Stir continuously, until cheese is melted and sauce is smooth. For a smoother sauce, briefly blend using an immersion blender.
4. Press Cancel and pour the dip into a storage container. Refrigerate until ready for use.

Per Serving
calories: 89 | fat: 7g | protein: 4g | carbs: 2g
net carbs: 2g | fiber: 0g

Three-Cheese Queso Dip

Prep time: 5 minutes | Cook time: 5 minutes
Serves 15

1 cup heavy whipping cream
2 tablespoons grass-fed butter, softened
1 cup full-fat Cheddar cheese, shredded
½ cup full-fat Mozzarella cheese, shredded
½ cup full-fat Gruyère cheese, thinly sliced

½ cup chili peppers, chopped
½ teaspoon cumin, ground
½ teaspoon cilantro, dried
½ teaspoon freshly ground black pepper
½ teaspoon kosher salt
¼ jalapeño, chopped, seeded

1. Preheat the Instant Pot by turning on Sauté mode.
2. Add the heavy whipping cream to the Instant Pot, then add in butter, Cheddar, Mozzarella, Gruyère, chili peppers, cumin, cilantro, black pepper, salt, and jalapeño.
3. Stir continuously, until cheese is melted and smooth. For a smoother sauce, briefly blend using an immersion blender.
4. Press Cancel and pour the dip into a storage container. Refrigerate until ready for use.

Per Serving
calories: 92 | fat: 8g | protein: 3g | carbs: 2g
net carbs: 2g | fiber: 0g

Mashed Cauliflower

Prep time: 5 minutes | Cook time: 5 minutes
Serves 6

4 cups chicken broth or vegetable broth
1 head cauliflower, cut into florets
Fine sea salt and ground black pepper, to taste

Unsalted butter, sour cream, or cream cheese, for serving (optional; omit for dairy-free)
Fresh thyme leaves, for garnish

1. Set a steamer basket in a 6-quart Instant Pot and pour in the broth. Place the cauliflower florets in the basket.
2. Seal the lid, press Manual, and set the timer for 5 minutes. Once finished, turn the valve to venting for a quick release.
3. Drain the liquid. Transfer the steamed cauliflower to a food processor or blender and purée until smooth. Season with salt and pepper to taste.
4. Place in a serving dish and top with butter, cream cheese, and/or sour cream, if desired. Garnish with thyme and freshly ground pepper.

Per Serving
calories: 57 | fat: 1g | protein: 9g | carbs: 5g
net carbs: 3g | fiber: 2g

Chicken Broth

Prep time: 5 minutes | Cook time: 2 hours
Makes 6 cups

2 pounds (907 g) chicken bones
2 celery stalks, chopped
2 medium halved carrots

1 medium onion, peeled and halved
2 bay leaves
2 sprigs fresh thyme
6 cups water

1. Add all ingredients to Instant Pot. Click lid closed. Press the Manual button and adjust time for 120 minutes.
2. When timer beeps, allow a full natural release. When pressure valve drops, remove large pieces of vegetables. Pour broth through fine-mesh strainer and store in closed containers in fridge or freezer.

Per Serving
calories: 21 | fat: 1g | protein: 2g | carbs: 0g
net carbs: 0g | fiber: 0g

Creamy Parmesan Alfredo Sauce

Prep time: 5 minutes | Cook time: 5 minutes
Serves 15

2 cups heavy whipping cream
3 cloves garlic, minced
2 tablespoons grass-fed butter, softened
1 tablespoon extra-virgin olive oil
½ cup full-fat Parmesan

cheese, grated
½ cup full-fat Mozzarella cheese, shredded
½ teaspoon freshly ground black pepper
½ teaspoon kosher salt

1. Preheat the Instant Pot by turning on Sauté mode.
2. Add the heavy whipping cream to the Instant Pot, then add in the garlic, butter, olive oil, Parmesan, Mozzarella, black pepper, and salt.
3. Stir continuously, until a smooth, even texture is obtained. For a smoother sauce, briefly blend using an immersion blender.
4. Press Cancel and pour the sauce into a storage container. Use immediately or refrigerate until ready for use.

Per Serving
calories: 106 | fat: 10g | protein: 3g | carbs: 1g
net carbs: 1g | fiber: 0g

Garlic-Red Pepper Marinara Sauce

Prep time: 5 minutes | Cook time: 5 minutes
Serves 10

1 (14-ounce / 397-g) can sugar-free or fire-roasted tomatoes
2 cloves garlic, minced
1 teaspoon kosher salt
½ cup extra-virgin olive

oil
½ teaspoon crushed red pepper
½ teaspoon oregano, dried

1. Preheat the Instant Pot by turning on Sauté mode.
2. Add the tomatoes to the Instant Pot, then add in garlic, salt, olive oil, red pepper, and oregano.
3. Stir continuously, until a smooth, even texture is obtained. For a smoother sauce, briefly blend using an immersion blender.
4. Press Cancel and pour the sauce into a storage container. Refrigerate until ready for use.

Per Serving
calories: 93 | fat: 10g | protein: 0g | carbs: 1g
net carbs: 1g | fiber: 0g

Soft Hard-Boiled Eggs

Prep time: 2 minutes | Cook time: 2 to 5 minutes | Makes 6 eggs

6 eggs
2 cups water, for

steaming

1. In the inner cooking pot of the Instant Pot, place a trivet or steamer basket. Pour in the water. Lay the eggs on the trivet or basket.
2. Lock the lid into place. Select Steam and adjust the pressure to High. Set the timer based on how you want your eggs to be cooked: Soft-boiled, runny yolks: 2 minutes; soft-boiled, half-set yolks: 3 minutes; hard-boiled, fully-set but soft yolks: 4 minutes; hard-boiled, fully-set hard yolks: 5 minutes.
3. While the eggs cook, make an ice bath by filling a medium-size bowl halfway with cold water, then add a handful of ice cubes. Set aside.
4. After cooking, quickly release the pressure. Unlock and remove the lid, and use tongs to transfer the eggs to the ice bath.
5. After about 5 minutes, drain the water. Peel and enjoy the eggs or store them in their shells in the refrigerator until ready to eat.

Per Serving (1 egg)
calories: 71 | fat: 5g | protein: 6g | carbs: 0g
net carbs: 0g | fiber: 0g

Asian Peanut Dressing

Prep time: 5 minutes | Cook time: 0 minutes
Makes about ¾ cup

⅓ cup creamy peanut butter
¼ cup hot water
2 tablespoons soy sauce
2 tablespoons white vinegar

Juice of 1 lime
1 teaspoon minced fresh ginger
1 teaspoon minced garlic
1 teaspoon freshly ground black pepper

1. Put the peanut butter, water, soy sauce, vinegar, lime juice, ginger, garlic, and pepper into a powerful blender and blend for 1 minute, until well emulsified.
2. Store in an airtight jar in the refrigerator for up to 1 week.

Per Serving (2 tablespoons)
calories: 99 | fat: 7g | protein: 4g | carbs: 5g
net carbs: 4g | fiber: 1g

Garam Masala

Prep time: 5 minutes | Cook time: 0 minutes
Makes about ¹/₃ cup

2 tablespoons coriander seeds	white pods
1 teaspoon cumin seeds	2 dried bay leaves
½ teaspoon whole cloves	3 dried red chiles or ½ teaspoon cayenne or red chile flakes
½ teaspoon cardamom seeds from green or	1 (2-inch) piece cinnamon stick

1. In a clean coffee or spice grinder, combine all the ingredients. Grind until the spices form a medium-fine powder. Stop the grinder several times and shake it so all the seeds and bits get under the blades and grind evenly.
2. Unplug the grinder. Holding the lid in place, turn the spice grinder upside down and shake the spice mixture into the lid. Pour the garam masala into a small jar with an airtight lid. Store in a cool, dry place for up to 3 to 4 weeks.

Per Serving (1 teaspoon)
calories: 2 | fat: 0g | protein: 0g | carbs: 1g
net carbs: 1g | fiber: 0g

Creamy Cilantro-Jalapeño Dressing

Prep time: 10 minutes | Cook time: 0 minutes
Makes about 1 cup

½ cup chopped fresh cilantro	spicy you want the dressing)
½ cup sour cream or Greek yogurt	6 garlic cloves
½ to 1 jalapeño (depending on how	1 teaspoon salt
	¼ cup water

1. Put the cilantro, sour cream, jalapeño, garlic, salt, and water into a powerful blender and blend for 1 minute, until well emulsified.
2. Store in an airtight jar in the refrigerator for up to 1 week.

Per Serving (2 tablespoons)
calories: 39 | fat: 3g | protein: 1g | carbs: 2g
net carbs: 2g | fiber: 0g

Homemade Ricotta

Prep time: 5 minutes | Cook time: 6 minutes
Makes about 4½ cups

3 cups whole milk	salt
1 cup heavy cream	3 tablespoons lemon juice
½ teaspoon fine sea	

1. Place the milk, cream, and salt in a 3-quart Instant Pot that has a Yogurt function. (A 6-quart will work, too.) Seal the lid, press Yogurt, and then press Adjust until the display reads Boil.
2. Once finished, remove the lid and use a candy thermometer to check the temperature of the ricotta to make sure it is between 170ºF (77ºC) and 180ºF (82ºC). If necessary, continue to heat it until it reaches that range.
3. Slowly add the lemon juice and gently stir to combine. Press Cancel to stop the cooking. Let the ricotta rest with the lid on the pot for at least 10 minutes.
4. Place the ricotta in a fine-mesh strainer or several layers of cheesecloth laid over a medium-sized bowl for 5 minutes to allow the liquid (known as whey) to drain; discard the whey. Taste the ricotta and add more salt, if desired.

Per Serving
calories: 154 | fat: 14g | protein: 4g | carbs: 5g
net carbs: 5g | fiber: 0g

Tomato Sauce

Prep time: 5 minutes | Cook time: 30 minutes
Makes 2½ cups

3 tablespoons butter	cans tomato paste
½ medium onion, finely diced	2 cups chicken broth
1 clove garlic, finely minced	1 teaspoon fresh parsley
2 (6-ounce / 170-g)	½ teaspoon oregano
	½ teaspoon basil

1. Press the Sauté button. Sauté onion until translucent. Add garlic and sauté for 30 seconds. Press the Cancel button.
2. Add remaining ingredients to Instant Pot and stir. Click lid closed. Press the Manual button and adjust time for 30 minutes. When timer beeps, quick-release the pressure.

Per Serving
calories: 65 | fat: 3g | protein: 2g | carbs: 7g
net carbs: 5g | fiber: 2g

Seafood Stock

Prep time: 5 minutes | Cook time: 120 minutes
Makes 6 cups

4 cups shellfish shells
6 cups water
1 medium onion, peeled and chopped

2 tablespoons apple cider vinegar
2 bay leaves
2 celery stalks, chopped

1. Add all ingredients to Instant Pot. Click lid closed. Press the Manual button and adjust time for 120 minutes.
2. Allow a 30-minute natural release, then quick-release the remaining pressure. When pressure valve drops, strain stock and store in sealed containers in fridge for 1 to 2 days or freeze.

Per Serving
calories: 10 | fat: 0g | protein: 2g | carbs: 0g
net carbs: 0g | fiber: 0g

Roasted Garlic

Prep time: 5 minutes | Cook time: 5 minutes
Serves 10

10 heads garlic
2 tablespoons extra-

virgin olive oil
Fine sea salt, to taste

1. Set a trivet in a 3-quart or larger Instant Pot and pour in 1 cup of cold water.
2. Remove the papery outer layers from the heads of garlic. With a sharp knife, cut ⅛ inch off the top of each head to expose the tops of the cloves. Rub the olive oil over the cloves and sprinkle with salt.
3. Place the garlic heads cut side up on the trivet in the Instant Pot. Seal the lid, press Manual, and set the timer for 5 minutes. Once finished, turn the valve to venting for a quick release.
4. Allow the garlic to cool enough that it is safe to handle, then remove from the pot and squeeze the bulbs to extract the roasted garlic as needed.

Per Serving
calories: 30 | fat: 3g | protein: 0g | carbs: 1g
net carbs: 1g | fiber: 0g

Low-Carb Loaf Bread

Prep time: 6 minutes | Cook time: 30 minutes
Serves 12

2 cups blanched almond flour
2 tablespoons coconut flour
1 tablespoon plus 1 teaspoon baking powder
1 tablespoon Swerve confectioners'-style sweetener or equivalent amount of liquid or powdered sweetener
1½ teaspoons garlic

powder
½ teaspoon fine sea salt
6 ounces (170 g) sharp Cheddar cheese, shredded (1½ cups)
1 cup unsweetened almond milk
2 tablespoons unsalted butter, melted but not hot
1 large egg, beaten

1. Set a trivet in a 6-quart Instant Pot and pour in ½ cup of cold water. Line a 6-inch round cake pan with parchment paper and grease the parchment.
2. Place the almond flour, coconut flour, baking powder, sweetener, garlic powder, and salt in a medium-sized bowl and whisk to combine well. Stir in the shredded cheese.
3. In another medium-sized bowl, stir together the almond milk, melted butter, and egg. Add the wet ingredients to the dry ingredients and mix until well combined. Spoon the dough into the prepared pan.
4. Use a foil sling to lower the pan onto the trivet in the Instant Pot. Tuck in the sides of the sling.
5. Seal the lid, press Manual, and set the timer for 30 minutes. Once finished, let the pressure release naturally. Lift the cake pan out of the Instant Pot using the foil sling.
6. Let the bread rest for 10 minutes, then invert onto a plate and peel off the parchment paper. Invert again onto a serving platter and let cool completely.
7. Once the bread is cool, cut into 1-inch-thick slices and serve.

Per Serving
calories: 199 | fat: 17g | protein: 9g | carbs: 6g
net carbs: 3g | fiber: 3g

Shawarma Spice Mix

Prep time: 5 minutes | Cook time: 0 minutes
Makes about 3 tablespoons

2 teaspoons dried oregano
1 teaspoon ground cinnamon
½ teaspoon ground allspice
½ teaspoon cayenne
1 teaspoon ground cumin
1 teaspoon ground coriander
1 teaspoon salt

1. Place all the ingredients in a jar with an airtight lid. Shake to combine. Store in a cool, dark place. Give the jar a shake or two before using.

Per Serving (1 teaspoon)
calories: 3 | fat: 0g | protein: 0g | carbs: 1g
net carbs: 1g | fiber: 0g

Herbed Marinara Sauce

Prep time: 4 minutes | Cook time: 15 minutes
Serves 10

2 tablespoons unsalted butter (or coconut oil for dairy-free)
1 medium onion, diced
1½ teaspoons minced garlic
6 cups crushed tomatoes
1 (6-ounce / 170-g) can tomato paste
1 tablespoon Swerve confectioners'-style sweetener or equivalent
amount of liquid or powdered sweetener
1 tablespoon coconut vinegar or balsamic vinegar
2 bay leaves
1 tablespoon dried basil leaves
1½ teaspoons dried oregano leaves
1 teaspoon fine sea salt
½ teaspoon ground black pepper

1. Place the butter in a 6-quart Instant Pot and press Sauté. Once melted, add the onion and garlic and cook, stirring, until the onion is soft, about 5 minutes. Press Cancel to stop the Sauté.
2. Add the tomatoes, tomato paste, sweetener, vinegar, herbs, salt, and pepper to the Instant Pot. Stir well to combine.
3. Seal the lid, press Manual, and set the timer for 10 minutes. Once finished, turn the valve to venting for a quick release.
4. Remove the lid, stir the sauce, and discard the bay leaves. Season with additional salt to taste. Enjoy the marinara over your favorite keto pasta, or use it in one of my recipes!

Per Serving
calories: 75 | fat: 3g | protein: 2g | carbs: 10g
net carbs: 7g | fiber: 3g

Traditional Ghee

Prep time: 5 minutes | Cook time: 10 minutes
Serves 20

1 pound (454 g) grass-fed butter, softened

1. Preheat the Instant Pot by turning on Sauté mode.
2. Add the butter and set the Instant Pot for 10 minutes. Stir occasionally.
3. Press Cancel and let the butter cool.
4. Strain the butter using a cheesecloth (or other fine-mesh filter).
5. Store the ghee in a container, and enjoy!

Per Serving
calories: 176 | fat: 19g | protein: 0g | carbs: 0g
net carbs: 0g | fiber: 0g

Keto "Rice"

Prep time: 5 minutes | Cook time: 5 minutes
Serves 4

8 large eggs
½ cup full-fat coconut milk
2 tablespoons beef broth or vegetable broth
1 teaspoon fine sea salt
½ teaspoon ground black pepper
Chopped fresh cilantro, rosemary, or thyme, for garnish (optional)

1. Place the eggs, coconut milk, broth, salt, and pepper in a medium-sized bowl and whisk until well combined.
2. Pour the egg mixture into a 6-quart Instant Pot and press Sauté. Cook until the mixture thickens and small curds form, continuously whisking and scraping the bottom of the pot to keep larger curds from forming, about 5 minutes. Press Cancel to stop the Sauté.
3. Place the "rice" on a platter. If it has released excess liquid, soak up the liquid with a paper towel before serving. Garnish the "rice" with fresh herbs, if desired.

Per Serving
calories: 194 | fat: 14g | protein: 13g | carbs: 1g
net carbs: 1g | fiber: 0g

Tzatziki Sauce

Prep time: 10 minutes | Cook time: 0 minutes
Makes about 2 cups

1 large cucumber, peeled and grated (about 2 cups)
1 cup sour cream
2 or 3 garlic cloves, minced

1 tablespoon tahini
Dash freshly squeezed lemon juice
Salt, for seasoning
Chopped parsley, for garnish (optional)

1. In a medium bowl, stir together the cucumber, sour cream, garlic, tahini, lemon juice, and salt. Garnish the sauce with parsley (if using).

Per Serving (¼ cup)
calories: 56 | fat: 4g | protein: 2g | carbs: 3g
net carbs: 3g | fiber: 0g

Best-Ever Savory Thyme Dip

Prep time: 5 minutes | Cook time: 0 minutes
Makes about ²/₃ cup

½ cup mayonnaise
2 tablespoons minced fresh thyme
2 tablespoons minced

red onion
1½ teaspoons freshly squeezed lemon juice

1. In a small bowl, mix the mayonnaise, thyme, onion, and lemon juice together. Cover the bowl with plastic wrap and let the mixture rest in the refrigerator for 2 hours before serving.
2. This dip will keep for 3 to 5 days in your refrigerator.

Per Serving (2 tablespoons)
calories: 87 | fat: 7g | protein: 0g | carbs: 6g
net carbs: 6g | fiber: 0g

Beef Broth

Prep time: 5 minutes | Cook time: 120 minutes
Makes 6 cups

2 pounds (907 g) beef bones
2 celery stalks, chopped
2 medium halved carrots

1 medium onion, peeled and halved
2 bay leaves
2 sprigs fresh thyme
6 cups water

1. Add all ingredients to Instant Pot. Click lid closed. Press the Manual button and adjust time for 120 minutes.
2. When timer beeps, allow a full natural release. When pressure valve drops, remove large pieces of vegetables. Pour broth through fine-mesh strainer and store in closed containers in fridge or freezer.

Per Serving
calories: 23 | fat: 2g | protein: 1g | carbs: 0g
net carbs: 0g | fiber: 0g

Mustard Dressing

Prep time: 5 minutes | Cook time: 0 minutes
Makes about 2 cups

1 cup extra-virgin olive oil
¾ cup apple cider vinegar
¼ cup Dijon mustard or other prepared mustard

1 tablespoon soy sauce
1 tablespoon Truvia
4 garlic cloves, minced
1 teaspoon salt
1 teaspoon freshly ground black pepper

1. Place the ingredients in a powerful blender and blend for 1 minute until well emulsified.
2. Store in an airtight jar in the refrigerator for up to 2 weeks, shaking the jar before each use.

Per Serving (2 tablespoons)
calories: 121 | fat: 13g | protein: 0g | carbs: 1g
net carbs: 1g | fiber: 0g

Chaptr 4 Breakfast

Protein Scramble

Prep time: 5 minutes | Cook time: 20 minutes
Serves 2

4 eggs
4 slices no-sugar-added bacon, cooked and finely cut
½ cup full-fat Cheddar cheese, shredded
1 cup spinach, chopped
2 tablespoons coconut oil
¼ cup full-fat coconut milk
½ teaspoon parsley, dried
½ teaspoon chili powder
½ teaspoon cumin, ground
½ teaspoon basil, dried
½ teaspoon kosher salt
½ teaspoon freshly ground black pepper

1. Grease the stainless steel inner pot of the Instant Pot, and pour in all ingredients. Mix thoroughly.
2. Add 1 cup of filtered water into the Instant Pot.
3. Close the lid, set the pressure release to Sealing, and select Manual. Set the Instant Pot to 20 minutes on High Pressure.
4. Once cooked, let the pressure naturally disperse from the Instant Pot for about 10 minutes, then carefully switch the pressure release to Venting.
5. Open the Instant Pot, serve, and enjoy!

Per Serving
calories: 767 | fat: 66g | protein: 38g | carbs: 6g
net carbs: 4g | fiber: 2g

Pumpkin Pie Fat Bombs

Prep time: 5 minutes | Cook time: 5 minutes
Serves 12

3 tablespoons grass-fed butter, softened
1 cup raw coconut butter
½ cup pecans, chopped
1 cup organic pumpkin purée
½ teaspoon pumpkin pie spice (or more, to taste)

1. Set the Instant Pot to Sauté and melt the grass-fed butter.
2. Add the coconut butter, pecans, pumpkin purée, and pumpkin pie spice to the Instant Pot. Mix thoroughly, until smooth and melted.
3. Pour mixture evenly into a silicone mini-muffin mold.
4. Refrigerate (or freeze) until firm. Serve and enjoy! Store any leftovers in the freezer.

Per Serving
calories: 199 | fat: 22g | protein: 0g | carbs: 2g
net carbs: 1g | fiber: 1g

Chocolate Butter Pecan Fat Bombs

Prep time: 5 minutes | Cook time: 5 minutes
Serves 5 to 6

2 tablespoons salted grass-fed butter, softened
1 cup raw coconut butter
1 cup sugar-free chocolate chips
½ cup pecans, chopped (or more, to taste)

1. Set the Instant Pot to Sauté and melt the butter.
2. Add the coconut butter, chocolate chips, and pecans to the Instant Pot, and mix thoroughly, until melted and smooth.
3. Pour mixture into a silicone mini-muffin mold. Freeze until firm. Remove from the muffin mold and store in an airtight container until ready to serve!

Per Serving
calories: 366 | fat: 32g | protein: 4g | carbs: 15g
net carbs: 8g | fiber: 7g

Bacon and Spinach Quiche

Prep time: 5 minutes | Cook time: 35 minutes
Serves 3

½ cup full-fat coconut milk
½ cup full-fat Cheddar cheese, shredded
½ cup spinach, chopped
5 eggs
2 slices no-sugar-added bacon, cooked and finely chopped
½ teaspoon basil, dried
½ teaspoon parsley, dried
½ teaspoon freshly ground black pepper
¼ teaspoon kosher salt

1. Pour 1 cup of filtered water into the inner pot of the Instant Pot, then insert the trivet.
2. Combine the coconut milk, cheese, spinach, eggs, bacon, basil, parsley, pepper, and salt, in an Instant Pot-safe dish. Mix thoroughly, then cover loosely with aluminum foil.
3. Using a sling if desired, gently place the covered dish on top of the trivet.
4. Close the lid, set the pressure release to Sealing, and hit Cancel to stop the current program. Select Manual, set the Instant Pot to 35 minutes on High Pressure, and let cook.
5. Once cooked, let the pressure naturally disperse from the Instant Pot for about 10 minutes, then carefully switch the pressure release to Venting.
6. Open the Instant Pot, serve, and enjoy!

Per Serving
calories: 343 | fat: 28g | protein: 20g | carbs: 4g
net carbs: 3g | fiber: 1g

Chocolate Cinnamon Roll Fat Bombs

Prep time: 5 minutes | Cook time: 5 minutes
Serves 5 to 6

2 tablespoons coconut oil
2 cups raw coconut butter
1 cup sugar-free chocolate chips
1 cup heavy whipping cream

½ cup Swerve, confectioners (or more, to taste)
½ teaspoon cinnamon, ground (or more, to taste)
½ teaspoon vanilla extract

1. Set the Instant Pot to Sauté and melt the oil.
2. Add the butter, chocolate chips, whipping cream, Swerve, cinnamon, and vanilla to the Instant Pot and cook. Stir occasionally until the mixture reaches a smooth consistency.
3. Pour mixture into a silicone mini-muffin mold.
4. Freeze until firm. Serve, and enjoy!

Per Serving
calories: 372 | fat: 32g | protein: 4g | carbs: 15g
net carbs: 8g | fiber: 7g

Feta Stuffed Chicken

Prep time: 15 minutes | Cook time: 17 minutes
Serves 5

1 pound (454 g) chicken breast, skinless, boneless
1 tablespoon Italian seasonings

1 teaspoon olive oil
3 ounces (85 g) feta cheese, crumbled
1 cup water, for cooking

1. Beat the chicken breast gently with the help of the kitchen hammer.
2. Then make a cut in the breast (to get the pocket).
3. Rub the chicken with Italian seasonings and olive oil.
4. Then fill the "chicken pocket" with crumbled feta.
5. After this, wrap the chicken breast in the foil.
6. Pour water and insert the trivet in the Instant Pot.
7. Place the chicken on the trivet; close and seal the lid
8. Cook the meal on Manual mode at High Pressure for 17 minutes; allow the natural pressure release for 5 minutes.

Per Serving
calories: 165 | fat: 7g | protein: 22g | carbs: 1g
net carbs: 1g | fiber: 0g

Grass-Fed Beef Breakfast Bowl

Prep time: 5 minutes | Cook time: 10 minutes
Serves 4

2 tablespoons avocado oil
1 pound (454 g) grass-fed beef, ground
½ teaspoon turmeric, ground
½ teaspoon crushed red pepper

½ teaspoon cayenne pepper
½ teaspoon cilantro, dried
½ teaspoon kosher salt
½ teaspoon freshly ground black pepper

1. Set the Instant Pot to Sauté and melt the oil. Place the grass-fed beef into the Instant Pot, breaking it up gently. Add the turmeric, red pepper, cayenne pepper, cilantro, salt, and black pepper. Mix thoroughly.
2. Pour in ½ cup of filtered water, close the lid, set the pressure release to Sealing, and hit Cancel to stop the current program. Select Manual, set the Instant Pot to 10 minutes on High Pressure, and let cook.
3. Once cooked, let the pressure naturally disperse from the Instant Pot for about 10 minutes, then carefully switch the pressure release to Venting.
4. Open the Instant Pot, serve over vegetable of your choice, and enjoy!

Per Serving
calories: 212 | fat: 12g | protein: 23g | carbs: 1g
net carbs: 1g | fiber: 0g

Cauliflower Hash

Prep time: 5 minutes | Cook time: 10 minutes
Serves 4

2 tablespoons grass-fed butter, softened
1 pound (454 g) cauliflower, chopped into small pieces
½ teaspoon paprika,

fresh
½ teaspoon freshly ground black pepper
½ teaspoon garlic
½ teaspoon kosher salt

1. Set the Instant Pot to Sauté and melt the butter.
2. Add the cauliflower to the Instant Pot, then mix in paprika, ground pepper, garlic, and salt. Continue to stir until fully cooked (hash will be cooked when browned).
3. Remove from the Instant Pot, serve, and enjoy!

Per Serving
calories: 85 | fat: 6g | protein: 3g | carbs: 6g
net carbs: 3g | fiber: 3g

Sirloin Steak and Eggs

**Prep time: 5 minutes | Cook time: 20 minutes
Serves 2 to 3**

2 tablespoons avocado oil
½ pound (227 g) sirloin steak
6 eggs
½ teaspoon parsley, dried
½ teaspoon freshly ground black pepper
½ teaspoon kosher salt

1. Set the Instant Pot to Sauté and heat the oil. Sear the steak for 2 to 5 minutes on each side, until reaching desired texture.
2. Add the eggs, parsley, black pepper, and salt to the Instant Pot. Stir thoroughly.
3. Close the lid, set the pressure release to Sealing, and hit Cancel to stop the current program. Select Manual, set the Instant Pot to 20 minutes on High Pressure, and let cook.
4. Once cooked, carefully switch the pressure release to Venting. Open the Instant Pot, serve, and enjoy!

Per Serving
calories: 280 | fat: 15g | protein: 34g | carbs: 2g
net carbs: 2g | fiber: 0g

Vanilla Bean Custard

**Prep time: 5 minutes | Cook time: 7 minutes
Serves 4**

½ cup powdered erythritol
5 egg yolks
1 cup heavy cream
1 vanilla bean
1 cup water

1. In large bowl, use a rubber spatula to mix erythritol and egg yolks until smooth. (Do not use a whisk; it will add too much air to the mixture.)
2. Slowly pour in heavy cream while stirring gently until just combined. Scrape vanilla bean seeds into mixture and slowly combine.
3. Pour mixture into four (4-inch) ramekins and cover with foil. Pour water into Instant Pot and place trivet in pot. Place ramekins on trivet. Click lid closed.
4. Press the Manual button and adjust time for 7 minutes. When timer beeps, allow a 10-minute natural release then quick-release the remaining pressure. Allow to cool completely uncovered then refrigerate, covered with plastic wrap, at least 2 hours.

Per Serving
calories: 273 | fat: 26g | protein: 5g | carbs: 15g
net carbs: 6g | fiber: 9g

Sausage Pepper Gravy

**Prep time: 5 minutes | Cook time: 15 minutes
Makes 2 cups**

1 pound (454 g) ground breakfast sausage
2 tablespoons butter
2 ounces (57 g) cream cheese
1 cup heavy cream
½ teaspoon xanthan gum
½ teaspoon pepper
¼ teaspoon salt

1. Press the Sauté button and add breakfast sausage to Instant Pot. Brown sausage until no pink remains, approximately 10 minutes. Add butter and cream cheese, stirring quickly until cream cheese is soft and smooth.
2. Press the Cancel button and add heavy cream. Continue stirring frequently as sauce begins to thicken. Add xanthan gum, pepper, and salt and stir until desired thickness, approximately 5 to 10 minutes. Serve warm with low-carb biscuits or eggs.

Per Serving
calories: 316 | fat: 27g | protein: 10g | carbs: 2g
net carbs: 2g | fiber: 0g

Egg Cups

**Prep time: 15 minutes | Cook time: 13 minutes
Serves 4**

4 eggs
¼ cups spinach, chopped
½ teaspoon chili flakes
2 ounces (57 g)
Mozzarella, sliced
1 teaspoon butter, melted
1 cup water, for cooking

1. Brush the muffin molds with butter.
2. Then crack the egg in every mold and sprinkle them with chili flakes and spinach.
3. Top the eggs with sliced Mozzarella.
4. Pour water and insert the trivet in the Instant Pot.
5. Put the egg cups on the trivet and close the lid.
6. Cook the meal on Manual mode at High Pressure for 3 minutes. Make a quick pressure release.
7. Let the cooked egg cups cool to room temperature. Remove the eggs from the muffin molds.

Per Serving
calories: 112 | fat: 8g | protein: 10g | carbs: 1g
net carbs: 1g | fiber: 0g

Cheddar Egg Muffins

Prep time: 5 minutes | Cook time: 10 minutes
Serves 6

4 eggs
2 tablespoons heavy cream
¼ teaspoon salt

⅛ teaspoon pepper
⅓ cup shredded Cheddar
1 cup water

1. In large bowl, whisk eggs and heavy cream. Add salt and pepper.
2. Pour mixture into 6 silicone cupcake baking molds. Sprinkle cheese into each cup.
3. Pour water into Instant Pot and place trivet in bottom of pot. Carefully set filled silicone molds steadily on trivet. If all do not fit, separate into two batches.
4. Click lid closed. Press the Manual button and adjust time for 10 minutes. When timer beeps, allow a quick release and remove lid. Egg bites will look puffy at first, but will become smaller once they begin to cool. Serve warm.

Per Serving
calories: 60 | fat: 6g | protein: 6g | carbs: 1g
net carbs: 1g | fiber: 0g

Sausage and Buffalo Egg Sandwich

Prep time: 10 minutes | Cook time: 15 minutes
Serves 1

2 uncooked breakfast sausage patties
1 egg
2 tablespoons cream cheese

2 tablespoons shredded sharp Cheddar cheese
½ teaspoon hot sauce
¼ avocado, sliced

1. Press the Sauté button and add sausage patties to pot. Sear each side and continue cooking until no pink remains. Remove and set aside on a plate. Crack egg into hot Instant Pot in leftover grease. Fry egg for approximately 3 minutes.
2. Press the Cancel button. Place egg onto one sausage patty. In small bowl, mix cream cheese, Cheddar, and hot sauce. Microwave for 30 seconds and stir until smooth. Spread on second sausage patty. Place avocado slices on top of egg. Close sandwich by placing sausage patty on top of avocado.

Per Serving
calories: 426 | fat: 33g | protein: 20g | carbs: 5g
net carbs: 3g | fiber: 2g

Mini Sausage Breakfast Bites

Prep time: 10 minutes | Cook time: 15 minutes
Makes 32 balls

1 pound (454 g) breakfast sausage
1 ounce (28 g) cream cheese, softened

1 egg
½ cup shredded sharp Cheddar
1 cup water

1. Mix all ingredients except water thoroughly and shape into round balls. Pour water into Instant Pot. Place an Instant Pot-safe bowl into pot and carefully put in sausage bites. Depending on your cooking vessel and pot size, this may require multiple batches. Click lid closed and adjust time for 15 minutes.
2. When timer beeps, quick-release pressure and remove meatballs. You may sear them on Sauté for a crunchy exterior or eat them as is. Serve warm.

Per Serving
calories: 239 | fat: 20g | protein: 11g | carbs:0 g
net carbs: 0g | fiber: 0g

Spaghetti Squash Fritters

Prep time: 20 minutes | Cook time: 15 minutes
Serves 4

½ cooked spaghetti squash
2 tablespoons cream cheese
½ cup shredded whole-milk Mozzarella cheese
1 egg
½ teaspoon salt

¼ teaspoon pepper
1 stalk green onion, sliced
4 slices cooked bacon, crumbled
2 tablespoons coconut oil

1. Remove seeds from cooked squash and use fork to scrape strands out of shell. Place strands into cheesecloth or kitchen towel and squeeze to remove as much excess moisture as possible.
2. Place cream cheese and Mozzarella in small bowl and microwave for 45 seconds to melt together. Mix with spoon and place in large bowl. Add all ingredients except coconut oil to bowl. Mixture will be wet like batter.
3. Press the Sauté button and then press the Adjust button to set heat to Less. Add coconut oil to Instant Pot. When fully preheated, add 2 to 3 tablespoons of batter to pot to make a fritter. Let fry until firm and completely cooked through.

Per Serving
calories: 202 | fat: 16g | protein: 9g | carbs: 2g
net carbs: 2g | fiber: 0g

Frittata with Greens

**Prep time: 10 minutes | Cook time: 10 minutes
Serves 2**

2 eggs, beaten
¼ cup heavy cream
½ teaspoon white pepper
1 tablespoon chives, chopped
1 teaspoon ground

paprika
1 teaspoon butter, softened
1 tablespoon scallions, chopped
1 cup water, for cooking

1. In the mixing bowl, mix up eggs, heavy cream, white pepper, chives, ground paprika, and scallions.
2. Then grease the frittata ramekin with softened butter.
3. Pour the egg mixture in the prepared ramekin and place it on the trivet.
4. Then pour water in the Instant Pot and insert the trivet inside.
5. Cook the frittata for 10 minutes on Manual mode at High Pressure.
6. Then make a quick pressure release and cut the meal into halves.

Per Serving
calories: 137 | fat: 12g | protein: 6g | carbs: 2g
net carbs: 1g | fiber: 1g

Morning Burritos

**Prep time: 10 minutes | Cook time: 15 minutes
Serves 4**

4 keto tortillas
1 cup ground beef
¼ cup crushed tomatoes
1 teaspoon olive oil

3 ounces (85 g) scallions, diced
½ teaspoon dried cilantro

1. In the mixing bowl mix up ground beef, crushed tomatoes, olive oil, scallions, and dried cilantro.
2. Put the meat mixture in the Instant Pot.
3. Close and seal the lid.
4. Cook the beef mixture for 15 minutes on Manual mode at High Pressure.
5. Then make a quick pressure release and stir the meat well.
6. Fill the tortillas with the cooked mixture and roll them in the shape of burritos.

Per Serving
calories: 238 | fat: 13g | protein: 19g | carbs: 11g
net carbs: 6g | fiber: 5g

Bacon Casserole

**Prep time: 10 minutes | Cook time: 10 minutes
Serves 6**

4 bacon slices, chopped
1 teaspoon olive oil
6 eggs, beaten
½ cup spinach, chopped
½ cup heavy cream
1 teaspoon chili flakes

3 ounces (85 g) Parmesan, grated
1 teaspoon ground paprika
1 cup water, for cooking

1. Preheat the Instant Pot on Sauté mode for 2 to 3 minutes.
2. Then put the chopped bacon inside and cook it on Sauté mode for 5 minutes or until it is crunchy.
3. Then transfer the cooked bacon in the mixing bowl. Add the eggs, spinach, heavy cream, chili flakes, paprika, and Parmesan. Carefully stir the. Clean the Instant Pot and pour water and insert the trivet inside.
4. After this, pour the mixture in the baking mold/ramekin and cover with foil. Cook the casserole on Manual at High Pressure for 15 minutes. Allow the natural pressure release for 10 minutes.

Per Serving
calories: 220 | fat: 17g | protein: 15g | carbs: 2g
net carbs: 2g | fiber: 0g

Margherita Egg Cups

**Prep time: 10 minutes | Cook time: 5 minutes
Serves 2**

2 eggs
4 ounces (113 g) Mozzarella, shredded
½ tomato, chopped
1 teaspoon butter,

softened
½ teaspoon fresh basil, chopped
1 cup water, for cooking

1. Grease the small ramekins with softened butter and crack the eggs inside.
2. Then top the eggs with chopped tomato, basil, and Mozzarella.
3. Pour water and insert the trivet in the Instant Pot.
4. Place the ramekins with eggs on the trivet. Close and seal the lid.
5. Cook the meal on Manual at High Pressure for 5 minutes. Allow the natural pressure release for 5 minutes.

Per Serving
calories: 243 | fat: 16g | protein: 22g | carbs: 3g
net carbs: 2g | fiber: 1g

Nut Yogurt

Prep time: 10 minutes | Cook time: 6 minutes
Serves 3

1 cup coconut yogurt
½ ounce (14 g) pistachio nuts, chopped
½ ounce (14 g) hazelnuts, chopped
½ ounce (14 g) macadamia nuts, chopped
1 teaspoon erythritol
½ teaspoon coconut oil

1. Preheat the coconut oil on Sauté mode for 1 minute.
2. When the oil is hot, add pistachio nuts, hazelnuts, and macadamia nuts. Cook them on Sauté mode for 5 minutes. Stir the nuts constantly.
3. Then cool the buts well and mix them up with erythritol and coconut yogurt.
4. Put the cooked meal in the serving jars.

Per Serving

calories: 132 | fat: 10g | protein: 3g | carbs: 9g net carbs: 8g | fiber: 1g

Spanakopita

Prep time: 20 minutes | Cook time: 15 minutes
Serves 4

½ cup coconut flour
3 eggs, beaten
2 tablespoons butter
1 cup spinach, chopped
1 ounce (28 g)
scallions, chopped
3 tablespoons cream cheese
4 egg whites, whisked
1 cup water, for cooking

1. Make the dough: In the mixing bowl mix up coconut flour, eggs, and butter. Knead the dough.
2. Then place the dough in the round mold and flatten in the shape of the pie crust.
3. Pour water in the Instant Pot and insert the trivet.
4. Put the mold with the pie crust on the trivet. Close and seal the lid. Cook the pie crust for 10 minutes on Manual mode at High Pressure. When the timer goes off, do a quick pressure release. Carefully open the lid.
5. After this, mix up spinach, scallions, cream cheese, and eggs,
6. Pour the mixture over the cooked pie crust.
7. Cook the spanakopita for 5 minutes more on Manual mode at High Pressure. Then allow the natural pressure release for 5 minutes.

Per Serving

calories: 157 | fat: 12g | protein: 9g | carbs: 2g net carbs: 1g | fiber: 1g

Sausage Puffs

Prep time: 15 minutes | Cook time: 10 minutes
Serves 6

9 ounces (255 g) ground sausages, fried
1 egg, beaten
¼ cup coconut flour
¼ teaspoon baking powder
3 ounces (85 g) Provolone cheese, grated
1 tablespoon cream cheese
1 cup water, for cooking

1. In the mixing bowl, mix up ground sausages, egg, coconut flour, baking powder, grated Parmesan, and cream cheese.
2. Make the small puff from the ground sausages and put in the nonstick baking pan.
3. Pour water and insert the pan with sausage puffs in the Instant Pot.
4. Close and seal the lid.
5. Cook the meal on Manual at High Pressure for 10 minutes. Make a quick pressure release.

Per Serving

calories: 230 | fat: 18g | protein: 14g | carbs: 3g net carbs: 1g | fiber: 2g

Lemon Cheddar Muffins

Prep time: 10 minutes | Cook time: 12 minutes
Serves 3

2 ounces (57 g) Cheddar cheese, shredded
2 tablespoons almond flour
2 tablespoon butter, softened
1 tablespoon heavy cream
¼ teaspoon baking powder
½ teaspoon lemon juice
1 cup water, for cooking

1. Pour water in the Instant Pot.
2. Then mix up together all remaining ingredients and stir until combined.
3. Put the muffin batter in the muffin molds and insert them in the Instant Pot.
4. Close and seal the lid.
5. Cook the Cheddar muffins for 12 minutes on Manual mode at High Pressure.
6. When the time is finished, make a quick pressure release.

Per Serving

calories: 269 | fat: 25g | protein: 9g | carbs: 5g net carbs: 3g | fiber: 2g

Starbucks Eggs

Prep time: 10 minutes | Cook time: 2 minutes
Serves 2

4 eggs
2 ounces (57 g) cottage cheese
⅓ cup Cheddar cheese, shredded
1 teaspoon chives, chopped
1 cup water

1. Crack the eggs in the bowl and mix them with chives.
2. Whisk the eggs and add shredded Cheddar cheese and cottage cheese. Stir well.
3. Then pour the eggs in the muffin molds.
4. Pour water in the Instant Pot and insert the trivet.
5. Place the eggs on the trivet and cook them for 2 minutes on Manual mode at High Pressure.
6. Make a quick pressure release and remove the eggs from the molds.

Per Serving
calories: 227 | fat: 15g | protein: 19g | carbs: 2g
net carbs: 2g | fiber: 0g

Hot Chocolate

Prep time: 5 minutes | Cook time: 2 minutes
Serves 2

2 tablespoons coconut oil
2 cups full-fat coconut milk
6 tablespoons sugar-free chocolate chips
4 tablespoons raw cacao nibs
½ teaspoon cinnamon, ground
¼ cup heavy whipping cream

1. Set the Instant Pot to Sauté and melt the coconut oil.
2. Pour in the coconut milk, and then add the chocolate chips, cacao nibs, cinnamon, and whipping cream. Stir thoroughly.
3. Close the lid, set the pressure release to Sealing, and hit Cancel to stop the current program. Select Manual, set the Instant Pot to 2 minutes on High Pressure, and let cook.
4. Once cooked, let the pressure naturally disperse from the Instant Pot for about 10 minutes, then carefully switch the pressure release to Venting.
5. Open the Instant Pot, serve, and enjoy!

Per Serving
calories: 451 | fat: 8g | protein: 0g | carbs: 22g
net carbs: 14g | fiber: 8g

Cauliflower Breakfast Pudding

Prep time: 5 minutes | Cook time: 5 minutes
Serves 2

2 tablespoons grass-fed butter
⅓ cup riced cauliflower
¼ cup Swerve confectioners (or more, to taste)
½ cup full-fat coconut milk
½ cup pecans, chopped
½ cup heavy whipping cream

1. Combine the butter, cauliflower, Swerve, and coconut milk into the inner pot of the Instant Pot, and stir thoroughly.
2. Close the lid, set the valve to Sealing, and select Manual. Set the Instant Pot to 5 minutes, on High Pressure.
3. Once cooked, allow the pressure to naturally disperse, then stir in the pecans and heavy whipping cream.

Per Serving
calories: 354 | fat: 36g | protein: 4g | carbs: 8g
net carbs: 5g | fiber: 3g

Avocado Breakfast Burger

Prep time: 5 minutes | Cook time: 10 minutes
Serves 2

2 tablespoons coconut oil
3 slices no-sugar-added bacon
2 eggs
½ cup full-fat Cheddar cheese, shredded
½ teaspoon freshly
ground black pepper
½ teaspoon kosher salt
1 cup lettuce, shredded
1 avocado, halved and pitted
2 tablespoons sesame seeds

1. Set the Instant Pot to Sauté and melt the coconut oil.
2. Add bacon, eggs, cheese, pepper, and salt. Stir thoroughly and continuously.
3. Once fully cooked, remove from the Instant Pot. Use the avocado as your bun, placing the food on top, then add the lettuce. Complete the breakfast burger by adding the other half of the avocado on top, then sprinkling with the sesame seeds.

Per Serving
calories: 612 | fat: 55g | protein: 21g | carbs: 13g
net carbs: 5g | fiber: 8g

Zucchini Roll

Prep time: 8 minutes | Cook time: 12 minutes
Serves 2

½ zucchini, grated
9 ounces (255 g) chicken breast, skinless, boneless

1 tablespoon butter
½ teaspoon white pepper
¼ teaspoon thyme

1. Beat the chicken breast well with the help of the kitchen hammer to get the tender piece.
2. Then sprinkle the chicken breast with the white pepper and thyme.
3. Put the grated zucchini over the chicken breast and flatten it well.
4. Roll up the chicken breast.
5. Wrap the zucchini roll in the foil.
6. Select the Poultry mode and place the zucchini roll in the Instant Pot.
7. Cook the zucchini roll for 12 minutes. Then make naturally pressure release.
8. Slice the cooked zucchini roll.

Per Serving
calories: 206 | fat: 9g | protein: 28g | carbs: 2g
net carbs: 1g | fiber: 1g

Cheese Jalapeños

Prep time: 10 minutes | Cook time: 5 minutes
Serves 2

2 jalapeño pepper
2 ounces (57 g) Provolone cheese, grated

1 egg, beaten
½ teaspoon ground paprika
1 cup water

1. In the mixing bowl, mix up cheese, eggs, and ground paprika.
2. Then cut the jalapeño peppers into halves and remove the seeds.
3. Fill the peppers with cheese mixture.
4. Pour water in the Instant Pot. Insert the trivet.
5. Place the jalapeños on the trivet. Close and seal the lid.
6. Cook the meal on Manual mode at High Pressure for 5 minutes. Then make quick pressure release.

Per Serving
calories: 137 | fat: 10g | protein: 10g | carbs: 2g
net carbs: 1g | fiber: 1g

Fat Burning Coffee

Prep time: 5 minutes | Cook time: 5 minutes
Serves 2

6 tablespoons salted grass-fed butter, softened
1 cup full-fat coconut milk
2 cups cold brew coffee
¼ cup Swerve,

confectioners (or more, to taste)
3 tablespoons unflavored MCT oil
½ teaspoon cinnamon, ground (or more, to taste)

1. Set the Instant Pot to Sauté and begin to melt the butter.
2. Add in the milk, followed by the coffee, Swerve, oil, and cinnamon. Stir continuously until the ingredients are melted into a smooth consistency. Hit Cancel to stop the current program.
3. Serve and enjoy!

Per Serving
calories: 760 | fat: 86g | protein: 3g | carbs: 7g
net carbs: 4g | fiber: 3g

Blackberry Cake

Prep time: 10 minutes | Cook time: 25 minutes
Serves 8

1 cup almond flour
2 eggs
½ cup erythritol
2 teaspoons vanilla extract
1 cup blackberries

4 tablespoons melted butter
¼ cup heavy cream
½ teaspoon baking powder
1 cup water

1. In large bowl, mix all ingredients except water. Pour into 7-inch round cake pan or divide into two 4-inch pans, if needed. Cover with foil.
2. Pour water into Instant Pot and place trivet in bottom. Place pan on trivet and click lid closed. Press the Manual button and press the Adjust button to set heat to Less. Set time for 25 minutes.
3. When timer beeps, allow a 15-minute natural release then quick-release the remaining pressure. Let cool completely.

Per Serving
calories: 174 | fat: 15g | protein: 10g | carbs: 17g
net carbs: 2g | fiber: 15g

Egg Bake

Prep time: 5 minutes | Cook time: 30 minutes
Serves 4 to 5

6 eggs
2 tablespoons coconut oil
1 avocado, mashed
1 cup full-fat Monterey Jack cheese, shredded
1 cup spinach, chopped
½ pound (227 g) no-sugar-added bacon, sliced finely, cooked
½ teaspoon basil, dried
½ teaspoon turmeric, ground
½ teaspoon cayenne pepper, ground
½ teaspoon crushed red pepper
½ teaspoon freshly ground black pepper
½ teaspoon kosher salt

1. Pour 1 cup of filtered water into the inner pot of the Instant Pot, and place the trivet inside. In a large bowl, combine the eggs, coconut oil, avocado, cheese, spinach, bacon, basil, turmeric, cayenne pepper, red pepper, black pepper, and salt. Mix thoroughly. Transfer this mixture into a well-greased, Instant Pot-friendly dish. Cover loosely with aluminum foil. Using a sling if desired, place this dish on top of the trivet.
2. Close the lid, set the pressure release to Sealing, and hit Cancel to stop the current program. Select Manual, set the Instant Pot to 30 minutes on High Pressure, and let cook.
3. Once cooked, perform a quick release by carefully switching the pressure valve to Venting. Open the Instant Pot, serve, and enjoy!

Per Serving
calories: 537 | fat: 44g | protein: 30g | carbs: 5g
net carbs: 2g | fiber: 3g

Crustless Kale Quiche

Prep time: 5 minutes | Cook time: 20 minutes
Serves 4 to 5

½ cup whole-milk ricotta cheese
½ cup full-fat Cheddar cheese, shredded
½ cup kale, chopped
6 eggs
6 slices no-sugar-added bacon, cooked and finely chopped
¼ cup full-fat coconut milk
2 tablespoons coconut oil
½ teaspoon freshly ground black pepper
½ teaspoon parsley, dried
½ teaspoon kosher salt
½ teaspoon basil, dried
¼ (4-ounce / 113-g) small onion, thinly sliced

1. Pour 1 cup of filtered water into the inner pot of the Instant Pot, then insert the trivet.
2. In a large bowl, combine the ricotta cheese, Cheddar cheese, kale, eggs, bacon, milk, oil, black pepper, parsley, salt, basil, coconut, and onion, and stir thoroughly. Then, transfer this mixture to a well-greased Instant Pot-friendly dish.
3. Place the dish onto the trivet, and cover loosely with aluminum foil. Close the lid, set the pressure release to Sealing, and select Manual. Set the Instant Pot to 20 minutes on High Pressure and let cook.
4. Once cooked, let the pressure naturally disperse from the Instant Pot for about 10 minutes, then carefully switch the pressure release to Venting.
5. Open the Instant Pot, serve, and enjoy!

Per Serving
calories: 340 | fat: 23g | protein: 13g | carbs: 3g
net carbs: 2g | fiber: 1g

Coconut Yogurt

Prep time: 5 minutes | Cook time: 8 to 10 hours | Serves 8

6 (13-ounce / 369-g) cans full-fat coconut milk
20 ounces (567 g) full-fat, grass-fed Greek yogurt
1 cup dark berries, to serve (optional)

1. From each coconut milk can, scrape the cream layer off the top, then place the cream into the inner pot of the Instant Pot. Cover and reserve the remaining coconut milk in the refrigerator.
2. Close the lid of the Instant Pot, set the pressure release to Sealing, and press Yogurt and then press Adjust until the screen reads Boil. Once boiled, remove the inner pot and let cool. Use a food thermometer to check when the mixture reaches 100ºF (38ºC), then stir in Greek yogurt.
3. Return the inner pot to the Instant Pot, seal the lid, and press the Yogurt button, setting the time for 8 to 10 hours. A longer cook time will result in a yogurt that has a slightly more sour taste.
4. Once done, mix in desired amount of refrigerated coconut milk, to achieve preferred consistency. Place the yogurt in an airtight container and refrigerate until ready to serve. When ready to consume, stir in berries (if desired). The yogurt will keep for 5 days.

Per Serving
calories: 446 | fat: 50g | protein: 10g | carbs: 4g
net carbs: 4g | fiber: 0g

Zucchini Fries with Bacon and Eggs

Prep time: 5 minutes | Cook time: 20 minutes
Serves 4

Zucchini Fries:

4 zucchinis, sliced into wedges

2 tablespoons blanched almond flour

1 cup full-fat Parmesan cheese

½ teaspoon kosher salt

½ teaspoon garlic powder

½ teaspoon crushed red pepper

Bacon and Eggs:

2 tablespoons coconut oil

6 eggs

6 slices no-sugar-added bacon

1. Pour 1 cup of filtered water into the inner pot of the Instant Pot, then insert the trivet. In a large bowl, thoroughly combine the zucchini fry ingredients and transfer this mixture to a well-greased, Instant Pot-friendly dish.
2. Using a sling if desired, place the dish onto the trivet, and cover loosely with aluminum foil. Close the lid, set the pressure release to Sealing, and select Manual. Set the Instant Pot to 20 minutes on High Pressure and let cook.
3. Once cooked, carefully switch the pressure release to Venting. Open the lid and remove the dish. Set the zucchini fries aside, loosely covered with foil to keep them warm.
4. Pour out the remaining water and set the Instant Pot to Sauté. Melt the coconut oil.
5. Add in the eggs and bacon to the Instant Pot, and stir thoroughly, continuously.
6. Once bacon and eggs are both fully cooked (about 5 to 7 minutes) remove from the Instant Pot, and serve alongside the zucchini fries.

Per Serving

calories: 522 | fat: 38g | protein: 40g | carbs: 10g
net carbs: 8g | fiber: 2g

Greens Power Bowl

Prep time: 10 minutes | Cook time: 10 minutes
Serves 1

1 cup water

2 eggs

1 tablespoon coconut oil

1 tablespoon butter

1 ounce (28 g) sliced almonds

1 cup fresh spinach, sliced into strips

½ cup kale, sliced into strips

½ clove garlic, minced

½ teaspoon salt

⅛ teaspoon pepper

½ avocado, sliced

⅛ teaspoon red pepper flakes

1. Pour water into Instant Pot and place trivet in bottom. Place eggs on trivet. Click lid closed. Press the Egg button and adjust time for 6 minutes. When timer beeps, quick-release the pressure. Set eggs aside.
2. Pour water out, clean pot, and replace. Press the Sauté button and add coconut oil, butter, and almonds. Sauté for 2 to 3 minutes until butter begins to turn golden and almonds soften. Add spinach, kale, garlic, salt, and pepper to Instant Pot.
3. Sauté for 4 to 6 minutes until greens begin to wilt. Press the Cancel button. Place greens in bowl for serving. Peel eggs, cut in half, and add to bowl. Slice avocado and place in bowl. Sprinkle red pepper flakes over all. Serve warm.

Per Serving

calories: 649 | fat: 55g | protein: 21g | carbs: 15g
net carbs: 6g | fiber: 9g

Breakfast Burritos

Prep time: 5 minutes | Cook time: 15 minutes
Serves 4

2 tablespoons avocado oil

¼ cup grass-fed bone broth

1 pound (454 g) chicken, ground

½ teaspoon cumin, ground

½ teaspoon cayenne pepper, ground

½ teaspoon chili powder

½ teaspoon kosher salt

½ teaspoon freshly ground black pepper

¼ cup full-fat Cheddar cheese, shredded (optional)

Lettuce, to wrap

½ cup avocado, mashed

½ cup sugar-free or low-sugar salsa, (optional)

¼ cup sour cream, at room temperature (optional)

1. Set the Instant Pot to Sauté and heat the oil.
2. Pour in bone broth and ¾ cup of filtered water. Add the chicken, cumin, cayenne pepper, chili powder, salt, black pepper, and cheese to the Instant Pot, and mix thoroughly.
3. Close the lid, set the pressure release to Sealing, and hit Cancel to stop the current program. Select Manual, set the Instant Pot to 15 minutes on High Pressure, and let cook.
4. Once cooked, carefully switch the pressure release to Venting. Drain the meat of any excess liquid, spoon the chicken mixture onto a lettuce wrap to make the burrito. Top with avocado and, if using, salsa and sour cream.

Per Serving

calories: 293 | fat: 15g | protein: 37g | carbs: 6g
net carbs: 4g | fiber: 2g

Granola

Prep time: 5 minutes | Cook time: 2 minutes
Serves 12

2 cups chopped raw pecans
½ cup chopped raw walnuts
½ cup slivered almonds
1 cup sunflower seeds
½ cup sesame seeds
1¾ cups vanilla-flavored egg white protein powder
1¼ cups (2½ sticks) unsalted butter or coconut oil, softened

½ cup Swerve confectioners'-style sweetener or equivalent amount of liquid or powdered sweetener
1 teaspoon ground cinnamon
½ teaspoon fine sea salt
Unsweetened vanilla-flavored almond milk, for serving (optional)

1. Place all of the ingredients in a 3-quart or larger Instant Pot. Stir well to combine.
2. Seal the lid, press Manual, and set the timer for 2 minutes. (The pressure ball may not rise much, but it needs only enough heat to create a crispy granola after cooling.) Once finished, let the pressure release naturally.
3. Stir well and pour the granola onto a sheet of parchment paper to cool. It will become crispy when completely cool.
4. Serve the granola in bowls. Pour almond milk over the granola, if desired.

Per Serving
calories: 492 | fat: 44g | protein: 17g | carbs: 9g
net carbs: 4g | fiber: 5g

Cauliflower Egg Muffins

Prep time: 5 minutes | Cook time: 20 minutes
Serves 4

6 eggs
2 tablespoons grass-fed butter, softened
1 tablespoon coconut milk
1 cup Mozzarella cheese, shredded
½ cup full-fat Cheddar cheese, shredded
16 uncured pepperoni slices (optional)
½ cup riced cauliflower,

cooked
½ cup spinach, chopped
½ cup bell peppers, chopped
½ teaspoon basil, dried
½ teaspoon oregano, dried
½ teaspoon parsley, dried
½ teaspoon freshly ground black pepper
½ teaspoon kosher salt

1. Pour 1 cup of filtered water into the inner pot of the Instant Pot, then insert the trivet. In a large bowl, mix the eggs, butter, milk, Mozzarella, Cheddar, pepperoni, cauliflower, spinach, bell peppers, basil, oregano, parsley, black pepper, and salt.
2. Once mixed, transfer into a well-greased Instant Pot-friendly muffin pan, filling evenly.
3. Place the pan onto the trivet, and cover loosely with aluminum foil. Close the lid, set the pressure release to Sealing, and select Manual. Set the Instant Pot to 20 minutes on High Pressure, and let cook.
4. Once cooked, let the pressure naturally disperse from the Instant Pot for about 10 minutes, then carefully switch the pressure release to Venting.
5. Open the Instant Pot, serve, and enjoy!

Per Serving
calories: 354 | fat: 30g | protein: 20g | carbs: 3g
net carbs: 2g | fiber: 1g

Huevos Rancheros

Prep time: 5 minutes | Cook time: 20 minutes
Serves 4

2 tablespoons coconut oil
6 eggs
1 (14-ounce / 397-g) can sugar-free or low-sugar crushed tomatoes
1 cup full-fat Cheddar cheese, shredded
½ teaspoon cilantro,

dried
½ teaspoon chili powder
½ jalapeño, finely chopped
½ teaspoon kosher salt
½ teaspoon freshly ground black pepper

1. Pour ½ cup of filtered water into the Instant Pot and insert the trivet. In a large bowl, combine the coconut oil, eggs, tomatoes, cheese, cilantro, chili powder, jalapeño, salt, and black pepper. Mix thoroughly. Transfer this mixture into a well-greased, Instant Pot-friendly dish. Cover dish loosely with aluminum foil.
2. Using a sling, transfer the dish to the Instant Pot and place on top of the trivet.
3. Close the lid, set the pressure release to Sealing, and hit Cancel to stop the current program. Select Manual, set the Instant Pot to 20 minutes on High Pressure, and let cook.
4. Once cooked, carefully switch the pressure release to Venting.
5. Open the Instant Pot, remove the dish, serve, and enjoy!

Per Serving
calories: 278 | fat: 23g | protein: 15g | carbs: 3g
net carbs: 2g | fiber: 1g

Fast and Easy Canja de Galinha

Prep time: 5 minutes | Cook time: 5 minutes
Serves 4

4 cups grass-fed bone broth
1 pound (454 g) chicken breasts, cooked and shredded
1 cup cauliflower, chopped
2 tablespoons grass-fed butter, softened
½ teaspoon parsley, dried
½ teaspoon garlic
¼ (4-ounce / 113-g) small onion, thinly sliced
2 bay leaves

1. Add the bone broth, chicken, cauliflower, butter, parsley, garlic, onion, and bay leaves to the Instant Pot. Stir thoroughly.
2. Close the lid, set the pressure release to Sealing, and hit Cancel to stop the current program. Select Manual, set the Instant Pot to 5 minutes on High Pressure, and let cook.
3. Once cooked, perform a quick release by carefully switching the pressure valve to Venting. Open the Instant Pot, serve, and enjoy!

Per Serving
calories: 217 | fat: 9g | protein: 31g | carbs: 3g net carbs: 2g | fiber: 1g

Denver Omelet

Prep time: 5 minutes | Cook time: 20 minutes
Serves 2

2 tablespoons avocado oil
¼ cup onion, chopped
¼ cup green bell pepper, finely chopped
¼ cup red bell pepper, finely chopped
6 eggs
2 slices no-sugar-added bacon, cooked and finely cut (optional)
½ cup full-fat Cheddar cheese, shredded
½ teaspoon basil, dried
½ teaspoon crushed red pepper
½ teaspoon parsley, dried
½ teaspoon kosher salt
½ teaspoon freshly ground black pepper

1. Set the Instant Pot to Sauté and heat the oil. Add the onion and peppers, and sauté for 4 minutes.
2. In a medium bowl, combine eggs, bacon, cheese, and spices. Pour mixture into a greased, Instant Pot-friendly dish. Add in the sautéed onion and peppers, thoroughly scraping out all the bits from the pot, and mix thoroughly.
3. Pour 1 cup of filtered water into the inner pot of the Instant Pot, then insert the trivet. Using a sling, place the glass dish inside the Instant Pot.

4. Close the lid, set the pressure release to Sealing, and hit Cancel to stop the current program. Select Manual, set the Instant Pot to 20 minutes on High Pressure, and let cook.
5. Once cooked, let the pressure naturally disperse from the Instant Pot for about 10 minutes, then carefully switch the pressure release to Venting.
6. Open the Instant Pot, remove the dish, serve, and enjoy!

Per Serving
calories: 439 | fat: 32g | protein: 31g | carbs: 5g net carbs: 3g | fiber: 2g

Mug Cakes

Prep time: 5 minutes | Cook time: 20 minutes
Serves 3 to 4

Base:
2 eggs
1 tablespoon salted grass-fed butter, softened
1 teaspoon smooth almond butter
1 teaspoon vanilla
extract
⅔ cup blanched almond flour
½ cup Swerve, confectioners (or more, to taste)

Flavors:
Blueberry: ¼ cup blueberries
Chocolate chip: ¼ cup sugar-free chocolate chips
Strawberry: 4 strawberries, hulled and chopped

1. In a large bowl, mix the eggs, grass-fed butter, almond butter, vanilla, almond flour, Swerve, and any desired flavors, thoroughly. Working in batches if needed, pour the mixed ingredients evenly into preferred size of heatproof mugs, ramekins, or mason jars, filling each about halfway. Cover each loosely with aluminum foil.
2. Pour 1 cup of filtered water into the inner pot of the Instant Pot, then insert the trivet. Place filled mugs on top of the trivet.
3. Close the lid, set the pressure release to Sealing, and select Manual. Set the Instant Pot to 20 minutes on High Pressure and let cook.
4. Release the pressure immediately by switching the valve to Venting, then place the mugs on a cooling rack. Be careful, as they will be hot. Let cool completely before serving.

Per Serving
calories: 94 | fat: 7g | protein: 4g | carbs: 3g net carbs: 2g | fiber: 1g

Cheddar-Herbed Strata

Prep time: 5 minutes | Cook time: 40 minutes
Serves 4

6 eggs
1 cup full-fat Cheddar cheese, shredded
1 cup spinach, chopped
½ tablespoon salted grass-fed butter, softened
¼ (4-ounce / 113-g) small onion, thinly sliced
½ teaspoon freshly ground black pepper
½ teaspoon kosher salt
½ teaspoon Dijon mustard
½ teaspoon paprika
½ teaspoon cayenne pepper
½ teaspoon cilantro, dried
½ teaspoon sage, dried
½ teaspoon parsley, dried

1. Pour 1 cup of filtered water into the inner pot of the Instant Pot, then insert the trivet. In a large bowl, combine the eggs, cheese, spinach, butter, onion, black pepper, salt, mustard, paprika, cayenne pepper, cilantro, sage, and parsley. Mix thoroughly. Transfer this mixture into a well-greased, Instant Pot-friendly dish.
2. Using a sling if desired, place the dish onto the trivet, and cover loosely with aluminum foil. Close the lid, set the pressure release to Sealing, and select Manual. Set the Instant Pot to 40 minutes on High Pressure and let cook.
3. Once cooked, let the pressure naturally disperse from the Instant Pot for about 10 minutes, then carefully switch the pressure release to Venting.
4. Open the Instant Pot and remove the dish. Let cool, serve, and enjoy!

Per Serving
calories: 179 | fat: 14g | protein: 10g | carbs: 2g net carbs: 2g | fiber: 0g

Chocolate Pumpkin Balls

Prep time: 5 minutes | Cook time: 5 minutes
Serves 5 to 6

2 tablespoons salted grass-fed butter, softened
2 cups sugar-free chocolate chips
¾ cup raw coconut butter
½ cup organic pumpkin purée (or more, to taste)
⅓ cup Swerve, confectioners (or more, to taste)
2 teaspoons coconut, shredded (optional)
⅛ teaspoon cinnamon, ground

1. Set the Instant Pot to Sauté and melt the grass-fed butter.
2. Add the chocolate chips, coconut butter, pumpkin, Swerve, coconut, and cinnamon to the Instant Pot. Mix thoroughly until melted.
3. Pour mixture into a silicone mini-muffin mold.
4. Freeze until firm. Serve and enjoy! For leftovers, store in an airtight container in the freezer for up to one month.

Per Serving
calories: 494 | fat: 46g | protein: 5g | carbs: 22g net carbs: 10g | fiber: 12g

Mini Pancake Bites

Prep time: 5 minutes | Cook time: 20 minutes
Serves 7

2 eggs
1 cup blanched almond flour
⅔ cup Swerve, confectioners (or more, to taste)
¼ cup full-fat coconut
milk
1 tablespoon salted grass-fed butter, softened
½ teaspoon kosher salt
¼ teaspoon baking soda

1. Pour 1 cup of filtered water into the inner pot of the Instant Pot, then insert the trivet. In a large bowl, combine the eggs, flour, Swerve, milk, butter, salt and baking soda. Mix thoroughly. Transfer this mixture into a well-greased, Instant Pot-friendly egg bites mold, working in batches if need be. I prefer to stack two egg bites molds on top of each other, separating them with Mason jar lids (or similar dividers).
2. Using a sling if desired, place the pan onto the trivet and cover loosely with aluminum foil. Close the lid, set the pressure release to Sealing, and select Manual. Set the Instant Pot to 20 minutes on High Pressure and let cook.
3. Once cooked, let the pressure naturally disperse from the Instant Pot for about 10 minutes, then carefully switch the pressure release to Venting.
4. Open the Instant Pot and remove the pan. Let cool, serve with your favorite toppings, and enjoy!

Per Serving
calories: 187 | fat: 17g | protein: 5g | carbs: 4g net carbs: 2g | fiber: 2g

Shakshuka

Prep time: 5 minutes | Cook time: 5 minutes
Serves 2 to 4

2 tablespoons coconut oil
2 cups full-fat Cheddar cheese, shredded
1 garlic clove, minced
½ teaspoon cilantro, dried
½ teaspoon cayenne pepper, ground
½ teaspoon cumin, ground
½ teaspoon oregano, dried
½ teaspoon freshly ground black pepper
½ teaspoon kosher salt
1 (14-ounce / 397-g) can roasted sugar-free or low-sugar tomatoes
6 eggs

1. Set the Instant Pot to Sauté and melt the coconut oil.
2. Add the cheese, garlic, cilantro, cayenne pepper, cumin, oregano, black pepper, salt, and tomatoes to the Instant Pot, and stir thoroughly.
3. Once combined, carefully crack the eggs into the mixture, maintaining the yolks. Make sure they are spaced evenly apart.
4. Close the lid, set the pressure release to Sealing, and hit Cancel to stop the current program. Select Manual, set the Instant Pot to 1 minute on High Pressure, and let cook.
5. Once cooked, perform a quick release by carefully switching the pressure valve to Venting.
6. Open the Instant Pot, serve, and enjoy!

Per Serving
calories: 397 | fat: 32g | protein: 23g | carbs: 5g net carbs: 4g | fiber: 1g

Chocolate Chip Mini Muffins

Prep time: 5 minutes | Cook time: 20 minutes
Serves 7

1 cup blanched almond flour
2 eggs
¾ cup sugar-free chocolate chips
1 tablespoon vanilla extract
½ cup Swerve, confectioners (or more, to taste)
2 tablespoons salted grass-fed butter, softened
½ teaspoon salt
¼ teaspoon baking soda

1. Pour 1 cup of filtered water into the inner pot of the Instant Pot, then insert the trivet. Using an electric mixer, combine flour, eggs, chocolate chips, vanilla, Swerve, butter, salt, and baking soda. Mix thoroughly. Transfer this mixture into a well-greased Instant Pot-friendly muffin (or egg bites) mold.

2. Using a sling if desired, place the pan onto the trivet and cover loosely with aluminum foil. Close the lid, set the pressure release to Sealing, and select Manual. Set the Instant Pot to 20 minutes on High Pressure and let cook.
3. Once cooked, let the pressure naturally disperse from the Instant Pot for about 10 minutes, then carefully switch the pressure release to Venting.
4. Open the Instant Pot and remove the pan. Let cool, serve, and enjoy!

Per Serving
calories: 204 | fat: 17g | protein: 3g | carbs: 10g net carbs: 9g | fiber: 1g

Mini Bacon and Kale Frittatas

Prep time: 5 minutes | Cook time: 20 minutes
Serves 4

6 eggs
4 slices no-sugar-added bacon, finely cut, cooked
1 cup kale, finely chopped
2 tablespoons coconut oil
½ teaspoon basil, dried
½ teaspoon chili powder (optional)
½ teaspoon cilantro, dried
½ teaspoon full-fat coconut milk
½ teaspoon freshly ground black pepper
½ teaspoon kosher salt
½ teaspoon parsley, dried

1. Pour 1 cup of filtered water into the inner pot of the Instant Pot, then insert the trivet. In a large bowl, thoroughly mix the eggs, bacon, kale, oil, basil, chili powder, cilantro, milk, pepper, salt, and parsley.
2. Once mixed, ladle mixture evenly inside four well-greased ramekins, or other small, heat-proof containers. Make sure to leave room on top of each for possible expansion during cooking. Place all ramekins or containers on the trivet.
3. Close the lid, set the pressure release to Sealing, and select Manual. Set the Instant Pot to 20 minutes on High Pressure and let cook.
4. Once cooked, let the pressure naturally disperse from the Instant Pot for about 10 minutes, then carefully switch the pressure release to Venting. Open the Instant Pot, remove the ramekins with oven mitts, and let cool for 5 to 10 minutes. Serve, and enjoy!

Per Serving
calories: 276 | fat: 21g | protein: 16g | carbs: 5g net carbs: 4g | fiber: 1g

Deconstructed Chicken Breakfast Tacos

Prep time: 5 minutes | Cook time: 10 minutes
Serves 4

2 tablespoons avocado oil	1 teaspoon hot sauce
1 pound (454 g) chicken, ground	½ teaspoon kosher salt
½ cup full fat Cheddar cheese, shredded (optional)	½ teaspoon freshly ground black pepper
1 jalapeño pepper, finely chopped	1 cup avocado, mashed
1 teaspoon lime juice	¾ cup sugar-free or low-sugar salsa
	1 tablespoon sour cream, at room temperature (optional)

1. Set the Instant Pot to Sauté and heat the oil.
2. Add the chicken, cheese (if using), jalapeño, lime juice, hot sauce, salt, black pepper, and ½ cup of filtered water.
3. Close the lid, set the pressure release to Sealing, and hit Cancel to stop the current program. Select Manual, set the Instant Pot to 10 minutes on High Pressure, and let cook.
4. Once cooked, perform a quick release by carefully switching the pressure valve to Venting.
5. Open the Instant Pot and serve, topped with the avocado, salsa, sour cream (if using).

Per Serving
calories: 334 | fat: 17g | protein: 38g | carbs: 8g
net carbs: 4g | fiber: 4g

Pumpkin Porridge

Prep time: 5 minutes | Cook time: 10 minutes
Serves 2 to 4

¼ cup unsweetened coconut flakes	½ teaspoon ginger, finely grated
2 cups full-fat coconut milk	½ teaspoon cinnamon, ground
1 cup pecans, chopped	Swerve, confectioners to taste (optional)
1 cup organic pumpkin purée	½ cup dark berries, to serve (optional)
¼ cup organic coconut flour	

1. Set the Instant Pot to Sauté, and toast the coconut flakes, stirring frequently so that they do not burn. Add in 2 cups of filtered water, as well as the milk.
2. Close the lid, set the pressure release to Sealing, and select Manual, with High Pressure. The timer should be set to 0.
3. When the Instant Pot beeps, very carefully switch the pressure release to Venting. Stir in the pecans, pumpkin, flour, ginger, cinnamon, and Swerve (if using). Let sit for about 2 to 4 minutes (or until desired consistency is reached), stirring occasionally.
4. Serve with the dark berries (if desired), and enjoy!

Per Serving
calories: 506 | fat: 41g | protein: 8g | carbs: 30g
net carbs: 13g | fiber: 17g

Cinnamon Roll Cakes

Prep time: 5 minutes | Cook time: 20 minutes
Serves 7

Base:

2 cups blanched almond flour	1 tablespoon vanilla extract
2 eggs	½ teaspoon cinnamon, ground (or more, to taste)
½ cup Swerve, confectioners	½ teaspoon salt
2 tablespoons salted grass-fed butter, softened	¼ teaspoon baking soda

Frosting:
1 cup heavy whipping cream
½ cup Swerve, confectioners (or more, to taste)

1. Pour 1 cup of filtered water into the inner pot of the Instant Pot, then insert the trivet. In a large bowl, combine the flour, eggs, Swerve, butter, vanilla, cinnamon, salt, and baking soda. Mix thoroughly. Transfer this mixture into a well-greased Instant Pot-friendly egg bites mold, working in batches if needed. I prefer to stack two egg bites molds on top of each other, separating them with Mason jar lids (or similar dividers).
2. Using a sling if desired, place the pan onto the trivet, and cover loosely with aluminum foil. Close the lid, set the pressure release to Sealing, and select Manual. Set the Instant Pot to 20 minutes on High Pressure and let cook.
3. Once cooked, let the pressure release naturally for about 10 minutes.
4. Carefully switch the pressure release on the Instant Pot to Venting. Open the Instant Pot and remove the pan. While the food cools, mix frosting ingredients thoroughly in a small bowl, and set aside.
5. Once cooled, top each cake evenly with the frosting mixture.

Per Serving
calories: 225 | fat: 21g | protein: 4g | carbs: 3g
net carbs: 2g | fiber: 1g

Bacon and Egg Bake

Prep time: 5 minutes | Cook time: 19 minutes
Serves 2 to 3

5 eggs
3 slices no-sugar-added bacon, cooked and finely chopped
2 tablespoons avocado oil
½ cup kale, chopped
½ cup broccoli, chopped

½ cup heavy whipping cream
½ teaspoon cayenne pepper, ground
½ teaspoon basil, dried
½ teaspoon kosher salt
½ teaspoon freshly ground black pepper

1. Pour in 1 cup of filtered water into the inner pot of the Instant Pot, then insert trivet. In a large bowl, combine the eggs, bacon, oil, kale, broccoli, whipping cream, cayenne pepper, basil, salt, and black pepper. Mix thoroughly.
2. Transfer mixture into a well-greased Instant Pot-friendly dish, and cover loosely with aluminum foil.
3. Close the lid, set the pressure release to Sealing, and hit Cancel to stop the current program. Select Manual, set the Instant Pot to 19 minutes on High Pressure, and let cook.
4. Once cooked, let the pressure naturally disperse from the Instant Pot for about 10 minutes, then carefully switch the pressure release to Venting.
5. Open the Instant Pot, serve, and enjoy!

Per Serving
calories: 302 | fat: 24g | protein: 17g | carbs: 5g
net carbs: 4g | fiber: 1g

Gluten-Free Zucchini Bread

Prep time: 5 minutes | Cook time: 40 minutes
Serves 5 to 6

3 eggs
1 cup blanched almond flour
¾ cup zucchini, grated
1 teaspoon vanilla extract
¼ teaspoon baking soda

½ cup Swerve, confectioners (or more, to taste)
½ teaspoon nutmeg, ground
½ teaspoon cinnamon, ground
½ teaspoon salt

1. In a large bowl, mix the eggs, flour, zucchini, vanilla, baking soda, Swerve, nutmeg, cinnamon, and salt. Stir thoroughly.
2. Pour 1 cup of filtered water into the Instant Pot, and insert the trivet. Transfer the mixture from the bowl into a well-greased Instant Pot-friendly pan (or dish).

3. Using a sling if desired, place the pan onto the trivet, and cover loosely with aluminum foil. Close the lid, set the pressure release to Sealing, and select Manual. Set the Instant Pot to 40 minutes on High Pressure, and let cook.
4. Once cooked, let the pressure naturally leave the Instant Pot, for about 10 minutes, then switch the pressure release to Venting.
5. Open the Instant Pot and remove the pan. If desired, finish bread by removing foil and placing pan on a baking sheet. Place the baking sheet in a 350ºF (180ºC) oven for 2 to 3 minutes (or until desired texture is reached).
6. Let cool, and enjoy!

Per Serving
calories: 207 | fat: 19g | protein: 6g | carbs: 4g
net carbs: 3g | fiber: 1g

Chocolate Pumpkin Treat

Prep time: 5 minutes | Cook time: 22 minutes
Serves 5 to 6

3 eggs
1 (14-ounce / 397-g) can organic pumpkin purée
1 cup almond flour
⅔ cup heavy whipping

cream
½ cup Swerve, confectioners (or more, to taste)
¼ cup sugar-free chocolate chips

1. In a large bowl, whisk the eggs, then mix in the pumpkin, flour, whipping cream, Swerve, and chocolate chips. Pour this mixture into a greased, Instant Pot-friendly pan (or dish).
2. Pour 1 cup of filtered water into the inner pot of the Instant Pot, then insert the trivet. Place the pan on top of the trivet and cover loosely with aluminum foil.
3. Close the lid, set the pressure release to Sealing, and select Manual. Set the Instant Pot to 22 minutes on High Pressure and let cook.
4. Once cooked, let the pressure naturally disperse from the Instant Pot for about 10 minutes, then carefully switch the pressure release to Venting.
5. Freeze until firm, then enjoy. Keep leftovers stored in freezer for up to one month.

Per Serving
calories: 112 | fat: 7g | protein: 4g | carbs: 8g
net carbs: 6g | fiber: 2g

Blueberry Cereal

Prep time: 5 minutes | Cook time: 2 minutes
Serves 4

2 tablespoons Swerve confectioners'-style sweetener or equivalent amount of liquid or powdered sweetener
$^1/_3$ cup crushed roasted almonds, pecans, or walnuts
¼ cup blanched almond flour
¼ cup vanilla-flavored egg white protein powder
¼ cup (½ stick) unsalted butter (or coconut oil for dairy-free), softened
1 teaspoon blueberry extract
1 teaspoon ground cinnamon
Unsweetened vanilla-flavored almond milk, for serving (optional)

1. Place all of the ingredients in a 3-quart or larger Instant Pot. Stir well to combine.
2. Seal the lid, press Manual, and set the timer for 2 minutes. (The pressure ball may not rise much, but it needs only enough heat to create a crispy cereal after cooling.) Once finished, let the pressure release naturally.
3. Stir well, then pour the cereal onto a sheet of parchment paper to cool. It will be crispy when completely cool. Serve the cereal in bowls. Pour almond milk over the cereal, if desired.

Per Serving
calories: 283 | fat: 25g | protein: 10g | carbs: 7g
net carbs: 3g | fiber: 4g

Egg Bites

Prep time: 5 minutes | Cook time: 10 minutes
Serves 2 to 4

6 eggs
½ cup spinach, finely chopped
½ cup bell peppers, finely chopped
½ cup full-fat Cheddar cheese, shredded
½ teaspoon kosher salt
½ teaspoon freshly ground black pepper
½ teaspoon cilantro, dried

1. Pour 1 cup of filtered water into the inner pot of the Instant Pot, then insert the trivet. In a large bowl, combine the eggs, spinach, bell peppers, cheese, salt, black pepper, and cilantro. Mix thoroughly. Transfer this mixture into a well-greased Instant Pot-friendly egg bites mold.
2. Using a sling if desired, place the pan onto the trivet, and cover loosely with aluminum foil. Close the lid, set the pressure release to Sealing, and select Manual. Set the Instant Pot to 10 minutes on High Pressure and let cook.

3. Once cooked, perform a quick release by carefully switching the pressure valve to Venting. Open the Instant Pot and remove the pan. Let cool, serve, and enjoy! Store any leftovers in the refrigerator.

Per Serving
calories: 152 | fat: 11g | protein: 12g | carbs: 2g
net carbs: 1g | fiber: 1g

Breakfast Cake

Prep time: 5 minutes | Cook time: 40 minutes
Serves 5 to 6

Base:
3 eggs
2 tablespoons salted grass-fed butter, softened
1 cup blanched almond flour
¾ cup walnuts, chopped
½ cup organic pumpkin purée
¼ cup heavy whipping cream
½ teaspoon salt
½ teaspoon baking powder
½ teaspoon cinnamon, ground
½ teaspoon nutmeg, ground

Toppings:
¼ cup heavy whipping cream
½ cup Swerve, confectioners (or more, to taste)
½ cup unsweetened coconut flakes

1. Pour 1 cup of filtered water into the inner pot of the Instant Pot, then insert the trivet. Using an electric mixer, combine the eggs, butter, flour, walnuts, pumpkin, cream, salt, baking powder, cinnamon, and nutmeg. Mix thoroughly. Transfer this mixture into a well-greased, Instant Pot-friendly pan (or dish).
2. Using a sling if desired, place the pan onto the trivet, and cover loosely with aluminum foil. Close the lid, set the pressure release to Sealing, and select Manual. Set the Instant Pot to 40 minutes on High Pressure, and let cook.
3. While cooking, mix all topping ingredients thoroughly in a large bowl.
4. Once cooked, let the pressure naturally disperse from the Instant Pot for about 10 minutes, then carefully switch the pressure release to Venting.
5. Open the Instant Pot and remove the pan. Sprinkle the topping mixture evenly over the cake. Let cool, serve, and enjoy!

Per Serving
calories: 334 | fat: 30g | protein: 8g | carbs: 8g
net carbs: 3g | fiber: 5g

Chaptr 5 Appetizers and Side

Deviled Eggs

Prep time: 15 minutes | Cook time: 8 minutes
Serves 3

6 eggs
1 cup water
¼ cup mayo
½ teaspoon salt
⅛ teaspoon pepper
½ teaspoon yellow mustard
¼ teaspoon paprika

1. Place eggs on steamer basket and add to Instant Pot. Pour water into pot and click lid closed. Press the Egg button and adjust time for 8 minutes.
2. When timer beeps, quick-release the pressure and remove steamer basket. Place eggs in cold water and peel when cooled. Slice eggs in half lengthwise.
3. Remove yolks and set egg whites aside. Place yolks, mayo, salt, pepper, and mustard in food processor and blend until smooth. (Alternatively, press with fork until all ingredients are smooth.) Place filling into egg whites. Sprinkle with paprika and refrigerate at least 30 minutes or until chilled.

Per Serving
calories: 268 | fat: 22g | protein: 13g | carbs: 1g
net carbs: 1g | fiber: 0g

Nutty "Noodles"

Prep time: 5 minutes | Cook time: 8 minutes
Serves 4

4 cups thinly sliced cabbage
¼ cup sunflower seed butter or creamy peanut butter
¼ cup chicken broth or vegetable broth
2 tablespoons coconut aminos, or 1½ teaspoons wheat-free tamari
1½ tablespoons Swerve confectioners'-style sweetener or equivalent amount of liquid or powdered sweetener
¼ teaspoon cayenne pepper
1½ teaspoons lemon juice
For Garnish:
Sliced green onions
Lime wedges

1. Place all of the ingredients except the garnishes in a 6-quart Instant Pot. Stir well to combine. Seal the lid, press Manual, and set the timer for 8 minutes. Once finished, turn the valve to venting for a quick release. The cabbage "noodles" should be soft.
2. Serve warm or chilled. Garnish with green onions and lime wedges.

Per Serving
calories: 128 | fat: 8g | protein: 5g | carbs: 9g
net carbs: 6g | fiber: 3g

Salsa Verde

Prep time: 5 minutes | Cook time: 25 minutes
Makes 2½ cups

1 pound (454 g) tomatillos
3 cloves garlic
2 whole serrano peppers
2 whole jalapeños
½ medium onion, chopped
1 teaspoon salt
¼ cup chopped cilantro
1 cup chicken broth
¼ teaspoon xanthan gum
2 teaspoons avocado oil

1. Remove husks from tomatillos. Peel garlic. Slice jalapeños and serrano peppers in half lengthwise, cut off stems, and remove most seeds. Peel and chop onion. Place all into Instant Pot.
2. Add salt, cilantro, and chicken broth to Instant Pot. Click lid to close. Press the Manual button and set timer to 10 minutes. When timer goes off, natural-release the pressure for 5 minutes. Quick-release the remaining steam.
3. Pour Instant Pot contents into food processor and pulse until desired texture. Stir in xanthan gum and allow a few minutes to thicken. Return mixture to Instant Pot and press the Sauté button. Add avocado oil. Allow salsa to reduce for 15 minutes. Store in sealed container in fridge.

Per Serving
calories: 58 | fat: 6g | protein: 1g | carbs: 7g
net carbs: 5g | fiber: 2g

Quick Steamed Cauliflower

Prep time: 3 minutes | Cook time: 1 minute
Serves 2

1 cup water
½ large head of cauliflower, chopped

1. Add water to Instant Pot and place steamer basket inside pot. Put cauliflower into steamer basket.
2. Click lid closed. Press the Steam button and adjust time for 1 minute. When timer beeps, quick-release the steam. When pressure indicator drops, remove steamer basket. Feel free to season with your choice of herbs, salt, and butter (adjust the nutritional stats accordingly).

Per Serving
calories: 52 | fat: 0g | protein: 4g | carbs: 10g
net carbs: 6g | fiber: 4g

Cauliflower Queso

Prep time: 10 minutes | Cook time: 30 minutes
Serves 5

2 cups cauliflower, chopped
⅓ cup cream cheese
½ cup Cheddar cheese
1 jalapeño, chopped
2 ounces (57 g)

scallions, diced
1 tablespoon nutritional yeast
1 tablespoon olive oil
2 garlic cloves, diced

1. Put chopped cauliflower, cream cheese, Cheddar cheese, jalapeño, diced scallions, nutritional yeast, olive oil, and diced garlic clove.
2. Stir the mixture well with the help of the spoon and close the lid.
3. Cook the queso for 30 minutes on Sauté mode. Stir meal every 5 minutes to avoid burning.

Per Serving
calories: 146 | fat: 12g | protein: 6g | carbs: 5g
net carbs: 3g | fiber: 2g

Cheese Stuffed Shishito Peppers

Prep time: 20 minutes | Cook time: 7 minutes
Serves 4

8 ounces (227 g) shishito peppers
1 cup Cheddar cheese, shredded
4 tablespoons cream cheese
1 tablespoon fresh

parsley, chopped
¼ teaspoon minced garlic
1 tablespoon butter, melted
1 cup water, for cooking

1. Cut the ends of the peppers and remove the seeds.
2. After this, in the mixing bowl mix up shredded cheese, cream cheese, parsley, and minced garlic.
3. Then fill the peppers with cheese mixture and put in the baking mold.
4. Sprinkle the peppers with melted butter.
5. After this, pour water and insert the trivet.
6. Place the mold with peppers on the trivet. Close and seal the lid.
7. Cook the meal on Manual at High Pressure for 7 minutes. Allow the natural pressure release for 5 minutes.

Per Serving
calories: 194 | fat: 16g | protein: 9g | carbs: 5g
net carbs: 2g | fiber: 3g

Queso Fundido

Prep time: 5 minutes | Cook time: 10 minutes
Serves 20

1 pound (454 g) ground hot sausage or Mexican chorizo
1 pound (454 g) processed yellow melting cheese (such as Velveeta), cubed

8 ounces (227 g) cream cheese, cubed
1 can (10 ounces / 283 g) diced tomatoes with green chiles
¾ cup heavy cream

1. Turn the pot to Sauté mode. Once hot, add the sausage and cook until no longer pink, 3 to 4 minutes. If your meat produces more than 1 tablespoon of grease, drain off the excess.
2. In this order, add the yellow cheese, cream cheese, and tomatoes (with juice). This will ensure that the cheese and tomatoes do not scorch terribly on the bottom of the pot. Do not stir the mixture.
3. Close the lid and seal the vent. Cook on Low Pressure for 3 minutes. Quick release the steam.
4. Open the lid and stir the mixture until all of the cheese is melted and incorporated. There may be a little bit stuck to the bottom, but that is okay. Add the cream and stir to combine.

Per Serving
calories: 163 | fat: 13g | protein: 6g | carbs: 2g
net carbs: 2g | fiber: 0g

Spinach Dip

Prep time: 10 minutes | Cook time: 6 hours
Serves 4

2 cups spinach, chopped
1 cup Mozzarella, shredded
2 artichoke hearts, chopped

1 teaspoon ground ginger
1 teaspoon butter
½ teaspoon white pepper
½ cup heavy cream

1. Put the spinach, artichoke hearts, and butter in the Instant Pot.
2. Add Mozzarella, ground ginger, white pepper, and heavy cream. Stir the mixture gently.
3. Cook it in Manual mode at Low Pressure for 6 hours. Then stir well and transfer in the serving bowl.

Per Serving
calories: 124 | fat: 8g | protein: 5g | carbs: 10g
net carbs: 5g | fiber: 5g

BLT Dip

Prep time: 10 minutes | Cook time: 20 minutes
Serves 3

2 teaspoons cream cheese
3 ounces (85 g) bacon, chopped
2 tablespoons sour cream
2 ounces (57 g) Cheddar cheese,

shredded
¼ teaspoon minced garlic
1 teaspoon smoked paprika
1 tomato, chopped
¼ cup lettuce, chopped

1. Preheat the Instant Pot on Sauté mode.
2. Put the chopped bacon in the Instant Pot and cook it for 5 minutes. Stir it from time to time.
3. Then add cream cheese, sour cream, Cheddar cheese, garlic, smoked paprika, and tomato.
4. Close the lid and cook the dip on Sauté mode for 15 minutes.
5. Then stir it well and mix up with lettuce.

Per Serving
calories: 261 | fat: 20g | protein: 16g | carbs: 2g
net carbs: 2g | fiber: 0g

Paprika-Lemon Brussels Sprouts

Prep time: 5 minutes | Cook time: 3 minutes
Serves 4

2 tablespoons extra-virgin olive oil
1 pound (454 g) Brussels sprouts, outer leaves removed, and washed
1 lemon, juiced

½ teaspoon kosher salt
½ teaspoon black ground pepper
½ teaspoon paprika, fresh
1 cup grass-fed bone broth

1. Set the Instant Pot to Sauté, and gently heat the extra-virgin olive oil. Add the Brussels sprouts, followed by the lemon juice, salt, pepper, and paprika.
2. Cook for 1 minute, then pour in the bone broth.
3. Close the Instant Pot, set the pressure release to Sealing, and select Manual. Set the Instant Pot to 3 minutes on Low Pressure and let cook.
4. Once cooked, carefully release the pressure. Open the lid, remove the Brussels sprouts, and enjoy!

Per Serving
calories: 121 | fat: 7g | protein: 5g | carbs: 12g
net carbs: 7g | fiber: 5g

Sausage Dip

Prep time: 10 minutes | Cook time: 25 minutes
Serves 7

12 ounces (340 g) Italian sausages
1 chili pepper, chopped
5 ounces (142 g) Cheddar cheese,

shredded
1 teaspoon coconut oil
1 teaspoon tomato paste
¼ cup heavy cream

1. Heat up coconut oil in the Instant Pot.
2. Then add Italian sausages and cook them on Sauté mode for 10 minutes. Mix up the sausages every 3 minutes.
3. Then add chili pepper, shredded Cheddar cheese, tomato paste, and heavy cream.
4. Close the lid and cook the dip on Manual mode at High Pressure for 10 minutes. Make a quick pressure release.

Per Serving
calories: 271 | fat: 24g | protein: 12g | carbs: 1g
net carbs: 1g | fiber: 0g

Artichoke with Buttery Garlic Dipping Sauce

Prep time: 5 minutes | Cook time: 5 minutes
Serves 2

1 artichoke, fresh
5 tablespoons salted grass-fed butter
1 teaspoon garlic, minced
¼ teaspoon lime juice,

fresh
¼ teaspoon cilantro, dried
¼ teaspoon oregano, dried

1. Prepare the artichoke by removing the stem, top, and thorns. Pour ½ cup of filtered water into the Instant Pot, then insert the trivet. Place the artichoke on the trivet, then set the valve to Sealing and close the lid. Use the Manual setting, and set the cook time for 5 minutes. Let cook.
2. Immediately, when cooking is complete, perform a quick release by carefully switching the pressure valve to Venting, and remove the artichoke. Mix butter, garlic, lime juice, cilantro, and oregano in a small bowl, and microwave briefly, until melted, about 30 to 40 seconds. Serve the sauce alongside the artichoke for dipping, and enjoy!

Per Serving
calories: 289 | fat: 29g | protein: 2g | carbs: 8g
net carbs: 4g | fiber: 4g

Almond Butter Cheese Jalapeños

Prep time: 10 minutes | Cook time: 7 minutes
Serves 4

4 jalapeño peppers
1 egg, beaten
½ cup Monterey Jack cheese, shredded

1 teaspoon almond butter, softened
1 cup water, for cooking

1. Cut the jalapeños into halves and remove the seeds.
2. In the mixing bowl, mix up softened almond butter, cheese, and egg.
3. Then fill the jalapeño halves with cheese mixture.
4. Put the jalapeños in the ramekin.
5. Then pour water and insert the trivet in the Instant Pot.
6. Put the ramekin with jalapeños on the trivet and close the lid.
7. Cook the meal for 7 minutes on Manual at High Pressure. Make a quick pressure release.

Per Serving
calories: 99 | fat: 8g | protein: 6g | carbs: 2g
net carbs: 1g | fiber: 1g

Red Cauliflower Rice

Prep time: 10 minutes | Cook time: 3 minutes
Serves 4

1 cup cauliflower, shredded
1 teaspoon tomato paste
½ cup coconut cream

½ teaspoon salt
¼ cup chicken broth
1 teaspoon dried cilantro

1. Put all ingredients in the Instant Pot and stir until you get the red color of the cauliflower.
2. Close and seal the lid.
3. Cook the meal on Manual at High Pressure for 3 minutes. Make a quick pressure release.

Per Serving
calories: 79 | fat: 7g | protein: 2g | carbs: 3g
net carbs: 2g | fiber: 1g

Steamed Savoy Cabbage

Prep time: 5 minutes | Cook time: 7 minutes
Serves 4

1 pound (454 g) cabbage, chopped
⅓ cup butter
1 teaspoon salt

½ teaspoon white pepper
1 cup chicken broth

1. Put all ingredients in the Instant Pot and stir them well.
2. After this, close and seal the lid.
3. Cook the cabbage on Manual mode at High Pressure for 7 minutes.
4. Then make a quick pressure release and open the lid.
5. Stir the meal well before serving.

Per Serving
calories: 174 | fat: 16g | protein: 3g | carbs: 7g
net carbs: 4g | fiber: 3g

Shrimp Sandwich

Prep time: 5 minutes | Cook time: 5 minutes
Serves 2

4 lettuce leaves
4 king shrimps, peeled
1 teaspoon lemon juice
½ teaspoon white

pepper
2 tablespoons butter
½ teaspoon salt

1. Sprinkle the shrimps with white pepper and salt and put in the Instant Pot.
2. Add butter and cook the seafood for 3 minutes on Sauté mode.
3. Then flip the shrimps on another side and cook them for 2 minutes more.
4. Sprinkle the cooked shrimps with lemon juice and transfer on lettuce leaves (2 shrimps per one lettuce leaf).
5. Cover them with the remaining lettuce.

Per Serving
calories: 165 | fat: 13g | protein: 13g | carbs: 2g
net carbs: 2g | fiber: 0g

Buttery Spinach

Prep time: 5 minutes | Cook time: 10 minutes
Serves 2

4 cups fresh spinach
4 tablespoons butter
½ teaspoon salt
¼ teaspoon pepper

¼ teaspoon garlic powder
⅛ teaspoon red pepper flakes

1. Press the Sauté button and press the Adjust button to set heat to Less. Place all ingredients in Instant Pot and sauté until greens are soft, approximately 10 minutes.

Per Serving
calories: 218 | fat: 1g | protein: 2g | carbs: 3g
net carbs: 1g | fiber: 2g

Sautéed Green Mix

Prep time: 5 minutes | Cook time: 5 minutes
Serves 2

2 cups spinach, chopped
1 cup kale, chopped
½ cup chicken stock
1 teaspoon cream

cheese
½ teaspoon salt
½ cup broccoli raab, chopped

1. Pour the chicken stock in the Instant Pot.
2. Add cream cheese, salt, spinach, kale, and broccoli raab.
3. Cook the meal on the Sauté mode for 5 minutes. Stir well.
4. Discard the greens from the chicken stock gravy and transfer on the plates.

Per Serving
calories: 37 | fat: 1g | protein: 3g | carbs: 6g
net carbs: 5g | fiber: 1g

Creamed Spinach

Prep time: 5 minutes | Cook time: 16 minutes
Serves 5

1 teaspoon avocado oil
2 ounces (57 g) onion, diced
2 cloves garlic, minced
12 ounces (340 g) fresh spinach
½ cup grated Parmesan

cheese
3 ounces (85 g) cream cheese, softened
2 tablespoons heavy cream
1 teaspoon salt
½ cup water

1. Turn the pot to Sauté mode. Once hot, add the avocado oil, onion, and garlic. Sauté until translucent, 2 to 3 minutes, and then add the spinach.
2. Cook until the spinach is wilted and the water is cooked out, about 5 minutes. Place the spinach on top of a paper towel and squeeze any excess water out.
3. Return the spinach to the pot and add the Parmesan, cream cheese, cream, and salt. Stir until the cheese is melted, 2 to 3 minutes.
4. Transfer the spinach mixture to the baking dish and cover with aluminum foil. Rinse out the inner pot and place back in the base. Add the water to the pot and place the trivet inside. Place the baking dish on the trivet.
5. Close the lid and seal the vent. Cook on High Pressure for 5 minutes. Quick release the steam.

Per Serving
calories: 145 | fat: 11g | protein: 6g | carbs: 5g
net carbs: 3g | fiber: 2g

Garlic Asparagus

Prep time: 6 minutes | Cook time: 4 minutes
Serves 2

9 ounces (255 g) asparagus
½ teaspoon garlic powder
1 teaspoon butter

¾ teaspoon minced garlic
2 ounces (57 g) Parmesan, shredded
1 cup water, for cooking

1. Grease the springform pan with butter.
2. Place the asparagus in the springform pan.
3. Sprinkle the vegetables with the garlic powder, and minced garlic.
4. Add water in the Instant Pot. Insert the springform with asparagus inside.
5. Close the lid and set the Manual mode at High Pressure for 4 minutes.
6. When the asparagus is cooked, make a quick pressure release.
7. Transfer the asparagus on the serving plates immediately and sprinkle with the shredded cheese.

Per Serving
calories: 137 | fat: 8g | protein: 12g | carbs: 7g
net carbs: 4g | fiber: 3g

Avocado Egg Salad

Prep time: 10 minutes | Cook time: 8 minutes
Serves 2

1 cup water
6 eggs
1 avocado
2 tablespoons lime juice
½ teaspoon chili

powder
¼ teaspoon salt
2 tablespoons mayo
2 tablespoons chopped cilantro

1. Pour water into Instant Pot. Place eggs on trivet or in steamer basket inside pot.
2. Click lid closed. Press the Egg button and adjust time for 8 minutes. While egg is cooking, cut avocado in half and scoop out flesh. Place in food processor and blend until smooth.
3. Transfer avocado to medium bowl and add lime juice, chili powder, salt, mayo, and cilantro.
4. When timer beeps, carefully remove eggs and place in bowl of cold water for 5 minutes. Peel eggs and chop into bite-sized pieces. Fold chopped eggs into avocado mixture. Serve chilled.

Per Serving
calories: 426 | fat: 33g | protein: 20g | carbs: 9g
net carbs: 4g | fiber: 5g

Steamed Artichoke

Prep time: 1 minute | Cook time: 30 minutes
Serves 2

1 large artichoke	¼ teaspoon salt
1 cup water	¼ teaspoon red pepper
¼ cup grated Parmesan cheese	flakes

1. Trim artichoke. Remove stem, outer leaves and top. Gently spread leaves.
2. Add water to Instant Pot and place trivet in bottom. Place artichoke on trivet and sprinkle with Parmesan, salt, and red pepper flakes. Click lid closed. Press the Steam button and adjust time for 30 minutes.
3. When timer beeps, allow a 15-minute natural release and then quick-release the remaining pressure. Enjoy warm topped with additional Parmesan.

Per Serving
calories: 90 | fat: 3g | protein: 6g | carbs: 10g
net carbs: 6g | fiber: 4g

Bacon Brussels Sprouts

Prep time: 5 minutes | Cook time: 10 minutes
Serves 4

½ pound (227 g) bacon	1 teaspoon salt
1 pound (454 g) Brussels sprouts	½ teaspoon pepper
	½ cup water
4 tablespoons butter	

1. Press the Sauté button and press the Adjust button to lower heat to Less. Add bacon to Instant Pot and fry for 3 to 5 minutes or until fat begins to render. Press the Cancel button.
2. Press the Sauté button, with heat set to Normal, and continue frying bacon until crispy. While bacon is frying, wash Brussels sprouts and remove damaged outer leaves. Cut in half or quarters.
3. When bacon is done, remove and set aside. Add Brussels sprouts to hot bacon grease and add butter. Sprinkle with salt and pepper. Sauté for 8 to 10 minutes until caramelized and crispy, adding a few tablespoons of water at a time as needed to deglaze pan. Serve warm.

Per Serving
calories: 387 | fat: 32g | protein: 11g | carbs: 11g
net carbs: 7g | fiber: 4g

Cheesy Cauliflower Rice

Prep time: 3 minutes | Cook time: 1 minute
Serves 4

1 head fresh cauliflower, chopped into florets	1 cup shredded sharp Cheddar cheese
1 cup water	½ teaspoon salt
3 tablespoons butter	¼ teaspoon pepper
1 tablespoon heavy cream	¼ teaspoon garlic powder

1. Place cauliflower in steamer basket. Pour water into Instant Pot and lower it into pot. Click lid closed. Press the Steam button and adjust time for 1 minute. When timer beeps, quick-release the pressure.
2. Remove steamer basket and place cauliflower in food processor. Pulse until cauliflower is broken into small pearls. Place cauliflower into large bowl, and add remaining ingredients. Gently fold until fully combined.

Per Serving
calories: 241 | fat: 18g | protein: 10g | carbs: 8g
net carbs: 5g | fiber: 3g

Bacon-Lime Guacamole

Prep time: 5 minutes | Cook time: 10 minutes
Serves 8

2 tablespoons avocado oil	sliced
	1 avocado, mashed
½ pound (227 g) no-sugar-added bacon, sliced into small pieces	½ teaspoon kosher salt
	¼ teaspoon cilantro, dried
¼ (4-ounce / 113-g) small onion, thinly	1 tablespoon lime juice

1. Set the Instant Pot to Sauté mode. Add the oil to the Instant Pot, melting it gently.
2. Add the bacon, and cook until crisp. Once cooked, remove the bacon with tongs, and drain on a paper towel-lined plate. Sprinkle the onion into the Instant Pot and let cook for 1 minute (or until translucent). Hit Cancel on the Instant Pot.
3. Spoon the onion into a large bowl, along with the avocado, salt, and cilantro. Crumble the cooled bacon into the bowl, then mix in the lime juice. Stir thoroughly, until desired consistency is reached.

Per Serving
calories: 237 | fat: 20g | protein: 11g | carbs: 3g
net carbs: 1g | fiber: 2g

Creamy Chorizo Dip

Prep time: 5 minutes | Cook time: 10 minutes
Serves 4

1 pound (454 g) ground chorizo
1 cup chicken broth
½ cup salsa
8 ounces (227 g) cream cheese
½ cup shredded white American cheese

1. Press the Sauté button and add chorizo to Instant Pot. Cook thoroughly and drain or pat with paper towel to absorb grease.
2. Add broth and salsa. Place cream cheese on top of meat. Click lid closed. Press the Manual button to adjust time for 5 minutes.
3. When timer beeps, quick-release the pressure and stir in white American cheese. Serve warm.

Per Serving
calories: 688 | fat: 53g | protein: 28g | carbs: 7g
net carbs: 7g | fiber: 0g

Buffalo Chicken Meatballs

Prep time: 25 minutes | Cook time: 10 minutes
Makes 20 meatballs

1 pound (454 g) ground chicken
1 rib celery, finely diced
1 scallion, finely diced
1 egg
2 tablespoons plus 1 cup buffalo wing sauce,
divided
½ teaspoon garlic powder
½ teaspoon salt
Pinch of black pepper
½ cup chicken broth

1. In a bowl, combine the chicken, celery, scallion, egg, 2 tablespoons of the buffalo wing sauce, garlic powder, salt, and pepper. Stir with a wooden spoon until the mixture is well combined.
2. Use a medium-size cookie scoop to measure out 20 meatballs and place them on a large plate or baking sheet. Each meatball should weigh about 1 ounce (28 g).
3. Put the plate of meatballs in the freezer for 15 minutes to flash freeze them. This will help them retain their shape during cooking.
4. Add the broth and ½ cup of the buffalo wing sauce to the pot. Remove the meatballs from the freezer and place them into the pot.
5. Close the lid and seal the vent. Cook on High Pressure for 10 minutes. Quick release the steam.
6. Use a slotted spoon to remove the meatballs from the pot and transfer to a serving plate or bowl. Top them with the remaining ½ cup buffalo wing sauce.
7. If desired, place the meatballs on a baking sheet and put them under the broiler for 3 to 5 minutes for a stickier buffalo coating.

Per Serving
calories: 39 | fat: 2g | protein: 5g | carbs: 0g
net carbs: 0g | fiber: 0g

Faux Mac and Cheese

Prep time: 5 minutes | Cook time: 5 minutes
Serves 6

1 large head cauliflower (about 2 pounds / 907 g)
½ cup water
½ cup heavy cream
2 ounces (57 g) cream cheese, softened
1 teaspoon Dijon
mustard
¼ teaspoon Worcestershire sauce
¼ teaspoon salt
Pinch of black pepper
2 cups shredded Cheddar cheese

1. Place the cauliflower on a cutting board. Remove the core and leaves but do not completely de-core. The head should remain intact for cooking.
2. Place the cauliflower in the steamer basket and lower into the Instant Pot. Add the water to the pot.
3. Close the lid and seal the vent. Cook on Low Pressure for 3 minutes. Quick release the steam. Press Cancel.
4. Remove the lid and use a fork to check for doneness. The fork should easily penetrate the cauliflower, but it should not fall apart. If it is still very firm, cook for 1 additional minute on Low Pressure.
5. Place the cauliflower back on the cutting board and remove the florets from the stems. Place the florets in the baking dish and set aside.
6. Drain the water from the pot. Turn the pot to Sauté mode. Add the cream to the pot.
7. Add the cream cheese, mustard, Worcestershire, salt, and pepper. Whisk until the cream cheese is completely melted, 1 to 2 minutes.
8. Add the Cheddar and whisk until all the cheese is melted and the consistency is smooth, 1 to 2 minutes.
9. Pour the cheese sauce over the cauliflower and toss to coat.

Per Serving
calories: 387 | fat: 31g | protein: 21g | carbs: 8g
net carbs: 6g | fiber: 2g

Game Day Meatballs

Prep time: 3 minutes | Cook time: 7 minutes
Serves 30

¼ cup water
2 packages (14 ounces / 397 g each) frozen meatballs (60 meatballs total)
8 ounces (227 g) sugar-free blackberry jam
½ cup sugar-free BBQ sauce
¼ cup Sriracha

1. Pour the water into the pot and add the meatballs.
2. In a small bowl, whisk together the jam, BBQ sauce, and sriracha. Pour the sauce over the meatballs.
3. Close the lid and seal the vent. Cook on High Pressure for 7 minutes. Quick release the steam.
4. Stir the meatballs to make sure they are evenly coated with sauce. Transfer to a serving bowl. Let rest for a few minutes so the sauce thickens up a bit before serving.

Per Serving
calories: 75 | fat: 4g | protein: 5g | carbs: 6g
net carbs: 4g | fiber: 2g

Extra Crispy Parmesan Crisps

Prep time: 5 minutes | Cook time: 4 minutes
Serves 7 to 8

6 slices no-sugar-added bacon, sliced into small pieces
2 cups full-fat Parmesan cheese, grated
1 cup full-fat Cheddar cheese, shredded
½ teaspoon paprika, fresh
½ teaspoon chili powder
½ teaspoon freshly ground black pepper
½ teaspoon kosher salt

1. Set the Instant Pot to Sauté, and add the bacon to cook. In a large bowl, mix the Parmesan and Cheddar, paprika, chili powder, and salt and pepper. Using a spoon, transfer cheese mixture into a greased, Instant Pot-friendly dish.
2. Make sure bacon is cooked, then press Cancel. Briefly drain the bacon on a paper towel-lined plate, break into large pieces, and divide evenly over the cheese.
3. Pour 1 cup of filtered water into the inner pot of the Instant Pot, then insert the trivet. Place the dish with the cheese and bacon on top of the trivet. Close the Instant Pot, set the pressure release to Sealing, and select Manual. Set the Instant Pot to 4 minutes on High Pressure and let cook.

4. Once cooked, quickly release the pressure. Use a spatula to transfer crisp mixture to a baking sheet, and separate into 7 or 8 individual crisps. Finish the crisps on the baking sheet in the oven at 350ºF (180ºC) for about 5 to 7 minutes (or until crunchy). Let cool, and enjoy!

Per Serving
calories: 315 | fat: 23g | protein: 27g | carbs: 2g
net carbs: 2g | fiber: 0g

Perfect Zucchini Noodles

Prep time: 5 minutes | Cook time: 4 minutes
Serves 2

1 tablespoon coconut oil
2 large zucchini, spiralized
½ teaspoon salt

1. Press the Sauté button and press the Adjust button to set heat to Less. Add coconut oil to Instant Pot.
2. Sprinkle zucchini with salt. Toss in coconut oil until just beginning to soften, 3 to 6 minutes, depending on zoodle thickness. (Watch them carefully, overcooking will cause them to release excess water and get soggy.) Serve warm in favorite sauce.

Per Serving
calories: 113 | fat: 7g | protein: 4g | carbs: 10g
net carbs: 7g | fiber: 3g

Garlic Butter Steamed Broccoli

Prep time: 3 minutes | Cook time: 1 minute
Serves 2

1 cup water
2 cups broccoli, chopped
½ teaspoon salt
½ teaspoon garlic powder
2 tablespoons butter

1. Add water to Instant Pot and place steamer basket inside pot. Add broccoli to basket.
2. Click lid closed. Press the Steam button and adjust time for 1 minute. When timer beeps, quick-release the steam. Wait until pressure indicator drops and open lid.
3. Remove basket and place broccoli in large bowl. Sprinkle with salt and garlic powder. Toss with butter until melted. Serve warm.

Per Serving
calories: 123 | fat: 11g | protein: 2g | carbs: 4g
net carbs: 4g | fiber: 0g

Pesto Zucchini Noodles

Prep time: 5 minutes | Cook time: 3 minutes
Serves 2

2 large zucchini, spiralized
½ teaspoon salt
¼ teaspoon pepper
2 tablespoons butter
¼ cup pesto
⅛ cup grated Parmesan

1. Sprinkle zucchini with salt and pepper. Press the Sauté button and add butter to Instant Pot. Let butter melt then add spiralized zucchini. Sauté for 2 to 3 minutes only. (Overcooking them will cause them to release excess water and get soggy.)
2. Press the Cancel button and add pesto. Sprinkle with grated Parmesan. Serve warm.

Per Serving
calories: 182 | fat: 23g | protein: 7g | carbs: 14g
net carbs: 10g | fiber: 4g

Smoky Bacon Sliders

Prep time: 5 minutes | Cook time: 10 minutes
Serves 4 to 5

2 tablespoons coconut oil
½ pound (227 g) no-sugar-added bacon, sliced into small pieces
1 pound (454 g) grass-fed beef, ground
½ teaspoon black ground pepper
½ teaspoon kosher salt
½ teaspoon chili powder
½ teaspoon crushed red pepper
½ teaspoon cayenne pepper, ground
1 cup full-fat Cheddar cheese, shredded
1 cup full-fat Mozzarella cheese, shredded

1. Set the Instant Pot to Sauté, and gently melt the coconut oil. Add the bacon and cook until crisp. Remove bacon and drain on a paper towel-lined plate. Set aside.
2. Meanwhile, in a large bowl, combine the beef with pepper and salt, chili powder, red pepper, and cayenne pepper, until the spices are evenly distributed throughout the beef. Avoid overmixing, as this might cause the patties to become tough.
3. In a greased, Instant Pot-friendly dish, mold the beef mixture into 4 to 5 thin, flat sliders.
4. Pour ¾ cup of filtered water into the Instant Pot, then insert the trivet. Set the dish with the sliders on top of the trivet. Close the Instant Pot, set the pressure release to Sealing, and select Manual. Set the Instant Pot to 10 minutes on High Pressure and let cook.

5. Once cooked, let the pressure naturally disperse for 5 to 10 minutes. Open the lid and remove the food. In a small bowl, mix the cheeses. Sprinkle the cheeses and cooked bacon over the sliders, and enjoy!

Per Serving
calories: 526 | fat: 41g | protein: 36g | carbs: 1g
net carbs: 1g | fiber: 0g

Sautéed Radishes

Prep time: 5 minutes | Cook time: 15 minutes
Serves 4

1 pound (454 g) radishes, quartered (remove leaves and ends)
2 tablespoons butter
¼ teaspoon dried thyme
¼ teaspoon minced garlic
⅛ teaspoon salt
⅛ teaspoon garlic powder
⅛ teaspoon dried rosemary

1. Press the Sauté button and then press the Adjust button to lower heat to Less.
2. Place radishes into Instant Pot with butter and seasoning.
3. Sauté, stirring occasionally until tender, about 10 to 15 minutes. Add a couple of teaspoons of water if radishes begin to stick.

Per Serving
calories: 62 | fat: 5g | protein: 0g | carbs: 3g
net carbs: 2g | fiber: 1g

Buttery Cabbage

Prep time: 5 minutes | Cook time: 5 minutes
Serves 4

1 medium head white cabbage, sliced into strips
4 tablespoons butter
½ teaspoon salt
¼ teaspoon pepper
1 cup water

1. Place cabbage in 7-cup glass bowl with butter, salt, and pepper.
2. Pour water into Instant Pot and place trivet in bottom. Place bowl on trivet. Click lid closed. Press the Manual button and adjust time for 5 minutes. When timer beeps, quick-release the pressure.

Per Serving
calories: 158 | fat: 11g | protein: 3g | carbs: 13g
net carbs: 8g | fiber: 5g

10-Minute Kale Chips

**Prep time: 5 minutes | Cook time: 5 minutes
Serves 4**

½ cup extra-virgin olive oil

4 tablespoons grass-fed butter, softened

4 cups kale, in large pieces, washed and

dried, stems removed

½ cup full-fat Parmesan cheese, grated

½ teaspoon freshly ground black pepper

½ teaspoon kosher salt

1. Set the Instant Pot to Sauté mode. Add the oil and grass-fed butter, melting it gently, and mix together.
2. Insert the trivet, and place the kale on top of it. In a small dish, mix together the Parmesan cheese, black pepper, and salt; then sprinkle mixture over the kale.
3. After 5 minutes, remove the chips. Finish the chips on a baking sheet in the oven at 350ºF (180ºC), for about 5 to 7 minutes (or until crisp). Allow to cool before enjoying.

Per Serving
calories: 215 | fat: 20g | protein: 3g | carbs: 7g
net carbs: 6g | fiber: 1g

Warm Cabbage and Broccoli Slaw

**Prep time: 5 minutes | Cook time: 10 minutes
Serves 6**

2 cups broccoli slaw

½ head cabbage, thinly sliced

¼ cup chopped kale

4 tablespoons butter

1 teaspoon salt

¼ teaspoon pepper

1. Press the Sauté button and add all ingredients to Instant Pot. Stir-fry for 7 to 10 minutes until cabbage softens. Serve warm.

Per Serving
calories: 97 | fat: 7g | protein: 2g | carbs: 6g
net carbs: 4g | fiber: 2g

Pizza Dip

**Prep time: 5 minutes | Cook time: 30 minutes
Serves 4**

¾ cup whole-milk ricotta cheese (6 ounces / 170 g)

¾ cup marinara sauce

Topping Options:
Sliced cooked sausage
Sliced pepperoni
Sliced bell peppers
Sliced black olives

1 clove garlic, minced

6 ounces (170 g) Italian cheeses, finely grated (¾ cup)

Sliced mushrooms
Sliced onions
Pork rinds, for serving

1. Set a trivet in a 6-quart Instant Pot and pour in ½ cup of cold water. Grease a 1-quart round casserole dish. Spread the ricotta in an even layer in the greased dish.
2. In a medium-sized bowl, stir together the marinara and garlic. Pour the sauce over the ricotta and spread evenly. Layer the shredded cheese over the sauce, then layer your favorite pizza toppings on top.
3. Use a foil sling to lower the casserole dish onto the trivet in the Instant Pot. Tuck in the sides of the sling.
4. Seal the lid, press Manual, and set the timer for 30 minutes. Once finished, let the pressure release naturally. Lift the casserole dish out of the Instant Pot using the foil sling.
5. Serve with pork rinds.

Per Serving
calories: 262 | fat: 21g | protein: 17g | carbs: 4g
net carbs: 3g | fiber: 1g

Turmeric Egg Salad

**Prep time: 5 minutes | Cook time: 7 minutes
Serves 2**

6 eggs

¼ cup mayonnaise

½ teaspoon paprika, fresh

½ teaspoon freshly ground black pepper

½ teaspoon turmeric, ground

½ teaspoon kosher salt

¼ cup green onions, thinly sliced

1. Crack the eggs in an Instant Pot-friendly bowl, and scramble. Pour 1 cup of filtered water into the inner pot of the Instant Pot, then insert the trivet. Place the bowl with the eggs on top of the trivet.
2. Close the lid, set the pressure release to Sealing, and select Manual. Set the Instant Pot to 7 minutes on High Pressure and let cook.
3. Once cooked, let the pressure naturally disperse from the Instant Pot for about 10 minutes, then carefully switch the pressure release to Venting.
4. Meanwhile, in a small bowl, mix together mayonnaise, paprika, black pepper, turmeric, and salt, until well combined.
5. Open the lid, remove the eggs, and allow to cool. Stir in the mayo mixture and serve with the green onions on top.

Per Serving
calories: 398 | fat: 37g | protein: 17g | carbs: 3g
net carbs: 2g | fiber: 1g

Mini Pizza Bites

Prep time: 5 minutes | Cook time: 5 minutes
Serves 4 to 5

2 cups full-fat
Mozzarella cheese,
shredded
1 (14-ounce / 397-g)
can sugar-free or low-
sugar diced tomatoes,
drained

1 cup full-fat Parmesan
cheese, grated
16 uncured pepperoni
slices, cut in half
1 teaspoon basil, dried
1 teaspoon oregano,
dried

1. Pour 1 cup of filtered water into the inner
   pot of the Instant Pot, then insert the trivet.
   In a large bowl, combine the Mozzarella,
   tomatoes, Parmesan, pepperoni, basil, and
   oregano. Mix thoroughly. Transfer this mixture
   into a well-greased, Instant Pot-friendly egg
   bites mold. Work in batches, if needed. I
   prefer to stack 2 egg bites molds on top of
   each other, separated by Mason jar lids (or
   similar dividers).
2. Place the molds onto the trivet, and cover
   loosely with aluminum foil. Close the lid, set
   the pressure release to Sealing, and select
   Manual. Set the Instant Pot to 5 minutes on
   High Pressure, and let cook.
3. Once cooked, let the pressure release
   naturally, for about 10 minutes. Then, switch
   the pressure release to Venting. Open the
   Instant Pot, and remove the molds. Serve
   warm, and enjoy!

Per Serving
calories: 328 | fat: 25g | protein: 22g | carbs: 6g
net carbs: 5g | fiber: 1g

Pizza Hit Breadsticks

Prep time: 15 minutes | Cook time: 30 minutes
Serves 6

Seasoning:
¼ cup grated Parmesan
cheese
3 tablespoons garlic
powder

1 tablespoon onion
powder
1 tablespoon dried
oregano leaves

Breadsticks:
1¼ cups whole-milk
ricotta cheese (10
ounces / 283 g)
½ cup coconut flour
1 teaspoon baking
powder

5 large eggs
½ teaspoon fine sea
salt
Marinara sauce, for
serving

1. Set a trivet in a 6-quart Instant Pot and pour
   in ½ cup of cold water. Line a 7-inch round
   cake pan or springform pan with parchment
   paper, then grease the parchment.

2. Make the seasoning: Put the Parmesan
   cheese, garlic powder, onion powder, and
   oregano in a small bowl and stir well to
   combine.
3. Make the breadsticks: Place the ricotta,
   coconut flour, baking powder, eggs, salt, and
   ¼ cup of the seasoning in a large bowl and
   mix using a hand mixer until very smooth.
   Scoop the dough into the prepared pan and
   smooth the top. Sprinkle with the remaining
   seasoning.
4. Use a foil sling to lower the pan onto the
   trivet in the Instant Pot. Tuck in the sides of
   the sling.
5. Seal the lid, press Manual, and set the
   timer for 30 minutes. Once finished, let the
   pressure release naturally. Lift the pan out of
   the Instant Pot using the foil sling.
6. Let the bread rest for 10 minutes, then invert
   onto a plate and peel off the parchment. Then
   invert again onto a cutting board. Once cool,
   cut the bread into 1-inch-wide sticks. Serve
   with marinara.

Per Serving
calories: 214 | fat: 13g | protein: 12g | carbs: 10g
net carbs: 6g | fiber: 4g

Cauliflower Mashed "Potatoes"

Prep time: 5 minutes | Cook time: 4 minutes
Serves 4

1 head cauliflower,
broken into florets
2 tablespoons grass-fed
butter
¼ cup heavy whipping
cream

Pinch of kosher salt
Pinch of freshly ground
black pepper
¼ cup full-fat Cheddar
cheese, shredded

1. Pour 1 cup of filtered water into the inner pot
   of the Instant Pot, then add the cauliflower.
   Move the valve to Sealing and close the lid.
2. Cook for 4 minutes at High Pressure, then
   perform a quick release. Using a potato
   masher, mash cauliflower carefully, while
   inside inner pot. Strain out excess liquid, if
   desired.
3. Once mashed, mix in butter, and whipping
   cream, and season with salt and pepper.
   Gently stir, until a uniform texture forms.
   Transfer to a serving bowl, sprinkle cheese on
   top, and serve.

Per Serving
calories: 126 | fat: 11g | protein: 3g | carbs: 4g
net carbs: 2g | fiber: 2g

Twice-Baked Mashed Cauliflower

**Prep time: 10 minutes | Cook time: 5 minutes
Serves 4**

½ cup water
1 head cauliflower
(about 2 pounds / 907
g)
2 ounces (57 g) cream
cheese

½ teaspoon salt
¼ teaspoon garlic
powder
¼ cup shredded
Cheddar cheese
¼ cup bacon bits

1. Pour the water into the pot. Add the steamer
    basket.
2. Cut the cauliflower into quarters. Cut out the
    stems on each quarter. Cut the quarters into
    small florets and place them in the steamer
    basket.
3. Close the lid and seal the vent. Cook on
    Steam mode for 2 minutes. Quick release the
    steam.
4. Transfer the cauliflower to a food processor.
    Add the cream cheese, salt, and garlic
    powder. Pulse until smooth.
5. Transfer the cauliflower mixture to the baking
    dish. Fold in the Cheddar cheese and bacon
    bits.
6. Cover the dish tightly with aluminum foil.
    Place it on the trivet and carefully lower it
    into the pot. Cook on Low Pressure for 3
    minutes. Quick release the steam.

Per Serving
calories: 130 | fat: 8g | protein: 6g | carbs: 8g
net carbs: 5g | fiber: 3g

Buffalo Wings with Blue Cheese Dressing

**Prep time: 5 minutes | Cook time: 10 minutes
Serves 16**

3 pounds (1.4 kg) chicken wingettes
Fine sea salt and ground black pepper, to taste
Sauce:
3 cups Buffalo wing
sauce
2 tablespoons unsalted

butter or coconut oil,
melted
1 teaspoon hot sauce

Blue Cheese Dressing:
2½ ounces (71 g) blue
cheese, crumbled
3 tablespoons beef
broth
3 tablespoons sour
cream
2 tablespoons
mayonnaise
2 teaspoons white wine

vinegar
⅛ teaspoon garlic
powder
Fine sea salt and
ground black pepper, to
taste
Celery sticks, for
serving

1. Pat the chicken wings dry and season well
    with salt and pepper.
2. Set a trivet in a 6-quart Instant Pot and pour
    in ½ cup of cold water. Set the wings on the
    trivet. Seal the lid, press Manual, and set the
    timer for 5 minutes. Once finished, let the
    pressure release naturally.
3. Meanwhile, place an oven rack one notch
    above the center position and preheat the
    oven to broil. Lay a sheet of parchment paper
    on a rimmed baking sheet.
4. Make the sauce: Place the wing sauce,
    butter, and hot sauce in a large bowl and mix
    together. Remove the chicken wings from the
    Instant Pot and add to the sauce; toss to coat
    the wings with the sauce.
5. Place the coated wings on the lined baking
    sheet and broil for 5 minutes, or until crispy
    on the edges.
6. Meanwhile, make the dressing: Place all of
    the dressing ingredients in a medium-sized
    bowl and stir well to combine.
7. Serve the wings with the blue cheese dressing
    and celery sticks.

Per Serving
calories: 213 | fat: 15g | protein: 15g | carbs: 6g
net carbs: 3g | fiber: 3g

Ginger Ale Soda

**Prep time: 5 minutes | Cook time: 25 minutes
Serves 4**

2 lemons, juiced
¼ cup ginger, diced
¼ lime, juiced
½ teaspoon lavender,
dried
½ teaspoon mint, finely

chopped
4 cups carbonated
water
1 cup erythritol, powder
(or more, to taste)

In a blender, blend the lemon juice, ginger, lime,
lavender, and mint, until it becomes a purée.
Pour the carbonated water and erythritol into the
Instant Pot, then add the purée.
Close the lid, set the pressure release to Sealing,
and select Manual. Set the Instant Pot to 25
minutes on High Pressure and let cook.
Once cooked, let the pressure naturally disperse,
strain the ginger ale, then refrigerate until ready
to serve.

Per Serving
calories: 30 | fat: 0g | protein: 1g | carbs: 7g
net carbs: 6g | fiber: 1g

Garlic-Parmesan Chicken Wings

Prep time: 5 minutes | Cook time: 13 minutes
Serves 4

3 pounds (1.4 kg) chicken wings (drummettes, flats, or whole wings)
2 teaspoons avocado oil
1 tablespoon grated Parmesan cheese, divided
½ teaspoon salt,
divided
½ teaspoon onion powder, divided
½ teaspoon garlic powder, divided
Pinch of black pepper
½ cup water
1 tablespoon butter, melted

1. Heat the broiler.
2. Place the wings on a large plate or baking sheet. Pat both sides dry with a paper towel. Drizzle the avocado oil on top of the wings and use your hands to coat them evenly.
3. In a small bowl, mix half the cheese, half the salt, half the onion powder, half the garlic powder, and a pinch of pepper. Toss the wings in the rub.
4. Place the wings in the steamer basket. Add the water to the pot.
5. Close the lid and seal the vent. Cook on High Pressure for 8 minutes. Quick release the steam.
6. Use tongs to carefully remove the wings from the basket and place them flat on a clean baking sheet. Broil the wings to crisp up the skins, about 5 minutes.
7. In a small bowl, combine the remaining cheese and spices with the melted butter. Brush the mixture on top of the wings before serving.

Per Serving
calories: 57 | fat: 6g | protein: 1g | carbs: 0g
net carbs: 0g | fiber: 0g

Crab Rangoon Dip

Prep time: 5 minutes | Cook time: 30 minutes
Serves 4

2 (8-ounce / 227-g) packages cream cheese, softened
4 green onions, chopped
2 tablespoons peeled and grated fresh ginger
1½ teaspoons coconut aminos
½ teaspoon lemon juice
2 tablespoons Swerve confectioners'-style sweetener or equivalent
amount of liquid or powdered sweetener
½ teaspoon garlic powder
2 cups fresh lump crab meat, or 3 (6-ounce / 170-g) cans lump crab meat
Sliced green onions, for garnish
Pork rinds and/or sliced bell peppers (any color), for serving

1. Place the cream cheese, green onions, ginger, coconut aminos, lemon juice, sweetener, and garlic powder in a food processor and blend until smooth. Gently stir in the crab meat.
2. Set a trivet in a 6-quart Instant Pot and pour in ½ cup of cold water. Grease a 1-quart round casserole dish, then spread the dip mixture in an even layer in the dish. Use a foil sling to lower the casserole dish onto the trivet in the Instant Pot. Tuck in the sides of the sling.
3. Seal the lid, press Manual, and set the timer for 30 minutes. Once finished, let the pressure release naturally. Lift the casserole dish out of the Instant Pot using the foil sling.
4. Garnish with sliced green onions. Serve with pork rinds and/or bell pepper strips.

Per Serving
calories: 491 | fat: 40g | protein: 24g | carbs: 5g
net carbs: 4g | fiber: 1g

Sesame Broccoli

Prep time: 12 minutes | Cook time: 5 minutes
Serves 4

2 cups broccoli florets
2 cups cauliflower florets
2 tablespoons toasted sesame seeds, for garnish
Sauce:
½ cup beef broth
¼ cup Swerve confectioners'-style sweetener or equivalent amount of liquid or powdered sweetener
2 tablespoons coconut aminos, or 1½
teaspoons wheat-free tamari
2 tablespoons lemon juice
1 tablespoon peeled and grated fresh ginger
1 clove roasted garlic
1 teaspoon guar gum (optional, for thickening)
1 teaspoon dark (toasted) sesame oil
½ teaspoon fine sea salt

1. Place all of the sauce ingredients in a large bowl and stir well to combine. Add the broccoli and cauliflower and toss well to coat with the sauce.
2. Transfer the vegetable mixture to a 6-quart Instant Pot. Seal the lid, press Manual, and set the timer for 5 minutes. Once finished, turn the valve to venting for a quick release.
3. Garnish with toasted sesame seeds. Best served warm.

Per Serving
calories: 78 | fat: 4g | protein: 3g | carbs: 9g
net carbs: 4g | fiber: 5g

Alfredo Veggies

**Prep time: 12 minutes | Cook time: 5 minutes
Serves 6**

3 broccoli crowns, cut into florets
½ head cauliflower, cut into florets
Sauce:
½ cup shredded sharp Cheddar cheese (about 2 ounces / 57 g)
2 ounces (57 g) cream cheese (¼ cup), softened
¼ cup grated Parmesan cheese
½ cup chicken broth or vegetable broth
Cloves squeezed from 1 head roasted garlic
1 teaspoon fine sea salt
For Garnish:
Fresh oregano or basil leaves
Ground black pepper

1. Set a trivet in a 6-quart Instant Pot and pour in ½ cup of cold water.
2. Place the broccoli and cauliflower in a 1-quart casserole dish.
3. Make the sauce: Place the cheeses, broth, garlic, and salt in a food processor or blender and purée until smooth. Reserve ¼ cup of the sauce for serving. Pour the remaining sauce over the vegetables and stir well to coat. Cover the dish with the lid or a piece of aluminum foil.
4. Use a foil sling to lower the casserole dish onto the trivet in the Instant Pot. Tuck in the sides of the sling.
5. Seal the lid, press Manual, and set the timer for 5 minutes. Once finished, turn the valve to venting for a quick release. Lift the casserole dish out of the pot using the foil sling.
6. Top with the reserved sauce and garnish with fresh oregano or basil leaves and freshly ground pepper. Serve warm.

Per Serving
calories: 128 | fat:6 g | protein: 8g | carbs: 10g
net carbs: 7g | fiber: 3g

Green Bean Casserole

**Prep time: 5 minutes | Cook time: 8 minutes
Serves 4**

4 tablespoons butter
½ medium onion, diced
½ cup chopped button mushrooms
1 cup chicken broth
1 teaspoon salt
¼ teaspoon pepper
1 pound (454 g) green beans, edges trimmed
½ cup heavy cream
1 ounce (28 g) cream cheese
¼ teaspoon xanthan gum

1. Press the Sauté button and add butter to Instant Pot. Sauté onions and mushrooms for 3 minutes or until onions become translucent. Press the Cancel button.
2. Add broth, salt, pepper, and green beans. Click lid closed. Adjust time for 5 minutes. When timer beeps, quick-release the pressure. Stir in remaining ingredients. Serve warm.

Per Serving
calories: 275 | fat: 24g | protein: 4g | carbs: 10g
net carbs: 7g | fiber: 3g

Ham and Cauliflower au Gratin

**Prep time: 12 minutes | Cook time: 5 minutes
Serves 6**

6 ounces (170 g) cream cheese (¾ cup), softened
¼ cup chicken broth
2 tablespoons grated Parmesan cheese
½ teaspoon fine sea salt
¼ teaspoon ground black pepper
1 medium head cauliflower, cut into bite-sized pieces
3 cups diced ham
¼ cup thinly sliced green onions
¾ cup shredded provolone cheese (about 3 ounces / 85 g)

1. Place the softened cream cheese in a large bowl and whisk to loosen. (If you don't use a whisk to loosen the cream cheese, you will end up with clumps.) Slowly pour in the broth while whisking to combine. Mix in the Parmesan cheese, salt, and pepper.
2. Add the cauliflower, ham, and green onions to the bowl and stir well to combine. Scoop the mixture into a 1-quart round casserole dish.
3. Set a trivet in a 6-quart Instant Pot and pour in ½ cup of cold water. Use a foil sling to lower the casserole dish onto the trivet. Tuck in the sides of the sling.
4. Seal the lid, press Manual, and set the timer for 5 minutes. Once finished, turn the valve to venting for a quick release. Lift the casserole dish out of the Instant Pot using the foil sling.
5. Top with the provolone cheese. Loosely cover the pot and allow the cheese to melt, about 8 minutes. Best served warm.

Per Serving
calories: 308 | fat: 17g | protein: 29g | carbs: 8g
net carbs: 6g | fiber: 2g

Tender Mexican Spice Wings

Prep time: 5 minutes | Cook time: 10 minutes
Serves 10

30 chicken wingettes or drumettes
3 tablespoons melted coconut oil or bacon fat
Taco Seasoning:

1 tablespoon chili powder	½ teaspoon garlic powder
½ tablespoon ground cumin	½ teaspoon onion powder
1 teaspoon fine sea salt	½ teaspoon paprika

For Serving:

Guacamole	Lime wedges

1. Pat the chicken dry and place in a large bowl. Pour the melted coconut oil over the chicken and toss to coat.
2. Make the taco seasoning: Place the ingredients in a small bowl and stir to combine. Sprinkle on all sides of the wings.
3. Set a trivet in a 6-quart Instant Pot and pour in ½ cup of cold water. Place the chicken on the trivet. Seal the lid, press Manual, and set the timer for 5 minutes. Once finished, let the pressure release naturally.
4. Meanwhile, place an oven rack one notch above the center position and preheat the oven to broil. Place a piece of parchment paper on a rimmed baking sheet.
5. Place the chicken on the lined baking sheet and broil for 5 minutes, or until crispy on the edges. Serve with guacamole and lime wedges.

Per Serving
calories: 164 | fat: 14g | protein: 10g | carbs: 2g
net carbs: 1g | fiber: 1g

Crab-Stuffed Mushrooms

Prep time: 5 minutes | Cook time: 6 minutes
Serves 6

18 medium-sized button mushrooms	1 (6½-ounce / 184-g) can lump crab meat, rinsed and drained well, or 1 cup fresh crab meat
¼ cup plus 2 tablespoons grated Parmesan cheese (about 1 ounce / 28 g)	Dash or two of hot sauce, to taste
3 tablespoons mayonnaise	Ground black pepper, to taste
3 tablespoons sour cream	Sliced green onions, for garnish
1 teaspoon minced garlic	

1. Wash the mushrooms and remove the stems. Set the caps aside on a paper towel to dry. Discard the stems.
2. Put the Parmesan cheese, mayonnaise, sour cream, and garlic in a small bowl and stir to combine. Fold in the crab meat. Add the hot sauce and pepper and stir gently. Spoon a heaping teaspoon of the crab filling into each mushroom cap.
3. Set a trivet in a 6-quart Instant Pot and pour in ½ cup of cold water. Arrange the mushroom caps, filling side up, in a 1-quart round casserole dish. Use a foil sling to lower the casserole dish onto the trivet. Tuck in the sides of the sling.
4. Seal the lid, press Manual, and set the timer for 6 minutes. Once finished, turn the valve to venting for a quick release. Lift the casserole dish out of the Instant Pot using the foil sling.
5. Garnish with sliced green onions. Best served warm.

Per Serving
calories: 113 | fat: 8g | protein: 8g | carbs: 2g
net carbs: 1g | fiber: 1g

Buttery Mushrooms

Prep time: 5 minutes | Cook time: 5 minutes
Serves 4

1 pound (454 g) button mushrooms, quartered	vinegar
½ cup (1 stick) unsalted butter (or coconut oil for dairy-free), melted	1 tablespoon fresh thyme or marjoram leaves
½ cup chicken broth or vegetable broth	1 teaspoon dried chives
2 tablespoons red wine	Fine sea salt and ground black pepper, to taste

1. Place the mushrooms, butter, broth, vinegar, thyme, and chives in a 3-quart or larger Instant Pot. Seal the lid, press Manual, and set the timer for 5 minutes. Once finished, turn the valve to venting for a quick release. Season with salt and pepper to taste. Serve warm.

Per Serving
calories: 256 | fat: 28g | protein: 3g | carbs: 3g
net carbs: 2g | fiber: 1g

Chaptr 6 Soups, Stews, and Chilies

Chicken Zoodle Soup

Prep time: 15 minutes | Cook time: 20 minutes
Serves 6

3 stalks celery, diced
2 tablespoons diced pickled jalapeño
1 cup bok choy, sliced into strips
½ cup fresh spinach
3 zucchini, spiralized
1 tablespoon coconut oil
¼ cup button mushrooms, diced

¼ medium onion, diced
2 cups cooked diced chicken
3 cups chicken broth
1 bay leaf
1 teaspoon salt
½ teaspoon garlic powder
⅛ teaspoon cayenne pepper

1. Place celery, jalapeño, bok choy, and spinach into medium bowl. Spiralize zucchini; set aside in a separate medium bowl. (The zucchini will not go in the pot during the pressure cooking.)
2. Press the Sauté button and add the coconut oil to Instant Pot. Once the oil is hot, add mushrooms and onion. Sauté for 4 to 6 minutes until onion is translucent and fragrant. Add celery, jalapeños, bok choy, and spinach to Instant Pot. Cook for additional 4 minutes. Press the Cancel button.
3. Add cooked diced chicken, broth, bay leaf, and seasoning to Instant Pot. Click lid closed. Press the Soup button and set time for 20 minutes.
4. When timer beeps, allow a 10-minute natural release, and quick-release the remaining pressure. Add spiralized zucchini on Keep Warm mode and cook for additional 10 minutes or until tender. Serve warm.

Per Serving
calories: 111 | fat: 4g | protein: 13g | carbs: 5g
net carbs: 3g | fiber: 2g

Buffalo Chicken Soup

Prep time: 5 minutes | Cook time: 25 minutes
Serves 4

2 tablespoons diced onion
2 tablespoons butter
3 cups chicken broth
2 (6-ounce / 170-g) boneless, skinless chicken breasts, cubed
1 teaspoon salt
¼ teaspoon garlic powder

¼ teaspoon pepper
2 celery stalks, chopped
½ cup hot sauce
4 ounces (113 g) cream cheese
½ cup shredded Cheddar cheese
¼ teaspoon xanthan gum

1. Press the Sauté button and add onion and butter to Instant Pot. Sauté 2 to 3 minutes until onions begin to soften. Press the Cancel button.
2. Add broth and chicken to Instant Pot. Sprinkle salt, garlic powder, and pepper on chicken. Add celery and hot sauce and place cream cheese on top of chicken. Click lid closed.
3. Press the Manual button and adjust time for 25 minutes. When timer beeps, quick-release the pressure and stir in Cheddar and xanthan gum. Serve warm.

Per Serving
calories: 332 | fat: 20g | protein: 26g | carbs: 3g
net carbs: 2g | fiber: 1g

Chicken Bacon Chowder

Prep time: 10 minutes | Cook time: 20 minutes
Serves 6

½ pound (227 g) bacon
1 teaspoon salt
½ teaspoon pepper
½ teaspoon garlic powder
¼ teaspoon dried thyme
3 (6-ounce / 170-g) boneless, skinless chicken breasts

½ cup button mushrooms, sliced
½ medium onion, diced
1 cup broccoli florets
½ cup cauliflower florets
4 ounces (113 g) cream cheese
3 cups chicken broth
½ cup heavy cream

1. Press the Sauté button and then press the Adjust button to lower heat to Less. Add bacon to Instant Pot and fry for a few minutes until fat begins to render, working in multiple batches if necessary. Press the Cancel button.
2. Press the Sauté button and then press the Adjust button to set heat to Normal. Continue frying bacon until fully cooked and crispy. Remove from pot and set aside. Sprinkle salt, pepper, garlic powder, and thyme over chicken breasts. Sear each side of the chicken for 3 to 5 minutes or until dark and golden. Press the Cancel button.
3. Add mushrooms, onion, broccoli, cauliflower, cream cheese, and broth to pot with chicken. Click lid closed. Press the Manual button and adjust time for 12 minutes. When timer beeps, quick-release the pressure. Remove chicken and shred or dice; add to pot. Crumble cooked bacon and stir into pot with heavy cream. Serve warm.

Per Serving
calories: 407 | fat: 28g | protein: 26g | carbs: 5g
net carbs: 4g | fiber: 1g

Red Chili

Prep time: 10 minutes | Cook time: 35 minutes
Serves 6

4 slices bacon
½ pound (227 g) 85% lean ground beef
½ pound (227 g) 84% lean ground pork
1 green pepper, diced
½ medium onion, diced
2 cups beef broth
1 (14½-ounce / 411-g) can diced tomatoes

1 (6-ounce / 170-g) can tomato paste
1 tablespoon chili powder
2 teaspoons salt
½ teaspoon pepper
⅛ teaspoon cayenne
¼ teaspoon xanthan gum (optional)

1. Press the Sauté button and cook bacon. Remove bacon, crumble, and set aside. In bacon grease, brown beef and pork until fully cooked. Add green pepper and onion to Instant Pot and allow to soften for 1 minute.
2. Press the Cancel button and add remaining ingredients except xanthan gum to pot. Click lid closed. Press the Soup button and adjust time for 30 minutes. Allow a 10-minute natural release and then quick-release the remaining pressure. Stir in cooked bacon and xanthan gum then allow to thicken for 10 minutes. Serve warm with favorite chili toppings.
3. For thicker chili, remove lid when timer goes off and press the Sauté button. Add xanthan gum and reduce chili, stirring frequently, until desired thickness. Top with additional diced onions or other toppings.

Per Serving
calories: 294 | fat: 18g | protein: 19g | carbs: 12g
net carbs: 9g | fiber: 3g

Lobster Bisque

Prep time: 5 minutes | Cook time: 10 minutes
Serves 4

4 tablespoons butter
½ medium onion, diced
1 clove garlic, finely minced
1 pound (454 g) cooked lump lobster meat
½ teaspoon salt
¼ teaspoon pepper
¼ teaspoon paprika

⅛ teaspoon cayenne
2 tablespoons tomato paste
1 cup seafood stock
1 cup chicken broth
½ cup heavy cream
½ teaspoon xanthan gum

1. Press the Sauté button and add butter and onions to Instant Pot. Sauté for 2 to 3 minutes until onions begin to soften. Add garlic and sauté 30 seconds. Press the Cancel button.

2. Add lobster, seasonings, tomato paste, and broths. Press the Manual button and adjust time for 7 minutes. When timer beeps, quick-release the pressure. Stir in heavy cream and xanthan gum. Allow a few minutes to thicken. Serve warm.

Per Serving
calories: 328 | fat: 22g | protein: 24g | carbs:5 g
net carbs: 4g | fiber: 1g

15-Minute Vegetable Soup

Prep time: 5 minutes | Cook time: 10 minutes
Serves 4

½ cup dried porcini mushrooms
1 tablespoon coconut or avocado oil
1 medium yellow onion, diced
2 medium stalks celery, diced
2 medium carrots, diced
1 cup white mushrooms, sliced
4 cloves garlic, minced or finely grated
1 tablespoon fresh rosemary, finely

chopped
1 teaspoon Italian seasoning
½ teaspoon smoked paprika
2 cups bite-size broccoli florets
3 cups kale, chopped
1 medium zucchini, diced
1 (14-ounce / 397-g) can sugar-free or low-sugar diced tomatoes
4 cups chicken or vegetable broth

1. Place the porcini mushrooms in a bowl and cover with boiling water. Soak for 15 to 30 minutes. Drain and chop.
2. Meanwhile, set the Instant Pot to Sauté. Add the oil. When hot, add the onion, celery, and carrots. Cook, stirring often, for 2 to 3 minutes.
3. Add the rehydrated porcini mushrooms and white mushrooms. Sauté for 1 to 2 minutes.
4. Add the garlic, rosemary, Italian seasoning, and paprika. Sauté for 1 minute.
5. Add the broccoli, kale, and zucchini. Stir to combine.
6. Add the tomatoes and broth. Close the lid, set the pressure release to Sealing, and select Manual. Set the Instant Pot to 10 minutes on High Pressure and let cook.
7. Once cooked, let the pressure naturally disperse from the Instant Pot for 2 to 3 minutes, then carefully switch the pressure release to Venting.
8. Remove the lid. Season to taste with salt and pepper.

Per Serving
calories: 342 | fat: 5g | protein: 46g | carbs: 17g
net carbs: 10g | fiber: 7g

Greek Lemon Soup

Prep time: 5 minutes | Cook time: 15 minutes
Serves 4

4 cups chicken broth   1 lemon
4 eggs, separated

1. Press the Sauté button. Add chicken broth to Instant Pot to warm.
2. In two medium bowls, separate egg yolks and egg whites. Beat egg yolks and stir into broth. Press the Cancel button so Instant Pot switches to Keep Warm mode.
3. Using whisk or hand mixer, whisk egg whites until they form soft peaks. Add into Instant Pot. Squeeze in juice from lemon. Foam may stay at the top of soup initially, but with continued occasional stirring, will dissipate by the end of cooking.

Per Serving
calories: 93 | fat: 5g | protein: 8g | carbs: 1g
net carbs: 1g | fiber: 0g

Spicy Bacon Cheeseburger Soup

Prep time: 5 minutes | Cook time: 15 minutes
Serves 6

1 pound (454 g) 85% lean ground beef
½ medium onion, sliced
½ (14½-ounce / 411-g) can fire-roasted tomatoes
3 cups beef broth
¼ cup cooked crumbled bacon
1 tablespoon chopped pickled jalapeños
1 teaspoon salt
½ teaspoon pepper
½ teaspoon garlic powder
2 teaspoons Worcestershire sauce
4 ounces (113 g) cream cheese
1 cup sharp Cheddar cheese
1 pickle spear, diced

1. Press the Sauté button and add ground beef. Brown beef halfway and add onion. Continue cooking beef until no pink remains. Press the Cancel button. Add tomatoes, broth, bacon, jalapeños, salt, pepper, garlic powder, and Worcestershire sauce, and stir. Place cream cheese on top in middle.
2. Click lid closed. Press the Soup button and adjust time for 15 minutes. When timer beeps, quick-release the pressure. Top with diced pickles. Feel free to add additional cheese and bacon.

Per Serving
calories: 358 | fat: 24g | protein: 24g | carbs: 6g
net carbs: 5g | fiber: 1g

Chicken Cordon Bleu Soup

Prep time: 5 minutes | Cook time: 15 minutes
Serves 6

2 (6-ounce / 170-g) boneless, skinless chicken breasts, cubed
4 cups chicken broth
½ cup cubed ham
8 ounces (227 g) cream cheese
1 teaspoon salt
½ teaspoon pepper
½ teaspoon garlic powder
½ cup heavy cream
2 cups grated Swiss cheese
2 teaspoons Dijon mustard

1. Place all ingredients except heavy cream, cream cheese, and mustard into Instant Pot. Click lid closed.
2. Press the Soup button and adjust time for 15 minutes. When timer beeps, quick-release the pressure. Stir in heavy cream, cheese, and mustard. Serve warm.

Per Serving
calories: 439 | fat: 30g | protein: 29g | carbs: 5g
net carbs:5 g | fiber: 0g

Creamy Tuscan Soup

Prep time: 5 minutes | Cook time: 17 minutes
Serves 4

4 slices bacon
1 pound (454 g) ground Italian sausage
4 tablespoons butter
½ medium onion, diced
2 cloves garlic, finely minced
3 cups chicken broth
4 ounces (113 g) cream cheese
2 cups kale, chopped
½ cup heavy cream
1 teaspoon salt
½ teaspoon pepper

1. Press the Sauté button and fry bacon until crispy. Remove bacon and chop into pieces, then set aside. Add Italian sausage to Instant Pot and sauté until no pink remains.
2. Add butter and onion to Instant Pot. Sauté until onions are translucent. Add garlic and sauté for 30 seconds. Press the Cancel button.
3. Add broth and cream cheese to pot. Click lid closed. Press the Soup button and adjust time for 7 minutes.
4. When timer beeps, quick-release the pressure and add remaining ingredients to pot. Leave Instant Pot on Keep Warm setting and allow to cook additional 10 minutes, stirring occasionally until kale is wilted. Serve warm.

Per Serving
calories: 836 | fat: 74g | protein: 24g | carbs: 6g
net carbs: 5g | fiber: 1g

Italian Chicken Soup

Prep time: 5 minutes | Cook time: 10 minutes
Serves 6

4 cups grass-fed bone broth
1 pound (454 g) chicken, ground
½ teaspoon hot peppers, chopped
½ teaspoon rosemary, ground
½ teaspoon oregano, dried

½ teaspoon basil, dried
½ teaspoon kosher salt
½ teaspoon freshly ground black pepper
2 tablespoons coconut oil
1 (14-ounce / 397-g) can sugar-free or low-sugar fire roasted tomatoes

1. Add the bone broth, chicken, hot peppers, rosemary, oregano, basil, salt, black pepper, oil, and tomatoes to the Instant Pot.
2. Close the lid, set the pressure release to Sealing, and select Manual. Set the Instant Pot to 10 minutes on High Pressure, and let cook.
3. Once cooked, immediately switch the pressure release to Venting. Do this carefully, as hot steam may rise up.
4. Open the Instant Pot, pour soup evenly into bowls, and enjoy!

Per Serving
calories: 183 | fat: 7g | protein: 25g | carbs: 3g
net carbs: 3g | fiber: 0g

5-Ingredient Minestrone Soup

Prep time: 5 minutes | Cook time: 5 minutes
Serves 2

2 cups grass-fed bone broth
½ stalk celery, chopped
1 (14-ounce / 397-g) can sugar-free or low-sugar fire roasted

tomatoes
½ cup green beans, cut up into pieces
¼ cup full-fat Parmesan cheese, grated

1. Pour bone broth into the inner pot, then add the celery, tomatoes, and green beans.
2. Close the lid, set the pressure release to Sealing, and select Manual. Set the Instant Pot to 5 minutes on High Pressure and let cook.
3. Once cooked, perform a quick release by carefully switching the pressure valve to Venting. Stir in the Parmesan cheese and serve.

Per Serving
calories: 154 | fat: 6g | protein: 14g | carbs: 10g
net carbs: 8g | fiber: 2g

Traditional Egg Drop Soup

Prep time: 5 minutes | Cook time: 5 minutes
Serves 5 to 6

8 cups grass-fed bone broth
4 tablespoons grass-fed butter, softened
1 scallion, thinly sliced
½ teaspoon basil, dried

½ teaspoon cayenne pepper, ground
½ teaspoon parsley, dried
½ teaspoon kosher salt
6 eggs, whisked

1. Pour the bone broth, butter, scallion, basil, cayenne pepper, parsley, and salt into the Instant Pot.
2. Close the lid, set the pressure release to Sealing, and select Manual. Set the Instant Pot to 5 minutes on High Pressure and let cook.
3. Once cooked, let the pressure naturally disperse from the Instant Pot for about 10 minutes, then carefully switch the pressure release to Venting.
4. Gently pour in the eggs, and let sit for 1 minute, until they form ribbon-like strands.
5. Stir, serve, and enjoy!

Per Serving
calories: 177 | fat: 12g | protein: 12g | carbs: 3g
net carbs: 3g | fiber: 0g

5-Ingredient Albondigas Soup

Prep time: 5 minutes | Cook time: 15 minutes
Serves 2

2 cups grass-fed bone broth
1 (14-ounce / 397-g) can sugar-free or low-sugar fire roasted tomatoes

½ teaspoon paprika, fresh
½ teaspoon chili powder, dried
½ pound (227 g) grass-fed beef, ground

1. Pour bone broth into the inner pot of the Instant Pot, then add the tomatoes, paprika, and chili powder.
2. Form 6 meatballs with the grass-fed beef, then add them in with the other ingredients.
3. Close the lid, set the pressure release to Sealing, and select Manual. Set the Instant Pot to 15 minutes on High Pressure and let cook.
4. Once cooked, perform a quick release by carefully switching the pressure valve to Venting, and serve.

Per Serving
calories: 298 | fat: 17g | protein: 26g | carbs: 7g
net carbs: 5g | fiber: 2g

Broccoli and Cheddar Soup

Prep time: 5 minutes | Cook time: 10 minutes
Serves 4

4 tablespoons grass-fed butter, softened
4 cups grass-fed bone broth
2 cups broccoli, chopped
1 cup celery, chopped
½ teaspoon garlic
½ teaspoon parsley, dried
½ teaspoon freshly ground black pepper
½ teaspoon kosher salt
¼ (4-ounce / 113-g) small onion, thinly sliced
2 cups full-fat Cheddar cheese, shredded

1. Set the Instant Pot to Sauté. Add the butter, melting it gently.
2. Pour in the bone broth, then add the broccoli, celery, garlic, parsley, black pepper, salt, and onion to the Instant Pot. Close the lid, set the pressure release to Sealing, and select Manual. Set the Instant Pot to 10 minutes on High Pressure and let cook.
3. Once cooked, perform a quick release. Open the lid and stir in the cheese until melted. Serve, and enjoy!

Per Serving
calories: 391 | fat: 31g | protein: 21g | carbs: 7g net carbs: 5g | fiber: 2g

Cream of Chicken Soup

Prep time: 5 minutes | Cook time: 10 minutes
Serves 1

½ cup heavy cream
½ cup chicken broth
3 tablespoons butter
¼ teaspoon poultry seasoning
¼ teaspoon salt
Pinch of black pepper
2 ounces (57 g) cream cheese, softened
¾ teaspoon xanthan gum

1. Combine the cream, chicken broth, butter, poultry seasoning, salt, and pepper in the pot.
2. Turn the pot to Sauté mode and whisk as the ingredients heat up and the butter melts.
3. Add the cream cheese and continue whisking until it is completely melted and combined. The soup will begin to bubble or foam up.
4. Add the xanthan gum and continue whisking until a thick consistency is reached, 2 to 3 minutes.

Per Serving
calories: 948 | fat: 95g | protein: 9g | carbs: 7g net carbs: 5g | fiber: 2g

Lasagna Soup

Prep time: 5 minutes | Cook time: 5 minutes
Serves 2

1 cup full-fat Cheddar cheese, shredded
½ cup full-fat Parmesan cheese, grated
½ cup heavy whipping cream
½ teaspoon basil, dried
½ teaspoon oregano, dried
¼ zucchini, grated
1 (14-ounce / 397-g) can sugar-free or low-sugar fire roasted tomatoes

1. Pour 1½ cups of filtered water into the inner pot of the Instant Pot. Then add the Cheddar, Parmesan, whipping cream, basil, oregano, zucchini, and tomatoes. Mix together thoroughly.
2. Set the Instant Pot to Sauté and let cook for 5 minutes (or until cheese is melted), stirring occasionally.

Per Serving
calories: 545 | fat: 42g | protein: 34g | carbs: 10g net carbs: 9g | fiber: 1g

Garlic Tomato-Basil Soup

Prep time: 5 minutes | Cook time: 20 minutes
Serves 4

2 tablespoons coconut oil
2 cloves garlic, minced
1 cup full-fat Cheddar cheese, shredded (optional)
1 teaspoon basil, dried
½ teaspoon kosher salt
¼ (4-ounce / 113-g) small onion, thinly sliced
2 (14-ounce / 397-g) cans sugar-free or low-sugar diced tomatoes
½ cup heavy whipping cream

1. Set the Instant Pot to Sauté mode. Add the oil, melting it gently.
2. Mix in the garlic, cheese, basil, salt, onion, and tomatoes. Close the lid, set the pressure release to Sealing, and select Manual. Set the Instant Pot to 20 minutes on High Pressure and let cook.
3. Once cooked, let the pressure naturally disperse from the Instant Pot for about 10 minutes, then carefully switch the pressure release to Venting.
4. Open the lid and stir in the heavy whipping cream. Blend with an immersion blender to achieve a smooth texture, if desired.
5. Serve, and enjoy!

Per Serving
calories: 264 | fat: 22g | protein: 9g | carbs: 9g net carbs: 6g | fiber: 3g

White Chicken Chili

Prep time: 15 minutes | Cook time: 20 minutes
Serves 6

4 tablespoons butter
¼ cup chopped onions
1 (4-ounce / 113-g) can green chilies, drained
2 cloves garlic, minced
1 green pepper, chopped
1½ cups chicken broth

1 pound (454 g) boneless, skinless chicken breasts, cubed
1 teaspoon salt
¼ teaspoon pepper
4 ounces (113 g) cream cheese
¼ cup heavy cream

1. Press the Sauté button and place butter and onions into Instant Pot. Sauté until onions are fragrant and translucent. Add chilies, garlic, and green pepper. Sauté for 3 minutes, stirring frequently.
2. Press the Cancel button and add broth, chicken, seasoning, and cream cheese to pot. Press the Manual button and adjust time for 30 minutes.
3. When timer beeps allow a 10-minute natural release and quick-release the remaining pressure. Stir in heavy cream.

Per Serving
calories: 274 | fat: 27g | protein: 20g | carbs: 5g
net carbs: 4g | fiber: 1g

French Onion Soup

Prep time: 10 minutes | Cook time: 35 minutes
Serves 10

1 ounce (28 g) butter
1 pound (454 g) chopped onions
6 cups beef broth
2 tablespoons Worcestershire sauce

1 teaspoon dried thyme
1 teaspoon salt
Pinch of black pepper
Gruyère cheese, shredded or sliced (optional)

1. Turn the pot to Sauté mode and add the butter. Once melted, add the onions and sauté until soft and translucent, 5 minutes. Alternatively, you may sauté the onions in a cast-iron skillet to fully caramelize them.
2. Press Cancel. Add the broth, Worcestershire, thyme, salt, and pepper and stir to combine.
3. Close the lid and seal the vent. Cook on High Pressure for 30 minutes. Quick release the steam.
4. If desired, top each serving of soup with cheese and broil until brown and bubbly.

Per Serving
calories: 121 | fat: 1g | protein: 2g | carbs: 5g
net carbs: 4g | fiber: 1g

Jalapeño Popper Soup

Prep time: 5 minutes | Cook time: 25 minutes
Serves 4

2 tablespoons butter
½ medium diced onion
¼ cup sliced pickled jalapeños
¼ cup cooked crumbled bacon
2 cups chicken broth
2 cups cooked diced chicken

4 ounces (113 g) cream cheese
1 teaspoon salt
½ teaspoon pepper
¼ teaspoon garlic powder
$1/_3$ cup heavy cream
1 cup shredded sharp Cheddar cheese

1. Press the Sauté button. Add butter, onion, and sliced jalapeños to Instant Pot. Sauté for 5 minutes, until onions are translucent. Add bacon and press the Cancel button.
2. Add broth, cooked chicken, cream cheese, salt, pepper, and garlic to Instant Pot. Click lid closed. Press the Soup button and adjust time for 20 minutes.
3. When timer beeps, quick-release the steam. Stir in heavy cream and Cheddar. Continue stirring until cheese is fully melted. Serve warm.

Per Serving
calories: 524 | fat: 36g | protein: 35g | carbs: 9g
net carbs: 8g | fiber: 1g

Creamy Mushroom Soup

Prep time: 10 minutes | Cook time: 10 minutes
Serves 4

1 pound (454 g) sliced button mushrooms
3 tablespoons butter
2 tablespoons diced onion
2 cloves garlic, minced

2 cups chicken broth
½ teaspoon salt
¼ teaspoon pepper
½ cup heavy cream
¼ teaspoon xanthan gum

1. Press the Sauté button and then press the Adjust button to set heat to Less. Add mushrooms, butter, and onion to pot. Sauté for 5 to 8 minutes or until onions and mushrooms begin to brown. Add garlic and sauté until fragrant. Press the Cancel button.
2. Add broth, salt, and pepper. Click lid closed. Press the Manual button and adjust time for 3 minutes. When timer beeps, quick-release the pressure. Stir in heavy cream and xanthan gum. Allow a few minutes to thicken and serve warm.

Per Serving
calories: 219 | fat: 19g | protein: 5g | carbs: 6g
net carbs: 4g | fiber: 2g

Herby Chicken "Noodle" Soup

Prep time: 5 minutes | Cook time: 12 minutes
Serves 6

7 cups grass-fed chicken bone broth
1 pound (454 g) chicken breasts, cubed, cooked
2 tablespoons avocado oil
1 teaspoon oregano, dried

1 carrot, chopped
½ teaspoon basil, dried
½ teaspoon parsley, dried
½ teaspoon kosher salt
½ teaspoon freshly ground black pepper
2 zucchinis, spiralized

1. Pour the chicken broth into the inner pot of the Instant Pot. Add in the chicken, avocado oil, oregano, carrot, basil, parsley, salt, black pepper, and zucchinis. Stir to combine.
2. Close the lid, set the pressure release to Sealing, and hit Cancel to stop the current program. Select Manual, set the Instant Pot to 5 minutes on High Pressure, and let cook.
3. Once cooked, immediately switch the pressure release to Venting (do this carefully).
4. Remove the lid, stir in the zucchini noodles, and enjoy!

Per Serving
calories: 200 | fat: 6g | protein: 29g | carbs: 6g net carbs: 5g | fiber: 1g

Immune-Boosting Soup

Prep time: 7 minutes | Cook time: 10 minutes
Serves 4

4 large boneless, skinless chicken breasts, cut into 1-inch cubes
1 (1-inch) piece fresh ginger, unpeeled, cut into 4 thick slices
Cloves squeezed from 1

head roasted garlic, or 2 cloves garlic, crushed to a paste
8 cups chicken broth
Fine sea salt and ground black pepper
Fresh thyme or parsley leaves, for garnish

1. Place the chicken, ginger, garlic, and broth in a 6-quart Instant Pot. Stir to combine.
2. Seal the lid, press Manual, and set the timer for 10 minutes. Once finished, let the pressure release naturally.
3. Remove the lid and discard the ginger. Shred the chicken with two forks. Season with salt and pepper to taste.
4. Ladle the soup into bowls and garnish with fresh thyme.

Per Serving
calories: 230 | fat: 7g | protein: 23g | carbs: 10g net carbs: 9g | fiber: 1g

10-Minute Pizza Soup

Prep time: 5 minutes | Cook time: 5 minutes
Serves 2

2 cups full-fat Cheddar cheese, shredded
1 (14-ounce / 397-g) can sugar-free or low-sugar fire roasted tomatoes

½ cup heavy whipping cream
½ teaspoon basil, dried
½ teaspoon oregano, dried

1. Start by pouring 2 cups of filtered water into the inner pot of the Instant Pot, then add cheese, tomatoes, whipping cream, basil, and oregano, mixing together thoroughly.
2. Set the Instant Pot to Sauté and let cook for 5 minutes (or until cheese is melted), stirring occasionally. Ladle soup into bowls and enjoy!

Per Serving
calories: 585 | fat: 48g | protein: 28g | carbs: 7g net carbs: 6g | fiber: 1g

Georgia Brunswick Stew

Prep time: 5 minutes | Cook time: 30 minutes
Serves 16

1 cup chicken broth
1 pound (454 g) boneless, skinless chicken breasts (fresh or frozen)
1 pound (454 g) boneless pork chops (fresh or frozen)
1 teaspoon salt
½ teaspoon black

pepper
12 ounces (340 g) frozen okra
5 ounces (142 g) chopped yellow onion (about 1 small onion)
1½ cups sugar-free BBQ sauce
1 can (28 ounces / 794 g) crushed tomatoes

1. Pour the broth into the pot. Place the chicken breasts and pork chops inside.
2. Sprinkle the salt and pepper on top of the meat. Add the okra and onion.
3. Pour the BBQ sauce on top. Pour the crushed tomatoes on top of the sauce but do not stir the mixture.
4. Close the lid and seal the vent. Cook on High Pressure for 30 minutes. Quick release the steam.
5. Remove the lid. Use a slotted spoon to remove the pork chops and chicken breasts from the stew to a plate. Shred the meat with two forks and transfer back to the stew. Stir to combine.

Per Serving
calories: 121 | fat: 4g | protein: 13g | carbs: 7g net carbs: 6g | fiber: 1g

Pumpkin and Bacon Soup

Prep time: 5 minutes | Cook time: 10 minutes
Serves 4

2 tablespoons coconut oil
4 slices no-sugar-added bacon, finely chopped and cooked
2 cups grass-fed bone broth
2 cups organic pumpkin purée
2 cups full-fat coconut milk
½ cup full-fat Cheddar cheese, shredded (optional)
½ teaspoon crushed red pepper
½ teaspoon kosher salt
½ teaspoon freshly ground black pepper
¼ cup heavy whipping cream

1. Add all ingredients to the Instant Pot. Stir and mix thoroughly.
2. Close the lid, set the pressure release to Sealing, and hit Cancel to stop the current program. Select Manual, set the Instant Pot to 10 minutes on Low Pressure, and let cook.
3. Once cooked, let the pressure naturally disperse from the Instant Pot for about 10 minutes, then carefully switch the pressure release to Venting. Open the Instant Pot, serve, and enjoy!

Per Serving
calories: 578 | fat: 51g | protein: 17g | carbs: 16g net carbs: 10g | fiber: 6g

Hearty Hamburger Soup

Prep time: 5 minutes | Cook time: 25 minutes
Serves 4

2 tablespoons coconut oil
1 pound (454 g) grass-fed beef, ground
4 cups grass-fed bone broth
3 slices no-sugar-added bacon, cooked and finely chopped (optional)
1 cup full-fat Cheddar cheese, shredded (optional)
1 carrot, chopped
1 celery stalk, chopped
½ teaspoon parsley, dried
½ teaspoon crushed red pepper
½ teaspoon basil, dried
½ teaspoon kosher salt
½ teaspoon freshly ground black pepper
1 (14-ounce / 397-g) can sugar-free or low-sugar diced tomatoes

1. Set the Instant Pot to Sauté and melt the oil. Add the beef and brown for 2 to 5 minutes.
2. Pour in bone broth, then add the bacon, cheese, carrot, celery, parsley, red pepper, basil, salt, black pepper, and tomatoes to the Instant Pot.

3. Close the lid, set the pressure release to Sealing and hit Cancel to stop the current program. Select Manual, set the Instant Pot to 25 minutes on High Pressure, and let cook.
4. Once cooked, let the pressure naturally disperse from the Instant Pot for about 10 minutes, then carefully switch the pressure release to Venting.
5. Open the Instant Pot, serve, and enjoy!

Per Serving
calories: 514 | fat: 30g | protein: 49g | carbs: 10g net carbs: 8g | fiber: 2g

Creamy Bacon Soup

Prep time: 5 minutes | Cook time: 10 minutes
Serves 4

10 slices no-sugar-added bacon
6 cups grass-fed bone broth
6 ounces (170 g) full-fat cream cheese, softened
5 tablespoons sugar-free or low-sugar tomato paste
4 tablespoons grass-fed butter, softened
2 teaspoons cumin, ground
2 teaspoons chili powder
1 garlic clove, chopped
½ teaspoon basil, dried
½ teaspoon parsley, dried
½ teaspoon cayenne pepper, ground
½ teaspoon freshly ground black pepper
1 cup heavy whipping cream
1 cup full-fat Cheddar cheese, shredded

1. Set the Instant Pot to Sauté. Add the bacon, and let cook until it is slightly crispy. Using tongs, place the bacon onto paper towels.
2. Add the bone broth, cream cheese, tomato paste, butter, cumin, chili powder, garlic, basil, parsley, cayenne pepper, and black pepper to the Instant Pot. Stir thoroughly. Close the lid, set the pressure release to Sealing, and select Manual. Set the Instant Pot to 10 minutes on High Pressure, and let cook.
3. Once cooked, perform a quick release by switching the valve to Venting. You may want to cover the valve with a towel, to avoid spilling the soup. Turn off the heat, remove the lid, stir in whipping cream, and let soup sit for 10 minutes.
4. Serve soup into bowls and crumble bacon on top. Sprinkle in Cheddar cheese, as desired.

Per Serving
calories: 804 | fat: 67g | protein: 37g | carbs: 11g net carbs: 10g | fiber: 1g

Hot and Sour Soup

Prep time: 10 minutes | Cook time: 13 minutes
Serves 8

5 cups low-sodium chicken broth
1 pound (454 g) boneless pork center loin chop, thinly sliced
1 cup dried wood ear mushrooms
3 tablespoons soy sauce
1 tablespoon black vinegar or white vinegar
2 tablespoons rice vinegar or white vinegar
1 teaspoon salt
½ teaspoon xanthan gum
2 teaspoons freshly ground black pepper
3 tablespoons water
1 pound (454 g) extra-firm tofu, diced
4 eggs, lightly beaten

1. In the inner cooking pot of the Instant Pot, put the broth, pork, mushrooms, soy sauce, black vinegar, rice vinegar, salt, xanthan gum, pepper, and water.
2. Lock the lid into place. Select Soup and adjust the pressure to High. Cook for 10 minutes. When the cooking is complete, let the pressure release naturally for 10 minutes, then quick-release any remaining pressure. Unlock the lid.
3. Turn the Instant Pot on Sauté and adjust to high heat to allow the soup to stay hot.
4. Using tongs, remove the mushrooms to a cutting board. Cut them into thin slices, then stir them back into the soup.
5. Add the tofu to the pot and stir. Slowly pour in the eggs. Mix the eggs three times around with chopsticks. Cover the pot and let the eggs cook in the broth for about 1 minute, then serve.

Per Serving
calories: 251 | fat: 15g | protein: 19g | carbs: 10g
net carbs: 10g | fiber: 0g

Chicken Tortilla Soup

Prep time: 5 minutes | Cook time: 30 minutes
Serves 4

½ cup roughly chopped onion
1 cup canned diced tomatoes and their juices
2 garlic cloves
1 chipotle chile in adobo sauce from a can
1 teaspoon adobo sauce
½ jalapeño pepper
¼ cup fresh cilantro
1 to 2 teaspoons salt
1 tablespoon olive oil
4 cups water
2 corn tortillas, diced (optional)
2 (6-ounce / 170-g) boneless, skinless chicken breasts, each cut into 4 to 6 pieces
½ cup sour cream
½ cup Mexican blend shredded cheese

1. In a blender, purée the onion, tomatoes, garlic, chipotle chile, adobo sauce, jalapeño, cilantro, and salt.
2. Preheat the Instant Pot by selecting Sauté and adjusting to high heat. When the inner cooking pot is hot, add the oil and heat until it is shimmering. Add the puréed vegetables and stir well. Cook, stirring occasionally, for about 10 minutes, or until the mixture is relatively thickened.
3. Add the water, tortillas (if using), and chicken.
4. Lock the lid into place. Select Manual and adjust the pressure to High. Cook for 20 minutes. When the cooking is complete, let the pressure release naturally for 10 minutes, then quick-release any remaining pressure. Unlock the lid.
5. Use tongs to transfer the chicken to a bowl. Shred the chicken, then stir it back into the soup. Ladle the soup into bowls and serve with the sour cream and cheese.

Per Serving
calories: 256 | fat: 17g | protein: 22g | carbs: 4g
net carbs: 3g | fiber: 1g

Reuben Soup

Prep time: 5 minutes | Cook time: 20 minutes
Serves 4

1 (8-ounce / 227-g) package cream cheese (or Kite Hill brand cream cheese style spread for dairy-free), softened
2½ cups beef broth
2 cups corned beef, sliced into thin strips (to resemble noodles)
1½ cups sauerkraut
1 cup finely grated Swiss cheese (omit for dairy-free)
¼ cup finely chopped onions
1 teaspoon fine sea salt
½ teaspoon ground black pepper
Fresh oregano sprigs, for garnish

1. Place the cream cheese in a 6-quart Instant Pot. Slowly add the broth while whisking. Stir in the corned beef, sauerkraut, Swiss cheese (if using), onions, salt, and pepper.
2. Seal the lid, press Soup/Broth, and set the timer for 20 minutes. Once finished, let the pressure release naturally.
3. Remove the lid and stir well. Taste and season with additional salt and pepper, if desired. Ladle the soup into bowls and garnish with oregano sprigs.

Per Serving
calories: 427 | fat: 34g | protein: 20g | carbs: 4g
net carbs: 3g | fiber: 1g

Taco Soup

Prep time: 10 minutes | Cook time: 34 minutes
Serves 5

1 pound (454 g) ground beef
3½ ounces (99 g) diced onion
2 cloves garlic, minced
1 tablespoon ground cumin
1 tablespoon chili powder
2 teaspoons dried

oregano
2 teaspoons salt
2 cups chicken broth
1 can (14½ ounces / 411 g) diced tomatoes with green chiles
3½ ounces (99 g) diced green bell pepper
1 jalapeño, seeded and diced

1. Turn the pot to Sauté mode. Once hot, add the ground beef and cook until most of the pink is gone, 3 to 4 minutes. Use a wooden spoon to break up the beef into small pieces as it cooks.
2. Add the onion and garlic and sauté until the beef is no longer pink, 3 to 4 minutes. Press Cancel.
3. Add the cumin, chili powder, oregano, and salt and stir to coat. Add the broth, tomatoes (with juice), bell pepper, and jalapeño.
4. Close the lid and seal the vent. Cook on High Pressure for 30 minutes. Quick release the steam.

Per Serving
calories: 208 | fat: 12g | protein: 20g | carbs: 8g net carbs: 6g | fiber: 2g

Pumpkin Soup

Prep time: 5 minutes | Cook time: 8 minutes
Serves 8

1 sugar pumpkin
4 cups chicken broth
½ cup heavy whipping cream
½ teaspoon cinnamon, ground
½ cup full-fat coconut

milk
½ teaspoon kosher salt
½ teaspoon freshly ground black pepper
1 teaspoon parsley, dried

1. Place the pumpkin on a stable work surface. Cut off the stem, slice pumpkin in half, and scoop out any seeds. Pour 1 cup of filtered water into the inner pot of the Instant Pot, then insert the trivet. Place the pumpkin on top of the trivet.
2. Close the lid, set the pressure release to Sealing, and select Manual. Set the Instant Pot to 8 minutes on High Pressure, and let cook.

3. Once cooked, let the pressure naturally disperse from the Instant Pot for about 10 minutes, then carefully switch the pressure release to Venting. Remove pumpkin.
4. In a blender, add the pumpkin, along with the chicken broth, whipping cream, cinnamon, milk, salt, and pepper. Blend until desired consistency. Set the Instant Pot to Sauté and return soup to the inner pot.
5. When warm enough (usually after 2 to 5 minutes), serve with the parsley, and enjoy!

Per Serving
calories: 100 | fat: 4g | protein: 1g | carbs: 7g net carbs: 5g | fiber: 2g

Sichuan Pork Soup

Prep time: 10 minutes | Cook time: 23 minutes
Serves 6

2 tablespoons olive oil
1 tablespoon minced garlic
1 tablespoon minced fresh ginger
2 tablespoons soy sauce
2 tablespoons black vinegar
1 to 2 teaspoons Truvia or Swerve
2 teaspoons Sichuan peppercorns, crushed

1 to 2 teaspoons salt
½ onion, sliced
1 pound (454 g) pork shoulder, cut into 2-inch chunks
2 tablespoons doubanjiang
3 cups water
3 to 4 cups chopped bok choy
¼ cup chopped fresh cilantro

1. Preheat the Instant Pot by selecting Sauté and adjusting to high heat. When the inner cooking pot is hot, add the oil and heat until it is shimmering. Add the garlic and ginger and sauté for 1 to 2 minutes.
2. Add the soy sauce, vinegar, sweetener, peppercorns, salt, onion, pork, doubanjiang, and water. Stir well.
3. Lock the lid into place. Select Manual and adjust the pressure to High. Cook for 20 minutes. When the cooking is complete, let the pressure release naturally for 10 minutes, then quick-release any remaining pressure. Unlock the lid.
4. Open the pot and add the bok choy. Close the lid and let it cook in the residual heat for about 10 minutes, or until softened but not mushy.
5. Ladle the soup into bowls and top with the cilantro. Serve and enjoy!

Per Serving
calories: 256 | fat: 20g | protein: 14g | carbs: 5g net carbs: 4g | fiber: 1g

Creamy Cauliflower Soup

Prep time: 5 minutes | Cook time: 20 minutes
Serves 4

2 tablespoons grass-fed butter, softened
2 cups grass-fed bone broth
6 slices no-sugar-added bacon, sliced, crumbled, cooked
1 cup full-fat Cheddar cheese, shredded
1 head cauliflower, chopped
1 cup celery, chopped
½ cup heavy whipping cream
½ cup full-fat coconut milk
¼ cup green onion, thinly sliced
½ teaspoon garlic powder
½ teaspoon freshly ground black pepper
½ teaspoon kosher salt

1. Set the Instant Pot to Sauté mode. Add the butter, melting it gently.
2. Pour in bone broth, then mix in bacon, cheese, cauliflower, celery, whipping cream, milk, onion, garlic powder, black pepper, salt, and 1 cup of filtered water. Close the lid, set the pressure release to Sealing, and select Manual. Set the Instant Pot to 10 minutes on High Pressure and let cook.
3. When cooking is complete, perform a quick release. Open the lid. Using an immersion blender, blend the soup until achieving your desired consistency. Add an extra tablespoon (or two) of heavy whipping cream for a thicker texture. Serve, and enjoy!

Per Serving
calories: 485 | fat: 40g | protein: 23g | carbs: 9g
net carbs: 6g | fiber: 3g

High-Protein Chili

Prep time: 5 minutes | Cook time: 18 minutes
Serves 5

2 tablespoons avocado oil
2 garlic cloves, minced
1 pound (454 g) grass-fed beef, ground
½ teaspoon crushed red pepper
½ teaspoon chili powder
½ cup full-fat Cheddar cheese, shredded
½ teaspoon basil, dried
½ teaspoon kosher salt
½ teaspoon freshly ground black pepper
1 (14-ounce / 397-g) can crushed sugar-free or low-sugar tomatoes

1. Set the Instant Pot to Sauté and heat the oil. Then add the garlic, sautéing for 2 to 3 minutes.
2. Pour in ½ cup of filtered water, then add the beef, red pepper, chili powder, cheese, basil, salt, black pepper, and tomatoes to the Instant Pot.

3. Close the lid, set the pressure release to Sealing, and hit Cancel to stop the current program. Select Manual, set the Instant Pot to 18 minutes on High Pressure, and let cook.
4. Once cooked, let the pressure naturally disperse from the Instant Pot for about 10 minutes, then carefully switch the pressure release to Venting. Open the Instant Pot, serve, and enjoy!

Per Serving
calories: 233 | fat: 10g | protein: 31g | carbs: 3g
net carbs: 2g | fiber: 1g

Curry Beef Stew

Prep time: 5 minutes | Cook time: 26 minutes
Serves 4

1 pound (454 g) beef stew meat
2 teaspoons fine sea salt
1 teaspoon ground black pepper
1 tablespoon coconut oil
1 cup diced onions
2 cloves garlic, minced
1 teaspoon peeled and chopped fresh ginger
1 jalapeño pepper, diced
1 tablespoon curry powder
2 cups beef broth
For Garnish:
Fresh cilantro leaves
Lime wedges
Sliced red jalapeño peppers

1. Cut the beef into 1-inch cubes and season on all sides with the salt and pepper.
2. Place the coconut oil in a 6-quart Instant Pot and press Sauté. Once melted, add the seasoned beef and cook for about 1 minute per side or until browned on all sides. Remove from the pot and set aside, leaving the drippings in the pot.
3. Add the onions, garlic, ginger, and jalapeño and sauté in the beef drippings for 2 minutes, until fragrant, then stir in the curry powder. Press Cancel to stop the Sauté.
4. Pour in the broth and return the browned beef to the pot. Stir to combine.
5. Seal the lid, press Manual, and set the timer for 20 minutes. Once finished, let the pressure release naturally.
6. Remove the lid and stir well. Serve the stew in bowls, garnish with cilantro, lime wedges, red jalapeño slices, and freshly ground black pepper.

Per Serving
calories: 394 | fat: 26g | protein: 33g | carbs: 5g
net carbs: 4g | fiber: 1g

Beef Stew

Prep time: 5 minutes | Cook time: 15 minutes
Serves 5

2 tablespoons avocado oil	mushrooms
1 pound (454 g) beef stew meat, cubed	2 carrots, cut up
1 clove garlic, minced	1 bay leaf
3 cups grass-fed bone broth	½ teaspoon parsley, dried
2 ounces (57 g) wild	½ teaspoon kosher salt
	½ teaspoon freshly ground black pepper

1. Set the Instant Pot to Sauté and heat the oil. Add the beef and cook until browned, stirring occasionally. Add the garlic and cook for an additional 1 minute.
2. Add the bone broth, mushrooms, carrots, bay leaf, parsley, salt, and black pepper to the Instant Pot.
3. Close the lid, set the pressure release to Sealing, and hit Cancel to stop the current program. Select Manual, set the Instant Pot to 15 minutes on High Pressure, and let cook.
4. Once cooked, let the pressure naturally disperse from the Instant Pot for about 10 minutes, then carefully switch the pressure release to Venting.
5. Open the Instant Pot, remove bay leaf, serve, and enjoy!

Per Serving
calories: 208 | fat: 6g | protein: 31g | carbs: 5g
net carbs: 4g | fiber: 1g

Coconut Butternut Squash Soup

Prep time: 5 minutes | Cook time: 10 minutes
Serves 5 to 6

2 tablespoons coconut oil	powder
4 cloves garlic, minced	½ teaspoon ginger, finely grated
6 cups grass-fed bone broth	½ teaspoon kosher salt
2 cups butternut squash, cubed	½ teaspoon freshly ground black pepper
½ teaspoon curry	2 cups full-fat coconut milk

1. Set the Instant Pot to Sauté and melt the oil, then add the garlic. Sauté for 2 minutes.
2. Pour in the bone broth, then add the butternut squash, curry powder, ginger, salt, and pepper to the Instant Pot. Close the lid, set the pressure release to Sealing, and hit Cancel to stop the current program. Select Manual, set the Instant Pot to 10 minutes on High Pressure, and let cook.

3. Once cooked, perform a quick release by carefully switching the pressure valve to Venting.
4. Open the lid and purée the coconut milk directly in the Instant Pot, using an immersion blender, until desired consistency is achieved.

Per Serving
calories: 278 | fat: 24g | protein: 7g | carbs: 13g
net carbs: 10g | fiber: 3g

Provolone Chicken Soup

Prep time: 7 minutes | Cook time: 13 minutes
Serves 4

4 strips bacon, chopped	into ¾-inch cubes
¼ cup chopped onions	4 cups chicken broth
2 cloves garlic, minced	1 cup provolone cheese, shredded
2 ounces (57 g) cream cheese (¼ cup), softened	½ teaspoon fine sea salt
1 pound (454 g) boneless, skinless chicken breasts, cut	½ teaspoon ground black pepper

For Garnish:

Sour cream	or ghee
Melted unsalted butter	Dried chives

1. Place the bacon in a 6-quart Instant Pot and press Sauté. Cook, stirring often, for 4 minutes, or until the bacon is crisp. Remove the bacon with a slotted spoon and set aside on a paper towel-lined plate to drain, leaving the drippings in the pot.
2. Add the onions and garlic to the Instant Pot and sauté in the bacon drippings for 4 minutes, or until the onions are soft. Press Cancel to stop the Sauté.
3. Add the cream cheese and whisk to loosen. (If you don't use a whisk to loosen the cream cheese, you will end up with clumps in your soup.) Add the chicken, broth, provolone, salt, and pepper and stir to combine.
4. Seal the lid, press Manual, and set the timer for 5 minutes. Once finished, let the pressure release naturally.
5. Remove the lid and stir well. Ladle the soup into bowls and garnish with sour cream, a drizzle of melted butter, the reserved bacon, and chives.

Per Serving
calories: 373 | fat: 18g | protein: 49g | carbs: 2g
net carbs: 1g | fiber: 1g

Broccoli Soup with Radishes

Prep time: 10 minutes | Cook time: 5 minutes
Serves 7

3 cups chicken broth
1 pound (454 g) broccoli florets
8 ounces (227 g) diced radishes
1½ ounces (43 g) diced carrot
1½ teaspoons salt
½ teaspoon black pepper
½ teaspoon garlic powder
2 cups shredded Cheddar cheese
½ cup heavy cream

1. Add the chicken broth, broccoli, radishes, carrot, salt, pepper, and garlic powder to the pot.
2. Close the lid and seal the vent. Cook on High Pressure for 5 minutes. Quick release the steam.
3. Add the cheese to the soup and stir until all the cheese is melted. Add the cream and stir until well combined.
4. Use an immersion blender to purée the soup until the desired consistency is reached. Alternatively, transfer to a standard blender and blend in batches.

Per Serving
calories: 190 | fat: 8g | protein: 4g | carbs: 6g
net carbs: 4g | fiber: 2g

New England Clam Chowder

Prep time: 5 minutes | Cook time: 13 minutes
Serves 8

1 pound (454 g) bacon, chopped
¼ cup chopped onions
1 leek, trimmed, halved lengthwise, and sliced
2 stalks celery, diced
4 cloves garlic, minced
1 (8-ounce / 227-g) package cream cheese (or Kite Hill brand cream cheese style spread for dairy-free), softened
3 (10-ounce / 283-g) cans baby clams, with liquid
2 cups cauliflower florets, chopped
1½ cups chicken broth
2 tablespoons unsalted butter (or butter-flavored coconut oil for dairy-free)
2 teaspoons fine sea salt
1 teaspoon ground black pepper
1 teaspoon dried thyme leaves
Fresh thyme sprigs, for garnish

1. Place the bacon in a 6-quart Instant Pot and press Sauté. Cook, stirring often, for 4 minutes, or until the bacon is crisp. Remove the bacon with a slotted spoon and set aside on a paper towel-lined plate to drain, leaving the drippings in the pot.
2. Add the onions, leek, celery, and garlic to the Instant Pot and sauté in the bacon drippings for 4 minutes, or until the onions are soft. Press Cancel to stop the Sauté.
3. Add the cream cheese to the Instant Pot and whisk to loosen. (If you don't use a whisk to loosen the cream cheese, you will end up with clumps in your soup.) Add the clams (including the liquid from the cans), cauliflower, broth, butter, salt, pepper, and thyme, along with three-quarters of the bacon; reserve the rest of the bacon for garnish.
4. Seal the lid, press Manual, and set the timer for 5 minutes. Once finished, let the pressure release naturally.
5. Remove the lid and stir well. Ladle the soup into bowls and garnish with thyme sprigs and the reserved bacon.

Per Serving
calories: 552 | fat: 41g | protein: 34g | carbs: 10g
net carbs: 9g | fiber: 1g

Chicken Zoodle Soup

Prep time: 5 minutes | Cook time: 30 minutes
Serves 6

1½ pounds (680 g) boneless, skinless chicken breasts
3½ ounces (99 g) chopped onion
1½ ounces (43 g) diced carrot
2 ribs celery, chopped
3 cups chicken broth
2 teaspoons salt
1½ teaspoons poultry seasoning
½ teaspoon black pepper
10½ ounces (298 g) zucchini noodles

1. Add the chicken, onion, carrot, celery, chicken broth, salt, poultry seasoning, and pepper to the pot.
2. Close the lid and seal the vent. Cook on High Pressure for 25 minutes. Quick release the steam. Press Cancel.
3. Remove the chicken from the soup and shred with two forks. Return the chicken to the soup.
4. Add the zucchini noodles to the hot soup and let sit until the noodles are soft, 5 to 10 minutes. If you'd like a softer noodle, you can cook the soup an additional 1 to 2 minutes on Low Pressure.

Per Serving
calories: 147 | fat: 2g | protein: 26g | carbs: 5g
net carbs: 4g | fiber: 1g

Cincinnati-Style Chili

Prep time: 10 minutes | Cook time: 24 minutes
Serves 6

1 tablespoon avocado oil	nutmeg
1 pound (454 g) ground beef	1 teaspoon ground allspice
5 ounces (142 g) chopped onion (about 1 cup)	¼ teaspoon black pepper
1 clove of garlic, minced	¾ teaspoon salt
1 tablespoon unsweetened cocoa powder	¼ teaspoon cayenne pepper
1 tablespoon chili powder	1 can (14½ ounces / 411 g) diced tomatoes
1½ teaspoons ground cinnamon	¼ cup beef broth
1 teaspoon ground	2 tablespoons Worcestershire sauce
	1 tablespoon red wine vinegar

1. Turn the pot to Sauté mode and add the avocado oil. Once hot, add the ground beef.
2. Brown the beef, breaking it apart into small pieces with a wooden spoon. When the meat is only slightly pink, 3 to 4 minutes, add the onion and garlic. Continue to sauté until the meat is browned. Press Cancel.
3. Add the cocoa powder and spices and stir well to coat the meat. Add the tomatoes (with juice), broth, Worcestershire, and vinegar.
4. Close the lid and seal the vent. Cook on High Pressure for 20 minutes. Quick release the steam.

Per Serving
calories: 227 | fat: 14g | protein: 15g | carbs: 8g net carbs: 6g | fiber: 2g

Cauliflower and Bacon Chowder

Prep time: 10 minutes | Cook time: 25 minutes
Serves 7

2 cups chicken broth	1 large head cauliflower (about 2 pounds / 907 g)
5 ounces (142 g) diced onion (about 1 small onion)	8 ounces (227 g) cream cheese, softened and cut into small cubes
8 ounces (227 g) diced bacon, uncooked	
1 teaspoon salt	½ cup heavy cream, at room temperature
½ teaspoon black pepper	

1. Pour the chicken broth into the pot. Add the onion, bacon, salt, and pepper. Stir to combine.

2. Remove the stems and core from the cauliflower but leave the florets in large pieces. Place the large florets in the pot.
3. Close the lid and seal the vent. Cook on High Pressure for 25 minutes. Quick release the steam.
4. Use a potato masher and gently break apart the cauliflower. It will be very soft. Be careful not to overmash the cauliflower. You want it to be in little pieces that resemble potatoes.
5. Add the cream cheese to the soup. Use a wooden spoon to stir the soup until all of the cream cheese is melted through. Add the cream and stir to combine.

Per Serving
calories: 328 | fat: 25g | protein: 16g | carbs: 9g net carbs: 6g | fiber: 3g

Vietnamese Bo Kho

Prep time: 10 minutes | Cook time: 15 minutes
Serves 6

1 onion, roughly chopped	garlic
1 pound (454 g) beef chuck stew meat cubes	1¾ cups water, divided
	½ cup coconut water
2 tablespoons tomato paste	1 teaspoon freshly ground black pepper
2 whole star anise	½ teaspoon Chinese five-spice powder
1 tablespoon lemongrass paste	½ teaspoon curry powder
1 tablespoon minced fresh ginger	1 turnip, quartered
1 tablespoon minced	2 carrots, chopped into large, thick chunks

1. In the inner cooking pot of the Instant Pot, add the onion, beef, tomato paste, star anise, lemongrass paste, ginger, garlic, 1½ cups of water, coconut water, pepper, Chinese five-spice powder, and curry powder. Place a trivet on top of the meat and spices.
2. In a smaller heatproof container, place the turnip, carrots, and remaining ¼ cup of water. Place on top of the trivet.
3. Lock the lid into place. Select Manual and adjust the pressure to High. Cook for 15 minutes. When the cooking is complete, let the pressure release naturally for 10 minutes, then quick-release any remaining pressure. Unlock the lid.
4. Remove the bowl with the vegetables and the trivet. Add the vegetables and any of their liquid to the soup, first cutting them into smaller pieces, if you like.

Per Serving
calories: 221 | fat: 14g | protein: 16g | carbs: 9g net carbs: 7g | fiber: 2g

Buffalo Chicken Chili

Prep time: 5 minutes | Cook time: 10 minutes
Serves 4

3 cups grass-fed bone broth
2 tablespoons avocado oil
2 tablespoons hot sauce (or more, to taste)
2 tablespoons buffalo sauce
1 pound (454 g) chicken breasts, cooked, shredded
1 cup full-fat Cheddar cheese, shredded

(optional)
½ teaspoon chili powder
½ teaspoon cayenne powder
½ teaspoon kosher salt
½ teaspoon freshly ground black pepper
1 (14-ounce / 397-g) can sugar-free or low-sugar fire roasted tomatoes

1. Add all ingredients to the Instant Pot. Stir and mix thoroughly.
2. Close the lid, set the pressure release to Sealing, and select Manual. Set the Instant Pot to 10 minutes on High Pressure and let cook.
3. Once cooked, carefully switch the pressure release to Venting. Open the Instant Pot, strain to your desired consistency, and enjoy!

Per Serving
calories: 383 | fat: 19g | protein: 44g | carbs: 6g net carbs: 4g | fiber: 2g

Broccoli and Leek Soup

Prep time: 5 minutes | Cook time: 7 minutes
Serves 4

¼ cup raw cashew nuts
2 tablespoons butter
1 cup sliced leek whites and tender greens
1 small onion, sliced
2 large cloves of garlic, crushed
2 cups broccoli florets and sliced stems
2 cups chicken broth
2 sprigs fresh tarragon,

leaves removed and stems discarded, or
2 teaspoons dried tarragon
Sea salt and pepper, to taste
¼ cup full-fat heavy cream, for topping
2 teaspoons chopped fresh chives, for garnish

1. Soak the raw cashews in cold water for 30 minutes. After they're soaked, drain the water and set the nuts aside. Discard the water.
2. Turn on the Instant Pot by pressing Sauté and set to More. Insert the inner pot and wait until the panel says Hot. Melt the butter and sauté the leek, onion and garlic for 3 minutes or until the leek is soft. Add the cashews, broccoli, chicken broth and tarragon to the inner pot.

3. Close the lid tightly and move the steam release handle to Sealing. Hit Cancel, and then press the Manual button and set the timer for 4 minutes on High Pressure. When the timer ends, carefully turn the steam release handle to the Venting position for the steam to escape and the float valve to drop down. Press Cancel and open the lid. Using an immersion blender, purée the soup until smooth. Add sea salt and pepper to taste, drizzle with the heavy cream and garnish with the chives before serving.

Per Serving
calories: 301 | fat: 24g | protein: 9g | carbs: 16g net carbs: 13g | fiber: 3g

Pumpkin Chili

Prep time: 5 minutes | Cook time: 12 minutes
Serves 4

2 tablespoons ghee or coconut oil
1 yellow onion, diced
1 bell pepper (any color), diced
2 cloves garlic, minced
1 pound (454 g) ground beef
1 (14½-ounce / 411-g) can diced tomatoes
2 (4-ounce / 113-g)

cans diced green chilies
1 (15-ounce / 425-g) can pumpkin purée
1 cup beef broth
1 teaspoon chili powder
1 teaspoon ground cinnamon
1 teaspoon fine sea salt
Ground black pepper
Chopped fresh Italian parsley, for garnish

1. Place the ghee in a 6-quart Instant Pot and press Sauté. Once melted, add the onion, bell pepper, and garlic and sauté for 4 minutes, or until the onion is soft. Add the ground beef and cook, breaking up the large chunks of meat, for 3 more minutes, or until the beef is starting to brown.
2. Add the tomatoes, chilies, pumpkin, broth, chili powder, cinnamon, and salt. Deglaze the pot, scraping up any bits stuck to the bottom, and stir the beef into the onion mixture well. Press Cancel to stop the Sauté.
3. Seal the lid, press Manual, and set the timer for 5 minutes. Once finished, let the pressure release naturally.
4. Remove the lid and stir well. Season with salt and pepper to taste. Ladle the soup into bowls and garnish with parsley.

Per Serving
calories: 431 | fat: 41g | protein: 23g | carbs: 15g net carbs: 11g | fiber: 4g

Hamburger Stew

Prep time: 10 minutes | Cook time: 7 minutes
Serves 6

1 pound (454 g) 80% lean ground beef
½ cup tomato sauce
2 tablespoons tomato paste
1 tablespoon powdered chicken broth base
2 cups frozen green beans

1 cup sliced onions
3 tablespoons apple cider vinegar
1 tablespoon soy sauce
1 teaspoon salt
2 teaspoons freshly ground black pepper
Juice of 1 lemon

1. Preheat the Instant Pot by selecting Sauté and adjusting to high heat. When the inner cooking pot is hot, add the ground beef. Break up any clumps and cook for 2 to 3 minutes. You do not need to brown the beef, as the Maillard reaction in the pressure cooker will take care of this for you.
2. Add the tomato sauce, tomato paste, chicken broth base, green beans, onions, vinegar, soy sauce, salt, and pepper.
3. Lock the lid into place. Select Manual and adjust the pressure to High. Cook for 5 minutes. When the cooking is complete, let the pressure release naturally for 10 minutes, then quick-release any remaining pressure. Unlock the lid.
4. Stir in the lemon juice and serve.

Per Serving
calories: 276 | fat: 20g | protein: 16g | carbs: 8g
net carbs: 5g | fiber: 3g

Cauliflower Clam Chowder

Prep time: 5 minutes | Cook time: 5 minutes
Serves 5 to 6

2 cups full-fat coconut milk
2 bay leaves
1 cup grass-fed bone broth
1 pound (454 g) cauliflower, chopped
1 cup celery, finely chopped
½ teaspoon freshly

ground black pepper
½ teaspoon kosher salt
¼ (4-ounce / 113-g) small onion, thinly sliced
2 (7-ounce / 198-g) cans clams, chopped, drained
1 cup heavy whipping cream

1. Add the coconut milk, bay leaves, bone broth, cauliflower, celery, black pepper, salt, and onion to the Instant Pot. Stir thoroughly.
2. Close the lid, set the pressure release to Sealing, and select Manual. Set the Instant Pot to 5 minutes on High Pressure and let cook.

3. Once cooked, let the pressure naturally disperse from the Instant Pot for about 3 minutes, then carefully switch the pressure release to Venting. Open the Instant Pot, remove bay leaves with tongs, and then stir in the clams and whipping cream.
4. Turn on Sauté mode, and let cook for 2 to 3 minutes (or until desired consistency). Serve, and enjoy!

Per Serving
calories: 314 | fat: 27g | protein: 5g | carbs: 18g
net carbs: 13g | fiber: 5g

Supreme Pizza Soup

Prep time: 10 minutes | Cook time: 13 minutes
Serves 6

1 tablespoon unsalted butter (or coconut oil for dairy-free)
¼ cup diced onions
1 cup button or cremini mushrooms (fresh or canned), thinly sliced
¼ cup diced red bell peppers
1½ pounds (680 g) bulk Italian sausage
5 cups marinara sauce
1 cup beef broth
½ cup sliced pepperoni

1 teaspoon dried oregano leaves
Fine sea salt and ground black pepper
½ cup sliced black olives, plus more for garnish
¼ cup shredded Mozzarella, for garnish (optional; omit for dairy-free)
Fresh oregano leaves, for garnish (optional)

1. Place the butter in a 6-quart Instant Pot and press Sauté. Once melted, add the onions and cook for 3 minutes, or until soft. Add the mushrooms and bell peppers and cook for another 3 minutes, or until the peppers are soft.
2. Add the sausage and cook, crumbling the meat to break up the large chunks, for 5 minutes, or until almost completely cooked through. Add the marinara, broth, pepperoni, and dried oregano and stir to combine. Press Cancel to stop the Sauté.
3. Seal the lid, press Manual, and set the timer for 2 minutes. Once finished, turn the valve to venting for a quick release.
4. Remove the lid and stir well. Season with salt and pepper to taste and stir in the olives. Ladle the soup into bowls and top each bowl with a couple of olive slices and some shredded cheese, if using. Garnish with oregano leaves, if desired.

Per Serving
calories: 260 | fat: 21g | protein: 6g | carbs: 6g
net carbs: 4g | fiber: 2g

Cabbage Roll Soup

Prep time: 10 minutes | Cook time: 8 minutes
Serves 4

½ pound (227 g) 84% lean ground pork
½ pound (227 g) 85% lean ground beef
½ medium onion, diced
½ medium head of cabbage, thinly sliced
2 tablespoons tomato paste
½ cup diced tomatoes
2 cups chicken broth
1 teaspoon salt
½ teaspoon thyme
½ teaspoon garlic powder
¼ teaspoon pepper

1. Press the Sauté button and add beef and pork to Instant Pot. Brown meat until no pink remains. Add onion and continue cooking until onions are fragrant and soft. Press the Cancel button.
2. Add remaining ingredients to Instant Pot. Press the Manual button and adjust time for 8 minutes.
3. When timer beeps, allow a 15-minute natural release and then quick-release the remaining pressure. Serve warm.

Per Serving
calories: 304 | fat: 15g | protein: 24g | carbs: 12g net carbs: 8g | fiber: 4g

Green Borscht

Prep time: 10 minutes | Cook time: 15 minutes
Serves 4

2 tablespoons unsalted butter (or coconut oil for dairy-free) (Instant Pot only)
½ cup diced onions
3 cups chopped sorrel or spinach
4 boneless, skinless chicken breasts, cut into ¾-inch chunks
1 head cauliflower, cut into ¾-inch pieces
6 cups chicken broth
1 tablespoon chopped fresh dill, plus more for garnish
1 tablespoon lemon juice
Fine sea salt and ground black pepper
6 hard-boiled eggs, halved (omit for egg-free)
Sour cream, for garnish (omit for dairy-free)

1. Place the butter in a 6-quart Instant Pot and press Sauté. Once melted, add the onions and cook for 2 minutes. Add the sorrel and cook for another 3 minutes, or until the onions are soft.
2. Add the chicken, cauliflower, broth, and dill and stir to combine. Press Cancel to stop the Sauté.
3. Seal the lid, press Manual, and set the timer for 10 minutes. Once finished, let the pressure release naturally.

4. Remove the lid and stir in the lemon juice. Season with salt and pepper to taste. Ladle the soup into bowls, then place the halved hard-boiled eggs in the bowls. Garnish with a dollop of sour cream (if using) and more dill.

Per Serving
calories: 519 | fat: 24g | protein: 52g | carbs: 23g net carbs: 19g | fiber: 4g

Seafood Chowder

Prep time: 5 minutes | Cook time: 13 minutes
Serves 8

2 strips bacon, chopped
2 tablespoons coconut oil, ghee, or unsalted butter (Instant Pot only)
2 cups chopped celery
½ cup diced onions
4 cloves garlic, minced
4 ounces (113 g) cream cheese (½ cup), softened
3 cups chicken broth
1 medium head cauliflower, cut into
small florets
1 pound (454 g) cod or other white fish fillets, cut into 1-inch cubes
2 cups frozen raw shrimp, peeled and deveined
½ teaspoon fine sea salt
½ teaspoon ground black pepper
Extra-virgin olive oil, for drizzling (optional)

1. Place the bacon in a 6-quart Instant Pot and press Sauté. Cook, stirring often, for 4 minutes, or until the bacon is crisp. Remove the bacon with a slotted spoon and set aside on a paper towel-lined plate to drain. Wipe the pot clean.
2. Place the coconut oil in the Instant Pot. Once melted, add the celery, onions, and garlic and cook for 4 minutes, or until the onions are soft. Press Cancel to stop the Sauté.
3. Add the cream cheese and whisk to loosen. (If you don't use a whisk to loosen the cream cheese, you will end up with clumps in your soup.) Slowly whisk in the broth. Add the cauliflower, fish, shrimp, salt, and pepper and stir to combine.
4. Seal the lid, press Manual, and set the timer for 5 minutes. Once finished, let the pressure release naturally.
5. Remove the lid and stir well. Serve the soup in bowls, garnished with the bacon, freshly ground pepper, and a drizzle of olive oil, if desired.

Per Serving
calories: 234 | fat: 15g | protein: 17g | carbs: 8g net carbs: 7g | fiber: 1g

Creamy Chicken and Tomato Soup

**Prep time: 10 minutes | Cook time: 19 minutes
Serves 4**

1 tablespoon unsalted butter (or coconut oil for dairy-free)
¼ cup finely chopped onions
2 cloves garlic, minced
2 large boneless, skinless chicken breasts
1 cup chicken broth
1 cup heavy cream (or full-fat coconut milk for dairy-free)
1 (14½-ounce / 411-

g) can diced tomatoes, drained
2 tablespoons tomato paste
3 tablespoons Italian seasoning
1 teaspoon fine sea salt
½ teaspoon ground black pepper
Chopped fresh basil leaves, for garnish
Extra-virgin olive oil, for drizzling

1. Place the butter in a 6-quart Instant Pot and press Sauté. Once melted, add the onions and garlic and sauté for 4 minutes, or until the onions are soft. Press Cancel to stop the Sauté.
2. Add the chicken, broth, cream, tomatoes, tomato paste, Italian seasoning, salt, and pepper to the Instant Pot and stir to combine. Seal the lid, press Manual, and set the timer for 15 minutes. Once finished, turn the valve to venting for a quick release.
3. Remove the lid and shred the chicken with two forks. Taste and adjust the seasoning to your liking. Ladle the soup into bowls and garnish with basil and a drizzle of olive oil.

Per Serving
calories: 382 | fat: 29g | protein: 24g | carbs: 11g
net carbs: 9g | fiber: 2g

Belgian Booyah

**Prep time: 10 minutes | Cook time: 16 minutes
Serves 8**

1 tablespoon unsalted butter (or coconut oil for dairy-free)
2 cups sliced button mushrooms
1 medium onion, diced
Cloves squeezed from 1 head roasted garlic, or 2 cloves garlic, minced
1 pound (454 g) ground beef
4 boneless, skinless chicken thighs, cut into ¾-inch pieces

1 head cauliflower, cut into 1-inch pieces
2 cups beef broth
2 cups tomato sauce
1 (14½-ounce / 411-g) can diced tomatoes
2 teaspoons dried basil leaves
2 teaspoons dried oregano leaves
1 teaspoon celery salt
1 teaspoon ground black pepper

1. Place the butter in a 6-quart Instant Pot and press Sauté. Once melted, add the mushrooms, onion, and garlic and cook for 4 minutes, or until the onions are soft.
2. Add the ground beef and continue to cook, crumbling the meat to break up the large chunks, for 2 minutes, or until the beef is starting to cook through. Press Cancel to stop the Sauté.
3. Add the chicken, cauliflower, broth, tomato sauce, tomatoes, basil, oregano, celery salt, and pepper. Stir well to combine.
4. Seal the lid, press Manual, and set the timer for 10 minutes. Once finished, turn the valve to venting for a quick release.
5. Remove the lid and stir well. Ladle the soup into bowls and serve.

Per Serving
calories: 273 | fat: 15g | protein: 22g | carbs: 13g
net carbs: 9g | fiber: 4g

Egg Roll Soup

**Prep time: 10 minutes | Cook time: 20 minutes
Serves 4**

1 pound (454 g) ground pork
2 cups thinly sliced cabbage, for "noodles"
4 cups beef broth
½ cup coconut aminos, or 2 tablespoons wheat-free tamari
½ teaspoon toasted sesame oil
¼ cup Swerve confectioners'-style sweetener or equivalent amount of liquid or

powdered sweetener
4 green onions, thinly sliced, plus more for garnish
Cloves squeezed from 1 head roasted garlic, or 2 teaspoons garlic paste
1 (2-inch) piece fresh ginger, peeled and finely grated
4 poached eggs, for serving

1. Place the ground pork and cabbage "noodles" in a 6-quart Instant Pot. Add the broth, coconut aminos, sesame oil, sweetener, green onions, garlic, and ginger. Stir well to break up the meat.
2. Seal the lid, press Manual, and set the timer for 20 minutes. Once finished, let the pressure release naturally.
3. Remove the lid and stir well. Ladle the soup into bowls and add a poached egg to each bowl. Garnish with more sliced green onions.

Per Serving
calories: 425 | fat: 30g | protein: 26g | carbs: 11g
net carbs: 3g | fiber: 8g

First Place Chili

Prep time: 5 minutes | Cook time: 24 minutes
Serves 8

1 pound (454 g) ground beef
3 ounces (85 g) chopped onion
3 ounces (85 g) chopped green bell pepper
3 tablespoons ground cumin
1½ tablespoons chili powder

2 teaspoons salt
1½ teaspoons garlic powder
¼ teaspoon ground coriander
¼ teaspoon cayenne pepper
Pinch of black pepper
½ cup water
1 can (28 ounces / 794 g) crushed tomatoes

1. Turn the pot to Sauté mode. Once hot, add the beef and cook until it is mostly cooked through, 3 to 4 minutes. Use a wooden spoon to break up the beef into small pieces. Press Cancel.
2. Add the onion, bell pepper, and spices and stir to combine. Add the water to the pot and stir to combine.
3. Add the tomatoes to the top of the beef mixture but do NOT stir.
4. Close the lid and seal the vent. Cook on High Pressure for 20 minutes. Quick release the steam.
5. Open the lid and stir the chili until thoroughly combined.

Per Serving
calories: 195 | fat: 12g | protein: 12g | carbs: 10g
net carbs: 7g | fiber: 3g

Cream of Asparagus Soup

Prep time: 5 minutes | Cook time: 14 minutes
Serves 4

1 tablespoon unsalted butter (or coconut oil for dairy-free) (Instant Pot only)
1½ pounds (680 g) fresh asparagus, woody ends trimmed, cut into 2-inch chunks, plus more for garnish
½ cup chopped onions
2 cups chopped cauliflower

4 cups chicken broth or vegetable broth
½ teaspoon fine sea salt
½ teaspoon ground black pepper
4 ounces (113 g) cream cheese (½ cup)
For Garnish (Optional):
Asparagus tips
Purple salt

1. Place the butter in a 6-quart Instant Pot and press Sauté. Once melted, add the asparagus and onions and cook, stirring occasionally, for 4 minutes, or until the onions are soft. Press Cancel to stop the Sauté.
2. Add the cauliflower, broth, salt, and pepper. Seal the lid, press Manual, and set the timer for 10 minutes. Once finished, let the pressure release naturally.
3. Remove the lid and add the cream cheese. Transfer the soup to a food processor and process until puréed (or purée the soup right in the pot with a stick blender). Season with additional salt and pepper before serving. Garnish with asparagus tips and purple salt, if desired.

Per Serving
calories: 270 | fat: 15g | protein: 13g | carbs: 20g
net carbs: 15g | fiber: 5g

Szechuan Beef Soup

Prep time: 10 minutes | Cook time: 30 minutes
Serves 6

1 pound (454 g) chuck roast beef, cut into 2-inch pieces
2 tablespoons dry white wine
2 tablespoons coconut aminos or tamari
1½ tablespoons minced fresh ginger
1½ tablespoons minced garlic
1 tablespoon spicy chili flakes
2 whole star anise

1 (3-inch) stick cinnamon
1 tablespoon rice vinegar
5 cups beef stock or bone broth
4 baby bok choy, cut in half lengthwise, for topping
5 cups raw zoodles or spiralized zucchini
3 chopped scallions, for topping

1. Season the beef with the wine and coconut aminos or tamari and marinate for 5 minutes. Turn on the Instant Pot by pressing the Manual button and set the timer for 30 minutes on High Pressure. Insert the inner pot and place all the ingredients except bok choy, zoodles and scallions.
2. Close the lid tightly and move the steam release handle to Sealing.
3. Meanwhile, place the zoodles in 6 bowls. When the timer goes off, allow the Instant Pot to cool down naturally until the float valve drops down. Press Cancel and open the lid. Add the bok choy and close the lid for 2 minutes. Ladle the soup over the raw zoodles and garnish with the chopped scallions. The hot broth should make the zoodles softer. Serve immediately.

Per Serving
calories: 351 | fat: 20g | protein: 27g | carbs: 18g
net carbs: 11g | fiber: 7g

Creamy Enchilada Soup

Prep time: 10 minutes | Cook time: 40 minutes
Serves 6

2 (6-ounce / 170-g) boneless, skinless chicken breasts
½ tablespoon chili powder
½ teaspoon salt
½ teaspoon garlic powder
¼ teaspoon pepper
½ cup red enchilada sauce
½ medium onion, diced

1 (4-ounce / 113-g) can green chilies
2 cups chicken broth
⅛ cup pickled jalapeños
4 ounces (113 g) cream cheese
1 cup uncooked cauliflower rice
1 avocado, diced
1 cup shredded mild Cheddar cheese
½ cup sour cream

1. Sprinkle seasoning over chicken breasts and set aside. Pour enchilada sauce into Instant Pot and place chicken on top.
2. Add onion, chilies, broth, and jalapeños to the pot, then place cream cheese on top of chicken breasts. Click lid closed. Adjust time for 25 minutes. When timer beeps, quick-release the pressure and shred chicken with forks.
3. Mix soup together and add cauliflower rice, with pot on Keep Warm setting. Replace lid and let pot sit for 15 minutes, still on Keep Warm. This will cook cauliflower rice. Serve with avocado, Cheddar, and sour cream.

Per Serving
calories: 318 | fat: 19g | protein: 21g | carbs: 10g
net carbs: 7g | fiber: 3g

Spicy Korean Chicken Stew

Prep time: 10 minutes | Cook time: 20 minutes
Serves 6

2 pounds (907 g) bone-in chicken thighs
⅓ cup coconut aminos or tamari
⅓ cup rice wine
¾ cup chicken stock
1 teaspoon sea salt
1 teaspoon black pepper
3 dried red chili peppers, or 2 tablespoons chili pepper flakes
2 tablespoons gochujang, or to taste

4 cloves of garlic, crushed
1 medium onion, sliced
1 green bell pepper, sliced
1 (1-inch) piece ginger, peeled and sliced
2 teaspoons sesame oil
3 scallions, cut into 2-inch pieces, reserve 1 tablespoon finely chopped for garnish
1 teaspoon toasted sesame seeds, for garnish

1. Turn on the Instant Pot by pressing the Manual button and set the timer for 20 minutes on High Pressure.
2. Cut the excess skin and fat from the chicken thighs. Place the chicken thighs in the inner pot. Except for the chopped scallions and sesame seeds, combine the rest of the ingredients in a small mixing bowl and mix well. Taste to see if it needs more gochujang, chili peppers or sea salt to your taste. Add the sauce over the chicken in the Instant Pot and mix well. Pat down the chicken thighs so they are well coated with the sauce.
3. Close the lid tightly and move the steam release handle to Sealing.
4. When the timer ends, allow the Instant Pot to cool down naturally until the float valve drops down. Press Cancel, and open the lid.
5. Stir, ladle the chicken pieces in a shallow bowl, top with the chopped scallions, sprinkle on sesame seeds and serve immediately.

Per Serving
calories: 333 | fat: 20g | protein: 23g | carbs: 10g
net carbs: 9g | fiber: 1g

Chicken and Cauliflower Rice Soup

Prep time: 5 minutes | Cook time: 20 minutes
Makes 4 cups

4 tablespoons butter
¼ cup diced onion
2 stalks celery, chopped
½ cup fresh spinach
½ teaspoon salt
¼ teaspoon pepper
¼ teaspoon dried thyme
¼ teaspoon dried

parsley
1 bay leaf
2 cups chicken broth
2 cups diced cooked chicken
¾ cup uncooked cauliflower rice
½ teaspoon xanthan gum (optional)

1. Press the Sauté button and add butter to Instant Pot. Add onions and sauté until translucent. Place celery and spinach into Instant Pot and sauté for 2 to 3 minutes until spinach is wilted. Press the Cancel button.
2. Sprinkle seasoning into Instant Pot and add bay leaf, broth, and cooked chicken. Click lid closed. Press the Soup button and adjust time for 10 minutes.
3. When timer beeps, quick-release the pressure and stir in cauliflower rice. Leave Instant Pot on Keep Warm setting to finish cooking cauliflower rice additional 10 minutes. Serve warm.
4. For a thicker soup, stir in xanthan gum.

Per Serving
calories: 228 | fat: 14g | protein: 22g | carbs: 3g
net carbs: 2g | fiber: 1g

Chicken Mulligatawny Soup

Prep time: 10 minutes | Cook time: 18 minutes
Serves 8

4 tablespoons butter	⅛ teaspoon dried
1 small onion, chopped	thyme
1-inch piece fresh	8 chicken thighs, bone-
ginger, minced	in and skinless
1 celery stalk, chopped	3 cups chicken broth
2 small carrots, diced	2 cups raw cauliflower
2 teaspoons curry	rice or minced florets
powder	2 cups full-fat coconut
1 teaspoon sea salt	milk
½ teaspoon freshly	¼ cup chopped
ground black pepper	fresh cilantro plus 1
⅛ teaspoon ground	tablespoon, for garnish
nutmeg	

1. Turn on the Instant Pot by pressing Sauté and set to More. Insert the inner pot and wait until the panel says Hot. Melt the butter in the inner pot and sauté the onion and ginger for 2 minutes or until the onion is soft. Add the celery and carrots and stir for 1 minute. Add the remaining ingredients except for the coconut milk and cilantro. Hit Cancel.
2. Close the lid tightly and move the steam release handle to Sealing.
3. Press the Manual button and set the timer for 15 minutes on High Pressure. When the timer ends, allow the Instant Pot to cool down naturally until the float valve drops down. Open the lid and stir in the coconut milk and cilantro. Press Cancel. Ladle the soup into bowls and garnish with the reserved cilantro. Serve immediately.

Per Serving
calories: 427 | fat: 35g | protein: 21g | carbs: 9g
net carbs: 6g | fiber: 3g

Brazilian Fish Stew

Prep time: 10 minutes | Cook time: 7 minutes
Serves 6

4 tablespoons extra-	1 teaspoon sea salt
virgin olive oil, divided	1 teaspoon freshly
2 dried whole bay	ground black pepper
leaves	¼ cup chopped fresh
2 teaspoons paprika	cilantro, divided
1 small onion, thinly	1 cup fish stock or
sliced	water
2 cloves garlic, crushed	1½ pounds (680 g)
1 small green bell	meaty fish, like cod or
pepper, chopped	striped bass, cut into
1½ cups diced tomatoes	2-inch chunks

1. Turn on the Instant Pot by pressing Sauté and set to More. Insert the inner pot and wait until the panel says Hot. Add the olive oil and, when the oil is hot, add the bay leaves and paprika. Sauté for about 30 seconds or until the paprika is moist. Add the onion, garlic, bell pepper, tomatoes, sea salt, pepper and 2 tablespoons of the cilantro.
2. Stir for 2 minutes until the onion is soft. Add the fish stock, then nestle the fish pieces among the vegetables in the pot. Close the lid tightly and move the steam release handle to Sealing.
3. Press the Manual button and set the timer for 5 minutes on High Pressure. When the time ends, you will hear a beeping sound, and then the Warm setting will start. At 5 minutes on Warm, carefully turn the steam release handle to the Venting position for the steam to escape and the float valve to drop down. Press Cancel, and open the lid carefully.
4. Divide the stew among bowls. Drizzle with the remaining 1 tablespoon of olive oil, sprinkle with the remaining 2 tablespoons of cilantro and serve immediately.

Per Serving
calories: 205 | fat: 11g | protein: 21g | carbs: 4g
net carbs: 3g | fiber: 1g

Loaded Taco Soup

Prep time: 10 minutes | Cook time: 10 minutes
Serves 4

1 pound (454 g) 85%	3 cups beef broth
lean ground beef	⅓ cup heavy cream
½ medium onion, diced	¼ teaspoon xanthan
1 (7-ounce / 198-g)	gum
can diced tomatoes and	1 avocado, diced
chilies	½ cup sour cream
1 teaspoon salt	1 cup shredded Cheddar
1 tablespoon chili	cheese
powder	¼ cup chopped cilantro
2 teaspoons cumin	

1. Press the Sauté button and brown ground beef in Instant Pot. When halfway done, add onion. Once beef is completely cooked, add diced tomatoes with chilies, seasoning, and broth.
2. Click lid closed. Press the Soup button and adjust time for 10 minutes. When timer beeps, quick-release the pressure. Stir in cream and xanthan gum. Serve warm and top with diced avocado, sour cream, Cheddar, and cilantro.

Per Serving
calories: 566 | fat: 41g | protein: 32g | carbs: 10g
net carbs: 6g | fiber: 4g

Chaptr 7 Vegetables

Spinach Casserole

Prep time: 5 minutes | Cook time: 20 minutes
Serves 4

6 eggs
1 cup spinach, chopped
½ cup full-fat coconut milk
½ teaspoon crushed red pepper

½ teaspoon basil, dried
½ teaspoon cilantro, dried
½ teaspoon kosher salt
½ teaspoon freshly ground black pepper

1. Pour 1 cup of filtered water into the inner pot of the Instant Pot, then insert the trivet. In a large bowl, combine the eggs, spinach, coconut milk, red pepper, basil, cilantro, salt, and black pepper. Mix thoroughly. Transfer this mixture into a well-greased, Instant Pot-friendly dish.
2. Using a sling if desired, place this dish onto the trivet, and cover loosely with aluminum foil. Close the lid, set the pressure release to Sealing, and select Manual. Set the Instant Pot to 20 minutes on High Pressure, and let cook.
3. Once cooked, let the pressure naturally disperse from the Instant Pot for about 10 minutes, then carefully switch the pressure release to Venting.
4. Open the Instant Pot, serve, and enjoy!

Per Serving
calories: 168 | fat: 14g | protein: 10g | carbs: 3g
net carbs: 2g | fiber: 1g

Butter Cabbage with Thyme

Prep time: 10 minutes | Cook time: 5 minutes
Serves 4

1 pound (454 g) white cabbage
2 tablespoons butter

1 teaspoon dried thyme
½ teaspoon salt
1 cup water

1. Cut the white cabbage on medium size petals and sprinkle with the butter, dried thyme and salt. Place the cabbage petals in the Instant Pot pan.
2. Pour the water and insert the trivet in the Instant Pot. Put the pan on the trivet.
3. Set the lid in place. Select the Manual mode and set the cooking time for 5 minutes on High Pressure. When the timer goes off, do a quick pressure release. Carefully open the lid.
4. Serve immediately.

Per Serving
calories: 81 | fat: 6g | protein: 1g | carbs: 6g
net carbs: 3g | fiber: 3g

Brussels Sprouts with Bacon

Prep time: 5 minutes | Cook time: 15 minutes
Serves 4

1 pound (454 g) Brussels sprouts
1 teaspoon sea salt
1 teaspoon garlic powder
1 tablespoon butter
1 small onion, diced
2 cloves garlic, crushed

3 strips uncured bacon, cut into ½-inch pieces
1 tablespoon extra-fine blanched almond slivers
½ cup chicken broth
2 tablespoons chopped scallions, for garnish

1. Wash the Brussels sprouts well and discard any old and rotten leaves. Trim the ends off and cut the Brussels sprouts in half vertically. Put any loose leaves with the rest of the Brussels sprouts, sea salt and garlic powder in a large mixing bowl and mix.
2. Turn on the Instant Pot by pressing Sauté and set to More. Insert the inner pot and wait until the panel says Hot.
3. Add the butter, onion and garlic and sauté for 2 minutes or until the onion is soft. Add the bacon and sauté for 3 minutes or until the bacon starts to shrivel. If there's too much bacon grease, you can spoon out some of it now. You want some bacon grease, but not so much that the Brussels sprouts won't brown.
4. Push the bacon to the side and add half of the Brussels sprouts to brown. Place the Brussels sprouts with their flat sides down on the inner pot. Do not to crowd them and don't mix until the sides turn brown.
5. When most of the sides are browned, take them out, place them in a bowl and set aside. Add the remaining Brussels sprouts to the inner pot to brown the sides. If needed, add more bacon grease back so as not to burn the Brussels sprouts. When they are browned, add the first batch of the browned Brussels sprouts back to the inner pot and add the almonds and the chicken broth and mix while scraping the bottom of the inner pot to loosen up all the bits and pieces.
6. Hit Cancel, then press the Manual button and set the timer for 8 minutes on High Pressure.
7. Close the lid tightly and move the steam release handle to Sealing. When the timer goes off, turn the steam release handle to the Venting position carefully for the steam to escape and the float valve to drop down. Press Cancel. Open the lid.
8. Garnish with the chopped scallions and serve immediately.

Per Serving
calories: 128 | fat: 6g | protein: 7g | carbs: 15g
net carbs: 10g | fiber: 5g

Butter Chanterelle Mushrooms

Prep time: 10 minutes | Cook time: 15 minutes
Serves 4

14 ounces (397 g) chanterelle mushrooms, chopped
½ cup heavy cream

3 tablespoons butter
1 teaspoon salt
½ teaspoon dried thyme

1. Melt the butter in the Instant Pot on Sauté mode and add chanterelle mushrooms.
2. Add dried thyme and salt and sauté the vegetables for 5 minutes.
3. Then stir them well and add heavy cream. Close and seal the lid.
4. Cook the mushrooms on Manual mode at High Pressure for 10 minutes.
5. Then do the quick pressure release.

Per Serving
calories: 130 | fat: 14g | protein: 1g | carbs: 1g
net carbs: 1g | fiber: 0g

Ginger Cabbage

Prep time: 10 minutes | Cook time: 8 minutes
Serves 6

1 tablespoon avocado oil
1 tablespoon butter or ghee (or more avocado oil)
½ medium onion, diced
1 medium bell pepper (any color), diced
1 teaspoon sea salt
½ teaspoon ground

black pepper
1 clove garlic, minced
1-inch piece fresh ginger, grated
1 pound (454 g) green or red cabbage, cored and leaves chopped
½ cup bone broth or vegetable broth

1. Set the Instant Pot to Sauté and heat the oil and butter together. When the butter has stopped foaming, add the onion, bell pepper, salt, and black pepper. Sauté, stirring frequently, until just softened, about 3 minutes. Add the garlic and ginger and cook 1 minute longer. Add the cabbage and stir to combine. Pour in the broth.
2. Secure the lid and set the steam release valve to Sealing. Press the Manual button and set the cook time to 2 minutes.
3. When the Instant Pot beeps, carefully switch the steam release valve to Venting to quick-release the pressure. When fully released, open the lid. Stir the cabbage and transfer it to a serving dish. Serve warm.

Per Serving
calories: 73 | fat: 5g | protein: 2g | carbs: 7g
net carbs: 5g | fiber: 2g

Masala Cauliflower

Prep time: 6 minutes | Cook time: 5 minutes
Serves 4

2 tablespoons olive oil
½ cup chopped scallions
2 cloves garlic, pressed
1 tablespoon garam masala
1 teaspoon curry powder
1 red chili pepper, minced
½ teaspoon ground cumin

Sea salt and ground black pepper, to taste
1 tablespoon chopped fresh coriander
2 tomatoes, puréed
1 pound (454 g) cauliflower, broken into florets
½ cup water
½ cup almond yogurt

1. Press the Sauté button to heat up your Instant Pot. Now, heat the oil and sauté the scallions for 1 minute.
2. Add garlic and continue to cook an additional 30 seconds or until aromatic.
3. Add garam masala, curry powder, chili pepper, cumin, salt, black pepper, coriander, tomatoes, cauliflower, and water.
4. Secure the lid. Choose Manual mode and High Pressure; cook for 3 minutes. Once cooking is complete, use a quick pressure release; carefully remove the lid.
5. Pour in the almond yogurt, stir well and serve warm. Bon appétit!

Per Serving
calories: 140 | fat: 8g | protein: 6g | carbs: 11g
net carbs: 7g | fiber: 4g

Turnip Roast

Prep time: 10 minutes | Cook time: 10 minutes
Serves 2

2 turnips, peeled, chopped
½ teaspoon ground paprika

1 tablespoon olive oil
¼ teaspoon salt
¼ teaspoon ground black pepper

1. Sprinkle the chopped turnip with ground paprika, salt, and ground black pepper.
2. Then heat up olive oil in the Instant Pot on Sauté mode and add chopped turnip.
3. Cook the turnip on Sauté mode for 3 minutes from each side.
4. Then close the lid and sauté it for 4 minutes more.

Per Serving
calories: 97 | fat: 7g | protein: 1g | carbs: 9g
net carbs: 7g | fiber: 2g

Cream of Asparagus and Mushroom Soup

Prep time: 10 minutes | Cook time: 7 minutes
Serves 4

2 tablespoons coconut oil
½ cup chopped shallots
2 cloves garlic, minced
1 pound (454 g) asparagus, washed, trimmed, and chopped
4 ounces (113 g) button mushrooms, sliced

4 cups vegetable broth
2 tablespoons balsamic vinegar
Himalayan salt, to taste
¼ teaspoon ground black pepper
¼ teaspoon paprika
¼ cup vegan sour cream

1. Press the Sauté button to heat up your Instant Pot. Heat the oil and cook the shallots and garlic for 2 to 3 minutes.
2. Add the remaining ingredients, except for sour cream, to the Instant Pot.
3. Secure the lid. Choose Manual mode and High Pressure; cook for 4 minutes. Once cooking is complete, use a quick pressure release; carefully remove the lid.
4. Spoon into four soup bowls; add a dollop of sour cream to each serving and serve immediately. Bon appétit!

Per Serving
calories: 171 | fat: 12g | protein: 10g | carbs: 9g net carbs: 6g | fiber: 3g

Summer Squash Gratin

Prep time: 15 minutes | Cook time: 10 minutes
Serves 4

2 zucchinis, sliced
½ cup coconut milk
3 ounces (85 g) tofu, shredded

1 teaspoon chili flakes
½ teaspoon dried dill
1 teaspoon coconut oil
1 cup water, for cooking

1. Grease the gratin mold with coconut oil.
2. Then place the sliced zucchini inside.
3. Add coconut milk, tofu, chili flakes, and dried dill.
4. Cover the gratin with foil and place it on the trivet.
5. Pour water in the Instant Pot.
6. Then transfer the trivet with gratin in the Instant Pot and close the lid.
7. Cook the gratin on Manual mode at High Pressure for 10 minutes.
8. When the time is finished, allow the natural pressure release for 10 minutes.

Per Serving
calories: 110 | fat: 9g | protein: 4g | carbs: 5g net carbs: 3g | fiber: 2g

Green Beans with Bacon

Prep time: 10 minutes | Cook time: 9 minutes
Serves 6

6 slices bacon, diced
1 cup diced onion
4 cups halved green beans
¼ cup water

1 teaspoon salt, plus more for seasoning
1 teaspoon freshly ground black pepper, plus more for seasoning

1. Preheat the Instant Pot by selecting Sauté and adjusting to high heat. Add the bacon and onion and sauté for 2 to 3 minutes.
2. Add the green beans, water, salt, and pepper to the pot.
3. Lock the lid into place. Select Manual and adjust the pressure to High. Cook for 4 minutes. When the cooking is complete, quick-release the pressure. Unlock the lid.
4. Taste and season with additional salt and pepper if needed before serving.

Per Serving
calories: 165 | fat: 13g | protein: 6g | carbs: 6g net carbs: 3g | fiber: 3g

Vodka Mushroom Stroganoff

Prep time: 8 minutes | Cook time: 8 minutes
Serves 4

2 tablespoons olive oil
½ teaspoon crushed caraway seeds
½ cup chopped onion
2 garlic cloves, smashed
¼ cup vodka
¾ pound (340 g) button

mushrooms, chopped
1 celery stalk, chopped
1 ripe tomato, puréed
1 teaspoon mustard seeds
Sea salt and freshly ground pepper, to taste
2 cups vegetable broth

1. Press the Sauté button to heat up your Instant Pot. Now, heat the oil and sauté caraway seeds until fragrant, about 40 seconds.
2. Then, add the onion and garlic, and continue sautéing for 1 to 2 minutes more, stirring frequently.
3. After that, add the remaining ingredients and stir to combine.
4. Secure the lid. Choose Manual mode and High Pressure; cook for 5 minutes. Once cooking is complete, use a quick pressure release; carefully remove the lid.
5. Ladle into individual bowls and serve warm. Bon appétit!

Per Serving
calories: 128 | fat: 9g | protein: 6g | carbs: 7g net carbs: 4g | fiber: 3g

Cauliflower Gnocchi

Prep time: 5 minutes | Cook time: 2 minutes
Serves 4

2 cups cauliflower, boiled
½ cup almond flour
1 tablespoon sesame oil
1 teaspoon salt
1 cup water

1. In a bowl, mash the cauliflower until puréed. Mix it up with the almond flour, sesame oil and salt.
2. Make the log from the cauliflower dough and cut it into small pieces.
3. Pour the water in the Instant Pot and add the gnocchi.
4. Lock the lid. Select the Manual mode and set the cooking time for 2 minutes on High Pressure. Once the timer goes off, perform a natural pressure release for 5 minutes, then release any remaining pressure. Carefully open the lid.
5. Remove the cooked gnocchi from the water and serve.

Per Serving
calories: 128 | fat: 10g | protein: 4g | carbs: 5g
net carbs: 2g | fiber: 3g

Portobello Cheese Sandwiches

Prep time: 15 minutes | Cook time: 6 minutes
Serves 2

4 Portobello mushrooms caps
¼ teaspoon minced garlic
1 tablespoon olive oil
2 Cheddar cheese slices
1 cup water, for cooking

1. In the shallow bowl, mix up garlic and olive oil.
2. Brush the mushrooms with garlic mixture and place them on the trivet.
3. Pour water in the Instant Pot. Transfer the trivet with mushroom caps inside.
4. Close and seal the lid and cook the vegetables for 6 minutes on Manual mode at High Pressure.
5. Then make a quick pressure release and open the lid.
6. Place the cheese slices on 2 mushroom caps and cover them with remaining mushroom to get the shape of sandwiches.

Per Serving
calories: 188 | fat: 16g | protein: 8g | carbs: 2g
net carbs: 2g | fiber: 0g

Sauerkraut and Mushroom Casserole

Prep time: 6 minutes | Cook time: 15 minutes
Serves 6

1 tablespoon olive oil
1 celery rib, diced
½ cup chopped leeks
2 pounds (907 g) canned sauerkraut, drained
6 ounces (170 g) brown
mushrooms, sliced
1 teaspoon caraway seeds
1 teaspoon brown mustard
1 bay leaf
1 cup dry white wine

1. Press the Sauté button to heat up your Instant Pot. Now, heat the oil and cook celery and leeks until softened.
2. Add the sauerkraut and mushrooms and cook for 2 minutes more.
3. Add the remaining ingredients and stir to combine well.
4. Secure the lid. Choose Manual mode and High Pressure; cook for 10 minutes. Once cooking is complete, use a natural pressure release; carefully remove the lid. Bon appétit!

Per Serving
calories: 90 | fat: 3g | protein: 2g | carbs: 8g
net carbs: 3g | fiber: 5g

Turmeric Green Cabbage Stew

Prep time: 5 minutes | Cook time: 4 minutes
Serves 4

2 tablespoons olive oil
½ cup sliced yellow onion
1 teaspoon crushed garlic
Sea salt and freshly ground black pepper, to taste
1 teaspoon turmeric
powder
1 serrano pepper, chopped
1 pound (454 g) green cabbage, shredded
1 celery stalk, chopped
2 tablespoons rice wine
1 cup roasted vegetable broth

1. Place all of the above ingredients in the Instant Pot.
2. Secure the lid. Choose Manual mode and High Pressure; cook for 4 minutes. Once cooking is complete, use a quick pressure release; carefully remove the lid.
3. Divide between individual bowls and serve warm. Bon appétit!

Per Serving
calories: 114 | fat: 8g | protein: 3g | carbs: 8g
net carbs: 5g | fiber: 3g

Mediterranean Zoodles

Prep time: 10 minutes | Cook time: 5 minutes
Serves 2

1 tablespoon olive oil
2 tomatoes, chopped
½ cup water
½ cup roughly chopped fresh parsley
3 tablespoons ground almonds
1 tablespoon fresh rosemary, chopped
1 tablespoon apple

cider vinegar
1 teaspoon garlic, smashed
2 zucchinis, spiralized and cooked
½ avocado, pitted and sliced
Salt and ground black pepper, to taste

1. Add the olive oil, tomatoes, water, parsley, ground almonds, rosemary, apple cider vinegar and garlic to the Instant Pot.
2. Lock the lid. Select the Manual mode and set the cooking time for 5 minutes on High Pressure. When the timer beeps, perform a natural pressure release for 10 minutes, then release any remaining pressure. Carefully open the lid.
3. Divide the cooked zucchini spirals between two serving plates. Spoon the sauce over each serving. Top with the avocado slices and season with salt and black pepper.
4. Serve immediately.

Per Serving
calories: 264 | fat: 20g | protein: 7g | carbs: 19g
net carbs: 10g | fiber: 9g

Red Wine Braised Collards

Prep time: 5 minutes | Cook time: 2 minutes
Serves 4

1 pound (454 g) Collards, torn into pieces
¾ cup water
¼ cup dry red wine
1½ tablespoons sesame oil
1 teaspoon ginger-

garlic paste
½ teaspoon fennel seeds
½ teaspoon mustard seeds
Sea salt and ground black pepper, to taste

1. Add all the ingredients to the Instant Pot and stir to combine.
2. Lock the lid. Select the Manual mode and set the cooking time for 2 minutes on High Pressure. When the timer goes off, perform a quick pressure release. Carefully open the lid.
3. Ladle into individual bowls and serve warm.

Per Serving
calories: 86 | fat: 5g | protein: 3g | carbs: 7g
net carbs: 2g | fiber: 5g

Garlic Cabbage with Tempeh

Prep time: 8 minutes | Cook time: 10 minutes
Serves 3

2 tablespoons sesame oil
½ cup chopped scallions
2 cups shredded cabbage
6 ounces (170 g) tempeh, cubed
1 tablespoon coconut aminos

1 cup vegetable stock
2 garlic cloves, minced
1 tablespoon lemon juice
Salt and pepper, to taste
¼ teaspoon paprika
¼ cup roughly chopped fresh cilantro

1. Press the Sauté button to heat up your Instant Pot. Heat the sesame oil and sauté the scallions until tender and fragrant.
2. Then, add the cabbage, tempeh, coconut aminos, vegetable stock, garlic, lemon juice, salt, pepper, and paprika.
3. Secure the lid. Choose Manual mode and Low Pressure; cook for 3 minutes. Once cooking is complete, use a quick pressure release; carefully remove the lid.
4. Press the Sauté button to thicken the sauce if desired. Divide between serving bowls, garnish with fresh cilantro, and serve warm. Bon appétit!

Per Serving
calories: 172 | fat: 12g | protein: 10g | carbs: 9g
net carbs: 7g | fiber: 2g

Zucchini Noodles with Almond Butter

Prep time: 10 minutes | Cook time: 4 minutes
Serves 4

2 tablespoons coconut oil
1 yellow onion, chopped
2 zucchini, julienned
1 cup shredded Chinese cabbage
2 garlic cloves, minced

2 tablespoons almond butter
Sea salt and freshly ground black pepper, to taste
1 teaspoon cayenne pepper

1. Press the Sauté button to heat up your Instant Pot. Heat the coconut oil and sweat the onion for 2 minutes.
2. Add the other ingredients.
3. Secure the lid. Choose Manual mode and High Pressure; cook for 2 minutes. Once cooking is complete, use a quick pressure release; carefully remove the lid. Bon appétit!

Per Serving
calories: 145 | fat: 15g | protein: 1g | carbs: 4g
net carbs: 2g | fiber: 2g

Lemon Broccoli

Prep time: 5 minutes | Cook time: 4 minutes
Serves 4

2 cups broccoli florets
1 tablespoon ground paprika
1 tablespoon lemon juice
1 teaspoon grated

lemon zest
1 teaspoon olive oil
½ teaspoon chili powder
1 cup water

1. Pour the water in the Instant Pot and insert the trivet.
2. In the Instant Pot pan, stir together the remaining ingredients.
3. Place the pan on the trivet.
4. Set the lid in place. Select the Manual mode and set the cooking time for 4 minutes on High Pressure. When the timer goes off, do a quick pressure release. Carefully open the lid.
5. Serve immediately.

Per Serving
calories: 34 | fat: 1g | protein: 1g | carbs: 4g
net carbs: 2g | fiber: 2g

Cauliflower and Spinach Medley

Prep time: 10 minutes | Cook time: 3 minutes
Serves 4

1 pound (454 g) cauliflower, cut into florets
1 yellow onion, peeled and chopped
1 red bell pepper, deseeded and chopped
1 celery stalk, chopped
2 garlic cloves, crushed

2 tablespoons olive oil
1 tablespoon grated lemon zest
1 teaspoon Hungarian paprika
Sea salt and ground black pepper, to taste
2 cups spinach, torn into pieces

1. Add all the ingredients, except for the spinach, to the Instant Pot.
2. Close and secure the lid. Select the Manual setting and set the cooking time for 3 minutes at High Pressure. Once the timer goes off, use a quick pressure release. Carefully open the lid.
3. Stir in the spinach and lock the lid. Let it sit in the residual heat for 5 minutes, or until wilted.
4. Serve warm.

Per Serving
calories: 114 | fat: 7g | protein: 3g | carbs: 11g
net carbs: 7g | fiber: 4g

Parmesan Zoodles

Prep time: 5 minutes | Cook time: 5 minutes
Serves 2

1 large zucchini, trimmed and spiralized
1 tablespoon butter
1 garlic clove, diced

½ teaspoon chili flakes
3 ounces (85 g) Parmesan cheese, grated

1. Set the Instant Pot on the Sauté mode and melt the butter. Add the garlic and chili flakes to the pot. Sauté for 2 minutes, or until fragrant.
2. Stir in the zucchini spirals and sauté for 2 minutes, or until tender.
3. Add the grated Parmesan cheese to the pot and stir well. Continue to cook it for 1 minute, or until the cheese melts.
4. Transfer to a plate and serve immediately

Per Serving
calories: 217 | fat: 15g | protein: 15g | carbs: 7g
net carbs: 5g | fiber: 2g

Green Cabbage in Cream Sauce

Prep time: 10 minutes | Cook time: 13 minutes
Serves 4

1 tablespoon unsalted butter
½ cup diced pancetta
¼ cup diced yellow onion
1 cup chicken broth
1 pound (454 g) green cabbage, finely chopped
1 bay leaf

¹/₃ cup heavy cream
1 tablespoon dried parsley
1 teaspoon fine grind sea salt
¼ teaspoon ground nutmeg
¼ teaspoon ground black pepper

1. Press the Sauté button on the Instant Pot and melt the butter. Add the pancetta and onion to the pot and sauté for about 4 minutes, or until the onion is tender and begins to brown.
2. Pour in the chicken broth. Using a wooden spoon, stir and loosen any browned bits from the bottom of the pot. Stir in the cabbage and bay leaf.
3. Lock the lid. Select the Manual mode and set the cooking time for 4 minutes on High Pressure. When the timer goes off, perform a quick pressure release. Carefully open the lid.
4. Select Sauté mode and bring the ingredients to a boil. Stir in the remaining ingredients and simmer for 5 additional minutes.
5. Remove and discard the bay leaf. Spoon into serving bowls. Serve warm.

Per Serving
calories: 211 | fat: 17g | protein: 7g | carbs: 7g
net carbs: 5g | fiber: 2g

Moroccan Zucchini

Prep time: 10 minutes | Cook time: 6 minutes
Serves 4

2 tablespoons avocado oil
½ medium onion, diced
1 clove garlic, minced
¼ teaspoon cayenne pepper
¼ teaspoon ground coriander
¼ teaspoon ground cumin
¼ teaspoon ground ginger
Pinch of ground cinnamon
1 Roma (plum) tomato, diced
2 medium zucchini, cut into 1-inch pieces
½ tablespoon fresh lemon juice
¼ cup bone broth or vegetable stock

1. Set the Instant Pot to Sauté. When hot, add the oil. Add the onion and sauté, stirring frequently, until translucent, about 2 minutes. Add the garlic, cayenne, coriander, cumin, ginger, and cinnamon and cook until fragrant, about 1 minute. Stir in the tomato and zucchini and cook 2 minutes longer.
2. Press Cancel. Add the lemon juice and broth. Secure the lid and set the steam release valve to Sealing. Press the Manual button, adjust the pressure to Low, and set the cook time to 1 minute.
3. When the Instant Pot beeps, carefully switch the steam release valve to Venting to quick-release the pressure. When fully released, open the lid. Stir and serve warm.

Per Serving
calories: 92 | fat: 7g | protein: 2g | carbs: 4g
net carbs: 3g | fiber: 1g

Lemon Asparagus

Prep time: 6 minutes | Cook time: 5 minutes
Serves 4

1 large bunch asparagus, woody ends cut off (medium-thick spears if possible)
1 cup water
2 tablespoons salted butter
2 large cloves garlic, minced
2 teaspoons fresh lemon juice (from ½ lemon)
¾ cup finely shredded Parmesan cheese (optional)
Salt, to taste

1. Cut the asparagus spears on a diagonal into 3 equal pieces, or trim the whole spears to fit your Instant Pot.
2. Pour the water into the Instant Pot. Place a metal steaming basket inside. Place the asparagus in the basket. Secure the lid and set the steam release valve to Sealing. Press the Manual button and set the cook time to 1 minute for tender (for softer, increase to 2 minutes; for crisp, decrease to 0). While it cooks, prepare a bowl with ice water.
3. When the Instant Pot beeps, carefully switch the steam release valve to Venting to quick-release the pressure. When fully released, open the lid and use tongs to transfer the asparagus to the ice bath. Let it sit for a minute, then drain and place the asparagus on a clean kitchen towel and pat dry.
4. Carefully remove the pot insert. Remove the steaming basket, drain the water, and wipe the pot insert dry.
5. Return the pot insert to the Instant Pot and press the Sauté button. Put the butter in the pot. When it has melted and starts to foam, add the garlic and sauté, stirring, for 1 minute.
6. Return the asparagus to the pot and stir well to coat it with the garlic-butter mixture. Add the lemon juice. Sauté until it reaches the desired doneness, about 1 minute more.
7. Transfer the asparagus to a serving bowl and stir in the Parmesan. Taste the asparagus and add salt to taste. Serve warm.

Per Serving
calories: 70 | fat: 11g | protein: 10g | carbs: 4g
net carbs: 3g | fiber: 1g

Vinegar Asparagus and Kale

Prep time: 5 minutes | Cook time: 3 minutes
Serves 4

8 ounces (227 g) asparagus, chopped
2 cups chopped kale
2 bell peppers, chopped
1 tablespoon avocado oil
1 teaspoon apple cider vinegar
½ teaspoon minced ginger
½ cup water

1. Pour the water into the Instant Pot.
2. In the Instant Pot pan, stir together the remaining ingredients.
3. Insert the trivet and place the pan on it.
4. Set the lid in place. Select the Manual mode and set the cooking time for 3 minutes on High Pressure. When the timer goes off, perform a quick pressure release. Carefully open the lid.
5. Serve immediately.

Per Serving
calories: 53 | fat: 1g | protein: 3g | carbs: 10g
net carbs: 7g | fiber: 3g

Creamy Broccoli and Mushroom Bake

Prep time: 10 minutes | Cook time: 3 minutes
Serves 4

½ cup sunflower seeds, soaked overnight
2 tablespoons sesame seeds
1 cup water
1 cup unsweetened almond milk
¼ teaspoon grated nutmeg
½ teaspoon sea salt
1 tablespoon nutritional yeast
2 tablespoons rice vinegar
1 pound (454 g)

broccoli, broken into florets
½ cup chopped spring onions
10 ounces (283 g) white fresh mushrooms, sliced
Sea salt and white pepper, to taste
1 tablespoon cayenne pepper
¼ teaspoon dried dill
¼ teaspoon ground bay leaf

1. Add sunflower seeds, sesame seeds, water, milk, nutmeg, ½ teaspoon of sea salt, nutritional yeast, and vinegar to your blender.
2. Blend until smooth and uniform.
3. Spritz a casserole dish with a nonstick cooking spray. Add broccoli, spring onions and mushrooms.
4. Sprinkle with salt, white pepper, cayenne pepper, dill, and ground bay leaf. Pour the prepared vegan béchamel over your casserole.
5. Add 1 cup of water and trivet to your Instant Pot. Place the dish on the trivet.
6. Secure the lid. Choose Manual mode and High Pressure; cook for 3 minutes. Once cooking is complete, use a quick pressure release; carefully remove the lid.
7. Allow the dish to stand for 5 to 10 minutes before slicing and serving. Bon appétit!

Per Serving
calories: 130 | fat: 8g | protein: 8g | carbs: 9g
net carbs: 3g | fiber: 6g

Parmesan Spaghetti Squash

Prep time: 5 minutes | Cook time: 18 minutes
Serves 4

2 pounds (907 g) spaghetti squash
1 cup water
3 garlic cloves
1 cup fresh basil leaves
½ cup olive oil
⅓ cup unsalted toasted almonds

¼ cup flat-leaf parsley
3 tablespoons grated Parmesan cheese
½ teaspoon fine grind sea salt
½ teaspoon ground black pepper

1. Using a knife, pierce all sides of the squash to allow the steam to penetrate during cooking.
2. Pour the water into the Instant Pot and put the trivet in the pot. Place the squash on the trivet.
3. Lock the lid. Select the Manual mode and set the cooking time for 18 minutes at High Pressure. When the timer goes off, use a natural pressure release for 10 minutes, then release any remaining pressure. Carefully open the lid.
4. Remove the trivet and squash from the pot. Set aside to cool for 15 minutes, or until the squash is cool enough to handle.
5. Make the pesto sauce by placing the remaining ingredients in a food processor. Pulse until the ingredients are well combined and form a thick paste. Set aside.
6. Cut the cooled spaghetti squash in half lengthwise. Using a spoon, scoop out and discard the seeds.
7. Using a fork, scrape the flesh of the squash to create the noodles. Transfer the noodles to a large bowl.
8. Divide the squash noodles among 4 serving bowls. Top each serving with the pesto sauce. Serve hot.

Per Serving
calories: 381 | fat: 32g | protein: 5g | carbs: 18g
net carbs: 10g | fiber: 8g

Chaptr 8 Poultry

TSO Chicken Drumsticks

Prep time: 10 minutes | Cook time: 20 minutes
Serves 6

6 chicken thighs
1 tablespoon apple cider vinegar
1 tablespoon coconut aminos
½ teaspoon ginger,

grated
1 teaspoon Splenda
½ teaspoon chili flakes
¼ cup avocado oil
⅓ cup water

1. Heat up avocado oil on Sauté mode for 3 minutes and add chicken thighs.
2. Sauté the chicken for 6 minutes.
3. Then add the rest of the ingredients and stir them gently.
4. Close and seal the lid and cook the meal on Poultry mode for 10 minutes.
5. Carefully stir the cooked chicken.

Per Serving
calories: 179 | fat: 11g | protein: 19g | carbs: 2g net carbs: 2g | fiber: 0g

Chicken Broccoli Casserole

Prep time: 8 minutes | Cook time: 9 minutes
Serves 6

1 (8-ounce / 227-g) package cream cheese, softened
1 cup chicken broth
1 cup mayonnaise
1 pound (454 g) boneless, skinless chicken breasts, cut into 1-inch cubes
4 cups frozen broccoli florets

1 teaspoon fine sea salt
½ teaspoon ground black pepper
4 ounces (113 g) Cheddar cheese, shredded (1 cup)
4 ounces (113 g) provolone cheese, shredded (1 cup)
Dried chives, for garnish

1. Place the cream cheese in a 6-quart Instant Pot and whisk to loosen. (If you don't use a whisk to loosen the cream cheese, you will end up with clumps in your casserole.) Slowly whisk in the broth, then the mayonnaise. Add the chicken, broccoli, salt, and pepper and stir to combine.
2. Seal the lid, press Manual, and set the timer for 9 minutes. Once finished, let the pressure release naturally.
3. Remove the lid and stir in the Cheddar and provolone cheeses until melted.
4. Spoon the casserole onto plates or into bowls and garnish with chives.

Per Serving
calories: 583 | fat: 49g | protein: 26g | carbs: 6g net carbs: 4g | fiber: 2g

Cajun Chicken

Prep time: 15 minutes | Cook time: 25 minutes
Serves 4

1 teaspoon Cajun seasoning
¼ cup apple cider vinegar

1 pound (454 g) chicken fillet
1 tablespoon sesame oil
¼ cup water

1. Put all ingredients in the Instant Pot. Close and seal the lid.
2. Cook the chicken fillets on Manual mode at High Pressure for 25 minutes.
3. Allow the natural pressure release for 10 minutes.

Per Serving
calories: 249 | fat: 12g | protein: 33g | carbs: 0g net carbs: 0g | fiber: 0g

Cheese and Mayo Turkey Breasts

Prep time: 5 minutes | Cook time: 26 minutes
Serves 8

2 pounds (907 g) turkey breasts
2 garlic cloves, halved
Sea salt and ground black pepper, to taste
1 teaspoon paprika
1 tablespoon butter

10 slices Colby cheese, shredded
1 cup grated Romano cheese, divided
⅔ cup mayonnaise
⅓ cup sour cream

1. Rub the turkey breasts with the garlic halves. Season with salt, black pepper, and paprika.
2. Set your Instant Pot to Sauté and melt the butter.
3. Add the turkey breasts and sear each side for 2 to 3 minutes.
4. Meanwhile, thoroughly combine the Colby cheese, ½ cup of Romano cheese, mayonnaise, and sour cream in a mixing bowl.
5. Spread this mixture over turkey breasts. Scatter the remaining ½ cup of Romano cheese on top.
6. Secure the lid. Select the Manual mode and set the cooking time for 20 minutes at High Pressure.
7. When the timer beeps, perform a quick pressure release. Carefully remove the lid.
8. Cool for 5 minutes before serving.

Per Serving
calories: 475 | fat: 33g | protein: 39g | carbs: 3g net carbs: 3g | fiber: 0g

Mushroom Chicken Alfredo

Prep time: 15 minutes | Cook time: 10 minutes
Serves 4

½ cup sliced cremini mushrooms
¼ cup chopped leek
1 tablespoon sesame oil
1 teaspoon chili flakes
1 cup heavy cream

1 pound (454 g) chicken fillet, chopped
1 teaspoon Italian seasoning
1 tablespoon cream cheese

1. Brush the Instant Pot boil with sesame oil from inside.
2. Put the chicken in the Instant Pot in one layer.
3. Then top it with mushrooms and leek.
4. Sprinkle the ingredients with chili flakes, heavy cream, Italian seasoning, and cream cheese.
5. Close and seal the lid.
6. Cook the meal on Manual mode at High Pressure for 10 minutes.
7. When the time is finished, allow the natural pressure release for 10 minutes.

Per Serving
calories: 367 | fat: 24g | protein: 34g | carbs: 2g
net carbs: 2g | fiber: 0g

Fiesta Chicken

Prep time: 20 minutes | Cook time: 15 minutes
Serves 4

1 cup cauliflower, shredded
1 teaspoon taco seasonings
¼ cup bell pepper, chopped
1 tomato, chopped

1 cup chicken broth
½ teaspoon chili flakes
1 tablespoon butter
1 pound (454 g) chicken thighs, skinless, boneless, chopped

1. Melt the butter in the Instant Pot on Sauté mode.
2. After this, add bell pepper, tomato, and cauliflower.
3. Sprinkle the vegetables with taco seasonings and cook them for 10 minutes on Sauté mode.
4. After this, add chicken thighs, chili flakes, and chicken broth.
5. Close and seal the lid and cook the meal on Manual mode at High Pressure for 15 minutes.
6. Allow the natural pressure release for 10 minutes.

Per Serving
calories: 265 | fat: 12g | protein: 35g | carbs: 4g
net carbs: 1g | fiber: 3g

Spicy Mexican Chicken

Prep time: 5 minutes | Cook time: 17 minutes
Serves 4

2 tablespoons avocado oil
1 pound (454 g) chicken, ground,
½ jalapeño, finely chopped
½ teaspoon coriander
½ teaspoon crushed red pepper
½ teaspoon curry powder

½ teaspoon chili powder
½ teaspoon kosher salt
½ teaspoon freshly ground black pepper
¼ poblano chili pepper, finely chopped
1 (14-ounce / 397-g) can sugar-free or low-sugar fire roasted tomatoes

1. Set the Instant Pot to Sauté and heat the oil. Pour in ½ cup water, then add the chicken, jalapeño, coriander, red pepper, curry powder, chili powder, salt, black pepper, chili pepper, and tomatoes.
2. Close the lid, set the pressure release to Sealing and hit Cancel to stop the current program. Select Manual, set the Instant Pot to 17 minutes on High Pressure, and let cook.
3. Immediately upon cooking, carefully switch the pressure release to Venting. Open the Instant Pot, serve, and enjoy!

Per Serving
calories: 269 | fat: 15g | protein: 30g | carbs: 4g
net carbs: 3g | fiber: 1g

Simple Keto Bruschetta Chicken

Prep time: 5 minutes | Cook time: 20 minutes
Serves 2

2 boneless, skinless chicken breasts
¼ teaspoon basil, dried
1 (14-ounce / 397-g) can sugar-free or low-

sugar crushed tomatoes
¼ cup heavy whipping cream
½ cup full-fat Cheddar cheese, shredded

1. Pour in ½ cup of filtered water, then add the chicken breasts, basil, and tomatoes. Close the lid, set the pressure release to Sealing, and select Manual. Set the Instant Pot to 20 minutes on High Pressure and let cook.
2. Immediately upon cooking completion, perform a quick release by carefully switching the pressure valve to Venting, and carefully stir in the whipping cream and cheese. When cheese is melted, serve, and enjoy.

Per Serving
calories: 591 | fat: 38g | protein: 57g | carbs: 6g
net carbs: 5g | fiber: 1g

Juicy Chicken Breast

Prep time: 10 minutes | Cook time: 15 minutes
Serves 2

8 ounces (227 g)
chicken breast, skinless,
boneless
1 cup water

¼ cup butter
1 teaspoon chili flakes
1 teaspoon olive oil

1. Heat up olive oil on Sauté mode for 2 minutes.
2. Then add the chicken breast and cook it for 3 minutes from each side.
3. Add water, butter, and chili flakes.
4. Close and seal the lid and cook the chicken for 10 minutes on High Pressure.
5. Then make a quick pressure release and open the lid.
6. Slice the cooked chicken breast and sprinkle it with liquid from the Instant Pot.

Per Serving
calories: 353 | fat: 28g | protein: 24g | carbs: 0g
net carbs: 0g | fiber: 0g

Cordon Bleu

Prep time: 20 minutes | Cook time: 7 minutes
Serves 4

1 cup coconut shred
4 deli ham slices
1 pound (454 g)
chicken breast, skinless,
boneless
4 tablespoons butter,

melted
1 teaspoon ground
black pepper
4 Cheddar cheese slices
1 cup beef broth

1. Cut the chicken breast into 4 fillets and beat them gently.
2. Then place the ham on the chicken fillets, add Cheddar cheese slices and roll them.
3. Mix up ground black pepper and melted butter.
4. Then dip the rolled chicken in the melted butter and coat in the coconut shred.
5. Pour beef broth and insert the trivet in the Instant Pot.
6. Put the chicken on the trivet and close the lid.
7. Cook the meal on Manual mode at High Pressure for 7 minutes.
8. Then allow the natural pressure release for 10 minutes.

Per Serving
calories: 601 | fat: 46g | protein: 37g | carbs: 10g
net carbs: 5g | fiber: 5g

Roast Chicken

Prep time: 5 minutes | Cook time: 28 minutes
Serves 6

1 (4-pound / 1.8-kg)
whole chicken
1 lemon, halved
1 medium onion,
quartered
1 tablespoon paprika
2 teaspoons fine sea

salt
1 teaspoon ground
black pepper
1 cup chicken broth
Fresh thyme leaves, for
garnish

1. Pat the chicken dry with a paper towel. Stuff the lemon halves and onion quarters inside the cavity. Rub the paprika all over the chicken. Sprinkle the chicken with the salt and pepper. Tie the legs together with kitchen twine.
2. Place the prepared chicken, breast side down, in a 6-quart Instant Pot. Pour the broth around the chicken.
3. Seal the lid, press Manual, and set the timer for 20 minutes. Once finished, let the pressure release naturally.
4. Preheat the oven to 425ºF (220ºC). Remove the chicken from the pot and place on a rimmed baking sheet. Roast for 8 minutes, or until the skin is crispy and golden brown. Place on a cutting board to rest for 10 minutes, then garnish with thyme before slicing and serving.

Per Serving
calories: 593 | fat: 23g | protein: 88g | carbs: 4g
net carbs: 3g | fiber: 1g

Chicken Fritters

Prep time: 10 minutes | Cook time: 10 minutes
Serves 4

1 zucchini, grated
1 cup ground chicken
1 teaspoon chili powder

1 tablespoon avocado
oil
1 egg, beaten

1. Mix up zucchini, ground chicken, chili powder, and egg. When the mixture is smooth, make the medium size fritters.
2. Heat up the avocado oil in the Instant Pot on Sauté mode for 3 minutes.
3. Place the chicken fritters in the hot oil and cook them for 5 minutes per side.

Per Serving
calories: 97 | fat: 4g | protein: 12g | carbs: 2g
net carbs: 1g | fiber: 1g

Thyme Chicken Gizzards

Prep time: 15 minutes | Cook time: 25 minutes
Serves 4

1 pound (454 g) chicken gizzards, chopped	1 tablespoon butter
1 cup water	1 teaspoon salt
1 teaspoon dried thyme	½ teaspoon peppercorns

1. Put all ingredients in the Instant Pot.
2. Close and seal the lid.
3. Cook the chicken gizzards on Manual mode at High Pressure for 25 minutes.
4. Allow the natural pressure release for 15 minutes before opening the lid.

Per Serving
calories: 50 | fat: 3g | protein: 4g | carbs: 0g net carbs: 0g | fiber: 0g

Turkey Meatballs

Prep time: 5 minutes | Cook time: 25 minutes
Serves 5

1 pound (454 g) ground turkey	½ teaspoon dried basil
¼ cup hot sauce, or more to taste	½ teaspoon chili powder
2 tablespoons coconut oil	½ teaspoon kosher salt
1 teaspoon finely grated ginger	½ teaspoon freshly ground black pepper
	1 cup filtered water

1. Shape the ground turkey into 1½ inch meatballs with your hands and place in a greased dish in a single layer.
2. Whisk together the hot sauce, oil, ginger, basil, chili powder, salt, and pepper in a small bowl until combined. Sprinkle evenly over the meatballs.
3. Pour the water into the Instant Pot and insert the trivet. Using a sling, put the dish with the meatballs on the trivet.
4. Lock the lid. Select the Manual mode and set the cooking time for 25 minutes at High Pressure.
5. When the timer beeps, perform a natural pressure release for 10 minutes, then release any remaining pressure. Carefully remove the lid.
6. Cool for 5 minutes and serve warm.

Per Serving
calories: 208 | fat: 10g | protein: 26g | carbs: 1g net carbs: 1g | fiber: 0g

Greek Burger

Prep time: 15 minutes | Cook time: 20 minutes
Serves 2

1 cup ground chicken	½ teaspoon minced garlic
1 tablespoon lemon juice	½ teaspoon dried parsley
2 tablespoons coconut flour	1 cup water, for cooking

1. In the mixing bowl, mix up ground chicken, lemon juice, coconut flour, minced garlic, and dried parsley.
2. Make 2 burgers and place them in the baking pan.
3. Pour water and insert the trivet in the Instant Pot.
4. Then place the pan with burgers on the trivet. Close and seal the lid.
5. Cook the meal on Manual mode at High Pressure for 20 minutes. Allow the natural pressure release for 10 minutes.

Per Serving
calories: 173 | fat: 7g | protein: 22g | carbs: 5g net carbs: 2g | fiber: 3g

Chicken Jalapenos Roll

Prep time: 15 minutes | Cook time: 20 minutes
Serves 4

16 ounces (454 g) chicken fillet	seasoning
2 jalapeños, trimmed, seeded	1 teaspoon ground paprika
1 tablespoon olive oil	½ teaspoon salt
1 teaspoon Italian	2 Cheddar cheese slices
	1 cup water, for cooking

1. Beat the chicken fillet with the help of the kitchen hammer.
2. Then sprinkle it with Italian seasonings, ground paprika, and salt.
3. After this, put the cheese on the fillet. Add jalapeños and roll the chicken fillet into a roll.
4. Brush it with the help of the olive oil and put it in the baking pan.
5. Pour water and insert the trivet in the Instant Pot.
6. Put the baking pan with chicken on the trivet. Close and seal the lid.
7. Cook the meal on Manual at High Pressure for 20 minutes. Make a quick pressure release.

Per Serving
calories: 309 | fat: 17g | protein: 37g | carbs: 1g net carbs: 1g | fiber: 0g

Parmesan Crusted Chicken Fillets

Prep time: 15 minutes | Cook time: 13 minutes
Serves 2

1 tomato, sliced
8 ounces (227 g) chicken fillets
2 ounces (57 g) Parmesan, sliced
1 teaspoon butter
4 tablespoons water, for sprinkling
1 cup water, for cooking

1. Pour water and insert the trivet in the Instant Pot.
2. Then grease the baking mold with butter.
3. Slice the chicken fillets into halves and put them in the mold.
4. Sprinkle the chicken with water and top with tomato and Parmesan.
5. Cover the baking mold with foil and place it on the trivet.
6. Close and seal the lid.
7. Cook the meal in Manual mode for 13 minutes. Then allow the natural pressure release for 10 minutes.

Per Serving
calories: 329 | fat: 16g | protein: 42g | carbs: 2g
net carbs: 2g | fiber: 0g

Whole Roast Chicken

Prep time: 5 minutes | Cook time: 25 minutes
Serves 6

4 tablespoons grass-fed butter, softened
1 teaspoon basil, dried
1 teaspoon cilantro, dried
½ teaspoon kosher salt
½ teaspoon freshly ground black pepper
½ cup grass-fed bone broth
1 whole chicken

1. In a large bowl, thoroughly mix the butter, basil, cilantro, salt, and pepper.
2. Pour bone broth into the Instant Pot. Add the chicken (with the breast facing down). Baste lightly with the buttery mixture.
3. Seal the valve and secure the lid of the Instant Pot. Cook for 25 minutes on the Meat setting. Once cooked, let the pressure naturally disperse from the Instant Pot for about 15 minutes, then carefully switch the pressure release to Venting.
4. Remove chicken, carve, and enjoy!

Per Serving
calories: 215 | fat: 13g | protein: 22g | carbs: 0g
net carbs: 0g | fiber: 0g

Cheese Chicken Kofte

Prep time: 10 minutes | Cook time: 10 minutes
Serves 4

1 ½ cup ground chicken
1 teaspoon chili flakes
1 teaspoon garlic powder
½ cup Cheddar cheese, shredded
1 egg, beaten
3 tablespoons coconut flour
1 tablespoon coconut oil

1. In the mixing bowl, mix up ground chicken, chili flakes, garlic powder, shredded cheese, egg, and coconut flour.
2. Then make the small meatballs and press them gently with the help of the hand palm.
3. Heat up coconut oil on Sauté mode for 2 minutes.
4. Then put the chicken kofte inside the Instant Pot in one layer and cook them for 4 minutes from each side.

Per Serving
calories: 227 | fat: 14g | protein: 21g | carbs: 5g
net carbs: 3g | fiber: 2g

Chicken Fingers

Prep time: 10 minutes | Cook time: 7 minutes
Serves 4

2 eggs, beaten
1 tablespoon coconut cream
½ teaspoon ground paprika
½ teaspoon ground turmeric
½ teaspoon salt
½ cup almond flour
1 pound (454 g) chicken fillet
1 tablespoon coconut oil

1. Cut the chicken fillet on the strips and sprinkle with salt, ground paprika, and ground turmeric.
2. In the mixing bowl, mix up coconut cream and eggs.
3. Then dip the chicken strips in the egg mixture. After this, coat the chicken in the almond flour.
4. Repeat the steps one more time.
5. Then preheat the coconut oil on Sauté mode for 2 minutes and put the chicken strips inside in one layer.
6. Cook the chicken strips on Sauté mode for 3 minutes from each side.

Per Serving
calories: 371 | fat: 22g | protein: 39g | carbs: 4g
net carbs: 2g | fiber: 2g

Chicken Lombardy

Prep time: 15 minutes | Cook time: 30 minutes
Serves 4

4 chicken thighs	flour
1 ounce (28 g) butter	3 ounces (85 g)
½ teaspoon garam	Parmesan, grated
masala	½ cup water
¼ cup apple cider	1 ounce (28 g)
vinegar	Mozzarella cheese,
2 tablespoons coconut	shredded

1. Heat up butter on Sauté mode.
2. When the butter is melted, add chicken thighs and sprinkle them with garam masala. Cook them for 3 minutes from each side.
3. After this, add apple cider vinegar, coconut flour, and ½ cup water.
4. Close and seal the lid and cook the chicken on Manual at High Pressure for 15 minutes.
5. Allow the natural pressure release for 10 minutes.
6. Then top the chicken with all cheese and sauté for 5 minutes more.

Per Serving
calories: 435 | fat: 23g | protein: 52g | carbs: 4g
net carbs: 2g | fiber: 2g

Pancetta Wings

Prep time: 15 minutes | Cook time: 7 minutes
Serves 4

4 chicken wings	black pepper
2 ounces (57 g)	½ teaspoon salt
pancetta, sliced	1 cup water, for cooking
1 teaspoon ground	

1. Put the sliced pancetta in the baking pan in one layer.
2. Then sprinkle the chicken wings with ground black pepper and salt and place them over the pancetta.
3. Cover the chicken with foil.
4. After this, pour water and insert the trivet in the Instant Pot.
5. Put the baking pan with chicken on the trivet. Close and seal the lid.
6. Cook the chicken wings on Manual mode at High Pressure for 7 minutes. Then allow the natural pressure release for 10 minutes.

Per Serving
calories: 177 | fat: 13g | protein: 14g | carbs: 1g
net carbs: 0g | fiber: 1g

Chicken Slaw Mix

Prep time: 10 minutes | Cook time: 15 minutes
Serves 2

½ cup slaw mix	1 teaspoon ground
1 tablespoon heavy	black pepper
cream	1 tablespoon olive oil
6 ounces (170 g)	1 teaspoon lemon juice
chicken, chopped	

1. Put the chicken in the Instant Pot and sprinkle with lemon juice, ground black pepper, and olive oil.
2. Stir gently and cook it on Sauté mode for 15 minutes. Stir it from time to time.
3. Then cool the cooked chicken gently and mix it up with slaw mix.
4. Add heavy cream and mix up well.

Per Serving
calories: 236 | fat: 12g | protein: 25g | carbs: 6g
net carbs: 6g | fiber: 0g

Pesto Turkey Breasts

Prep time: 5 minutes | Cook time: 26 minutes
Serves 6

2 pounds (907 g)	1 teaspoon paprika
turkey breasts	1 tablespoon olive oil
Sea salt and ground	1 cup water
black pepper, to taste	

Pesto Sauce:

⅓ cup olive oil	nuts, toasted
½ cup fresh basil leaves	1 garlic clove, halved
⅓ cup grated Parmesan	Salt and ground black
cheese	pepper, to taste
2 tablespoons pine	

1. Season the turkey breasts on both sides with salt, black pepper, and paprika.
2. Set your Instant Pot to Sauté and heat the olive oil.
3. Add the turkey breasts and sear each side for 2 to 3 minutes. Pour in the water.
4. Secure the lid. Select the Poultry mode and set the cooking time for 20 minutes at High Pressure.
5. Meanwhile, place all the ingredients for the pesto sauce into a food processor. Pulse until everything is well combined.
6. When the timer beeps, perform a quick pressure release. Carefully remove the lid.
7. Spoon the pesto sauce onto the turkey breasts and serve.

Per Serving
calories: 395 | fat: 26g | protein: 35g | carbs: 1g
net carbs: 1g | fiber: 0g

Tender Turkey Tetrazzini

Prep time: 15 minutes | Cook time: 20 minutes
Serves 4

14 ounces (397 g) turkey, breast, cooked, shredded
½ cup mushrooms, sliced
2 ounces (57 g) Parmesan, grated
1 cup spaghetti squash, chopped, cooked
2 tablespoons butter, melted
½ cup heavy cream
½ cup Mozzarella, shredded
½ cup water

1. Put shredded turkey, mushrooms, Parmesan, and spaghetti squash in the Instant Pot. Mix up well.
2. In the mixing bowl, mix up butter, heavy cream, Mozzarella, and water.
3. Pour the liquid over the turkey.
4. Close and seal the lid.
5. Cook the meal on Manual mode at High Pressure for 20 minutes. Allow the natural pressure release for 10 minutes.

Per Serving
calories: 337 | fat: 20g | protein: 35g | carbs: 3g
net carbs: 3g | fiber: 0g

Dijon Turkey

Prep time: 15 minutes | Cook time: 14 minutes
Serves 4

14 ounces (397 g) ground turkey
1 tablespoon Dijon mustard
½ cup coconut flour
1 teaspoon onion powder
1 teaspoon salt
½ cup chicken broth
1 tablespoon avocado oil

1. In the mixing bowl, mix up ground turkey, Dijon mustard, coconut flour, onion powder, and salt.
2. Make the meatballs with the help of the fingertips.
3. Then pour avocado oil in the Instant Pot and heat it up for1 minute.
4. Add the meatballs and cook them for 2 minutes from each side.
5. Then add chicken broth. Close and seal the lid.
6. Cook the meatballs for 10 minutes. Make a quick pressure release.

Per Serving
calories: 268 | fat: 13g | protein: 30g | carbs: 11g
net carbs: 5g | fiber: 6g

Crack Chicken

Prep time: 15 minutes | Cook time: 20 minutes
Serves 4

1 cup chicken broth
1 teaspoon dried dill
1 teaspoon dried oregano
½ teaspoon onion powder
1 pound (454 g) skinless, boneless chicken breast
½ teaspoon salt
2 tablespoons mascarpone cheese
2 ounces (57 g) Cheddar cheese, shredded

1. Pour the chicken broth in the Instant Pot.
2. Add dried ill, oregano, onion powder, chicken breast, and salt.
3. Close and seal the lid.
4. Cook the chicken breast on Manual mode at High Pressure for 15 minutes.
5. Then make a quick pressure release and transfer the cooked chicken in the bowl.
6. Blend the chicken broth mixture with the help of the immersion blender.
7. Add mascarpone cheese and Cheddar cheese. Sauté the liquid for 2 minutes on Sauté mode.
8. Meanwhile, shred the chicken.
9. Add it in the mascarpone mixture and mix it up. Sauté the meal for 3 minutes more.

Per Serving
calories: 212 | fat: 9g | protein: 30g | carbs: 1g
net carbs: 1g | fiber: 0g

Mascarpone Chicken with Tomato

Prep time: 10 minutes | Cook time: 20 minutes
Serves 2

8 ounces (227 g) chicken fillet, sliced
1 tomato, chopped
2 tablespoons mascarpone
1 teaspoon coconut oil
1 teaspoon ground paprika
½ teaspoon ground turmeric
1 tablespoon butter

1. Rub the chicken fillet with ground paprika, ground turmeric, and paprika.
2. Put the sliced chicken in the Instant Pot.
3. Add tomato, mascarpone, coconut oil, and butter.
4. Close the lid and cook the meal on Sauté mode for 20 minutes.
5. Stir it every 5 minutes to avoid burning.

Per Serving
calories: 323 | fat: 19g | protein: 35g | carbs: 3g
net carbs: 2g | fiber: 1g

Marry Me Chicken

Prep time: 15 minutes | Cook time: 25 minutes
Serves 4

4 chicken thighs
1 teaspoon olive oil
1 teaspoon garlic, diced
1 teaspoon dried thyme
1 tablespoon avocado oil
¼ cup chicken broth
½ cup heavy cream
1 teaspoon salt
1 teaspoon ground black pepper

1. Pour olive oil in the Instant Pot and add chicken thighs.
2. Sauté them for 4 minutes from each side. Sprinkle the chicken with salt and ground black pepper.
3. Then transfer the chicken on the plate.
4. Add avocado oil in the Instant Pot.
5. Then add dried thyme and garlic. Sauté the ingredients for 2 minutes. Add chicken thighs, chicken broth, and heavy cream. Sauté the chicken for 15 minutes.

Per Serving
calories: 232 | fat: 17g | protein: 20g | carbs: 2g
net carbs: 1g | fiber: 1g

Philadelphia Stuffed Chicken Breast

Prep time: 10 minutes | Cook time: 16 minutes
Serves 5

1 pound (454 g) chicken breast, skinless, boneless
2 tablespoons cream cheese
1 tablespoon chives, chopped
½ teaspoon minced garlic
½ teaspoon salt
1 tablespoon avocado oil
1 cup water, for cooking

1. Make the cut in the shape of the pocket in the chicken breast. Rub the chicken with salt.
2. After this, in the mixing bowl, mix up cream cheese, chives, and minced garlic.
3. Rub the chicken breast with salt and fill with the cream cheese.
4. Then secure the "chicken pocket" with the help of the toothpicks.
5. Pour water and insert the trivet in the Instant Pot.
6. Then put the chicken breast in the baking pan and transfer it on the trivet.
7. Cook the meal on Manual mode at High Pressure for 25 minutes. Allow the natural pressure release for 10 minutes.

Per Serving
calories: 122 | fat: 4g | protein: 20g | carbs: 0g
net carbs: 0g | fiber: 0g

Tuscan Chicken Drumsticks with Spinach

Prep time: 15 minutes | Cook time: 12 minutes
Serves 4

4 chicken drumsticks
1 cup chopped spinach
1 teaspoon minced garlic
1 teaspoon ground paprika
1 cup heavy cream
1 teaspoon cayenne pepper
1 ounce (28 g) sun-dried tomatoes, chopped

1. Put all ingredients in the Instant Pot.
2. Close and seal the lid.
3. Cook the meal on Manual mode at High Pressure for 12 minutes.
4. Then allow the natural pressure release for 10 minutes.
5. Serve the chicken with hot sauce from the Instant Pot.

Per Serving
calories: 188 | fat: 14g | protein: 14g | carbs: 2g
net carbs: 1g | fiber: 1g

Chicken Fajitas

Prep time: 10 minutes | Cook time: 5 minutes
Serves 4

1½ pounds (680 g) boneless, skinless chicken breasts
¼ cup avocado oil
2 tablespoons water
1 tablespoon Mexican hot sauce
2 cloves garlic, minced
1 teaspoon lime juice
1 teaspoon ground cumin
1 teaspoon salt
1 teaspoon erythritol
¼ teaspoon chili powder
¼ teaspoon smoked paprika
5 ounces (142 g) sliced yellow bell pepper strips
5 ounces (142 g) sliced red bell pepper strips
5 ounces (142 g) sliced green bell pepper strips

1. Slice the chicken into very thin strips lengthwise. Cut each strip in half again. Imagine the thickness of restaurant fajitas when cutting.
2. In a measuring cup, whisk together the avocado oil, water, hot sauce, garlic, lime juice, cumin, salt, erythritol, chili powder, and paprika to form a marinade. Add to the pot, along with the chicken and peppers.
3. Close the lid and seal the vent. Cook on High Pressure for 5 minutes. Quick release the steam.

Per Serving
calories: 319 | fat: 18g | protein: 34g | carbs: 6g
net carbs: 4g | fiber: 2g

Turkey Burger with Avocado Fries

Prep time: 5 minutes | Cook time: 10 minutes
Serves 4

2 tablespoons coconut oil
6 slices no-sugar-added bacon
1 avocado, sliced into thin strips
½ pound (227 g) turkey, ground
½ teaspoon freshly
ground black pepper
½ teaspoon parsley, dried
½ teaspoon turmeric, ground
½ teaspoon basil, dried
½ teaspoon kosher salt
2 cups broccoli, chopped

1. On a piece of aluminum foil, wrap the bacon around the avocado slices. If any bacon remains, wrap slices a second time, until no bacon is left. In a separate bowl, mix the turkey, black pepper, parsley, turmeric, basil, and salt. Once combined, form one large, thin patty with the seasoned turkey.
2. Sauté oil in Instant Pot, then pour in ¼ cup of filtered water, and place the turkey patty in the middle. Then add the broccoli.
3. Insert the trivet, then place the aluminum foil with the avocado fries on top. Be sure to fold the edges of the aluminum foil upward. Close the lid, set the pressure release to Sealing, and select Manual. Set the Instant Pot to 10 minutes on High Pressure and let cook.
4. Once cooked, let the pressure naturally disperse from the Instant Pot for about 10 minutes, then carefully switch the pressure release to Venting.
5. Open the lid and remove the food. Cut the patty into 4 equal parts and serve alongside the avocado fries.

Per Serving
calories: 429 | fat: 32g | protein: 29g | carbs: 8g
net carbs: 3g | fiber: 5g

Creamy Chicken with Tomatoes and Spinach

Prep time: 5 minutes | Cook time: 18 minutes
Serves 4

4 boneless, skinless chicken breasts (about 2 pounds / 907 g)
2½ ounces (71 g) sun-dried tomatoes, coarsely chopped (about 2 tablespoons)
¼ cup chicken broth
2 tablespoons creamy, no-sugar-added balsamic vinegar
dressing
1 tablespoon whole-grain mustard
2 cloves garlic, minced
1 teaspoon salt
8 ounces (227 g) fresh spinach
¼ cup sour cream
1 ounce (28 g) cream cheese, softened

1. Place the chicken breasts in the Instant Pot. Add the tomatoes, broth, and dressing.
2. Close the lid and seal the vent. Cook on High Pressure for 10 minutes. Quick release the steam. Press Cancel.
3. Remove the chicken from the pot and place on a plate. Cover with aluminum foil to keep warm while you make the sauce.
4. Turn the pot to Sauté mode. Whisk in the mustard, garlic, and salt and then add the spinach. Stir the spinach continuously until it is completely cooked down, 2 to 3 minutes. The spinach will absorb the sauce but will release it again as it continues to cook down.
5. Once the spinach is completely wilted, add the sour cream and cream cheese. Whisk until completed incorporated.
6. Let the sauce simmer to thicken and reduce by about one-third, about 5 minutes. Stir occasionally to prevent burning. Press Cancel.
7. Pour the sauce over the chicken. Serve.

Per Serving
calories: 357 | fat: 13g | protein: 52g | carbs: 7g
net carbs: 5g | fiber: 2g

Deconstructed Turkey and Bacon Pizza

Prep time: 5 minutes | Cook time: 10 minutes
Serves 4

2 tablespoons coconut oil
1 pound (454 g) turkey, ground
½ teaspoon kosher salt
½ teaspoon freshly ground black pepper
1 (14-ounce / 397-g)
can sugar-free or low-sugar crushed tomatoes
2 cups full-fat Cheddar cheese, shredded
4 slices no-sugar-added bacon, cut finely, cooked

1. Set the Instant Pot to Sauté and melt the oil. Add ground turkey, salt, and pepper. Cook until browned, stirring occasionally. Arrange the turkey so that it's in a single layer, acting as the "crust." In order, add the salt, black pepper, tomatoes, Cheddar, and bacon. Do not mix.
2. Close the lid, set the pressure release to Sealing and hit Cancel to stop the current program. Select Manual, set the Instant Pot to 10 minutes on High Pressure, and let cook.
3. Once cooked, let the pressure naturally disperse from the Instant Pot for about 10 minutes, then carefully switch the pressure release to Venting.
4. Open the Instant Pot, serve, and enjoy!

Per Serving
calories: 595 | fat: 39g | protein: 54g | carbs: 4g
net carbs: 3g | fiber: 1g

Chicken Thighs with Sage

Prep time: 10 minutes | Cook time: 16 minutes
Serves 4

1 teaspoon dried sage	4 skinless chicken
1 teaspoon ground	thighs
turmeric	1 cup water
2 teaspoons avocado oil	1 teaspoon sesame oil

1. Rub the chicken thighs with dried sage, ground turmeric, sesame oil, and avocado oil.
2. Then pour water in the Instant Pot and insert the trivet.
3. Place the chicken thighs on the trivet and close the lid.
4. Cook the meal on Manual at High Pressure for 16 minutes.
5. Then make a quick pressure release and open the lid.
6. Let the cooked chicken thighs cool for 10 minutes before serving.

Per Serving
calories: 293 | fat: 12g | protein: 42g | carbs: 1g
net carbs: 1g | fiber: 0g

Thai Green Curry

Prep time: 10 minutes | Cook time: 8 hours
Serves 6

1 tablespoon coconut oil	eggplant
2 tablespoons Thai	1 cup chopped green,
green curry paste	yellow, or orange bell
(adjust to your	pepper
preferred spice level)	½ cup fresh basil
1 tablespoon minced	leaves, preferably Thai
fresh ginger	basil
1 tablespoon minced	1½ cups unsweetened
garlic	coconut milk
½ cup sliced onion	1 tablespoon fish sauce
1 pound (454 g)	2 tablespoons soy
boneless, skinless	sauce
chicken thighs	2 teaspoons Truvia or
2 cups peeled, chopped	Swerve
	Salt, to taste

1. Preheat the Instant Pot by selecting Sauté and adjusting to high heat. When the inner cooking pot is hot, add the coconut oil and heat until it is shimmering. Add the curry paste and cook for 1 to 2 minutes, stirring occasionally.
2. Add the ginger and garlic and stir-fry for 30 seconds. Add the onion and stir it all together.
3. Add the chicken, eggplant, bell pepper, basil, coconut milk, fish sauce, soy sauce, and Truvia or Swerve. Stir to combine.

4. Press Cancel to turn off Sauté mode, and switch to Slow Cook mode. Adjust to cook for 8 hours on medium (not low).
5. When the curry has finished cooking, add salt to taste.

Per Serving
calories: 290 | fat: 20g | protein: 17g | carbs: 12g
net carbs: 9g | fiber: 3g

Chicken Asparagus Rolls

Prep time: 12 minutes | Cook time: 24 minutes
Serves 4

½ cup mayonnaise	butter or coconut oil
3 tablespoons Dijon	16 spears fresh
mustard	asparagus, trimmed
Zest and juice of 1	4 boneless, skinless
lemon	chicken breast halves
2 teaspoons dried	(about 4 ounces / 113
tarragon	g each)
1 teaspoon ground	2 ounces (57 g)
black pepper	provolone cheese,
½ teaspoon fine sea	shredded (½ cup)
salt	Fresh thyme leaves, for
1 tablespoon unsalted	garnish

1. Place the mayonnaise, mustard, lemon zest, lemon juice, tarragon, pepper, and salt in a medium-sized bowl and stir until well combined. Set aside.
2. Place the butter in a 6-quart Instant Pot and press Sauté. Once melted, add the asparagus and sauté for 4 minutes, or until tender. Press Cancel to stop the Sauté. Remove the asparagus from the pot and set aside.
3. Place a chicken breast between two sheets of parchment paper. Using a cast-iron skillet, a rolling pin, or the smooth side of a meat mallet, pound the chicken until it is about ¼ inch thick. Remove the parchment and repeat with the remaining chicken breasts.
4. Place a quarter of the shredded cheese on top of each chicken breast, then top with 4 asparagus spears. Roll the chicken around the asparagus and cheese. Secure with a few toothpicks.
5. Pour half of the mayonnaise mixture into the Instant Pot and add the chicken rolls. Seal the lid, press Manual, and set the timer for 20 minutes. Once finished, turn the valve to venting for a quick release.
6. Serve the chicken rolls with the sauce from the pot. Garnish with thyme leaves and the rest of the mayonnaise mixture.

Per Serving
calories: 392 | fat: 29g | protein: 26g | carbs: 5g
net carbs: 3g | fiber: 2g

Turmeric Chicken Nuggets

Prep time: 10 minutes | Cook time: 9 minutes
Serves 5

8 ounces (227 g) chicken fillet
1 teaspoon ground turmeric
½ teaspoon ground coriander
½ cup almond flour
2 eggs, beaten
½ cup butter

1. Chop the chicken fillet roughly into the medium size pieces.
2. In the mixing bowl, mix up ground turmeric, ground coriander, and almond flour.
3. Then dip the chicken pieces in the beaten egg and coat in the almond flour mixture.
4. Toss the butter in the Instant Pot and melt it on Sauté mode for 4 minutes.
5. Then put the coated chicken in the hot butter and cook for 5 minutes or until the nuggets are golden brown.

Per Serving
calories: 343 | fat: 29g | protein: 18g | carbs: 3g net carbs: 2g | fiber: 1g

Buffalo-Style Chicken Wings

Prep time: 5 minutes | Cook time: 15 minutes
Serves 12

2 cups hot sauce
¼ cup apple cider vinegar
1 tablespoon cayenne pepper
½ cup butter, melted
1 teaspoon sea salt
1 teaspoon black pepper
5 pounds (2.3 kg) chicken wings

1. In a medium-sized mixing bowl, combine the hot sauce, vinegar, cayenne pepper, butter, sea salt and black pepper, and whisk together. Reserve about ½ cup of the sauce for basting later. Remove the wing tips from the main wingettes and separate the drummettes. In the inner pot of the Instant Pot, combine the chicken wings and sauce and mix well. You can make the recipe up to this point and marinate overnight.
2. When ready to cook, turn on the Instant Pot by pressing the Manual button and set the timer for 10 minutes on High Pressure. Close the lid tightly and move the steam release handle to Sealing.
3. When the timer ends, you will hear a beeping sound. Allow the Instant Pot to cool down naturally until the float valve drops down. Meanwhile, turn on the oven to broil.
4. Press Cancel on the Instant Pot and open the lid. Take out the chicken wings and place them in a single layer on a roasting pan. Baste the chicken wings with the reserved hot sauce. Broil for about 1 minute or until browned, without burning them. Mix the wings with more hot sauce and serve immediately.

Per Serving
calories: 301 | fat: 24g | protein: 19g | carbs: 1g net carbs: 0g | fiber: 1g

Cumin Chicken with Red Salsa

Prep time: 10 minutes | Cook time: 20 minutes
Serves 8

2 pounds (907 g) boneless, skinless chicken thighs, cut into bite-size pieces
1½ tablespoons ground cumin
1½ tablespoons chili powder
1 tablespoon salt
2 tablespoons olive oil
1 (14½-ounce / 411-g) can diced tomatoes, undrained
1 (5-ounce / 142-g) can sugar-free tomato paste
1 small onion, chopped
3 garlic cloves, minced
2 ounces (57 g) pickled jalapeños from a can, with juice
½ cup sour cream

1. Preheat the Instant Pot by selecting Sauté and adjusting to high heat.
2. In a medium bowl, coat the chicken with the cumin, chili powder, and salt.
3. Put the oil in the inner cooking pot. When it is shimmering, add the coated chicken pieces. (This step lets the spices bloom a bit to get their full flavor.) Cook the chicken for 4 to 5 minutes.
4. Add the tomatoes, tomato paste, onion, garlic, and jalapeños.
5. Lock the lid into place. Select Manual and adjust the pressure to High. Cook for 15 minutes. When the cooking is complete, let the pressure release naturally for 10 minutes, then quick-release any remaining pressure. Unlock and remove the lid.
6. Use two forks to shred the chicken. Serve topped with the sour cream. This dish is good with mashed cauliflower, steamed vegetables, or a salad.

Per Serving
calories: 329 | fat: 24g | protein: 21g | carbs: 8g net carbs: 6g | fiber: 2g

Chicken Piccata

**Prep time: 8 minutes | Cook time: 3 minutes
Serves 2**

2 boneless, skinless chicken thighs
1 teaspoon Italian seasoning
½ teaspoon fine sea salt
2 tablespoons unsalted butter (or coconut oil for dairy-free)
½ cup chicken broth

2 tablespoons lemon juice
2 tablespoons capers, rinsed and drained
1 lemon, thinly sliced, for garnish
2 tablespoons chopped fresh Italian parsley leaves, for garnish

1. Place the chicken thighs between two sheets of parchment paper. Using a cast-iron skillet, a rolling pin, or the smooth side of a meat mallet, pound the thighs until they are about ¼ inch thick. Remove the parchment. Season the chicken on both sides with the Italian seasoning and salt.
2. Place the butter in a 6-quart Instant Pot and press Sauté. Once melted, add the chicken and cook for 2 minutes per side or until golden brown but not cooked through. Add the broth, lemon juice, and capers to the pot. Whisk the sauce well to scrape up the bits stuck to the bottom of the pot. Press Cancel to stop the Sauté.
3. Seal the lid, press Manual, and set the timer for 1 minute. Once finished, turn the valve to venting for a quick release.
4. Remove the chicken to a serving platter and pour the sauce over the thighs. Garnish with the lemon slices and parsley.

Per Serving
calories: 442 | fat: 23g | protein: 54g | carbs: 6g
net carbs: 5g | fiber: 1g

Thyme Turkey Salad

**Prep time: 5 minutes | Cook time: 20 minutes
Serves 6**

1½ cups water
2 pounds (907 g) turkey breasts, boneless and skinless
½ teaspoon crushed red pepper flakes
½ teaspoon black pepper
Salt, to taste
2 sprigs thyme

2 garlic cloves, pressed
1 sprig sage
1 leek, sliced
1 cucumber, chopped
½ cup finely diced celery
½ cup mayonnaise
1½ tablespoons Dijon mustard

1. Pour the water into the Instant Pot and insert the trivet.
2. Season the turkey breasts with red pepper flakes, black pepper, and salt. Place the turkey breasts on the trivet. Scatter the thyme, garlic, and sage on top.
3. Lock the lid. Select the Poultry mode and set the cooking time for 20 minutes at High Pressure.
4. When the timer beeps, perform a natural pressure release for 10 minutes, then release any remaining pressure. Carefully remove the lid.
5. Allow the turkey to cool completely, then slice it into strips. Transfer to a salad bowl.
6. Add the remaining ingredients to the bowl and gently toss until well combined. Serve immediately or serve chilled.

Per Serving
calories: 325 | fat: 17g | protein: 35g | carbs: 4g
net carbs: 3g | fiber: 1g

Creamed Chicken Meatballs with Cabbage

**Prep time: 15 minutes | Cook time: 4 minutes
Serves 4**

1 pound (454 g) ground chicken
¼ cup heavy (whipping) cream
2 teaspoons salt, divided
½ teaspoon ground caraway seeds
1½ teaspoons freshly

ground black pepper, divided
¼ teaspoon ground allspice
4 to 6 cups thickly chopped green cabbage
½ cup coconut milk
2 tablespoons unsalted butter

1. To make the meatballs, put the chicken in a bowl. Add the cream, 1 teaspoon of salt, the caraway, ½ teaspoon of pepper, and the allspice. Mix thoroughly. Refrigerate the mixture for 30 minutes. Once the mixture has cooled, it is easier to form the meatballs.
2. Using a small scoop, form the chicken mixture into small-to medium-size meatballs. Place half the meatballs in the inner cooking pot of your Instant Pot and cover them with half the cabbage. Place the remaining meatballs on top of the cabbage, then cover them with the rest of the cabbage.
3. Pour in the milk, place pats of the butter here and there, and sprinkle with the remaining 1 teaspoon of salt and 1 teaspoon of pepper.
4. Lock the lid into place. Select Manual and adjust the pressure to High. Cook for 4 minutes. When the cooking is complete, quick-release the pressure. Unlock the lid.
5. Serve the meatballs on top of the cabbage.

Per Serving
calories: 338 | fat: 23g | protein: 23g | carbs: 7g
net carbs: 4g | fiber: 3g

Chicken with Poblano Peppers and Cream

Prep time: 10 minutes | Cook time: 29 minutes
Serves 4

2 Poblano peppers, sliced
16 ounces (454 g) chicken fillet
½ teaspoon salt
½ cup coconut cream
1 tablespoon butter
½ teaspoon chili powder

1. Heat up the butter on Sauté mode for 3 minutes.
2. Add Poblano and cook them for 3 minutes.
3. Meanwhile, cut the chicken fillet into the strips and sprinkle with salt and chili powder.
4. Add the chicken strips to the Instant Pot.
5. Then add coconut cream and close the lid.
6. Cook the meal on Sauté mode for 20 minutes.

Per Serving
calories: 320 | fat: 18g | protein: 34g | carbs: 4g
net carbs: 3g | fiber: 1g

Lime Turkey Burgers

Prep time: 10 minutes | Cook time: 3 minutes
Serves 4

Burgers:
2 pounds (907 g) ground turkey
1½ ounces (43 g) diced red onion
2 cloves garlic, minced
1½ teaspoons minced
cilantro
1½ teaspoons salt
1 teaspoon Mexican chili powder
Juice and zest of 1 lime
½ cup water

Dipping Sauce:
½ cup sour cream
4 teaspoons sriracha
1 tablespoon chopped
cilantro, plus more for garnish
1 teaspoon lime juice

1. Make the burgers: In a large bowl, add the turkey, onion, garlic, cilantro, salt, chili powder, and lime juice and zest. Use a wooden spoon to mix until the ingredients are well distributed.
2. Divide the meat into four 8-ounce (227-g) balls. Use a kitchen scale to measure for accuracy. Pat the meat into thick patties, about 1 inch thick.
3. Add the water and trivet to the Instant Pot. Place the turkey patties on top of the trivet, overlapping if necessary.
4. Close the lid and seal the vent. Cook on High Pressure for 3 minutes. Quick release the steam.
5. Remove the patties from the pot.
6. Make the dipping sauce: In a small bowl, whisk together the sour cream, sriracha, cilantro, and lime juice.
7. Top each patty with 2 tablespoons of the sauce and garnish with fresh cilantro.

Per Serving
calories: 417 | fat: 25g | protein: 44g | carbs: 5g
net carbs: 4g | fiber: 1g

Chicken Cacciatore

Prep time: 10 minutes | Cook time: 29 minutes
Serves 8

1 tablespoon unsalted butter (or coconut oil for dairy-free)
2½ pounds (1.1 kg) bone-in, skin-on chicken thighs
1 cup chopped onions
1 medium-sized green bell pepper, chopped
8 ounces (227 g) cremini or button mushrooms, sliced
4 cloves garlic, minced
1 (14½-ounce / 411-g) can diced tomatoes
1 tablespoon Italian
seasoning
1 teaspoon fine sea salt
1 teaspoon ground black pepper
1 drop stevia glycerite (optional)
⅓ cup tomato sauce
⅓ cup grated Parmesan cheese (about 1 ounce / 28 g)
Capers, rinsed and drained, for garnish (optional)
Fresh thyme leaves, for garnish (optional)

1. Place the butter in a 6-quart Instant Pot and press Sauté. Season the chicken on all sides with salt and pepper. Once the butter is melted, place the chicken skin side down in the pot and cook for 4 minutes, or until the skin is golden brown. Remove from the pot and set aside, leaving the drippings in the pot.
2. Place the onions, bell pepper, mushrooms, and garlic in the pot and cook, stirring often, for 5 minutes, or until the onions are soft. Add the tomatoes, Italian seasoning, salt, and pepper and cook for another 10 minutes. Taste and adjust the seasonings; if the sauce tastes too acidic, add the stevia glycerite. Press Cancel to stop the Sauté.
3. Add the tomato sauce and Parmesan cheese and stir to combine. Return the chicken to the pot with the sauce.
4. Seal the lid, press Manual, and set the timer for 10 minutes. Once finished, turn the valve to venting for a quick release.
5. Transfer the chicken to a serving dish and top with the sauce from the pot. Garnish with capers and thyme leaves, if desired.

Per Serving
calories: 333 | fat: 22g | protein: 25g | carbs: 7g
net carbs: 6g | fiber: 1g

Bruschetta and Cheese Stuffed Chicken

Prep time: 10 minutes | Cook time: 10 minutes
Serves 4

6 ounces (170 g) diced Roma tomatoes
2 tablespoons avocado oil
1 tablespoon thinly sliced fresh basil, plus more for garnish
1½ teaspoons balsamic vinegar
Pinch of salt
Pinch of black pepper
4 boneless, skinless chicken breasts (about 2 pounds / 907 g)
12 ounces (340 g) goat cheese, divided
2 teaspoons Italian seasoning, divided
1 cup water

1. Prepare the bruschetta by mixing the tomatoes, avocado oil, basil, vinegar, salt, and pepper in a small bowl. Let it marinate until the chicken is done.
2. Pat the chicken dry with a paper towel. Butterfly the breast open but do not cut all the way through. Stuff each breast with 3 ounces (85 g) of the goat cheese. Use toothpicks to close the edges.
3. Sprinkle ½ teaspoon of the Italian seasoning on top of each breast.
4. Pour the water into the pot. Place the trivet inside. Lay a piece of aluminum foil on top of the trivet and place the chicken breasts on top. It is okay if they overlap.
5. Close the lid and seal the vent. Cook on High Pressure for 10 minutes. Quick release the steam.
6. Remove the toothpicks and top each breast with one-fourth of the bruschetta.

Per Serving
calories: 581 | fat: 34g | protein: 64g | carbs: 5g
net carbs: 4g | fiber: 1g

Turkey Breasts with Mushrooms

Prep time: 10 minutes | Cook time: 15 minutes
Serves 6

3 teaspoons butter
1½ pounds (680 g) turkey breasts, cubed
2 cloves garlic, minced
½ leek, chopped
1 cup thinly sliced white mushrooms
½ cup broth
½ teaspoon basil
½ teaspoon dried parsley flakes
¼ teaspoon ground allspice
Salt and black pepper, to taste
½ cup heavy cream

1. Set your Instant Pot to Sauté and melt the butter.
2. Add the turkey and sear for about 4 minutes, stirring constantly.
3. Remove the turkey and set aside on a plate.
4. Add the garlic, leek, and mushrooms to the Instant Pot and cook for 3 minutes, or until the garlic is fragrant.
5. Stir in the cooked turkey, broth, basil, parsley flakes, allspice, salt, and pepper.
6. Lock the lid. Select the Manual mode and set the cooking time for 8 minutes at High Pressure.
7. When the timer beeps, perform a quick pressure release. Carefully remove the lid.
8. Stir in the heavy cream until heated through. Ladle the turkey mixture into six bowls and serve warm.

Per Serving
calories: 251 | fat: 14g | protein: 26g | carbs: 3g
net carbs: 3g | fiber: 0g

African Chicken and Peanut Stew

Prep time: 10 minutes | Cook time: 10 minutes
Serves 6

1 cup chopped onion
2 tablespoons minced garlic
1 tablespoon minced fresh ginger
1 teaspoon salt
½ teaspoon ground cumin
½ teaspoon ground coriander
½ teaspoon freshly ground black pepper
½ teaspoon ground cinnamon
⅛ teaspoon ground
cloves
1 tablespoon sugar-free tomato paste
1 pound (454 g) boneless, skinless chicken breasts or thighs, cut into large chunks
3 to 4 cups chopped Swiss chard
1 cup cubed raw pumpkin
½ cup water
1 cup chunky peanut butter

1. In the inner cooking pot of the Instant Pot, stir together the onion, garlic, ginger, salt, cumin, coriander, pepper, cinnamon, cloves, and tomato paste. Add the chicken, chard, pumpkin, and water.
2. Lock the lid into place. Select Manual and adjust the pressure to High. Cook for 10 minutes. When the cooking is complete, let the pressure release naturally. Unlock the lid.
3. Mix in the peanut butter a little at a time. Taste with each addition, as your reward for cooking. The final sauce should be thick enough to coat the back of a spoon in a thin layer.
4. Serve over mashed cauliflower, cooked zucchini noodles, steamed vegetables, or with a side salad.

Per Serving
calories: 411 | fat: 27g | protein: 31g | carbs: 15g
net carbs: 10g | fiber: 5g

Spicy Mediterranean Chicken

Prep time: 15 minutes | Cook time: 15 minutes
Serves 5

1 small onion, chopped	for garnish
2 cloves garlic, crushed	1 cup green olives,
1 bell pepper, seeded	pitted and sliced
and chopped	½ cup hot cherry
1 cup diced tomatoes	pepper slices (in water)
3 pounds (1.4 kg)	¼ cup chicken broth or
boneless chicken	bone broth
breasts and thighs	¼ cup white wine
1 teaspoon smoked	½ teaspoon sea salt or
paprika	to taste
2 tablespoons chopped	½ teaspoon black
fresh flat leaf parsley,	pepper
reserve 1 tablespoon	

1. Place the onion, garlic, pepper and tomatoes into the Instant Pot and add the chicken on top. Add the herbs and spices on top, except for 1 tablespoon of parsley. Then add the olives, hot cherry pepper slices, chicken broth and white wine.
2. Close the lid tightly and move the steam release handle to Sealing.
3. Press Cancel, then the Manual button and set the timer for 15 minutes on High Pressure. When the timer ends, you will hear a beeping sound. Allow the Instant Pot to cool down naturally until the float valve drops down. Press Cancel and open the lid. Remove the chicken and vegetables to serving plates. Add sea salt and pepper to taste, garnish with parsley and serve immediately.

Per Serving
calories: 444 | fat: 23g | protein: 47g | carbs: 8g
net carbs: 6g | fiber: 2g

Two-Cheese Stuffed Chicken

Prep time: 15 minutes | Cook time: 20 minutes
Serves 4

12 ounces (340 g)	cheese
chicken fillet	½ teaspoon dried
4 ounces (113 g)	cilantro
provolone cheese,	½ teaspoon smoked
sliced	paprika
1 tablespoon cream	1 cup water, for cooking

1. Beat the chicken fillet well and rub it with dried cilantro and smoked paprika.
2. Then spread it with cream cheese and top with Provolone cheese.
3. Roll the chicken fillet into the roll and wrap in the foil.

4. Pour water and insert the trivet in the Instant Pot.
5. Place the chicken roll on the trivet. Close and seal the lid.
6. Cook it on Manual mode at High Pressure for 20 minutes.
7. Make a quick pressure release and slice the chicken roll into the servings.

Per Serving
calories: 271 | fat: 15g | protein: 32g | carbs: 1g
net carbs: 1g | fiber: 0g

Italian Chicken Cupcakes

Prep time: 6 minutes | Cook time: 22 minutes
Serves 5

1½ pounds (680 g)	seasoning
ground chicken	1 teaspoon dried
¾ cup finely chopped	oregano leaves
button or cremini	2 cloves garlic, minced
mushrooms	1½ cups (¼-inch
½ cup grated Parmesan	chunks) fontina or
cheese	Mozzarella cheese
½ cup chopped fresh	10 slices fresh
basil leaves	Mozzarella cheese, for
¼ cup marinara sauce,	topping (optional)
plus more for serving	Fresh oregano leaves,
1 teaspoon Italian	for garnish

1. Place the chicken, mushrooms, Parmesan cheese, basil, and marinara in a large bowl. Add the Italian seasoning, oregano, garlic, and chunks of cheese and stir well.
2. Divide the meat mixture into 10 equal portions and press each portion into a greased 4-ounce (113-g) ramekin or mason jar.
3. Set a trivet in an 8-quart Instant Pot and pour in 1 cup of cold water. Place eight of the ramekins on the trivet; cover and refrigerate or freeze the other two to cook later. Seal the lid, press Manual, and set the timer for 20 minutes. Once finished, let the pressure release naturally.
4. Remove the ramekins with tongs and preheat the oven to broil.
5. Remove the cupcakes from the ramekins. If desired, top each with a Mozzarella slice, place on a rimmed baking sheet, and broil for 2 minutes, or until the cheese is melted. To serve, spoon some warmed marinara onto a serving platter. Place the cupcakes on top of the sauce. Garnish with oregano.

Per Serving
calories: 637 | fat: 41g | protein: 74g | carbs: 1g
net carbs: 1g | fiber: 0g

Spanish Chicken

Prep time: 10 minutes | Cook time: 25 minutes
Serves 4

4 chicken thighs, skinless
1 teaspoon tomato paste
2 ounces (57 g) olives, sliced
½ cup chicken broth
1 teaspoon dried oregano
1 tablespoon butter

1. Put the butter in the Instant Pot and heat it up on Sauté mode for 2 minutes.
2. Then add chicken thighs and cook them for 4 minutes from each side.
3. Add dried oregano, olives, tomato paste, and chicken broth.
4. Close and seal the lid and cook the Spanish chicken on Manual mode at High Pressure for 15 minutes.
5. Make a quick pressure release.

Per Serving
calories: 328 | fat: 16g | protein: 43g | carbs: 2g net carbs: 1g | fiber: 1g

Hot Chicken Caesar Sandwiches

Prep time: 10 minutes | Cook time: 22 minutes
Serves 8

2 pounds (907 g) boneless, skinless chicken thighs
2 cups chicken broth
Caesar Dressing:
1 tablespoon Dijon mustard
1 tablespoon coconut vinegar or apple cider vinegar
Cloves squeezed from ½ head roasted garlic, or 1 clove garlic, minced
¼ teaspoon fine sea salt
¼ teaspoon ground black pepper
½ cup MCT oil or extra-virgin olive oil
For Serving:
8 romaine lettuce leaves
1 tomato, thinly sliced

1 teaspoon fine sea salt
1 teaspoon ground black pepper

2 tablespoons mayonnaise
1 teaspoon lemon juice
1 (2-ounce / 57-g) can anchovies, finely chopped
½ cup shredded Parmesan cheese (about 2 ounces / 57 g), plus more for garnish
¼ cup chopped fresh parsley
½ teaspoon ground black pepper, plus more for garnish

1. Place the chicken, broth, salt, and pepper in a 3-quart Instant Pot. Seal the lid, press Manual, and set the timer for 20 minutes. Once finished, turn the valve to venting for a quick release.
2. While the chicken is cooking, make the dressing: Place the mustard, vinegar, garlic, salt, and pepper in a blender and blend until smooth and thick. With the blender running on low speed, slowly add the oil, then the mayonnaise. Scrape down the sides of the jar as needed. Add the lemon juice and blend well. Add the anchovies and purée until smooth. Taste and add up to ¾ teaspoon more salt, adding it in ¼-teaspoon increments and blending and tasting after each addition. Season with additional pepper, if needed.
3. Remove the lid from the Instant Pot and drain the broth, leaving the chicken in the pot. Shred the chicken with two forks. Add ½ cup of the Caesar dressing, the Parmesan cheese, parsley, and pepper. (Refrigerate the remaining dressing for later use.) Stir until thoroughly combined.
4. Press Sauté and cook for 2 minutes, or until the Caesar chicken mixture is heated through and the cheese is melted.
5. To serve, spoon ¼ cup of the Caesar chicken onto a lettuce leaf. Top with extra shredded Parmesan, a slice of tomato, and freshly ground pepper. Repeat with the remaining ingredients to make 8 sandwiches.

Per Serving
calories: 577 | fat: 49g | protein: 32g | carbs: 10g net carbs: 6g | fiber: 4g

Chicken Pasta

Prep time: 10 minutes | Cook time: 20 minutes
Serves 4

¼ cup Monterey Jack cheese, shredded
1 tablespoon mascarpone cheese
½ cup coconut cream
1 teaspoon ground
black pepper
½ teaspoon salt
1 pound (454 g) chicken fillet, sliced
1 teaspoon olive oil

1. Sprinkle the chicken fillet with ground black pepper and salt.
2. Then put it in the Instant Pot, add olive oil and cook on Sauté mode for 10 minutes.
3. Stir the chicken and add coconut cream and mascarpone cheese. Mix up well.
4. Add shredded cheese and close the lid.
5. Sauté the chicken pasta for 10 minutes on Sauté mode.
6. Stir the cooked chicken pasta well before serving.

Per Serving
calories: 329 | fat: 19g | protein: 36g | carbs: 2g net carbs: 1g | fiber: 1g

15-Minute Fajitas

**Prep time: 5 minutes | Cook time: 10 minutes
Serves 4**

2 tablespoons avocado oil	½ teaspoon freshly ground black pepper
2 bell peppers, chopped	½ teaspoon cumin, ground
2 garlic cloves, minced	½ teaspoon kosher salt
1 pound (454 g) chicken breasts, cut into thin strips	1 avocado, mashed
1 teaspoon chili powder	1 cup full-fat Cheddar cheese, shredded
1 teaspoon oregano, dried	¾ cup sour cream, at room temperature

1. Set the Instant Pot to Sauté and heat the avocado oil. Add in the bell peppers, garlic, chicken, chili powder, oregano, black pepper, cumin, salt, and ½ cup of filtered water.
2. Close the lid, set the pressure release to Sealing, and select Manual. Set the Instant Pot to 10 minutes on High Pressure and let cook.
3. Once cooked, let the pressure naturally disperse from the Instant Pot for about 10 minutes, then carefully switch the pressure release to Venting.
4. Open the lid and remove the food. Serve inside of your favorite keto-friendly wraps, and top with the avocado, cheese, and sour cream.

Per Serving
calories: 610 | fat: 44g | protein: 43g | carbs: 12g
net carbs: 8g | fiber: 4g

Reuben Chicken

**Prep time: 5 minutes | Cook time: 15 minutes
Serves 6**

Dressing:

⅔ cup mayonnaise	salt
⅓ cup tomato sauce	½ teaspoon ground black pepper
¼ cup finely diced dill pickles or dill pickle relish	¼ teaspoon onion powder
½ teaspoon fine sea	

32 ounces (907 g) sauerkraut, with juices	taste
6 boneless, skinless chicken breast halves (about 4 ounces / 113 g each)	3 ounces (85 g) Swiss cheese, shredded (¾ cup) (omit for dairy-free)
Fine sea salt and ground black pepper, to	Prepared yellow mustard, for drizzling

1. Make the dressing: Put the mayonnaise, tomato sauce, dill pickles, salt, pepper, and onion powder in a medium-sized bowl and stir until well combined. Set aside in the fridge; the dressing can be made up to 3 days ahead.
2. Grease a 6-quart Instant Pot. Place the sauerkraut with juices in the pot. Season the chicken on all sides with salt and pepper. Place the chicken on top of the sauerkraut.
3. Seal the lid, press Manual, and set the timer for 15 minutes. (If you use larger chicken breasts, they may need closer to 20 minutes.) Once finished, turn the valve to venting for a quick release.
4. Divide the sauerkraut among 6 plates. Place a chicken breast on top of each serving, then add the shredded Swiss cheese and a scoop of the dressing. Garnish with a drizzle of mustard and some freshly ground pepper.

Per Serving
calories: 303 | fat: 22g | protein: 22g | carbs: 4g
net carbs: 4g | fiber: 0g

Sesame-Ginger Chicken

**Prep time: 5 minutes | Cook time: 10 minutes
Serves 6**

1½ pounds (680 g) boneless, skinless chicken thighs, cut into large pieces	1 tablespoon minced fresh ginger
2 tablespoons soy sauce	1 tablespoon minced garlic
1 tablespoon sesame oil	1 tablespoon Truvia
	1 tablespoon rice vinegar

1. Put the chicken in a heatproof bowl. Add the soy sauce, sesame oil, ginger, garlic, Truvia, and vinegar. Stir to coat the chicken. Cover the bowl with aluminum foil or a silicone lid.
2. Pour 2 cups of water into the inner cooking pot of the Instant Pot, then place a trivet in the pot. Place the bowl on the trivet.
3. Lock the lid into place. Select Manual and adjust the pressure to High. Cook for 10 minutes. When the cooking is complete, let the pressure release naturally for 10 minutes, then quick-release any remaining pressure. Unlock the lid.
4. Remove the chicken and shred it, then mix it back in with the liquid in the bowl. Serve.

Per Serving
calories: 272 | fat: 20g | protein: 19g | carbs: 4g
net carbs: 4g | fiber: 0g

Indian Chicken Butter Masala

Prep time: 15 minutes | Cook time: 15 minutes
Serves 4

1 (14½-ounce / 411-g) can diced tomatoes, undrained
5 or 6 garlic cloves, minced
1 tablespoon minced fresh ginger
1 teaspoon ground turmeric
1 teaspoon cayenne
1 teaspoon smoked paprika
2 teaspoons garam masala, divided
1 teaspoon ground cumin

1 teaspoon salt
1 pound (454 g) boneless, skinless chicken breasts or thighs
½ cup unsalted butter, cut into cubes, or ½ cup coconut oil
½ cup heavy (whipping) cream or full-fat coconut milk
¼ to ½ cup chopped fresh cilantro
4 cups cauliflower rice or cucumber noodles

1. Put the tomatoes, garlic, ginger, turmeric, cayenne, paprika, 1 teaspoon of garam masala, cumin, and salt in the inner cooking pot of the Instant Pot. Mix thoroughly, then place the chicken pieces on top of the sauce.
2. Lock the lid into place. Select Manual and adjust the pressure to High. Cook for 10 minutes. When the cooking is complete, let the pressure release naturally. Unlock the lid. Carefully remove the chicken and set aside.
3. Using an immersion blender in the pot, blend together all the ingredients into a smooth sauce. (Or use a stand blender, but be careful with the hot sauce and be sure to leave the inside lid open to vent.) After blending, let the sauce cool before adding the remaining ingredients or it will be thinner than is ideal.
4. Add the butter cubes, cream, remaining 1 teaspoon of garam masala, and cilantro. Stir until well incorporated. The sauce should be thick enough to coat the back of a spoon when you're done.
5. Remove half the sauce and freeze it for later or refrigerate for up to 2 to 3 days.
6. Cut the chicken into bite-size pieces. Add it back to the sauce.
7. Preheat the Instant Pot by selecting Sauté and adjust to Less for low heat. Let the chicken heat through. Break it up into smaller pieces if you like, but don't shred it.
8. Serve over cauliflower rice or raw cucumber noodles.

Per Serving
calories: 512 | fat: 36g | protein: 31g | carbs: 16g
net carbs: 10g | fiber: 6g

Chicken Pot Pie

Prep time: 5 minutes | Cook time: 15 minutes
Serves 4

Crust:
1 tablespoon grass-fed butter, softened
2 tablespoons sour cream, at room temperature

1 tablespoon psyllium husk
1 cup blanched almond flour

Filling:
2 cups boneless, skinless chicken breast, cubed, cooked
2 garlic cloves, minced
¼ cup green beans, cut into small pieces
½ teaspoon freshly ground black pepper
½ teaspoon kosher salt
½ teaspoon rosemary,

ground
½ teaspoon thyme, ground
½ teaspoon parsley, dried
½ teaspoon basil, dried
¼ (4-ounce / 113-g) small onion, thinly sliced

1. In a large bowl, thoroughly combine all crust ingredients.
2. Pour 1 cup filtered water into the Instant Pot, and insert the trivet. Transfer the mixture from the bowl to a well-greased Instant Pot-friendly dish (or pan), forming a crust on the bottom and lightly on the sides. Freeze the dish for 15 minutes. While freezing, in a large bowl, mix the chicken and other filling ingredients.
3. Remove the dish from freezer, then pour the filling into the center of the dish. Using a sling if desired, place the dish onto the trivet, and cover loosely with aluminum foil. Close the lid, set the pressure release to Sealing, and select Manual. Set the Instant Pot to 15 minutes on High Pressure, and let cook.
4. Once cooked, let the pressure naturally leave the Instant Pot, for about 10 minutes. Next, switch the pressure release to Venting. Open the Instant Pot, and remove the dish. Let cool, fold the crust into a covered pie (if desired), and serve.

Per Serving
calories: 247 | fat: 16g | protein: 22g | carbs: 4g
net carbs: 3g | fiber: 1g

Chicken and Bacon Lasagna Roll-Ups

Prep time: 10 minutes | Cook time: 26 minutes
Serves 8

Sauce:

1 (8-ounce / 227-g) package cream cheese, softened	2 teaspoons garlic powder
½ cup chicken broth	2 teaspoons onion powder
½ cup shredded Cheddar cheese (about 2 ounces / 57 g)	1 pound (454 g) bacon, chopped

Filling:

2 boneless, skinless chicken thighs	Cheddar cheese (about 2 ounces / 57 g)
½ cup diced yellow onions	8 long slices shaved deli chicken breast
6 cloves garlic, crushed	Ground black pepper, to taste
½ cup shredded	

1. Make the sauce: Place the cream cheese in a medium-sized bowl and whisk to loosen. (If you don't use a whisk to loosen the cream cheese, you will end up with clumps in your sauce.) Slowly whisk in the broth. Add the Cheddar cheese, garlic powder, and onion powder and stir well to combine. Set the sauce aside in the fridge.
2. Cook the bacon: Place the bacon in a 6-quart Instant Pot and press Sauté. Cook, stirring occasionally, until crisp, about 4 minutes. Remove the bacon using a slotted spoon, leaving the drippings in the pot. Reserve 3 tablespoons of the bacon for the topping and set the rest aside.
3. Make the filling: Add the chicken thighs, onions, and garlic to the Instant Pot. Seal the lid, press Manual, and set the timer for 20 minutes. Once finished, turn the valve to venting for a quick release.
4. Remove the lid. Shred the chicken with two forks and transfer to a medium-sized bowl or container. (The filling can be made up to 2 days ahead.)
5. Pour the sauce into the Instant Pot.
6. Lay a slice of shaved chicken on a clean work surface. Place a few tablespoons of the shredded chicken filling, 1½ teaspoons of the Cheddar cheese, and a teaspoon of the cooked bacon in the center. Wrap the shaved chicken around the filling and set in the sauce. Repeat with the remaining filling and chicken "tortillas." Top the roll-ups with the remaining Cheddar cheese.
7. Seal the lid, press Manual, and set the timer for 2 minutes. Once finished, let the pressure release naturally.
8. Remove the roll-ups to a serving plate or dish using a large serving spoon. Top with the reserved bacon and freshly ground pepper.

Per Serving
calories: 644 | fat: 46g | protein: 51g | carbs: 4g
net carbs: 4g | fiber: 0g

Thanksgiving Turkey

Prep time: 5 minutes | Cook time: 60 minutes
Serves 8

1 turkey breast (7 pounds / 3.2 kg), giblets removed	2 teaspoons black pepper
4 tablespoons butter, softened	½ onion, quartered
2 teaspoons ground sage	1 rib celery, cut into 3 or 4 pieces
2 teaspoons garlic powder	1 cup chicken broth
2 teaspoons salt	2 or 3 bay leaves
	1 teaspoon xanthan gum

1. Pat the turkey dry with a paper towel.
2. In a small bowl, combine the butter with the sage, garlic powder, salt, and pepper. Rub the butter mixture all over the top of the bird. Place the onion and celery inside the cavity.
3. Place the trivet in the pot. Add the broth and bay leaves to the pot.
4. Place the turkey on the trivet. If you need to remove the trivet to make the turkey fit, you can. The turkey will be near the top of the pot, which is fine.
5. Close the lid and seal the vent. Cook on High Pressure for 35 minutes. It is normal if it takes your pot a longer time to come to pressure.
6. Let the steam naturally release for 20 minutes before manually releasing. Press Cancel.
7. Heat the broiler.
8. Carefully remove the turkey to a sheet pan. Place under the broiler for 5 to 10 minutes to crisp up the skin.
9. While the skin is crisping, use the juices to make a gravy. Pour the juices through a mesh sieve, reserving 2 cups of broth. Return the reserved broth to the pot. Turn the pot to Sauté mode. When the broth starts to boil, add the xanthan gum and whisk until the desired consistency is reached. Add more xanthan gum if you like a thicker gravy.
10. Remove the turkey from the broiler and place on a platter. Carve as desired and serve with the gravy.

Per Serving
calories: 380 | fat: 18g | protein: 47g | carbs: 3g
net carbs: 1g | fiber: 2g

Better Butter Chicken

Prep time: 10 minutes | Cook time: 20 minutes
Serves 6

1 tablespoon avocado oil
1 cup chopped onion
4 cloves garlic, mashed
2 tablespoons peeled grated fresh ginger
½ teaspoon turmeric
½ teaspoon cumin
½ teaspoon garam masala
1 teaspoon curry powder
1 (14-ounce / 397-g) can diced tomatoes
1 teaspoon paprika
1 teaspoon cayenne pepper
1 cup chopped fresh cilantro, reserve ¼ cup for garnish
3 pounds (1.4 kg) bone-in chicken thighs
½ cup chicken broth
½ cup butter, cut in pieces
1 cup full-fat heavy cream
Sea salt, to taste

1. Turn on the Instant Pot by pressing Sauté and set to More. Insert the inner pot and wait until the panel says Hot. To the inner pot, add the avocado oil. Then, sauté the onion, garlic and ginger for 2 minutes or until the onion is soft. Add the turmeric, cumin, garam masala, curry powder, diced tomatoes, paprika, cayenne pepper and ¾ cup of cilantro. Add the chicken thighs and the chicken broth and stir well. Make sure all the thighs are coated. Pat down the ingredients and close the lid tightly. Move the steam release handle to Sealing.
2. Press Cancel, then press the Manual button and set the timer for 20 minutes on High Pressure.
3. When the timer ends, you will hear a beeping sound. Allow the Instant Pot to cool down naturally until the float valve drops down. Press Cancel and then Sauté. Open the lid, add the butter pieces, heavy cream and sea salt to taste. Stir and simmer for 2 minutes. Press Cancel. Serve immediately with the remaining cilantro as garnish.

Per Serving
calories: 713 | fat: 60g | protein: 34g | carbs: 10g
net carbs: 8g | fiber: 2g

Creamy Chicken and Broccoli

Prep time: 10 minutes | Cook time: 15 minutes
Serves 4

6 slices uncured bacon, chopped
½ cup chicken broth
8 ounces (227 g) full-fat cream cheese
½ cup full-fat buttermilk
2 pounds (907 g) boneless chicken breast, cut into 1-inch chunks
¼ cup fresh flat leaf parsley, reserve 1 tablespoon for garnish
1 teaspoon dried tarragon
½ teaspoon dried dill weed
½ teaspoon dried basil
½ teaspoon herbes de Provence
2 teaspoons onion powder
1 teaspoon garlic powder
1 teaspoon sea salt
½ teaspoon black pepper
2 cups broccoli florets
2 tablespoons blue cheese crumbles

1. Turn on the Instant Pot by pressing Sauté and set to More. Insert the inner pot and wait until the panel says Hot. Add the bacon pieces and sauté to brown, 3 minutes. Add the chicken broth and deglaze the bacon bits. Add the cream cheese and buttermilk, and stir. Add the chicken pieces and the rest of the ingredients except for the broccoli and 1 tablespoon of parsley.
2. Close the lid tightly and move the steam release handle to Sealing.
3. Press the Manual button and set the timer for 15 minutes on High Pressure. When the timer goes off, allow the Instant Pot to cool down naturally until the float valve drops down and you can open the lid. After cooking is finished, press Cancel. Add the broccoli and stir. Press the Manual button and set the timer to 0 minutes.
4. When you hear the beeping sound indicating that the time has ended, carefully turn the steam release handle to the Venting position for the steam to escape and the float valve to drop down. Press Cancel, and open the lid. Sprinkle blue cheese crumbles and garnish with remaining parsley before serving.

Per Serving
calories: 545 | fat: 28g | protein: 64g | carbs: 7g
net carbs: 6g | fiber: 1g

Asian Chicken Salad with Miso Dressing

Prep time: 10 minutes | Cook time: 15 minutes
Serves 6

1 pound (454 g) chicken breasts
1 teaspoon sea salt
½ teaspoon black pepper
½ teaspoon garlic powder
¼ cup white wine
1 cup water
½ head iceberg lettuce, sliced ½-inch (13-mm) thick
1 carrot, julienned
1 small purple onion, diced
3 scallions, chopped,
reserve 1 tablespoon for garnish
1 tablespoon grated fresh ginger
2 tablespoons rice vinegar
2 tablespoons miso paste, light or dark
1 tablespoon sesame oil
1½ teaspoons lime juice
¼ cup blanched almond slivers, for garnish
1 teaspoon toasted sesame seeds, for garnish

1. Season the chicken breast with the sea salt, black pepper, garlic powder and white wine and set aside.
2. Turn on the Instant Pot by pressing the Manual button and set the timer for 15 minutes on High Pressure. Put the water in the inner pot and place the trivet inside. Place the seasoned chicken breast in a shallow dish and place it on the trivet. Close the lid tightly and move the steam release handle to Sealing.
3. Meanwhile, cut the vegetables and transfer them to a large salad bowl. In a small mixing bowl, combine and whisk the ginger, rice vinegar, miso, sesame oil and lime juice. When the timer of the Instant Pot ends, you will hear a beeping sound. Allow the Instant Pot to cool down naturally until the float valve drops down. Press Cancel and open the lid. Remove the dish and using a fork, shred the chicken. Let the chicken cool for 5 minutes and then add it to the salad bowl with the vegetables. Add the salad dressing and mix well. Serve with the almond slivers, sesame seeds and remaining scallions on top.

Per Serving
calories: 207 | fat: 12g | protein: 16g | carbs: 9g
net carbs: 6g | fiber: 3g

Greek Chicken Salad

Prep time: 10 minutes | Cook time: 15 minutes
Serves 4

Marinade:
2 (6-ounce / 170-g) boneless, skinless chicken breasts
2 garlic cloves, minced
2 tablespoons avocado oil
Juice of 1 lemon
½ teaspoon dried oregano
½ teaspoon dried thyme
¼ teaspoon salt
¼ teaspoon pepper
1 cup chicken broth
Salad:
¼ cup halved kalamata olives
¼ cup sliced pepperoncini
½ cup cherry tomatoes, halved
1 cup chopped cucumber
½ cup crumbled feta cheese
Dressing:
½ cup mayo
¼ cup white or red wine vinegar
¼ teaspoon dried oregano
¼ teaspoon garlic powder
½ teaspoon Dijon mustard

1. Mix all marinade ingredients and chicken in resealable bag or covered container. Place in fridge to marinate for 2 hours.
2. Press the Sauté button and add chicken to Instant Pot. Sear chicken for 3 to 5 minutes or until each side is browned. Add broth to pot and press the Cancel button.
3. Place lid on Instant Pot and click to close. Press the Manual button and set timer for 10 minutes. When timer beeps, allow a natural release for 10 minutes and quick-release the remaining pressure.
4. To prepare salad, cut chicken into 1-inch bite-sized cubes. Add chicken and all salad ingredients except feta to large bowl and set aside.
5. In medium bowl, whisk together dressing ingredients and pour on top of salad, tossing to cover. Sprinkle feta on top.

Per Serving
calories: 377 | fat: 28g | protein: 23g | carbs: 3g
net carbs: 2g | fiber: 1g

Chaptr 9 Pork

Filipino Pork

Prep time: 10 minutes | Cook time: 40 minutes
Serves 4

1 pound (454 g) pork loin, chopped
½ cup apple cider vinegar
1 cup chicken broth
1 chili pepper, chopped
1 tablespoon coconut oil
1 teaspoon salt

1. Melt the coconut oil on Sauté mode.
2. When it is hot, and chili pepper and cook it for 2 minutes. Stir it.
3. Add chopped pork loin and salt. Cook the ingredients for 5 minutes.
4. After this, add apple cider vinegar and chicken broth.
5. Close and seal the lid and cook the Filipino pork for 30 minutes at High Pressure on Manual mode. Then make a quick pressure release.

Per Serving
calories: 320 | fat: 20g | protein: 32g | carbs: 1g
net carbs: 1g | fiber: 0g

Peperonata with Pork Sausages

Prep time: 15 minutes | Cook time: 10 minutes
Serves 4

1 teaspoon olive oil
8 pork sausages, casing removed
1 green bell pepper, seeded and sliced
1 red bell pepper, seeded and sliced
1 jalapeño pepper, seeded and sliced
1 red onion, chopped
2 garlic cloves, minced
2 Roma tomatoes, puréed
1 cup roasted vegetable broth
1 tablespoon Italian seasoning
2 tablespoons fresh Italian parsley
2 tablespoons ripe olives, pitted and sliced

1. Press the Sauté button to heat up the Instant Pot. Once hot, add the oil; sear your sausages until no longer pink in center.
2. Add the other ingredients, except for the olives and parsley; stir to combine well.
3. Secure the lid. Choose the Manual setting and cook for 8 minutes at High Pressure. Once cooking is complete, use a quick pressure release; carefully remove the lid.
4. Serve garnished with fresh parsley and olives. Bon appétit!

Per Serving
calories: 582 | fat: 49g | protein: 24g | carbs: 9g
net carbs: 7g | fiber: 2g

Asian Ribs

Prep time: 15 minutes | Cook time: 25 minutes
Serves 3

¼ teaspoon ground cardamom
½ teaspoon minced ginger
4 tablespoons apple cider vinegar
¼ teaspoon sesame
seeds
10 ounces (283 g) pork ribs, chopped
¼ teaspoon chili flakes
1 tablespoon avocado oil

1. In the mixing bowl, mix up ground cardamom. Minced ginger, apple cider vinegar, sesame seeds, chili flakes, and avocado oil.
2. Then brush the pork ribs with the cardamom mixture and leave for 10 minutes to marinate.
3. After this, heat up the Instant Pot on Sauté mode for 2 minutes.
4. Add the marinated pork ribs and all remaining marinade.
5. Cook the pork ribs on Sauté mode for 25 minutes. Flip the ribs on another side every 5 minutes.

Per Serving
calories: 271 | fat: 17g | protein: 25g | carbs: 1g
net carbs: 1g | fiber: 0g

Five-Ingredient Pork Roast

Prep time: 5 minutes | Cook time: 35 minutes
Serves 4

1 (2½-pound / 1.1-kg) boneless pork loin roast
2 teaspoons fine sea salt
1 large onion, cut into thick slices
2 cloves garlic, minced
2 cups chicken broth
Fresh herbs, such as rosemary, for garnish
Lemon wedges, for garnish

1. Season the pork roast on all sides with the salt, then place the roast in a 6-quart Instant Pot. Add the onion slices and garlic, then pour in the broth.
2. Seal the lid, press Manual, and set the timer for 35 minutes. Once finished, turn the valve to venting for a quick release.
3. Remove the roast to a serving platter and shred the meat with two forks. Serve with the onion slices and juices from the pot. Garnish with fresh herbs and lemon wedges.

Per Serving
calories: 560 | fat: 33g | protein: 58g | carbs: 5g
net carbs: 4g | fiber: 1g

Pork Dumpling Meatballs

Prep time: 10 minutes | Cook time: 19 minutes
Serves 2

6 ounces (170 g) ground pork
1 teaspoon minced garlic
½ teaspoon chives, chopped
1 teaspoon coconut

aminos
½ teaspoon cayenne pepper
1 tablespoon coconut oil
1 teaspoon ginger paste
½ cup chicken broth

1. In the bowl, mix up ground pork, minced garlic, chives, coconut aminos, cayenne pepper, and ginger paste.
2. Make the small balls (dumplings) from the meat mixture.
3. After this, melt the coconut oil and put the meatballs inside.
4. Roast them on Sauté mode for 1 minute from each side.
5. Then add chicken broth and close the lid.
6. Cook the meal on Sauté mode for 15 minutes.

Per Serving
calories: 199 | fat: 10g | protein: 24g | carbs: 2g
net carbs: 2g | fiber: 0g

Smoked Paprika Pulled Pork

Prep time: 7 minutes | Cook time: 40 minutes
Serves 3

1 pound (454 g) pork roast, chopped
½ teaspoon ground cumin
1 tablespoon smoked paprika

1 cup beef broth
1 tablespoon coconut oil
1 teaspoon garlic powder

1. Mix up together garlic powder and ground cumin.
2. Then combine together the spices and chopped pork roast. Add the smoked paprika.
3. Place the meat in the Instant Pot. Add coconut oil and beef broth.
4. Close the Instant Pot lid and seal it.
5. Set the Manual mode and set the timer to 30 minutes at High Pressure.
6. Make the natural-release pressure.
7. Transfer the cooked meat in the bowl and shred it. Serve the meal with meat liquid.

Per Serving
calories: 376 | fat: 20g | protein: 45g | carbs: 3g
net carbs: 2g | fiber: 1g

Pork Quiche

Prep time: 10 minutes | Cook time: 6 minutes
Serves 2

3 eggs, beaten
1 tablespoon coconut flour
4 ounces (113 g) Mozzarella, shredded

5 ounces (142 g) ground pork
¼ cup spinach
½ teaspoon salt
1 tablespoon butter

1. Whisk the eggs and coconut flour together.
2. add ground pork in the egg mixture.
3. After this, chop the spinach and add in the egg mixture too.
4. Add butter and mix up the mixture very carefully.
5. Place the mixture into the quiche pan. Sprinkle the mixture with Mozzarella over.
6. Then transfer the pan in the Instant Pot and close the lid.
7. Select Manual and cook quiche for 6 minutes on High Pressure. When the timer goes off, perform a quick pressure release. Carefully open the lid.
8. Cut the quiche into halves.

Per Serving
calories: 422 | fat: 26g | protein: 43g | carbs: 5g
net carbs: 3g | fiber: 2g

Ground Salisbury Steak

Prep time: 10 minutes | Cook time: 25 minutes
Serves 4

1 cup ground pork
1 teaspoon chili flakes
1 teaspoon dried cilantro
1 cup chicken broth

1 teaspoon olive oil
1 tablespoon mustard
1 cup white mushrooms, chopped

1. Put olive oil and mushrooms in the Instant Pot.
2. Add dried cilantro, and chili flakes and cook the ingredients for 10 minutes on Sauté mode.
3. Then add mustard and ground pork.
4. Add chicken broth. Close and seal the lid.
5. Cook the meat on Manual mode at High Pressure for 15 minutes.
6. Make a quick pressure release.

Per Serving
calories: 94 | fat: 6g | protein: 7g | carbs: 2g
net carbs: 1g | fiber: 1g

Perfect BBQ Pulled Pork

Prep time: 5 minutes | Cook time: 60 minutes
Serves 8

1 (5-pound / 2.3-kg) boneless pork shoulder roast
5 cloves garlic, sliced
1 medium onion, diced
2 cups chicken broth
1 cup tomato sauce
2 teaspoons liquid

smoke
2 tablespoons paprika
1 teaspoon fine sea salt
1 teaspoon ground black pepper
½ teaspoon chili powder

1. Use a sharp paring knife to cut deep slits in the pork roast. Push the garlic slices into the slits.
2. Place the roast in a 6-quart Instant Pot. Add the onion, broth, tomato sauce, liquid smoke, paprika, salt, pepper, and chili powder.
3. Seal the lid, press Manual, and set the timer for 60 minutes. Once finished, let the pressure release naturally.
4. Remove the lid and shred the meat with two forks. Stir before serving.

Per Serving
calories: 584 | fat: 34g | protein: 40g | carbs: 7g
net carbs: 6g | fiber: 1g

Smoked Sausages Cabbage

Prep time: 15 minutes | Cook time: 20 minutes
Serves 2

1 cup white cabbage, shredded
6 ounces (170 g) smoked sausages, chopped
1 teaspoon avocado oil

1 teaspoon ground paprika
½ teaspoon chili powder
1 cup chicken stock

1. Put the smoked sausages and avocado oil in the Instant Pot and cook the ingredients on Sauté mode for 5 minutes. Stir them from time to time.
2. After this, add ground paprika, chili powder, and shredded cabbage. Mix up well.
3. Add chicken stock. Close and seal the lid.
4. Cook the meal on Manual mode at High Pressure for 15 minutes.
5. Then make a quick pressure release.
6. Stir the meal well before serving.

Per Serving
calories: 310 | fat: 25g | protein: 17g | carbs: 4g
net carbs: 2g | fiber: 2g

Taco Casserole

Prep time: 20 minutes | Cook time: 30 minutes
Serves 4

1 cup ground pork
1 tablespoon taco seasonings
1 tablespoon coconut oil

½ teaspoon dried cilantro
¼ cup Cheddar cheese, shredded
½ cup beef broth

1. In the mixing bowl, mix up ground pork, taco seasonings, and dried cilantro.
2. Then grease the casserole mold with coconut oil and put the pork mixture inside. Flatten it well.
3. After this, top the casserole mixture with shredded cheese.
4. Add beef broth and cover the casserole with foil.
5. Pour water in the Instant Pot and place the casserole inside.
6. Close and seal the lid.
7. Cook the meal on Manual at High Pressure for 30 minutes.
8. Allow the natural pressure release for 10 minutes.

Per Serving
calories: 302 | fat: 22g | protein: 22g | carbs: 2g
net carbs: 2g | fiber: 0g

Apple Cider Vinegar Ham

Prep time: 10 minutes | Cook time: 10 minutes
Serves 6

1 pound (454 g) bone-in ham, cooked
1 cup apple cider vinegar
2 tablespoons erythritol

2 tablespoons butter
1 tablespoon avocado oil
½ teaspoon pumpkin pie spices

1. Pour apple cider vinegar in the Instant Pot and insert the trivet.
2. Then rub the ham with erythritol, butter, avocado oil, and pumpkin pie spices.
3. Put the ham on the trivet. Close and seal the lid.
4. Cook the ham on Manual mode at High Pressure for 10 minutes.
5. Allow the natural pressure release for 5 minutes and open the lid.
6. Slice the ham.

Per Serving
calories: 134 | fat: g | protein: 16g | carbs: 7g
net carbs: 7g | fiber: 0g

Pot Roast Pork

Prep time: 6 minutes | Cook time: 60 minutes
Serves 14

1 (4-pound / 1.8-kg) boneless pork loin roast
12 cloves garlic
½ cup sliced onions
1 cup ham or chicken broth
3 tablespoons lime or lemon juice
3 teaspoons fish sauce
3 bay leaves
2 teaspoons fine sea salt
½ teaspoon ground black pepper
Lime slices, for garnish
Fresh flat-leaf parsley, for garnish

1. Use a sharp paring knife to cut deep slits in the pork roast. Push the garlic cloves into the slits.
2. Place the roast in a 6-quart Instant Pot and lay the onions on top. Add the broth, lime juice, fish sauce, bay leaves, salt, and pepper.
3. Seal the lid, press Manual, and set the timer for 60 minutes. Once finished, let the pressure release naturally.
4. Remove the roast to a cutting board and allow to rest for 10 minutes, then cut into ½-inch slices. Season with additional salt and a squirt of lime juice, then garnish with lime slices and parsley.

Per Serving
calories: 261 | fat: 15g | protein: 27g | carbs: 2g
net carbs: 2g | fiber: 0g

Vietnamese Pork

Prep time: 10 minutes | Cook time: 20 minutes
Serves 2

6 ounces (170 g) pork tenderloin
½ cup water
¼ teaspoon ground clove
¼ teaspoon minced ginger
1 teaspoon coconut aminos
1 teaspoon olive oil

1. Heat up olive oil on Sauté mode.
2. Then chop the pork tenderloin roughly and add it in the Instant Pot.
3. Cook the meat for 2 minutes and flip it on another side.
4. After this, add coconut aminos, minced ginger, ground clove, and water.
5. Close and seal the lid and cook the meat on Manual at High Pressure for 15 minutes.
6. Allow the natural pressure release for 10 minutes and transfer the meat in the bowls.

Per Serving
calories: 146 | fat: 5g | protein: 22g | carbs: 1g
net carbs: 1g | fiber: 0g

Pork Chops Marsala

Prep time: 20 minutes | Cook time: 25 minutes
Serves 2

2 pork chops
½ cup cremini mushrooms, sliced
¼ cup apple cider vinegar
1 tablespoon coconut oil
1 teaspoon dried thyme
½ cup heavy cream
¼ cup chicken broth

1. Put all ingredients in the Instant Pot.
2. Close and seal the lid.
3. Cook the pork on Manual mode at High Pressure for 25 minutes.
4. Allow the natural pressure release for 15 minutes and open the lid.
5. Stir the pork chop marsala well before serving.

Per Serving
calories: 435 | fat: 38g | protein: 20g | carbs: 2g
net carbs: 2g | fiber: 0g

Smoky Baby Back Ribs

Prep time: 3 minutes | Cook time: 23 minutes
Serves 4

2 pounds (907 g) baby back pork ribs
2 teaspoons fine sea
Glaze:
½ cup tomato sauce
¼ cup Swerve confectioners'-style sweetener or equivalent
salt
2 teaspoons smoked paprika
amount of liquid or powdered sweetener
2 teaspoons liquid smoke

1. Season the ribs on all sides with the salt and paprika.
2. Place a trivet in an 8-quart Instant Pot and pour in 1 cup of cold water. Place the seasoned ribs on the trivet.
3. Seal the lid, press Manual, and set the timer for 20 minutes. Once finished, turn the valve to venting for a quick release.
4. Meanwhile, preheat the oven to broil. Place the glaze ingredients in a small bowl and stir well to combine.
5. Place the cooked ribs on a rimmed baking sheet. Brush the glaze over the ribs, reserving some to pour over the ribs after broiling, if desired. Broil the ribs for 3 minutes, or until crispy on the edges.
6. Serve with the reserved glaze poured over the top of the ribs, if desired.

Per Serving
calories: 518 | fat: 41g | protein: 37g | carbs: 2g
net carbs: 1g | fiber: 1g

Paprika Ribs

Prep time: 10 minutes | Cook time: 30 minutes
Serves 4

1 pound (454 g) pork ribs	turmeric
1 tablespoon ground paprika	3 tablespoons avocado oil
1 teaspoon ground	1 teaspoon salt
	½ cup beef broth

1. Rub the pork ribs with ground paprika, turmeric, salt, and avocado oil.
2. Then pour the beef broth in the Instant Pot.
3. Arrange the pork ribs in the Instant Pot. Close and seal the lid.
4. Cook the pork ribs for 30 minutes on Manual mode at High Pressure.
5. When the time is finished, make a quick pressure release and chop the ribs into servings.

Per Serving
calories: 335 | fat: 22g | protein: 31g | carbs: 2g
net carbs: 1g | fiber: 1g

Pork Florentine

Prep time: 20 minutes | Cook time: 45 minutes
Serves 6

12 ounces (340 g) pork roast, roll cut	shredded
1 cup spinach	1 tablespoon olive oil
3 ounces (85 g) Monterey Jack cheese,	½ teaspoon ground black pepper
	1 cup water, for cooking

1. Beet the pork roast with the help of the kitchen hammer.
2. After this, put the spinach in the blender and add olive oil, and ground black pepper. Blend the mixture until smooth.
3. Then transfer the mixture over the pork roast, spread it well and top with shredded cheese.
4. Roll the meat and wrap in the foil.
5. Pour water and insert the trivet in the Instant Pot.
6. Put the wrapped pork on the trivet. Close and seal the lid.
7. Cook the meal on Manual mode at High Pressure for 45 minutes.
8. Allow the natural pressure release for 15 minutes.

Per Serving
calories: 298 | fat: 20g | protein: 26g | carbs: 1g
net carbs: 1g | fiber: 0g

Tender Pork Liver

Prep time: 5 minutes | Cook time: 7 minutes
Serves 3

14 ounces (397 g) pork liver, chopped	chopped
½ cup heavy cream	1 teaspoon salt
3 tablespoons scallions,	1 teaspoon butter

1. Sprinkle the liver with the salt.
2. Toss the butter in the Instant Pot and melt it on the Sauté mode.
3. Add heavy cream, scallions, and liver.
4. Stir gently and close the lid.
5. Cook the meal on the Sauté mode for 12 minutes.

Per Serving
calories: 300 | fat: 14g | protein: 35g | carbs: 6g
net carbs: 6g | fiber: 0g

Melt-in-Your-Mouth Pork Belly

Prep time: 6 minutes | Cook time: 44 minutes
Serves 8

1 (2-pound / 907-g) pork belly	and grated fresh ginger
1 cup beef or chicken broth	1 tablespoon coconut oil
2 green onions, thinly sliced	2 teaspoons fine sea salt
2 tablespoons peeled	½ teaspoon ground black pepper

1. Place the pork belly, broth, green onions, and ginger in a 6-quart Instant Pot.
2. Seal the lid, press Manual, and set the timer for 35 minutes. Once finished, turn the valve to venting for a quick release.
3. Remove the pork belly from the pot and discard the cooking liquid. Place the coconut oil in the pot and press Sauté. Season the cooked pork belly on all sides with the salt and pepper. When the oil is hot, add the pork belly to the pot and sauté on all sides until crispy, about 2 minutes per side. Press Cancel to stop the Sauté.
4. Place the crispy pork belly on a cutting board and allow to rest for 5 minutes. Cut into ½-inch slices and serve.

Per Serving
calories: 349 | fat: 30g | protein: 18g | carbs: 2g
net carbs: 2g | fiber: 0g

Garlic Italian Sausages

Prep time: 15 minutes | Cook time: 20 minutes
Serves 4

1 teaspoon garlic powder	Italian sausages, chopped
1 cup water	½ teaspoon Italian seasonings
1 teaspoon butter	
12 ounces (340 g)	

1. Sprinkle the chopped Italian sausages with Italian seasonings and garlic powder and place in the Instant Pot.
2. Add butter and cook the sausages on Sauté mode for 10 minutes. Stir them from time to time with the help of the spatula.
3. Then add water and close the lid.
4. Cook the sausages on Manual mode at High Pressure for 10 minutes.
5. Allow the natural pressure release for 10 minutes more.

Per Serving
calories: 307 | fat: 28g | protein: 12g | carbs: 1g
net carbs: 1g | fiber: 0g

Ground Pork Pizza Crust

Prep time: 10 minutes | Cook time: 15 minutes
Serves 4

½ cup Cheddar cheese, shredded	1 tablespoon psyllium husk
1 cup ground pork	1 teaspoon olive oil
1 teaspoon Italian seasonings	1 cup water, for cooking

1. In the mixing bowl, mix up shredded cheese, ground pork, Italian seasonings, and Psyllium husk.
2. Line the round Instant Pot pan with baking paper and brush with olive oil.
3. Then put the ground pork mixture in the pan and flatten it in the shape of the pizza crust.
4. Pour water and insert the trivet in the Instant Pot.
5. Put the pan with pizza crust on the trivet. Close and seal the lid.
6. Cook the meal on Manual mode at High Pressure for 15 minutes. Make a quick pressure release.

Per Serving
calories: 324 | fat: 22g | protein: 24g | carbs: 9g
net carbs: 2g | fiber: 7g

Herbed Pork Tenderloin

Prep time: 15 minutes | Cook time: 18 minutes
Serves 4

¼ teaspoon ground cumin	coriander
½ teaspoon ground nutmeg	1 tablespoon sesame oil
½ teaspoon dried thyme	1 pound (454 g) pork tenderloin
½ teaspoon ground	2 tablespoons apple cider vinegar
	1 cup water

1. In the mixing bowl, mix up ground cumin, ground nutmeg, thyme, ground coriander, and apple cider vinegar.
2. Then rub the meat with the spice mixture.
3. Heat up sesame oil on Sauté mode for 2 minutes.
4. Put the pork tenderloin in the hot oil and cook it for 5 minutes from each side or until meat is light brown.
5. Add water.
6. Close and seal the lid. Cook the meat on Manual mode at High Pressure for 5 minutes.
7. When the time is finished, allow the natural pressure release for 15 minutes.

Per Serving
calories: 196 | fat: 7g | protein: 30g | carbs: 1g
net carbs: 1g | fiber: 0g

Pork Chops with Blue Cheese

Prep time: 5 minutes | Cook time: 20 minutes
Serves 2

2 pork chops	1 teaspoon coconut oil
2 ounces (57 g) blue cheese, crumbled	1 teaspoon lemon juice
	¼ cup heavy cream

1. Heat up coconut oil in the Instant Pot on Sauté mode.
2. Then put the pork chops in the Instant Pot and cook them on Sauté mode for 5 minutes from each side.
3. Then add lemon juice and crumbled cheese.
4. Stir the ingredients well.
5. Add heavy cream and close the lid.
6. Cook the pork chops on Sauté mode for 10 minutes more.

Per Serving
calories: 300 | fat: 26g | protein: 15g | carbs: 1g
net carbs: 1g | fiber: 0g

Pork and Sauerkraut Mix

Prep time: 10 minutes | Cook time: 15 minutes
Serves 4

4 pork chops, chopped
½ teaspoon cayenne pepper
½ teaspoon ground coriander

1 tablespoon coconut oil
1 tablespoon avocado oil
1 cup sauerkraut

1. Melt the coconut oil on Sauté mode.
2. Add cayenne pepper, ground coriander, and chopped pork chops.
3. Cook the meat on Sauté mode for 7 minutes from each side.
4. Then transfer the cooked meat in the bowl, add sauerkraut and mix up well.

Per Serving
calories: 297 | fat: 24g | protein: 20g | carbs: 2g
net carbs: 1g | fiber: 1g

Pork Chops in Mushroom Gravy

Prep time: 5 minutes | Cook time: 15 minutes
Serves 4

4 (5-ounce / 142-g) pork chops
1 teaspoon salt
½ teaspoon pepper
2 tablespoons avocado oil
1 cup chopped button mushrooms
½ medium onion, sliced

1 clove garlic, minced
1 cup chicken broth
¼ cup heavy cream
4 tablespoons butter
¼ teaspoon xanthan gum
1 tablespoon chopped fresh parsley

1. Sprinkle pork chops with salt and pepper. Place avocado oil and mushrooms in Instant Pot and press the Sauté button. Sauté 3 to 5 minutes until mushrooms begin to soften. Add onions and pork chops. Sauté additional 3 minutes until pork chops reach a golden brown.
2. Add garlic and broth to Instant Pot. Click lid closed. Press the Manual button and adjust time for 15 minutes. When timer beeps, allow a 10-minute natural release. Quick-release the remaining pressure.
3. Remove lid and place pork chops on plate. Press the Sauté button and add heavy cream, butter, and xanthan gum. Reduce for 5 to 10 minutes or until sauce begins to thicken. Add pork chops back into pot. Serve warm topped with mushroom sauce and parsley.

Per Serving
calories: 516 | fat: 40g | protein: 32g | carbs: 3g
net carbs: 2g | fiber: 1g

Ranch Pork Chops

Prep time: 15 minutes | Cook time: 15 minutes
Serves 4

1 teaspoon ranch seasonings
1 tablespoon olive oil

4 pork chops
1 cup water

1. Rub the pork chops with ranch seasonings and olive oil.
2. Then place the meat in the Instant Pot, add water. Close and seal the lid.
3. Cook the pork chops on Manual mode at High Pressure for 15 minutes.
4. Naturally release the pressure and transfer the meat on the plates.

Per Serving
calories: 289 | fat: 23g | protein: 18g | carbs: g
net carbs: 18g | fiber: 0g

Basil-Lime Carnitas

Prep time: 5 minutes | Cook time: 30 minutes
Serves 4

2 tablespoons avocado oil
1 pound (454 g) pork shoulder, chopped
½ jalapeño, finely chopped
½ teaspoon oregano, dried
½ teaspoon chili

powder
½ teaspoon cumin, ground
½ teaspoon basil, dried
½ teaspoon kosher salt
½ teaspoon freshly ground black pepper
½ teaspoon lime juice

1. Set the Instant Pot to Sauté and heat the oil. Brown pork shoulder (takes about 10 minutes).
2. Pour in 1 cup of filtered water, then add the jalapeño, oregano, chili powder, cumin, basil, salt, and black pepper to the Instant Pot.
3. Close the lid, set the pressure release to Sealing, and hit Cancel to stop the current program. Select Manual, set the Instant Pot to 30 minutes on High Pressure, and let cook.
4. Once cooked, let the pressure naturally disperse from the Instant Pot for about 10 minutes, then carefully switch the pressure release to Venting.
5. Open the Instant Pot, stir in lime juice, serve, and enjoy!

Per Serving
calories: 344 | fat: 25g | protein: 27g | carbs: 1g
net carbs: 0g | fiber: 1g

Chipotle Pork Chops

Prep time: 7 minutes | Cook time: 15 minutes
Serves 4

2 tablespoons coconut oil
3 chipotle chilies
2 tablespoons adobo sauce
2 teaspoons cumin
1 teaspoon dried thyme
1 teaspoon salt
4 (5-ounce / 142-g)

boneless pork chops
½ medium onion, chopped
2 bay leaves
1 cup chicken broth
½ (7-ounce / 198-g) can fire-roasted diced tomatoes
⅓ cup chopped cilantro

1. Press the Sauté button and add coconut oil to Instant Pot. While it heats, add chilies, adobo sauce, cumin, thyme, and salt to food processor. Pulse to make paste. Rub paste into pork chops. Place in Instant Pot and sear each side 5 minutes or until browned.
2. Press the Cancel button and add onion, bay leaves, broth, tomatoes, and cilantro to Instant Pot. Click lid closed. Press the Manual button and adjust time for 15 minutes. When timer beeps, allow a 10-minute natural release, then quick-release the remaining pressure. Serve warm with additional cilantro as garnish if desired.

Per Serving
calories: 375 | fat: 24g | protein: 31g | carbs: 5g
net carbs: 3g | fiber: 2g

Sweet Pork Tenderloin

Prep time: 15 minutes | Cook time: 30 minutes
Serves 2

9 ounces (255 g) pork tenderloin
1 teaspoon erythritol
½ teaspoon dried dill
½ teaspoon white

pepper
1 garlic clove, minced
3 tablespoons butter
¼ cup water

1. Rub the pork tenderloin with erythritol, dried dill, white pepper, and minced garlic.
2. Then melt the butter in the Instant Pot on Sauté mode.
3. Add pork tenderloin and cook it for 8 minutes from each side (use Sauté mode).
4. Then add water and close the lid.
5. Cook the meat on Sauté mode for 10 minutes.
6. Cool the cooked tenderloin for 10 to 15 minutes and slice.

Per Serving
calories: 339 | fat: 22g | protein: 34g | carbs: 4g
net carbs: 4g | fiber: 0g

Pork Chops

Prep time: 5 minutes | Cook time: 30 minutes
Serves 4 to 6

2 tablespoons coconut oil
4 pork chops, boneless
1 tablespoon grass-fed butter
1 teaspoon crushed red pepper
½ teaspoon parsley, dried
½ teaspoon garlic

powder
½ teaspoon chili powder
½ teaspoon basil, dried
½ teaspoon kosher salt
½ teaspoon freshly ground black pepper
¼ cup hot sauce (or other preferred sauce)

1. Set the Instant Pot to Sauté and melt the oil. Brown the sides of the pork chops; this should take about 5 minutes per side.
2. Add 1 cup of filtered water, butter, red pepper, parsley, garlic powder, chili powder, basil, salt, and black pepper to the Instant Pot. Close the lid, set the pressure release to Sealing, and hit Cancel to stop the current program. Select Manual, set the Instant Pot to 30 minutes on High Pressure, and let cook.
3. Once cooked, let the pressure naturally disperse from the Instant Pot for about 10 minutes, then carefully switch the pressure release to Venting. Remove the pork chops, and rub with the hot sauce (or other preferred sauce). Serve, and enjoy!

Per Serving
calories: 232 | fat: 20g | protein: 12g | carbs: 1g
net carbs: 1g | fiber: 0g

Wrapped Pork Cubes

Prep time: 15 minutes | Cook time: 20 minutes
Serves 4

6 ounces (170 g) bacon, sliced
10 ounces (283 g) pork tenderloin, cubed

½ teaspoon white pepper
3 tablespoons butter
¾ cup chicken stock

1. Melt the butter on Sauté mode.
2. Meanwhile, wrap the pork tenderloin cubes in the sliced bacon and sprinkle with white pepper.
3. Put the wrapped pork tenderloin in the melted butter and cook them for 3 minutes from each side.
4. Add chicken stock and close the lid.
5. Cook the pork cubes on Sauté mode for 14 minutes or until meat is tender.

Per Serving
calories: 410 | fat: 29g | protein: 35g | carbs: 1g
net carbs: 1g | fiber: 0g

Elegant Pork Shank with Cauliflower

Prep time: 15 minutes | Cook time: 55 minutes
Serves 6

2 pounds (907 g) pork shank, cubed
Sea salt, to taste
2 teaspoons coconut oil
1 cup chicken stock
1 leek, sliced
4 cloves garlic, sliced
½ teaspoon cumin powder
½ teaspoon porcini

powder
½ teaspoon oregano
½ teaspoon basil
4 cups cauliflower, broken into small florets
½ teaspoon salt
¼ teaspoon ground black pepper
¼ teaspoon red pepper flakes, crushed

1. Generously season the pork shank with sea salt.
2. Press the Sauté button to heat up the Instant Pot. Now, melt the coconut oil. Once hot, cook pork shank until delicately browned on all sides.
3. Add chicken stock, leeks, garlic, cumin powder, porcini powder, oregano, and basil to the Instant Pot.
4. Secure the lid. Choose the Meat/Stew setting and cook for 50 minutes under High Pressure. Once cooking is complete, use a natural pressure release; carefully remove the lid. Reserve the cooked meat.
5. Add the remaining ingredients to the Instant Pot.
6. Secure the lid. Choose the Manual setting and cook for 3 minutes under Low Pressure. Once cooking is complete, use a natural pressure release; carefully remove the lid.
7. Serve the cooked cauliflower with reserved pork shank. Bon appétit!

Per Serving
calories: 342 | fat: 20g | protein: 33g | carbs: 7g
net carbs: 5g | fiber: 2g

Cilantro Pork Shoulder

Prep time: 10 minutes | Cook time: 85 minutes
Serves 4

1 pound (454 g) pork shoulder, boneless
¼ cup fresh cilantro, chopped
1 cup water

1 teaspoon salt
1 teaspoon coconut oil
½ teaspoon mustard seeds

1. Pour water in the Instant Pot.
2. Add pork shoulder, fresh cilantro, salt, coconut oil, and mustard seeds.
3. Close and seal the lid. Cook the meat on Manual mode at High Pressure for 85 minutes.

4. Then make a quick pressure release and open the lid.
5. The cooked meat has to be served with the remaining liquid from the Instant Pot.

Per Serving
calories: 343 | fat: 25g | protein: 26g | carbs: 0g
net carbs: 0g | fiber: 0g

Crispy Bacon Bomb

Prep time: 10 minutes | Cook time: 20 minutes
Serves 4

1 pound (454 g) no-sugar-added bacon
¼ cup full-fat Cheddar cheese, shredded
6 slices full-fat provolone cheese
¼ cup full-fat Monterey Jack cheese, shredded

½ cup spinach, chopped
½ teaspoon chili powder
½ teaspoon cayenne pepper, ground
½ teaspoon freshly ground black pepper

1. On a large cookie sheet covered with aluminum foil, tightly weave the bacon, forming a bottom layer. Go over and then under, making it as tight as possible. If you are having trouble visualizing how to proceed, form a T shape with two pieces of bacon, and then continue to interlink.
2. Add the Cheddar, provolone, and Monterey Jack on top, followed by the spinach. Sprinkle on the chili powder, cayenne pepper, and black pepper. Push down gently on the top of the food, and then roll it into a ball. You want this to be done as tightly as possible. Transfer this ball into a well-greased, Instant Pot-friendly dish.
3. Pour 1 cup of filtered water into the inner pot of the Instant Pot, then insert the trivet. Using a sling if desired, place the dish on top of the trivet.
4. Close the lid, set the pressure release to Sealing, and select Manual. Set the Instant Pot to 20 minutes on High Pressure and let cook. While cooking, preheat the oven to 350°F (180°C), if you'd like to have a crispier dish.
5. Once cooked, let the pressure naturally disperse from the Instant Pot for about 10 minutes, then carefully switch the pressure release to Venting.
6. Open the lid and remove the food.
7. If desired, finish the bomb in the oven by returning it to the cookie sheet and cooking for 5 to 10 minutes (or until desired crispness is reached). Serve and enjoy!

Per Serving
calories: 395 | fat: 30g | protein: 27g | carbs: 2g
net carbs: 2g | fiber: 0g

Sausages and Kale

Prep time: 5 minutes | Cook time: 4 minutes
Serves 4

4 smoked sausages   ¼ cup water
6 cups chopped kale

1. Place the sausages in the inner cooking pot of the Instant Pot. Top with the kale and pour in the water.
2. Lock the lid into place. Select Manual and adjust the pressure to High. Cook for 4 minutes. When the cooking is complete, let the pressure release naturally for 5 minutes, then quick-release any remaining pressure. Unlock the lid.
3. Eat and enjoy!

Per Serving
calories: 259 | fat: 6g | protein: 11g | carbs: 11g
net carbs: 9g | fiber: 2g

Sausage Fajita Bowls

Prep time: 5 minutes | Cook time: 8 minutes
Serves 6

1 tablespoon unsalted butter (or coconut oil for dairy-free)
½ cup sliced onions
½ cup sliced orange bell peppers
½ cup sliced yellow bell peppers
2 cloves garlic, minced
6 (5-inch-long) smoked sausages, cut into ¼-inch slices
½ cup salsa, plus more for serving
1 teaspoon fine sea salt
½ teaspoon ground cumin
½ teaspoon smoked paprika
½ cup shredded sharp Cheddar cheese, for garnish (optional; omit for dairy-free)
Finely chopped fresh cilantro leaves, for garnish
Sour cream, for serving (optional; omit for dairy-free)

1. Place the butter in a 3-quart or larger Instant Pot and press Sauté. Once melted, add the onions, bell peppers, and garlic. Cook for 5 minutes, or until the onions and peppers are soft. Press Cancel to stop the Sauté. Add the sausage, salsa, salt, cumin, and paprika and stir to combine.
2. Seal the lid, press Manual, and set the timer for 3 minutes. Once finished, turn the valve to venting for a quick release.
3. Remove the lid and stir well. Place the sausage mixture in bowls, top with the shredded cheese (if using) and additional salsa, and garnish with cilantro. Serve with sour cream on the side, if desired.

Per Serving
calories: 204 | fat: 16g | protein: 9g | carbs: 4g
net carbs: 3g | fiber: 1g

Pork Saag

Prep time: 10 minutes | Cook time: 20 minutes
Serves 4

Marinade:
⅓ cup half-and-half, plus more as needed
1 teaspoon minced garlic
1 teaspoon minced fresh ginger
½ teaspoon ground turmeric
½ teaspoon cayenne
2 teaspoons garam masala
1 teaspoon salt
1 pound (454 g) pork shoulder, cut into bite-size cubes

For Finishing the Pork Saag:
1 tablespoon ghee
1 tablespoon tomato paste
¾ cup water
5 ounces (142 g) baby spinach, chopped
Salt, for seasoning

Marinate the Pork
1. In a large bowl, mix the half-and-half, garlic, ginger, turmeric, cayenne, garam masala, and salt. Add the pork and stir to coat.
2. Marinate the pork for at least 30 minutes or up to 8 hours. If you marinate for more than 30 minutes, cover and refrigerate the bowl until ready for use.

Finish the Pork Saag
1. Preheat the Instant Pot by selecting Sauté and adjusting to high heat. When the inner cooking pot is hot, add the ghee and heat until it is shimmering. Add the pork along with the marinade, and the tomato paste. Cook for 5 to 10 minutes, or until the pork is lightly seared and the tomato paste has been well incorporated. Pour in the water.
2. Lock the lid into place. Select Manual and adjust the pressure to High. Cook for 10 minutes. When the cooking is complete, quick-release the pressure. Carefully remove the lid and add the spinach. Mix well to incorporate.
3. Lock the lid into place. Select Manual and adjust the pressure to High. Cook for 2 minutes. Allow the pressure to release naturally. Unlock and remove the lid.
4. Mix well and adjust the seasoning, adding more salt and half-and-half if desired.

Per Serving
calories: 335 | fat: 24g | protein: 24g | carbs: 7g
net carbs: 4g | fiber: 3g

Sweet 'n' Sour Pork

Prep time: 6 minutes | Cook time: 15 minutes
Serves 4

6 ounces (170 g) tomato paste
1½ cups beef or chicken broth
⅓ cup Swerve confectioners'-style sweetener or equivalent amount of liquid or powdered sweetener
¼ cup coconut vinegar
¾ tablespoon lime or lemon juice
¾ teaspoon fish sauce
½ teaspoon fine sea salt

salt
½ teaspoon garlic powder
⅛ teaspoon peeled and grated fresh ginger
1 pound (454 g) boneless pork shoulder roast
½ cup (½-inch chunks) green bell peppers
Butter lettuce leaves, for serving
Sliced green onions, for garnish

1. Place the tomato paste, broth, sweetener, vinegar, lime juice, fish sauce, salt, garlic powder, and ginger in a 6-quart Instant Pot. Stir well. Add the pork roast and bell peppers and stir to coat in the sauce.
2. Seal the lid, press Manual, and set the timer for 15 minutes. Once finished, turn the valve to venting for a quick release.
3. Remove the lid and shred the meat with two forks. Serve the shredded pork wrapped in lettuce leaves. Garnish with sliced green onions.

Per Serving
calories: 294 | fat: 14g | protein: 27g | carbs: 11g
net carbs: 8g | fiber: 3g

Lime Pulled Pork

Prep time: 5 minutes | Cook time: 30 minutes
Serves 4

1 tablespoon chili adobo sauce
1 tablespoon chili powder
2 teaspoons salt
1 teaspoon garlic powder
1 teaspoon cumin
½ teaspoon pepper

1 (2½ to 3 pounds / 1.1 to 1.4 kg) cubed pork butt
1 tablespoon coconut oil
2 cups beef broth
1 lime, cut into wedges
¼ cup chopped cilantro

1. In a small bowl, mix adobo sauce, chili powder, salt, garlic powder, cumin, and pepper.
2. Press the Sauté button on Instant Pot and add coconut oil to pot. Rub spice mixture onto cubed pork butt. Place pork into pot and sear for 3 to 5 minutes per side. Add broth.

3. Press the Cancel button. Lock Lid. Press the Manual button and adjust time to 30 minutes.
4. When timer beeps, let pressure naturally release until the float valve drops, and unlock lid.
5. Shred pork with fork. Pork should easily fall apart. For extra-crispy pork, place single layer in skillet on stove over medium heat. Cook for 10 to 15 minutes or until water has cooked out and pork becomes brown and crisp. Serve warm with fresh lime wedges and cilantro garnish.

Per Serving
calories: 570 | fat: 36g | protein: 55g | carbs: 3g
net carbs: 2g | fiber: 1g

Carnitas for Every Day

Prep time: 10 minutes | Cook time: 30 minutes
Serves 8

1 (3-pound / 1.4-kg) skinless picnic shoulder pork, cut to fit the pot
1 teaspoon black pepper
1½ teaspoons dry adobo seasoning
½ teaspoon garlic powder
1 tablespoon cumin, divided
6 cloves garlic, crushed
½ cup bone broth

½ cup tomato sauce
1 small onion, chopped
2 jalapeños, sliced
½ tablespoon dried oregano
2 dried whole bay leaves
3 limes, 2 juiced and 1 cut into 8 wedges, for garnish
¼ cup chopped fresh cilantro, reserve 2 tablespoons for garnish

1. Pat the pork dry and rub the sides with the black pepper, adobo seasoning, garlic powder and 2 teaspoons of cumin. Set aside.
2. Turn on the Instant Pot by pressing the Manual button and set the timer for 30 minutes on High Pressure.
3. Add the pork shoulder and the remaining ingredients, except for the lime wedges and 2 tablespoons of cilantro into the inner pot. Close the lid tightly and move the steam release handle to Sealing. When the timer ends, you will hear a beeping sound. Allow the Instant Pot to cool down naturally until the float valve drops down. Press Cancel and open the lid.
4. Remove the pork and pull the meat apart with a fork. Serve immediately with lime wedges and the remaining cilantro.

Per Serving
calories: 337 | fat: 24g | protein: 24g | carbs: 7g
net carbs: 6g | fiber: 1g

Cabbage Egg Roll

Prep time: 15 minutes | Cook time: 5 minutes
Serves 4

1 pound (454 g) 84% lean ground pork
2 tablespoons soy sauce
½ teaspoon salt
½ cup diced onion

1 clove garlic, minced
2 stalks green onion, sliced
8 cabbage leaves
1 cup water

1. Press the Sauté button and add ground pork, soy sauce, and salt to Instant Pot. Brown pork until no pink remains. Carefully drain grease.
2. Add diced onion and continue cooking until translucent, 2 to 4 minutes. Add garlic and cook for additional 30 seconds. Press the Cancel button.
3. Pour mixture into large bowl; set aside. Mix green onions into pork. Rinse pot and replace. Add water and trivet.
4. Take 2 to 3 tablespoons of pork mixture and spoon it into cabbage leaf in rectangle shape, off to one side of the leaf. Fold the short ends of the leaf toward the middle. Complete the roll by starting at the filled edge and rolling toward the empty side, as you would a burrito.
5. Place rolls onto trivet. Click lid closed. Press the Manual button and adjust time for 1 minute. When timer beeps, quick-release the steam. Serve warm.

Per Serving
calories: 257 | fat: 16g | protein: 22g | carbs: 5g
net carbs: 4g | fiber: 1g

Pot Sticker Bowls

Prep time: 5 minutes | Cook time: 9 minutes
Serves 6

4 cups finely shredded cabbage
1 pound (454 g) ground pork
½ cup finely chopped red bell peppers
½ cup sliced green onions (about 1 bunch), plus more for garnish
2 cloves garlic, minced
½ teaspoon peeled and grated fresh ginger
½ cup coconut aminos, or 2 tablespoons wheat-

free tamari
¼ cup chicken broth
2 tablespoons lime juice
2 teaspoons coconut vinegar or unseasoned rice vinegar
⅛ teaspoon red pepper flakes
2 large eggs, lightly beaten
Fine sea salt, to taste
Black sesame seeds, for garnish

1. Place all of the ingredients, except the eggs, salt, and sesame seeds, in a 6-quart Instant Pot. Stir well.
2. Seal the lid, press Manual, and set the timer for 7 minutes. Once finished, let the pressure release naturally.
3. Remove the lid and make a well in the center of the pork mixture. Pour the eggs into the well and press Sauté. Scramble the eggs for 2 minutes, or until set. Stir the eggs into the pork mixture until well combined. Press Cancel to stop the Sauté.
4. Taste and season with salt, if needed. Serve in bowls, garnished with more sliced green onions and black sesame seeds.

Per Serving
calories: 267 | fat: 19g | protein: 17g | carbs: 8g
net carbs: 4g | fiber: 4g

Braised Collard Greens with Ham Hocks

Prep time: 10 minutes | Cook time: 20 minutes
Serves 4

3 strips uncured bacon, chopped into 1-inch pieces
1 medium onion, diced
5 cloves garlic, crushed
2 pounds (907 g) collard greens, stems removed
2 pounds (907 g) smoked ham hock

1 teaspoon liquid smoke
1 tablespoon apple cider vinegar
2 dried whole bay leaves
Juice from 1 lemon and its zest
½ cup chopped fresh flat leaf parsley, reserve 1 tablespoon for garnish

1. Turn on the Instant Pot by pressing Sauté and set to More. Insert the inner pot and wait until the panel says Hot. Add the bacon to the inner pot of the Instant Pot. Sauté for 5 minutes or until the bacon browns around the edges. Add the onion and garlic and sauté for 2 minutes until the onion is soft. Add the remaining ingredients except for the 1 tablespoon of parsley.
2. Close the lid tightly and move the steam release handle to Sealing.
3. Press Cancel, then the Manual button and set the timer for 20 minutes on High Pressure. When the timer ends, you will hear a beeping sound. Allow the Instant Pot to cool down naturally until the float valve drops down. Press Cancel and open the lid. Serve immediately with the remaining parsley as a garnish.

Per Serving
calories: 511 | fat: 26g | protein: 51g | carbs: 12g
net carbs: 6g | fiber: 6g

Smothered Pork Chops

Prep time: 10 minutes | Cook time: 33 minutes
Serves 4

½ teaspoon garlic powder
½ teaspoon onion powder
1 teaspoon paprika
1 teaspoon sea salt
½ teaspoon black pepper
4 (6-ounce / 170-g) boneless pork loin chops
2 strips of uncured bacon, finely chopped
1 tablespoon butter, more as needed
½ medium onion, sliced
12 ounces (340 g)
white mushrooms, sliced ¼-inch (6-mm) thick
½ cup white wine
½ cup full-fat heavy cream
1 teaspoon dried thyme
1 teaspoon dried tarragon
1 tablespoon Worcestershire sauce
1 tablespoon tapioca flour, more if needed
¼ cup fresh flat leaf parsley, chopped, reserve 1 tablespoon for garnish

1. In a small bowl, mix the garlic powder, onion powder, paprika, sea salt and black pepper. Sprinkle both sides of the pork chops with the garlic powder mixture and set aside.
2. Turn on the Instant Pot by pressing Sauté and set to More. Insert the inner pot and wait until the panel says Hot. Add the bacon and sauté for 3 minutes, then add the pork chops, two at a time, and brown both sides for 2 minutes per side. Add butter at this point if needed. Transfer the pork chops to a plate and set aside. Add the onion and mushrooms and sauté until the onion is soft. Add the white wine and stir and scrape the bottom for 1 minute. Place the pork chops on top of the onion and mushrooms.
3. Close the lid tightly and move the steam release handle to Sealing. Press Cancel, then the Manual button and set the timer for 20 minutes on High Pressure. When the timer ends, you will hear a beeping sound. Allow the Instant Pot to cool down naturally until the float valve drops down. Press Cancel and open the lid. Place the pork chops on plates to be served and let rest. Meanwhile, add the rest of the ingredients in the inner pot except 1 tablespoon of parsley and stir for 2 minutes or until it thickens. Add more tapioca flour if needed, depending on how much liquid was produced from the meat and vegetables from cooking. Top the pork chops with the mushroom gravy and garnish with parsley before serving.

Per Serving
calories: 343 | fat: 21g | protein: 23g | carbs: 12g
net carbs: 10g | fiber: 2g

Pork Carnitas

Prep time: 10 minutes | Cook time: 45 minutes
Serves 4

1 onion, sliced
4 garlic cloves, sliced
1 pound (454 g) pork shoulder, cut into cubes, visible fat removed
Juice of 1 lemon
¼ teaspoon ancho chili powder
¼ teaspoon chipotle chili powder
¼ teaspoon smoked paprika
½ teaspoon dried oregano
½ teaspoon roasted cumin powder
1 to 2 teaspoons salt
1 teaspoon freshly ground black pepper
½ cup water
1 to 2 tablespoons coconut oil
½ cup sour cream
½ avocado, diced

1. Place the onion and garlic in the inner cooking pot of the Instant Pot to help them release water when the meat is cooking.
2. In a large bowl, mix together the pork and lemon juice. Add the ancho chili powder, chipotle chili powder, paprika, oregano, cumin, salt, and pepper, and stir to combine.
3. Place the pork on top of the onions and garlic.
4. Pour the water into the bowl and swirl it around to get the last of the spices, then pour this onto the pork.
5. Lock the lid into place. Select Meat and adjust the pressure to High. Cook for 35 minutes. When the cooking is complete, let the pressure release naturally for 10 minutes, then quick-release any remaining pressure. Unlock the lid.
6. Remove the pork, leaving the liquid in the pot.
7. Switch the pot to Sauté and adjust the heat to high to reduce the sauce while you finish the next steps.
8. Place a cast iron skillet on the stove over medium-high heat. Once it is hot, add the oil.
9. Shred the pork, then place it in a single layer in the skillet. Let the meat brown, undisturbed, for 3 to 4 minutes.
10. When the meat is browned on the bottom, stir it and continue cooking until it's crisp in parts.
11. Once it's good and crisp, add in the sauce, a little at a time, from the pot. The skillet should be hot enough that most of it just evaporates, leaving behind the flavor. (I use almost all of my broth, small portions at a time, to flavor the meat.)
12. Serve with the sour cream and diced avocado.

Per Serving
calories: 332 | fat: 23g | protein: 26g | carbs: 5g
net carbs: 2g | fiber: 3g

Chaptr 10 Beef and Lamb

Mini BBQ Meatloaf

Prep time: 5 minutes | Cook time: 25 minutes
Serves 4

1 pound (454 g) 85%
lean ground beef
½ medium onion, diced
½ green pepper, diced
¼ cup almond flour
¼ cup shredded whole-
milk Mozzarella cheese

1 egg
1 teaspoon salt
¼ teaspoon pepper
1 teaspoon garlic
powder
¼ cup barbecue sauce

1. Mix all ingredients except barbecue sauce in
   large mixing bowl. Form into two small loaves
   and place into two (4-inch) loaf pans. Pour
   barbecue sauce on top of pans and cover with
   foil.
2. Pour water into Instant Pot and place trivet in
   bottom. Place one or both meatloaf pans on
   trivet, depending on the size of your Instant
   Pot, and click lid closed. Press the Manual
   button and adjust time to 25 minutes. When
   timer beeps, quick-release pressure.

Per Serving
calories: 340 | fat: 5g | protein: 26g | carbs: 6g
net carbs: 4g | fiber: 2g

BBQ Short Ribs

Prep time: 10 minutes | Cook time: 35 minutes
Serves 8

1 cup tomato sauce
⅓ cup Swerve
confectioners'-style
sweetener or equivalent
amount of liquid or
powdered sweetener
¼ cup beef broth

¼ cup apple cider
vinegar
2 teaspoons liquid
smoke
8 beef short ribs (about
4 pounds / 1.8 kg)

1. Place the tomato sauce, sweetener, broth,
   vinegar, and liquid smoke in a 6-quart Instant
   Pot and stir until smooth. Add the short ribs.
2. Seal the lid, press Manual, and set the
   timer for 35 minutes. Once finished, let the
   pressure release naturally.
3. Remove the ribs from the pot. If you prefer
   a thicker sauce, press Sauté and cook the
   sauce for 5 to 15 minutes, until thickened to
   your liking. Press Cancel to stop the Sauté.
4. To serve, place the short ribs on plates and
   spoon the sauce over the ribs.

Per Serving
calories: 569 | fat: 50g | protein: 26g | carbs: 2g
net carbs: 2g | fiber: 0g

Rosemary Lamb Shanks

Prep time: 15 minutes | Cook time: 35 minutes
Serves 2

2 lamb shanks
1 rosemary spring
1 teaspoon coconut
flour
¼ teaspoon onion
powder

¼ teaspoon chili
powder
¾ teaspoon ground
ginger
½ cup beef broth
½ teaspoon avocado oil

1. Put all ingredients in the Instant Pot. Stir to
   mix well.
2. Close the lid. Select Manual mode and
   set cooking time for 35 minutes on High
   Pressure.
3. When timer beeps, use a natural pressure
   release for 15 minutes, then release any
   remaining pressure. Open the lid.
4. Discard the rosemary sprig and serve warm.

Per Serving
calories: 179 | fat: 7g | protein: 25g | carbs: 2g
net carbs: 1g | fiber: 1g

Avocado-Cilantro Tacos

Prep time: 5 minutes | Cook time: 15 minutes
Serves 4

2 tablespoons coconut
oil
1 pound (454 g) grass-
fed beef, ground
1 teaspoon cilantro,
dried
½ teaspoon chili

powder
1 avocado, mashed
2 cups full-fat Cheddar
cheese, shredded
½ cup sour cream, at
room temperature
1 cup lettuce, shredded

1. Set the Instant Pot to Sauté, and melt the oil
   gently. Add the beef, cilantro, chili powder,
   and avocado. Stir in ½ cup of filtered water.
   Close the lid, set the pressure release to
   Sealing, and select Manual. Set the Instant
   Pot to 15 minutes on High Pressure and let
   cook.
2. Once cooked, let the pressure naturally
   disperse from the Instant Pot for about 10
   minutes, then carefully switch the pressure
   release to Venting.
3. Open the lid and remove the food. Serve
   inside your favorite keto-friendly tacos shells,
   and top with the cheese, sour cream, and
   lettuce.

Per Serving
calories: 664 | fat: 48g | protein: 50g | carbs: 7g
net carbs: 3g | fiber: 4g

Taco Stuffed Peppers

**Prep time: 5 minutes | Cook time: 10 minutes
Serves 6**

1 pound (454 g) 85%
lean ground beef
¼ cup diced tomatoes
and green chilies
¼ cup diced onion
1 teaspoon salt
1 teaspoon chili powder
1 teaspoon cumin

1 cup water
6 green bell peppers
cut in half lengthwise,
seeds removed
Toppings such as salsa,
sour cream, chopped
cilantro, chopped red
onion, and so on

1. Press the Sauté button and place ground beef
   into Instant Pot. Break into small pieces and
   cook until beef is no longer pink. Carefully
   drain grease if there is excess fat.
2. Replace pot and add tomatoes and chilies,
   onion, salt, chili powder, and cumin. Mix
   ingredients until fully combined. Spoon
   mixture into pepper halves and rinse pot with
   water.
3. Replace pot and add water. Place steamer
   basket into pot and carefully add pepper
   halves. Click lid closed. Press the Manual
   button and adjust timer for 4 minutes.
4. When timer beeps, quick-release the pressure
   and add favorite toppings to serve.

Per Serving
calories: 139 | fat: 6g | protein: 13g | carbs: 7g
net carbs: 5g | fiber: 2g

Beef Stew with Almond Butter

**Prep time: 10 minutes | Cook time: 60 minutes
Serves 3**

10 ounces (283 g) beef
chuck roast, chopped
½ cup almond butter
½ teaspoon cayenne

pepper
½ teaspoon salt
1 teaspoon dried basil
1 cup water

1. Place the almond butter in the Instant Pot
   and start to preheat it on the Sauté mode.
2. Meanwhile, mix up together the cayenne
   pepper, salt, and dried basil.
3. Sprinkle the beef with the spices and transfer
   the meat in the melted almond butter.
4. Close the Instant Pot lid and lock it.
5. Set the Manual mode and put a timer on 60
   minutes (Low Pressure).

Per Serving
calories: 360 | fat: 28g | protein: 25g | carbs: 1g
net carbs: 1g | fiber: 0g

Classic Beef Meatballs

**Prep time: 5 minutes | Cook time: 16 minutes
Serves 4**

2 tablespoons avocado
oil
2 tablespoons coconut
oil
1 pound (454 g) grass-
fed beef, ground
½ teaspoon cayenne
pepper, ground
½ teaspoon crushed

red pepper
½ teaspoon basil, dried
½ teaspoon kosher salt
½ teaspoon freshly
ground black pepper
2 (14-ounce / 397-
g) cans sugar-free or
low-sugar fire roasted
tomatoes

1. Set the Instant Pot to Sauté and heat the
   avocado oil. In a large bowl, mix together
   the coconut oil, beef, cayenne pepper, red
   pepper, basil, salt, and black pepper. Form
   the mixture into 1½ inch meatballs and place
   them into the Instant Pot. Then, pour the
   tomatoes evenly over the meatballs.
2. Close the lid, set the pressure release to
   Sealing, and hit Cancel to stop the current
   program. Select Manual, set the Instant Pot
   to 16 minutes on High Pressure, and let cook.
3. Once cooked, carefully switch the pressure
   release to Venting. Open the Instant Pot,
   serve by sprinkling your favorite shredded
   cheese over the meatballs (if desired), and
   enjoy!

Per Serving
calories: 347 | fat: 23g | protein: 26g | carbs: 6g
net carbs: 4g | fiber: 2g

Smoky BBQ Brisket

**Prep time: 5 minutes | Cook time: 70 minutes
Serves 12**

4 pounds (1.8 kg)
brisket
2 teaspoons celery salt
1½ teaspoons garlic
powder

½ teaspoon ground
black pepper
½ cup tomato sauce
½ cup liquid smoke

1. Place all of the ingredients in a 6-quart
   Instant Pot. Seal the lid, press Manual, and
   set the timer for 70 minutes. Once finished,
   let the pressure release naturally.
2. Place the brisket on a cutting board. Cut
   the meat across the grain into ¼-inch-thick
   slices.

Per Serving
calories: 522 | fat: 40g | protein: 38g | carbs: 1g
net carbs: 1g | fiber: 0g

Rosemary Lamb Stew

Prep time: 5 minutes | Cook time: 50 minutes
Serves 3

½ cup coconut milk	coriander
1 teaspoon butter	13 ounces (369 g) lamb
½ teaspoon dried	shoulder, chopped
rosemary	1 teaspoon ground
¼ teaspoon salt	anise
½ teaspoon ground	¾ cup water

1. Slice the mushrooms and place them in the Instant Pot.
2. Add all remaining ingredients. Close and seal the lid.
3. Set Manual mode for 45 minutes.
4. When the time is over, make natural pressure release for 10 minutes.

Per Serving
calories: 332 | fat: 20g | protein: 35g | carbs: 3g
net carbs: 2g | fiber: 1g

Spicy Brisket

Prep time: 5 minutes | Cook time: 110 minutes
Serves 6

3 teaspoons salt	1 tablespoon avocado
2 teaspoons pepper	oil
1 teaspoon garlic	1 cup beef broth
powder	½ cup pickled jalapeño
1 teaspoon dried thyme	juice
½ teaspoon dried	½ cup pickled jalapeños
rosemary	½ medium onion,
1 (4 to 5-pound / 1.8 to	chopped
2.3-kg) beef brisket	

1. In a small bowl combine salt, pepper, garlic powder, thyme, and rosemary. Sprinkle over brisket; set aside.
2. Press the Sauté button and add avocado oil to Instant Pot. Sear each side of brisket for 5 minutes.
3. Add beef broth, jalapeño juice, jalapeños, and onions to Instant Pot. Press the Cancel button and click to close lid.
4. Press the Manual button and adjust time to 100 minutes. When timer beeps, allow pot to naturally release, about 30 to 40 minutes. Don't do a quick release; it will result in tougher meat.
5. Remove brisket, slice, and pour all the strained broth over meat for additional flavor.

Per Serving
calories: 1001 | fat: 68g | protein: 62g | carbs: 9g
net carbs: 8g | fiber: 1g

Sloppy Joes

Prep time: 10 minutes | Cook time: 10 minutes
Serves 4

1 pound (454 g) 85%	½ teaspoon yellow
lean ground beef	mustard
½ green pepper, diced	½ cup beef broth
½ medium onion, diced	1 teaspoon salt
3 tablespoons tomato	½ teaspoon garlic
paste	powder
1 tablespoon erythritol	⅛ teaspoon pepper

1. Press the Sauté button and brown ground beef in Instant Pot. When no pink remains, add in remaining ingredients.
2. Stir frequently and reduce liquid until desired consistency. Serve warm.

Per Serving
calories: 263 | fat: 15g | protein: 22g | carbs: 7g
net carbs: 3g | fiber: 4g

Italian Meatballs

Prep time: 10 minutes | Cook time: 10 minutes
Serves 4

1½ pounds (680 g)	1 large egg, beaten
ground beef	1 tablespoon coconut
3½ cups marinara	flour, or 3 tablespoons
sauce, divided	powdered Parmesan
¼ cup chopped fresh	cheese
Italian parsley	1¼ teaspoons Italian
¼ cup chopped onions	seasoning
2 cloves garlic, minced	1 teaspoon fine sea salt

For Garnish:
Shredded Mozzarella cheese (omit for dairy-free)
Fresh basil and/or oregano leaves

1. Put the ground beef, ¼ cup of the marinara, the parsley, onions, garlic, egg, coconut flour, Italian seasoning, and salt in a large bowl and thoroughly combine using your hands. Shape the meat mixture into 16 balls about 1¼ inches in diameter.
2. Place the meatballs in a 6-quart Instant Pot, leaving a little space between them. Pour the remaining marinara around the meatballs.
3. Seal the lid, press Manual, and set the timer for 10 minutes. Once finished, let the pressure release naturally.
4. Serve the sauce and meatballs topped with shredded Mozzarella, if using, and fresh herbs.

Per Serving
calories: 583 | fat: 45g | protein: 33g | carbs: 10g
net carbs: 7g | fiber: 3g

Swedish Meatballs

Prep time: 5 minutes | Cook time: 10 minutes
Serves 12

Meatballs:

1½ pounds (680 g) ground beef
¼ pound (113 g) bulk pork sausage
1 large egg
¼ cup tomato sauce
¼ cup minced onions

1 tablespoon mustard powder
1 clove garlic, minced
2 teaspoons fine sea salt
1 teaspoon ground black pepper

Sauce:

1 cup beef broth
1 (8-ounce / 227-g) package cream cheese (1 cup), softened

⅛ teaspoon ground nutmeg
Zucchini noodles, for serving

1. Make the meatballs: Place all of the meatball ingredients in a large bowl and mix well with your hands. Shape the meat mixture into 1½-inch balls.
2. Put the meatballs in an 8-quart Instant Pot, leaving a little space around each meatball.
3. Make the sauce: Place the broth, cream cheese, and nutmeg in a medium-sized bowl and whisk to combine. Pour the sauce around the meatballs in the pot.
4. Seal the lid, press Manual, and set the timer for 10 minutes. Once finished, let the pressure release naturally.
5. Serve the meatballs with the sauce over zucchini noodles.

Per Serving

calories: 249 | fat: 20g | protein: 13g | carbs: 1g net carbs: 1g | fiber: 0g

Coconut Milk Beef Sirloin

Prep time: 10 minutes | Cook time: 15 minutes
Serves 2

1 cup water
¼ cup coconut milk
14 ounces (397 g) beef

sirloin, chopped
1 teaspoon dried oregano

1. Put all ingredients in the Instant Pot. Close and seal the lid.
2. Cook the meal on Manual mode at High Pressure for 15 minutes.
3. Use the quick pressure release.

Per Serving

calories: 440 | fat: 19g | protein: 61g | carbs: 2g net carbs: 1g | fiber: 1g

Mocha Pot Roast

Prep time: 6 minutes | Cook time: 30 minutes
Serves 4

2 tablespoons finely ground decaf coffee
2 tablespoons unsweetened cocoa powder
1 tablespoon smoked paprika
2 teaspoons fine sea salt

2 pounds (907 g) boneless beef chuck roast, cut into 1½- to 2-inch cubes
2 cups beef broth
1 cup chopped onions
3 tablespoons coconut vinegar or apple cider vinegar

1. Place the coffee, cocoa powder, paprika, and salt in a small bowl and stir to combine well. Add the beef cubes in batches and rub the seasoning mixture onto the meat with your hands.
2. Place the seasoned beef in a 6-quart Instant Pot. Add the broth, onions, and vinegar. Seal the lid, press Manual, and set the timer for 30 minutes. Once finished, turn the valve to venting for a quick release.
3. Remove the lid and shred the meat with two forks. Serve.

Per Serving

calories: 698 | fat: 56g | protein: 41g | carbs: 6g net carbs: 4g | fiber: 2g

Chili Beef Sticks

Prep time: 15 minutes | Cook time: 10 minutes
Serves 2

¼ teaspoon ground coriander
½ teaspoon salt
½ teaspoon chili powder

6 ounces (170 g) ground beef
1 tablespoon avocado oil

1. In the mixing bowl, mix up ground coriander, salt, chili powder, and ground beef.
2. Then brush the Instant Pot bowl with avocado oil and heat up on Sauté mode.
3. Meanwhile, make the small beef sticks.
4. Put them in the Instant Pot and cook on Sauté mode for 4 minutes from each side or until the beef sticks are light crunchy.
5. Dry the cooked meat sticks with the help of the paper towel.

Per Serving

calories: 169 | fat: 6g | protein: 26g | carbs: 1g net carbs: 1g | fiber: 0g

Cumin Chili

Prep time: 5 minutes | Cook time: 15 minutes
Serves 2

13 ounces (369 g) ground beef
1 tablespoon cumin seeds
½ teaspoon salt
1 tablespoon tomato paste
½ teaspoon garlic powder
1 cup water

1. Preheat the Instant Pot bowl on the Sauté mode until it is displayed "Hot".
2. Then place the ground beef there.
3. Sprinkle it with the cumin seeds, garlic powder, and salt.
4. Stir gently and sauté for 4 minutes.
5. After this, add tomato paste.
6. Add water and close the lid.
7. Sauté the chili for 10 minutes.
8. When the chili is cooked, transfer it directly into the serving bowls.

Per Serving
calories: 362 | fat: 12g | protein: 57g | carbs: 3g
net carbs: 2g | fiber: 1g

Harissa Lamb Shoulder

Prep time: 30 minutes | Cook time: 40 minutes
Serves 4

1 tablespoon keto-friendly Harissa sauce
1 teaspoon dried thyme
½ teaspoon salt
1 pound (454 g) lamb
shoulder
2 tablespoons sesame oil
2 cups water

1. In a bowl, mix the Harissa, dried thyme, and salt.
2. Rub the lamb shoulder with the Harissa mixture and brush with sesame oil.
3. Heat the the Instant Pot on Sauté mode for 2 minutes and put the lamb shoulder inside.
4. Cook the lamb for 3 minutes on each side, then pour in the water.
5. Close the lid. Select Manual mode and set cooking time for 40 minutes on High Pressure.
6. When timer beeps, use a natural pressure release for 25 minutes, then release any remaining pressure. Open the lid.
7. Serve warm.

Per Serving
calories: 284 | fat: 15g | protein: 32g | carbs: 1g
net carbs: 1g | fiber: 0g

Creamed Beef Brisket

Prep time: 6 minutes | Cook time: 20 minutes
Serves 3

½ teaspoon salt
14 ounces (397 g) beef brisket, cut into the strips
½ cup water
½ cup heavy cream
½ teaspoon ground black pepper
1 tablespoon avocado oil

1. Preheat the Instant Pot on the Sauté mode.
2. When it is displayed "Hot", pour avocado oil inside and heat it up.
3. Add the meat.
4. Sprinkle the meat with the ground black pepper and salt.
5. Sauté it for 5 minutes. Stir it once per cooking time.
6. Add water and heavy cream.
7. Seal the lid and set the Manual mode.
8. Put the timer on 15 minutes at High Pressure.
9. Make a quick pressure release.

Per Serving
calories: 322 | fat: 16g | protein: 41g | carbs: 1g
net carbs: 1g | fiber: 0g

Ginger Beef Flank Steak

Prep time: 8 minutes | Cook time: 13 minutes
Serves 2

14 ounces (397 g) beef flank steak, sliced
1 tablespoon almond flour
½ teaspoon minced ginger
1 ounce (28 g) scallions, sliced
1 tablespoon coconut oil
¾ cup water

1. Toss the beef strips in the almond flour and shake well.
2. Toss the coconut oil in the Instant Pot bowl and set the Sauté mode.
3. When the coconut oil is melted, add the beef flank steak slices and cook them for 3 minutes. Stir them from time to time.
4. Add minced ginger.
5. Pour the water over the meat and lock the Instant Pot lid.
6. Press the Manual mode and set the timer for 10 minutes at High Pressure.
7. Make a quick pressure release.
8. Top the cooked beef with sliced scallions.

Per Serving
calories: 513 | fat: 26g | protein: 63g | carbs: 4g
net carbs: 2g | fiber: 2g

Marjoram Beef

Prep time: 10 minutes | Cook time: 40 minutes
Serves 2

10 ounces (283 g) beef ribs
¾ cup water
2 tablespoons coconut oil
1 teaspoon dried marjoram
½ teaspoon salt
½ cup chicken broth

1. Rub the beef ribs with the dried marjoram and salt.
2. Place the beef ribs in the Instant Pot.
3. Add chicken broth and water.
4. Then add coconut oil.
5. Close the lid and set the Meat/Stew mode. Cook the ribs for 40 minutes.

Per Serving
calories: 391 | fat: 23g | protein: 44g | carbs: 0g
net carbs: 0g | fiber: 0g

Mushroom and Swiss Mini Meatloaves

Prep time: 5 minutes | Cook time: 20 minutes
Serves 8

1½ pounds (680 g) ground beef
1½ cups sliced mushrooms, plus more for topping
½ cup diced onions
½ cup powdered Parmesan cheese
¼ cup tomato sauce
2 tablespoons prepared
yellow mustard
1 large egg
1 clove garlic, crushed to a paste
2 teaspoons paprika
½ teaspoon fine sea salt
6 ounces (170 g) Swiss cheese, cut into ¼-inch chunks (1½ cups)

Special Equipment:
3 mini loaf pans (6 by 3½ inches) or 6 (4-ounce / 113-g) ramekins

1. Place all of the ingredients, except the Swiss cheese, in a large bowl and mix well with your hands. Press into 3 mini loaf pans or six 4-ounce (113-g) ramekins.
2. Set a trivet in an 8-quart Instant Pot and pour in 1 cup of cold water. Place the mini loaves on the trivet. Seal the lid, press Manual, and set the timer for 20 minutes (or 15 minutes if using ramekins). Once finished, let the pressure release naturally.
3. Preheat the oven to broil.
4. Remove the lid and lift the mini meatloaves out of the pot. Sprinkle the Swiss cheese over the tops of the loaves and top with extra mushroom slices. Place the loaves under the broiler for a few minutes to melt the cheese.

5. Cut into slices and serve.

Per Serving
calories: 282 | fat: 21g | protein: 20g | carbs: 3g
net carbs: 3g | fiber: 0g

Beef Stroganoff

Prep time: 5 minutes | Cook time: 34 minutes
Serves 4

1 tablespoon coconut oil
2 cups sliced mushrooms
½ cup diced onions
Cloves squeezed from 1 head roasted garlic, or 2 cloves garlic, minced
1 pound (454 g) boneless beef roast, cut into 2-inch cubes
1½ teaspoons fine sea salt
½ teaspoon ground black pepper
4 ounces (113 g) cream cheese (½ cup), softened
1 cup beef broth
1 teaspoon tomato paste
4 cups thinly sliced cabbage, for "noodles"
Fresh thyme leaves, for garnish

1. Place the coconut oil in a 6-quart Instant Pot and press Sauté. Once melted, add the mushrooms, onions, and garlic and cook for 4 minutes, or until the onions are soft. Remove the mushroom mixture to a small bowl and set aside.
2. Pat the beef cubes dry and season well on all sides with the salt and pepper. Place the beef in the Instant Pot, still on Sauté mode, and brown on all sides, about 4 minutes. Press Cancel to stop the Sauté.
3. Place the cream cheese in a medium-sized bowl and whisk to loosen. (If you don't use a whisk to loosen the cream cheese, you will end up with clumps in your sauce.) Slowly whisk in the broth and tomato paste until smooth. Pour the mixture into the Instant Pot. Add the mushroom mixture and stir to combine.
4. Seal the lid, press Manual, and set the timer for 20 minutes. Once finished, let the pressure release naturally.
5. Remove the lid and shred the beef with two forks. Lay the cabbage on top of the shredded beef.
6. Seal the lid, press Manual, and set the timer for 6 minutes. Once finished, turn the valve to venting for a quick release.
7. Transfer the stroganoff to a large serving dish, garnish with thyme, and enjoy!

Per Serving
calories: 469 | fat: 32g | protein: 34g | carbs: 9g
net carbs: 6g | fiber: 3g

Beef Burgers with Kale and Cheese

Prep time: 6 minutes | Cook time: 6 minutes
Serves 6

1 pound (454 g) ground beef
½ pound (227 g) beef sausage, crumbled
1½ cups chopped kale
¼ cup chopped scallions
2 garlic cloves, minced
½ cup grated Romano cheese

⅓ cup crumbled blue cheese
Salt and ground black pepper, to taste
1 teaspoon crushed dried sage
½ teaspoon oregano
½ teaspoon dried basil
1 tablespoon olive oil

1. Place 1½ cups of water and a steamer basket in your Instant Pot.
2. Mix all ingredients until everything is well incorporated.
3. Shape the mixture into 6 equal sized patties. Place the burgers in the steamer basket.
4. Secure the lid. Choose Manual mode and High Pressure; cook for 6 minutes. Once cooking is complete, use a quick pressure release; carefully remove the lid. Bon appétit!

Per Serving
calories: 323 | fat: 20g | protein: 30g | carbs: 6g
net carbs: 5g | fiber: 1g

Chili Cheese Dog Casserole

Prep time: 5 minutes | Cook time: 11 minutes
Serves 6

1 tablespoon unsalted butter or coconut oil
½ cup diced onions
Cloves squeezed from 1 head roasted garlic, or 2 cloves garlic, minced
1 pound (454 g) ground beef
1 cup diced tomatoes (fresh preferred)
1 cup tomato sauce
1 cup beef broth
2 teaspoons Swerve confectioners'-style sweetener or equivalent amount of liquid or

powdered sweetener (optional)
2 teaspoons chili powder
1 teaspoon fine sea salt
½ teaspoon ground cumin
¼ teaspoon ground black pepper
8 uncured hot dogs, sliced lengthwise and then cut in half
1 cup shredded Monterey Jack or Cheddar cheese

1. Place the butter in a 6-quart Instant Pot and press Sauté. Once melted, add the onions and garlic and cook, stirring often, for 4 minutes, or until the onions are soft.
2. Add the ground beef, tomatoes, tomato sauce, broth, sweetener (if using), chili powder, salt, cumin, and pepper and stir well.

3. Seal the lid, press Manual, and set the timer for 5 minutes. Once finished, turn the valve to venting for a quick release.
4. Remove the lid and stir well to combine. Lay the hot dog slices on top of the casserole mixture. Cover everything with the shredded cheese. Cover loosely with the lid, press Sauté, and cook for 2 minutes, or until the cheese is melted.
5. Scoop the casserole into bowls to serve.

Per Serving
calories: 541 | fat: 41g | protein: 33g | carbs: 7g
net carbs: 5g | fiber: 2g

Parmesan-Oregano Meatballs

Prep time: 5 minutes | Cook time: 20 minutes
Serves 4 to 5

2 tablespoons coconut oil
1 pound (454 g) grass-fed beef, ground
1 cup full-fat Parmesan cheese, grated
½ cup blanched almond flour
½ teaspoon oregano, dried
½ teaspoon cumin,

ground
½ teaspoon kosher salt
½ teaspoon freshly ground black pepper
½ teaspoon garlic powder
½ teaspoon parsley, dried
1 (14-ounce / 397-g) can sugar-free or low-sugar diced tomatoes

1. Set the Instant Pot to Sauté. Add the oil, melting it gently. Meanwhile, in a large bowl, combine the beef, Parmesan cheese, flour, oregano, cumin, salt, black pepper, garlic powder, parsley, and tomatoes. Once well-combined, form 1½ inch meatballs.
2. Place the meatballs inside the Instant Pot, then gently pour in any remaining tomatoes and liquid from the bowl. Close the lid, set the pressure release to Sealing, and select Manual. Set the Instant Pot to 20 minutes on High Pressure and let cook.
3. Once cooked, let the pressure naturally disperse from the Instant Pot for about 10 minutes, then carefully switch the pressure release to Venting.
4. Open the lid and remove the food. Serve, and enjoy! Store any leftovers in the refrigerator or freezer.

Per Serving
calories: 424 | fat: 28g | protein: 37g | carbs: 7g
net carbs: 5g | fiber: 2g

Cheeseburger Casserole

Prep time: 5 minutes | Cook time: 15 minutes
Serves 4

1 pound (454 g) 85%
lean ground beef
½ teaspoon salt
¼ teaspoon pepper
¼ teaspoon garlic
powder
2 tablespoons butter
¼ cup diced onion

¼ cup mayo
1 teaspoon yellow
mustard
1 tablespoon tomato
paste
1 egg
1 cup shredded Cheddar
cheese, divided

1. Press the Sauté button and add ground beef to Instant Pot. Brown meat until fully cooked. Add salt, pepper, garlic powder, butter, and onion to pot. Sauté until onions are translucent. Press the Cancel button.
2. Spoon meat mixture into 7-cup glass bowl and add mayo, mustard, tomato paste, egg, and ½ cup of Cheddar. Mix well. Top with remaining Cheddar. Cover with aluminum foil.
3. Pour water into Instant Pot and add trivet. Set bowl on trivet. Click lid closed. Press the Manual button and adjust time for 15 minutes. When timer beeps, quick-release the pressure.

Per Serving
calories: 442 | fat: 30g | protein: 30g | carbs: 2g
net carbs: 2g | fiber: 0g

Barbacoa

Prep time: 10 minutes | Cook time: 42 minutes
Serves 8

1 tablespoon coconut
oil (Instant Pot only)
1 large onion, diced
Cloves squeezed from 1
head roasted garlic, or
2 cloves garlic, minced
1 (3-pound / 1.4-kg)
boneless beef chuck
roast, cut into 4 equal
pieces
4 canned chipotle
chilies
2 cups beef broth
½ cup lime juice

1 teaspoon liquid smoke
(optional)
1½ tablespoons chili
powder
2 teaspoons dried
oregano leaves
1½ teaspoons ground
cumin
1 teaspoon fine sea salt
¼ teaspoon ground
black pepper
16 large Boston lettuce
leaves

Topping Suggestions:

Lime wedges
Diced tomatoes
Sliced olives
Shredded red cabbage
Guacamole

Sour cream (omit for
dairy-free)
Shredded Cheddar
cheese (omit for dairy-
free)

1. Place the coconut oil in a 6-quart Instant Pot and press Sauté. Once melted, add the onion and cook for 4 minutes, or until soft. If using raw garlic instead of roasted, add the garlic and cook for another minute. If using roasted garlic, add it with the other ingredients in Step 2.
2. Add the roast, chilies, broth, lime juice, liquid smoke (if using), chili powder, oregano, cumin, salt, and pepper and stir to combine.
3. Seal the lid, press Manual, and set the timer for 38 minutes. Once finished, let the pressure release naturally.
4. Transfer the roast to a cutting board and shred the meat with two forks.
5. Serve the barbacoa wrapped in lettuce leaves with your desired toppings.

Per Serving
calories: 539 | fat: 43g | protein: 32g | carbs: 4g
net carbs: 2g | fiber: 2g

Hot 'N' Spicy Meatloaf

Prep time: 5 minutes | Cook time: 35 minutes
Serves 4

1 pound (454 g) grass-
fed beef, ground
1 teaspoon curry
powder
½ teaspoon parsley,
dried
½ teaspoon turmeric,
ground
½ teaspoon paprika,
fresh

½ teaspoon chili
powder
½ teaspoon basil, dried
½ teaspoon crushed
red pepper
½ teaspoon coconut
aminos
½ teaspoon kosher salt
½ teaspoon freshly
ground black pepper

1. Pour 1 cup of filtered water into the inner pot of the Instant Pot, and insert the trivet.
2. On a piece of aluminum foil, mix together the beef, curry powder, parsley, turmeric, paprika, chili powder, basil, red pepper, coconut aminos, salt, and black pepper. Form into one large loaf. Move this (and the aluminum foil) to rest on top of the trivet.
3. Close the lid, set the pressure release to Sealing, and select Manual. Set the Instant Pot to 35 minutes on High Pressure and let cook.
4. Once cooked, let the pressure naturally disperse from the Instant Pot for about 10 minutes, then carefully switch the pressure release to Venting. Open the Instant Pot, serve, and enjoy!

Per Serving
calories: 253 | fat: 15g | protein: 26g | carbs: 1g
net carbs: 1g | fiber: 0g

Korean Short Rib Lettuce Wraps

Prep time: 7 minutes | Cook time: 25 minutes
Serves 4

¼ cup coconut aminos, or 1 tablespoon wheat-free tamari

2 tablespoons coconut vinegar

2 tablespoons sesame oil

3 green onions, thinly sliced, plus more for garnish

2 teaspoons peeled and

grated fresh ginger

2 teaspoons minced garlic

½ teaspoon fine sea salt

½ teaspoon red pepper flakes, plus more for garnish

1 pound (454 g) boneless beef short ribs, sliced ½ inch thick

For Serving:

1 head radicchio, thinly sliced

Butter lettuce leaves

1. Place the coconut aminos, vinegar, sesame oil, green onions, ginger, garlic, salt, and red pepper flakes in the Instant Pot and stir to combine. Add the short ribs and toss to coat well.
2. Seal the lid, press Manual, and set the timer for 20 minutes. Once finished, let the pressure release naturally.
3. Remove the ribs from the Instant Pot and set aside on a warm plate, leaving the sauce in the pot.
4. Press Sauté and cook the sauce, whisking often, until thickened to your liking, about 5 minutes.
5. Put the sliced radicchio on a serving platter, then lay the short ribs on top. Pour the thickened sauce over the ribs. Garnish with more sliced green onions and red pepper flakes. Serve wrapped in lettuce leaves.

Per Serving
calories: 547 | fat: 48g | protein: 18g | carbs: 9g
net carbs: 0g | fiber: 9g

Cardamom Beef with Broccoli

Prep time: 10 minutes | Cook time: 50 minutes
Serves 2

9 ounces (255 g) beef stew meat, chopped

1 teaspoon ground cardamom

½ teaspoon salt

1 cup chopped broccoli

1 cup water

1. Preheat the Instant Pot on the Sauté mode.
2. When it is displayed "Hot", add chopped beef stew meat and cook it for 4 minutes (for 2 minutes from each side).
3. Then add the ground cardamom, salt, and broccoli.

4. Add water and close the Instant Pot lid.
5. Sauté the stew for 45 minutes to get the tender taste.
6. Enjoy!

Per Serving
calories: 256 | fat: 8g | protein: 40g | carbs: 4g
net carbs: 2g | fiber: 2g

Mongolian Beef

Prep time: 10 minutes | Cook time: 18 minutes
Serves 6

2 pounds (907 g) flank steak or brisket, sliced ½-inch thick, 2 × 1-inch strips

½ teaspoon sea salt

½ teaspoon black pepper

6 cloves garlic, minced, divided

1 tablespoon avocado oil

¼ cup tamari or

coconut aminos

1 teaspoon minced fresh ginger

1 tablespoon dry sweetener

½ cup water, divided

2 tablespoons tapioca flour

½ cup scallions, chopped into 1-inch pieces

1. In a small bowl, combine the beef, sea salt, black pepper and 1 teaspoon of minced garlic. Set aside. Turn on the Instant Pot by pressing Sauté and set to More. Insert the inner pot and wait until the panel says Hot. Add the avocado oil into the pot and heat until hot. Add half of the beef and sauté for 3 minutes or until the meat is no longer pink. Take out the browned beef and add the other batch of beef to brown. When all of the beef is browned, add the first batch back to the pot with its juices and the rest of the ingredients, except ¼ cup of water, the tapioca flour and the scallions.
2. Close the lid tightly and move the steam release handle to Sealing. Press Cancel, then the Manual button and set the timer for 10 minutes on High Pressure. Mix the remaining water and the tapioca in a small bowl to make a slurry.
3. When the timer ends, you will hear a beeping sound. Allow the Instant Pot to cool down naturally until the float valve drops down. Press Cancel, then Sauté, and open the lid. Add the slurry and stir to thicken and simmer for 2 minutes. Press Cancel. Serve immediately with the chopped scallions as garnish.

Per Serving
calories: 310 | fat: 18g | protein: 31g | carbs: 4g
net carbs: 3g | fiber: 1g

Buttery Pot Roast

Prep time: 5 minutes | Cook time: 90 minutes
Serves 4

4 teaspoons onion powder
2 teaspoons dried parsley
1 teaspoon salt
1 teaspoon garlic powder
½ teaspoon dried oregano
½ teaspoon pepper

1 (2-pound / 907-g) chuck roast
1 tablespoon coconut oil
1 cup beef broth
½ packet dry ranch seasoning
1 stick butter
10 pepperoncini

1. Press the Sauté button and allow to heat. In small bowl, mix onion powder, parsley, salt, garlic powder, oregano, and pepper. Rub seasoning onto roast. Add coconut oil to Instant Pot. Place roast in pot and sear for 5 minutes each side; remove roast and set aside.
2. Press the Cancel button. Add broth to Instant Pot. Using rubber spatula or wooden spoon, scrape bottom to loosen any stuck-on seasoning or meat.
3. Place roast back into Instant Pot and sprinkle dry ranch powder on top. Place stick of butter on roast and add pepperoncini. Click lid closed. Press the Manual button and adjust time for 90 minutes.
4. When timer beeps, allow a natural release to retain meat tenderness. When pressure indicator drops, remove lid and remove cooked roast. Slice or shred and top with broth from pot.

Per Serving
calories: 561 | fat: 33g | protein: 51g | carbs: 5g
net carbs: 5g | fiber: 0g

Lamb Vindaloo

Prep time: 10 minutes | Cook time: 34 minutes
Serves 4

1 tablespoon unsalted butter (or coconut oil for dairy-free)
¼ cup diced onions
6 cloves garlic, minced
3 tablespoons grainy mustard
2 teaspoons ground cumin
2 teaspoons turmeric powder

½ teaspoon cayenne pepper
2 pounds (907 g) boneless lamb shoulder, cut into 1½-inch cubes
1 (14-ounce / 397-g) can full-fat coconut milk
1 tablespoon lime juice
Fresh cilantro leaves, for garnish

1. Place the butter in the Instant Pot and press Sauté. Once melted, add the onions and garlic and cook, stirring often, for 4 minutes, or until the onions are soft. Press Cancel to stop the Sauté.
2. Place the mustard, cumin, turmeric, and cayenne in a small bowl and stir well. Place the lamb in the Instant Pot and cover with the mustard mixture. Pour in the coconut milk.
3. Seal the lid, press Manual, and set the timer for 30 minutes. Once finished, let the pressure release naturally.
4. Remove the lid and stir in the lime juice. Garnish with cilantro and serve.

Per Serving
calories: 535 | fat: 35g | protein: 46g | carbs: 5g
net carbs: 4g | fiber: 1g

Leftover Brisket Loaded Cauliflower Bowl

Prep time: 5 minutes | Cook time: 15 minutes
Serves 4

1 cup water
2 cups fresh cauliflower, chopped into bite-sized pieces
3 tablespoons butter
¼ onion, diced
¼ cup pickled jalapeño slices
2 cups cooked brisket

2 ounces (57 g) cream cheese, softened
1 cup shredded sharp Cheddar cheese
¼ cup heavy cream
¼ cup cooked crumbled bacon
2 tablespoons sliced green onions

1. Add water to Instant Pot. Place steamer basket into pot and add cauliflower. Click lid closed.
2. Press the Steam button and adjust time for 1 minute. When timer beeps, quick-release the steam and remove steamer basket with cauliflower; set aside. Do not remove excess moisture from cauliflower. Carefully pick up inner pot, it may be hot, and pour out water. Then place back inside Instant Pot.
3. Press the Sauté button and add butter, onion, and jalapeño slices. Sauté for 4 minutes. Add cooked brisket and cream cheese. Continue cooking for 2 minutes. Add sharp Cheddar, heavy cream, and cauliflower. Press the Cancel button.
4. Gently fold mixture until all ingredients are incorporated and cheese has melted. Sprinkle with crumbled bacon and green onions. Serve warm.

Per Serving
calories: 574 | fat: 40g | protein: 33g | carbs: 9g
net carbs: 8g | fiber: 1g

Steak and Cauliflower Rice

Prep time: 5 minutes | Cook time: 20 minutes
Serves 4

1 ribeye steak
½ teaspoon paprika, fresh
½ teaspoon turmeric, ground
½ teaspoon parsley, dried
½ teaspoon cumin, ground

½ teaspoon freshly ground black pepper
½ teaspoon kosher salt
1 head cauliflower, chopped
2 tablespoons grass-fed butter, softened
1 avocado, mashed

1. Pour 1 cup of filtered water into the inner pot of the Instant Pot, then insert the trivet. In a small bowl, mix together the paprika, turmeric, parsley, cumin, black pepper, and salt. Coat the steak evenly with this mixture.
2. Once coated, place the steak onto a well-greased, Instant Pot-friendly dish. Arrange the cauliflower beside the steak.
3. Place the dish onto the trivet, and cover loosely with aluminum foil. Close the lid, set the pressure release to Sealing, and select Manual. Set the Instant Pot to 20 minutes on High Pressure, and let cook.
4. Once cooked, let the pressure naturally disperse from the Instant Pot for about 10 minutes, then carefully switch the pressure release to Venting.
5. Open the Instant Pot, and remove the dish. Add the butter to the steak, serve with the avocado, and enjoy!

Per Serving
calories: 418 | fat: 22g | protein: 54g | carbs: 8g
net carbs: 3g | fiber: 5g

Santa Fe Meatloaf

Prep time: 10 minutes | Cook time: 30 minutes
Serves 6

1½ pounds (680 g) ground beef
⅔ cup salsa, plus more for serving
½ cup finely chopped button or cremini mushrooms
½ cup chopped green onions
1 teaspoon fine sea salt
1 teaspoon chili powder
1 teaspoon smoked paprika
½ teaspoon ground cumin

½ teaspoon garlic powder
½ teaspoon onion powder
1 (4-ounce / 113-g) can chopped mild green chilies, drained well
1 large egg, lightly beaten
1 jalapeño pepper, thinly sliced (optional)
Fresh cilantro leaves, for garnish
Guacamole, for serving (optional)

1. Place a 15 by 9-inch sheet of parchment paper on a 15 by 9-inch piece of aluminum foil and set aside.
2. Place all of the ingredients, except the jalapeño slices and garnishes, in a large bowl and mix well with your hands. Shape the mixture into a 9 by 5-inch loaf, then place the loaf on the parchment-lined foil. Top the meatloaf with the jalapeño slices, if using.
3. To make the loaf pan, use the foil on the outside of the loaf to hold its shape, then tuck in the sides of the foil around the loaf.
4. Set a trivet in an 8-quart Instant Pot and pour in 1 cup of cold water. Grasp the sides of the foil loaf pan and place the meatloaf on the trivet.
5. Seal the lid, press Manual, and set the timer for 30 minutes. Once finished, let the pressure release naturally.
6. Remove the lid and lift the meatloaf out of the pot. Place on a serving dish and top with additional salsa or guacamole, if using. Garnish with cilantro, slice, and serve.

Per Serving
calories: 318 | fat: 24g | protein: 21g | carbs: 4g
net carbs: 3g | fiber: 1g

Hibachi Steak with Mushrooms

Prep time: 10 minutes | Cook time: 10 minutes
Serves 4

1 pound (454 g) beef sirloin, roughly chopped
1 teaspoon ground ginger
¼ teaspoon garlic powder
¼ cup cremini

mushrooms, sliced
2 tablespoons apple cider vinegar
1 tablespoon avocado oil
¼ cup water

1. Mix the beef sirloin, mushrooms, garlic powder, apple cider vinegar, ground ginger, and avocado oil in the Instant Pot. Pour in the water.
2. Close the lid and select Manual mode. Set cooking time for 10 minutes on High Pressure.
3. When timer beeps, allow a natural pressure release for 10 minutes, then release any remaining pressure. Open the lid.
4. Serve warm.

Per Serving
calories: 220 | fat: 7g | protein: 34g | carbs: 1g
net carbs: 1g | fiber: 0g

Corned Beef and Cabbage

Prep time: 5 minutes | Cook time: 94 minutes
Serves 9

3 pounds (1.4 kg) brisket
2 cups beef broth
1 teaspoon mustard seeds
3 bay leaves
10 allspice berries
Cloves squeezed from 2

heads roasted garlic, or
4 cloves garlic, minced
1 teaspoon fine sea salt
1 teaspoon ground black pepper
1 head red cabbage, cut into large wedges

1. Place all of the ingredients, except the cabbage wedges, in a 6-quart Instant Pot. Seal the lid, press Manual, and set the timer for 90 minutes. Once finished, let the pressure release naturally.
2. Remove the lid and lay the cabbage wedges on top of the corned beef. Seal the lid, press Manual, and set the timer for 4 minutes. Once finished, turn the valve to venting for a quick release.
3. Put the cabbage in a serving dish or on the outer edges of a serving platter. Place the corned beef on a cutting board and cut across the grain into ¼-inch-thick slices. Move the slices to the center of the serving dish with the cabbage.

Per Serving
calories: 548 | fat: 40g | protein: 39g | carbs: 7g
net carbs: 4g | fiber: 3g

Blue Cheese Stuffed Steak Roll-Ups

Prep time: 5 minutes | Cook time: 15 minutes
Serves 6

1 (1½-pound / 680-g) beef round tip roast, sliced into 6 steaks of equal thickness
6 ounces (170 g) blue cheese, crumbled
½ cup beef broth
¼ cup coconut aminos,

or 1 tablespoon wheat-free tamari
4 cloves garlic, minced
Chopped fresh Italian parsley, for garnish
Cracked black pepper, for garnish

1. Place each steak in a resealable plastic bag and pound with a rolling pin or meat mallet until it is ½ inch thick. Lay the pounded steaks flat on a cutting board or other work surface.
2. Divide the blue cheese evenly among the steaks, placing the cheese on one side. Roll up each steak, starting at a shorter end, and secure with toothpicks.

3. Combine the broth, coconut aminos, and garlic in the Instant Pot. Add the steak roll-ups to the broth mixture.
4. Seal the lid, press Manual, and set the timer for 15 minutes. Once finished, turn the valve to venting for a quick release.
5. Remove the toothpicks from the steak roll-ups before serving. Garnish the roll-ups with chopped parsley and cracked black pepper.

Per Serving
calories: 417 | fat: 28g | protein: 37g | carbs: 3g
net carbs: 1g | fiber: 2g

Steak Nachos

Prep time: 5 minutes | Cook time: 20 minutes
Serves 6

2 tablespoons grass-fed butter, softened
1 (14-ounce / 397-g) can sugar-free or low-sugar fire roasted tomatoes, drained
1 pound (454 g) beef steak, sliced into thin strips
½ pound (227 g) cauliflower, chopped
½ cup full-fat Cheddar cheese, shredded
½ cup full-fat Monterey Jack cheese, shredded

½ teaspoon chili powder
½ jalapeño, chopped, seeded
½ teaspoon turmeric, ground
½ teaspoon cumin, ground
½ teaspoon curry powder
¼ cup coconut oil
1 avocado, mashed
¼ cup sour cream, at room temperature

1. Pour 1 cup of filtered water into the inner pot of the Instant Pot, then insert the trivet. In a large bowl, combine butter, tomatoes, steak, cauliflower, Cheddar, Monterey Jack, chili powder, jalapeño, turmeric, cumin, curry powder, and coconut oil. Mix thoroughly. Transfer this mixture into a well-greased, Instant Pot-friendly dish.
2. Using a sling if desired, place the dish onto the trivet, and cover loosely with aluminum foil. Close the lid, set the pressure release to Sealing, and select Manual. Set the Instant Pot to 20 minutes on High Pressure, and let cook.
3. Once cooked, let the pressure naturally disperse from the Instant Pot for about 10 minutes, then carefully switch the pressure release to Venting.
4. Open the Instant Pot, and remove the dish. Let cool, add the avocado and sour cream atop the nachos, and enjoy!

Per Serving
calories: 449 | fat: 32g | protein: 30g | carbs: 10g
net carbs: 5g | fiber: 5g

Simple Ropa Vieja

Prep time: 5 minutes | Cook time: 85 minutes
Serves 8

3 pounds (1.4 kg) beef roast
½ cup grass-fed bone broth
½ teaspoon cumin, ground
½ teaspoon, oregano
½ teaspoon chili powder
1 (14-ounce / 397-g) can sugar-free or low-sugar crushed tomatoes
Salt and pepper, to taste

1. Pour all ingredients into the inner pot of the Instant Pot. Close the lid, set the pressure release to Sealing, and select Manual. Set the Instant Pot to 85 minutes on High Pressure and let cook.
2. Once cooked, let the pressure naturally disperse from the Instant Pot for about 10 minutes, then carefully switch the pressure release to Venting. Open the lid, shred the beef, and enjoy!

Per Serving
calories: 317 | fat: 15g | protein: 45g | carbs: 2g
net carbs: 2g | fiber: 0g

Bunless Bacon Cheeseburger

Prep time: 5 minutes | Cook time: 15 minutes
Serves 4

6 slices no-sugar-added bacon
2 tablespoons grass-fed butter, softened
1 pound (454 g) grass-fed beef, ground
½ teaspoon cayenne pepper, ground
½ teaspoon crushed red pepper
½ teaspoon paprika, fresh
½ teaspoon freshly ground black pepper
½ teaspoon kosher salt
½ cup full-fat Cheddar cheese, shredded
½ cup full-fat Monterey Jack cheese, shredded

1. Place the bacon slices on aluminum foil, laid out evenly.
2. Set the Instant Pot to Sauté. Add the grass-fed butter to the Instant Pot, melting it gently.
3. In a large bowl, mix the beef, cayenne pepper, red pepper, paprika, black pepper, and salt. Form 2 large, thin patties with the beef.
4. Add ½ cup of filtered water to the Instant Pot, then add the patties. Add the trivet to create a second cooking layer, and place the aluminum foil with the bacon on top. Be sure to fold the edges of the aluminum foil upward.

5. Close the lid, set the pressure release to Sealing, and select Manual. Set the Instant Pot to 15 minutes on High Pressure and let cook.
6. Once cooked, let the pressure naturally disperse from the Instant Pot for about 10 minutes, then carefully switch the pressure release to Venting.
7. Open the lid and remove the food. Top the burgers with the Cheddar, Monterey Jack, bacon, and serve.

Per Serving
calories: 591 | fat: 49g | protein: 33g | carbs: 4g
net carbs: 3g | fiber: 1g

Classic Lasagna

Prep time: 5 minutes | Cook time: 20 minutes
Serves 4

2 tablespoons coconut oil
1 pound (454 g) grass-fed beef, ground
1 egg
1 cup spinach, chopped
¾ cup Mozzarella cheese, shredded
½ cup full-fat Parmesan cheese, grated
½ teaspoon basil, dried
½ teaspoon fennel seeds
½ teaspoon garlic
½ teaspoon oregano, dried
½ teaspoon parsley, dried
¼ (4-ounce / 113-g) small onion, thinly sliced
1 ½ cups whole milk ricotta cheese
1 (14-ounce / 397-g) can sugar-free or low-sugar fire roasted tomatoes

1. Pour 1 cup of filtered water into the inner pot of the Instant Pot, then insert the trivet. In a large bowl, combine the coconut oil, beef, egg, spinach, Mozzarella, Parmesan, basil, fennel, garlic, oregano, parsley, onion, ricotta, and tomatoes. Mix thoroughly. Transfer this mixture into a well-greased, Instant Pot-friendly dish.
2. Place the dish onto the trivet, and cover loosely with aluminum foil. Close the lid, set the pressure release to Sealing and select Manual. Set the Instant Pot to 20 minutes on High Pressure, and let cook.
3. Once cooked, let the pressure naturally disperse from the Instant Pot for about 10 minutes, then carefully switch the pressure release to Venting.
4. Open the Instant Pot, and remove the dish. Let cool, serve, and enjoy!

Per Serving
calories: 533 | fat: 36g | protein: 43g | carbs: 10g
net carbs: 9g | fiber: 1g

Icelandic Lamb with Turnip and Celery

Prep time: 5 minutes | Cook time: 45 minutes
Serves 4

12 ounces (340 g) lamb fillet, chopped
4 ounces (113 g) turnip, chopped
3 ounces (85 g) celery ribs, chopped
1 teaspoon unsweetened tomato purée
¼ cup scallions, chopped
½ teaspoon salt
½ teaspoon ground black pepper
4 cups water

1. Put all ingredients in the Instant Pot and stir well.
2. Close the lid. Select Manual mode and set cooking time for 45 minutes on High Pressure.
3. When timer beeps, use a quick pressure release. Open the lid.
4. Serve hot.

Per Serving
calories: 173 | fat: 6g | protein: 24g | carbs: 3g
net carbs: 2g | fiber: 1g

Mushroom Burgers

Prep time: 5 minutes | Cook time: 20 minutes
Serves 2

1 pound (454 g) grass-fed beef, ground
½ teaspoon cayenne pepper, ground
½ teaspoon oregano, dried
½ teaspoon freshly ground black pepper
½ teaspoon kosher salt
4 portobello mushroom caps
1 cup lettuce, shredded
1 cup tomatoes, diced
1 teaspoon Dijon mustard
¼ (4-ounce / 113-g) small onion, thinly sliced
½ cup full-fat Cheddar cheese, shredded

1. Preheat your oven to 350ºF (180ºC). Place the mushroom caps on a lightly greased baking sheet.
2. Add ½ cup of filtered water to the Instant Pot, then insert the trivet. In a large bowl, mix the beef with the cayenne pepper, oregano, black pepper, and salt. Form two well-crafted patties, and place these patties on top of the trivet.
3. Close the lid, set the pressure release to Sealing, and select Manual. Set the Instant Pot to 20 minutes on High Pressure and let cook.
4. While cooking, heat the mushroom caps in the oven for 5 minutes per side. When done, remove and let cool.

5. Once cooked, let the pressure naturally disperse from the Instant Pot for about 10 minutes, then carefully switch the pressure release to Venting. Open the lid and remove the meat. Place burgers on top of two of the mushroom caps. Top the burgers with the remaining ingredients, and complete each burger with the remaining mushroom caps.

Per Serving
calories: 510 | fat: 33g | protein: 40g | carbs: 8g
net carbs: 6g | fiber: 2g

Braised Beef Brisket

Prep time: 10 minutes | Cook time: 60 to 75 minutes | Serves 8

1½ teaspoons salt
2 teaspoons freshly ground black pepper
2 pounds (907 g) beef brisket, cut against the grain into 4 pieces
½ cup water
2 tablespoons tomato paste
2 tablespoons Worcestershire sauce
1 to 2 teaspoons liquid smoke
2 cups sliced onions
1 tablespoon prepared mustard, or to taste
½ teaspoon xanthan gum

1. Sprinkle the salt and pepper over the brisket pieces and let them sit while you get your other ingredients together.
2. In a small bowl, mix together the water, tomato paste, Worcestershire sauce, and liquid smoke.
3. Put the onions in the inner cooking pot of the Instant Pot. Place the beef on top of the onions. Pour in the sauce.
4. Lock the lid into place. Select Manual and adjust the pressure to High. Cook for 60 minutes for a brisket with some chew, and 70 to 75 minutes for a more tender brisket. When the cooking is complete, let the pressure release naturally for 10 minutes, then quick-release any remaining pressure. Unlock the lid.
5. Open the pot and remove the brisket with tongs.
6. Tilting the pot slightly, use an immersion blender to blend together the onions and all the liquid in the pot. Add the mustard and stir until it is well mixed.
7. Switch the Instant Pot to Sauté and adjust the heat to high. Add the xanthan gum, stirring well, and allow the sauce to thicken.
8. Slice the beef across the grain and serve with the sauce.

Per Serving
calories: 332 | fat: 25g | protein: 21g | carbs: 4g
net carbs: 3g | fiber: 1g

Fast and Easy Gumbo

Prep time: 5 minutes | Cook time: 15 minutes
Serves 2

2 cups grass-fed bone broth
½ pound (227 g) grass-fed beef
¼ teaspoon arrowroot powder

½ stalk celery, chopped
¼ cup bell peppers, chopped
¼ (4-ounce / 113-g) small onion, finely chopped

1. Pour bone broth into the inner pot of the Instant Pot, then add the grass-fed beef, breaking it up thoroughly.
2. Close the lid, set the pressure release to Sealing, and select Manual. Set the Instant Pot to 15 minutes on High Pressure and let cook.
3. Once cooked, perform a quick release by carefully switching the pressure valve to Venting. Stir in the arrowroot powder, celery, bell peppers, and onion. Serve and enjoy!

Per Serving
calories: 239 | fat: 12g | protein: 26g | carbs: 5g net carbs: 4g | fiber: 1g

Not Your Mama's Meatloaf

Prep time: 10 minutes | Cook time: 30 minutes
Serves 8

½ pound (227 g) ground sirloin beef
½ pound (227 g) ground pork
2 large eggs, beaten
¼ cup finely chopped onion
1 clove garlic, minced
½ cup extra fine blanched almond flour
¼ cup coconut flour
½ cup your favorite homemade marinara sauce, reserve 2

tablespoons for topping
½ teaspoon sea salt
½ teaspoon black pepper
1 tablespoon Worcestershire sauce
1 teaspoon Italian seasoning
½ teaspoon dried tarragon
½ cup fresh flat leaf parsley, reserve 1 tablespoon for garnish
1 cup water

1. In a large mixing bowl, combine all of the ingredients except the water and mix well.
2. Transfer the mixture to a loaf pan big enough to fit into the inner pot of the Instant Pot. Cover the top of the meatloaf mixture with 2 tablespoons of marinara sauce. Loosely cover the pan with aluminum foil. Put the water in the inner pot and place the trivet inside. Place the pan containing the meatloaf mixture on top of the trivet.
3. Close the lid tightly and move the steam release handle to Sealing.

4. Press the Manual button and set the timer for 30 minutes on High Pressure. When the timer ends, you will hear a beeping sound. Allow the Instant Pot to cool down naturally until the float valve drops down. Press Cancel and open the lid. Carefully take out the trivet with the pan on top and let the meatloaf rest for 5 minutes. Garnish with the remaining fresh parsley and serve.

Per Serving
calories: 260 | fat: 17g | protein: 20g | carbs: 7g net carbs: 4g | fiber: 3g

Perfect Pot Roast

Prep time: 20 minutes | Cook time: 94 minutes
Serves 6

3 to 4 pounds (1.4 to 1.8 kg) chuck roast
1 tablespoon sea salt
1 tablespoon fresh ground black pepper
2 tablespoons butter
1 large onion, sliced
4 cloves garlic, crushed
2 carrots, cut diagonally about 1 inch in length
2 celery stalks, cut diagonally about 2 inch in length
2 long daikon or turnip or radish, cut into

2-inch large chunks
1 cup red wine
2 sprigs of fresh thyme
2 dried whole bay leaves
¼ cup chopped flat leaf fresh parsley with stems, reserve 1 teaspoon for garnish
2 sprigs of fresh tarragon
1 tablespoon Worcestershire sauce
¾ cup beef stock

1. Pat dry the meat, rub the sea salt and pepper on the outside and set aside.
2. Turn on the Instant Pot by pressing Sauté and set to More. Insert the inner pot and wait until the panel says Hot. Melt the butter and add the onion and garlic. Sauté for 2 minutes or until the onion is soft. Add the carrots and sauté for 2 minutes. Add the rest of the ingredients and stir around to mix. Place the chuck roast on top of the vegetables. Press Cancel, and then press the Manual button and set the timer for 90 minutes on High Pressure. Close the lid tightly and move the steam release handle to Sealing.
3. When the timer ends, you will hear a beeping sound. Allow the Instant Pot to cool down naturally until the float valve drops down. Press Cancel and open the lid.
4. Take out the roast and allow it to rest for 5 minutes. Slice the beef, top it with the cooked vegetables, sauce and garnish with parsley before serving.

Per Serving
calories: 646 | fat: 39g | protein: 58g | carbs: 11g net carbs: 7g | fiber: 3g

Balsamic Chuck Roast

Prep time: 5 minutes | Cook time: 20 minutes
Serves 4

1 pound (454 g) chuck roast	½ teaspoon kosher salt
2 cloves garlic, minced	½ teaspoon ground thyme
1 cup grass-fed bone broth	½ teaspoon crushed red pepper
½ teaspoon ground rosemary	¼ cup balsamic vinegar
½ teaspoon freshly ground black pepper	4 tablespoons grass-fed butter, softened
	1 cup chopped broccoli

1. Pour ½ cup filtered water into the Instant Pot, then add the chuck roast. Close the lid, set the pressure release to Sealing, and select Manual. Set the Instant Pot to 20 minutes on High Pressure, and let cook.
2. In a large bowl, combine the garlic, bone broth, rosemary, black pepper, salt, thyme, red pepper, vinegar, and 2 tablespoons of butter. Mix thoroughly.
3. Once cooked, let the pressure naturally disperse from the Instant Pot for about 10 minutes, then carefully switch the pressure release to Venting.
4. Open the Instant Pot, and remove the dish. Set the Instant Pot to Sauté mode, add in the broccoli, and mix in 2 additional tablespoons of grass-fed butter. Cook the broccoli, stirring continuously, until cooked.
5. Remove the broccoli, and serve alongside the roast. Spoon your prepared sauce over both, to taste.

Per Serving
calories: 323 | fat: 16g | protein: 40g | carbs: 3g
net carbs: 2g | fiber: 1g

Sesame Beef

Prep time: 5 minutes | Cook time: 20 minutes
Serves 4

½ cup grass-fed bone broth	finely grated
2 tablespoons coconut oil	½ teaspoon freshly ground black pepper
1 pound (454 g) chuck steak, sliced	½ teaspoon kosher salt
1 green onion, chopped	½ teaspoon crushed red pepper
1 jalapeño pepper, sliced thinly	½ teaspoon parsley, dried
½ teaspoon garlic	1 teaspoon sesame seeds
½ teaspoon ginger,	1 cup broccoli, chopped

1. Pour the bone broth into the Instant Pot, then add the oil, steak, green onion, jalapeño, garlic, ginger, black pepper, salt, red pepper, and parsley. Close the lid, set the pressure release to Sealing, and select Manual. Set the Instant Pot to 20 minutes on High Pressure, and let cook.
2. Once cooked, let the pressure naturally disperse from the Instant Pot for about 10 minutes, then carefully switch the pressure release to Venting.
3. Open the Instant Pot and remove the dish. Add broccoli, and let cook for 2 to 5 minutes (or until desired tenderness, sautéing with butter, if desired). Remove the broccoli.
4. Once beef is cooled, top with the sesame seeds, serve with the broccoli, and enjoy!

Per Serving
calories: 365 | fat: 22g | protein: 37g | carbs: 3g
net carbs: 2g | fiber: 1g

Classic Pot Roast

Prep time: 5 minutes | Cook time: 55 minutes
Serves 5 to 6

2 tablespoons coconut oil	dried
3 pounds (1.4 kg) beef chuck roast	½ teaspoon basil, dried
1 cup grass-fed butter	½ teaspoon chili powder
½ teaspoon paprika, fresh	½ teaspoon kosher salt
½ teaspoon parsley,	½ teaspoon freshly ground black pepper

1. Set the Instant Pot to Sauté and melt the oil. Sauté the pot roast briefly to sear the outside of the meat, then remove.
2. Pour 1 cup of filtered water into the inner pot of the Instant Pot, then add the butter, paprika, parsley, basil, chili powder, salt, and black pepper. Last, return the beef to the pot.
3. Once all ingredients are in the Instant Pot, close the lid, set the pressure release to Sealing, and hit Cancel to stop the current program. Select Manual, set the Instant Pot to 55 minutes on High Pressure, and let cook.
4. Once cooked, let the pressure naturally disperse from the Instant Pot for about 10 minutes, then carefully switch the pressure release to Venting. Open the Instant Pot, serve, and enjoy!

Per Serving
calories: 486 | fat: 40g | protein: 30g | carbs: 0g
net carbs: 0g | fiber: 0g

Beef Brisket with Green Cabbage

Prep time: 15 minutes | Cook time: 1 hour 7 minutes | Serves 8

3 pounds (1.4 kg) corned beef brisket
4 cups water
3 garlic cloves, minced
2 teaspoons yellow mustard seed
2 teaspoons black peppercorns
3 celery stalks, chopped
½ large white onion, chopped
1 green cabbage, cut into quarters

1. Add the brisket to the Instant Pot. Pour the water into the pot. Add the garlic, mustard seed, and black peppercorns.
2. Lock the lid. Select Meat/Stew mode and set cooking time for 50 minutes on High Pressure.
3. When cooking is complete, allow the pressure to release naturally for 20 minutes, then release any remaining pressure. Open the lid and transfer only the brisket to a platter.
4. Add the celery, onion, and cabbage to the pot.
5. Lock the lid. Select Soup mode and set cooking time for 12 minutes on High Pressure.
6. When cooking is complete, quick release the pressure. Open the lid, add the brisket back to the pot and let warm in the pot for 5 minutes.
7. Transfer the warmed brisket back to the platter and thinly slice. Transfer the vegetables to the platter. Serve hot.

Per Serving
calories: 357 | fat: 25g | protein: 26g | carbs: 7g net carbs: 5g | fiber: 2g

Spaghetti Bolognese

Prep time: 15 minutes | Cook time: 19 minutes Serves 8

Bolognese Sauce:

4 slices bacon, chopped
½ cup chopped onions
Cloves squeezed from 1 head roasted garlic, or 1 clove garlic, minced
¼ cup fresh flat-leaf parsley
3 tablespoons fresh oregano leaves
3 tablespoons fresh thyme leaves
2 bay leaves
1 teaspoon fine sea salt
½ teaspoon ground black pepper
1 pound (454 g) ground beef
½ pound (227 g) ground Italian sausage
2 cups marinara sauce
4 cups crushed tomatoes, with juices
1 cup beef broth
½ teaspoon stevia glycerite (optional)
¼ cup heavy cream (omit for dairy-free)
2 tablespoons unsalted butter (omit for dairy-free)

For Serving:

2 medium zucchini, cut into thin noodles, warmed
1 cup grated Parmesan cheese (about 4 ounces / 113 g) (omit for dairy-free)

1. Place the bacon in a 6-quart Instant Pot and press Sauté. Cook, stirring occasionally, for 4 minutes, or until the bacon is starting to crisp and the fat is rendered. Add the onions and cook, stirring frequently, for 4 more minutes, or until soft. Add the garlic, herbs, salt, and pepper. Cook, stirring, for 30 seconds.
2. Add the ground beef and Italian sausage and stir well to combine. Add the marinara, tomatoes, broth, and stevia, if using. Press Cancel to stop the Sauté.
3. Seal the lid, press Manual, and set the timer for 10 minutes. Once finished, let the pressure release naturally.
4. Remove the lid, add the cream and butter, if using, and stir to combine. Cover to keep warm until ready to serve. Before serving, adjust the seasoning to taste and discard the bay leaves. Serve the Bolognese sauce over the zucchini noodles and top with the Parmesan cheese, if desired.

Per Serving
calories: 460 | fat: 34g | protein: 24g | carbs: 13g net carbs: 10g | fiber: 3g

Sirloin Roast

Prep time: 10 minutes | Cook time: 55 minutes Serves 4

1 teaspoon pot roast seasonings
16 ounces (454 g) beef sirloin, roughly chopped
1 cup water
1 tablespoon sesame oil

1. Rub the beef sirloin with pot roast seasonings and sesame oil and wrap in the foil.
2. After this, pour water and insert the trivet in the Instant Pot.
3. Place the wrapped meat on the trivet. Close and seal the lid.
4. Cook the sirloin on Manual mode at High Pressure for 55 minutes.
5. Then make a quick pressure release and open the lid.
6. Slice the sirloin roast into the servings.

Per Serving
calories: 245 | fat: 10g | protein: 35g | carbs: 0g net carbs: 0g | fiber: 0g

Blackberry Beef

Prep time: 15 minutes | Cook time: 30 minutes
Serves 2

15 ounces (425 g) beef loin, chopped
1 tablespoon blackberries
1 cup water
½ teaspoon ground cinnamon
⅓ teaspoon ground black pepper
½ teaspoon salt
1 tablespoon butter

1. Pour water in the Instant Pot.
2. Add chopped beef loin, blackberries, ground cinnamon, salt, and ground black pepper. Add butter.
3. Close the Instant Pot lid and set the Meat/Stew mode.
4. Cook the meat for 30 minutes. Then remove the meat from the Instant Pot. Blend the remaining blackberry mixture.
5. Pour it over the meat.

Per Serving
calories: 372 | fat: 21g | protein: 39g | carbs: 4g
net carbs: 3g | fiber: 1g

Thyme Beef Brisket

Prep time: 10 minutes | Cook time: 25 minutes
Serves 3

1 teaspoon dried thyme
12 ounces (340 g) beef brisket, chopped
½ cup water
½ teaspoon salt
1 teaspoon coconut oil

1. Sprinkle the beef brisket with salt and dried thyme.
2. Then melt the coconut oil in the Instant Pot on Sauté mode and add beef brisket.
3. Add water and close the lid.
4. Cook the meat on Manual mode at High Pressure for 25 minutes.
5. Then allow the natural pressure release for 10 minutes.

Per Serving
calories: 225 | fat: 8g | protein: 25g | carbs: 0g
net carbs: 0g | fiber: 0g

Lamb Korma

Prep time: 15 minutes | Cook time: 25 minutes
Serves 6

1 (6-inch) Anaheim chile, minced
1 clove garlic, grated
½ medium onion, chopped
2 tablespoons coconut oil
½ teaspoon grated fresh ginger
1 teaspoon garam masala
¼ teaspoon ground cardamom
Pinch of ground cinnamon
2 teaspoons ground cumin
1 teaspoon coriander seeds
1 teaspoon sea salt
½ teaspoon cayenne pepper
½ tablespoon unsweetened tomato purée
1 cup chicken broth
3 pounds (1.4 kg) lamb shoulder, cut into 1-inch cubes
¼ cup full-fat coconut milk
½ cup full-fat Greek yogurt

1. Preheat the Instant Pot on Sauté mode. Add the chile, garlic, onion, coconut oil, and ginger and sauté for 2 minutes.
2. Add the garam masala, cardamom, cinnamon, cumin, coriander seeds, salt, cayenne, and unsweetened tomato purée and sauté for a minute or until fragrant.
3. Pour in the broth. Add the lamb and stir well.
4. Secure the lid. Press the Manual button and set cooking time for 15 minutes on High Pressure.
5. When timer beeps, quick release the pressure. Open the lid.
6. Stir in the coconut milk and yogurt. Switch to Sauté mode and bring the mixture to a simmer for 5 minutes, stirring occasionally until thickened.
7. Serve hot.

Per Serving
calories: 450 | fat: 26g | protein: 48g | carbs: 5g
net carbs: 4g | fiber: 1g

Chaptr 11 Fish and Seafood

Simple Crab Legs

Prep time: 5 minutes | Cook time: 3 minutes
Serves 5

2 pounds (907 g) crab legs, thawed

1. Pour 1 cup of water into the Instant Pot and insert trivet.
2. Place the crab legs on top of the trivet.
3. Select Manual, set the Instant Pot to 3 minutes on High Pressure, and let cook.
4. Immediately after cook time completes, carefully switch the pressure release to Venting.
5. Set crab legs on a plate, and serve with whatever desired!

Per Serving
calories: 152 | fat: 5g | protein: 19g | carbs: 0g
net carbs: 0g | fiber: 0g

Fish Taco Bowls

Prep time: 15 minutes | Cook time: 5 minutes
Serves 4

4 cups shredded cabbage
¼ cup mayo
2 tablespoons sour cream
1 lime, halved
2 tablespoons chopped pickled jalapeños
3 (4-ounce / 113-g) tilapia fillets
2 teaspoons chili powder
1 teaspoon cumin
1 teaspoon garlic powder
1 teaspoon salt
2 tablespoons coconut oil
1 avocado, diced
4 tablespoons fresh chopped cilantro

1. In large bowl, mix cabbage, mayo, sour cream, juice from half lime, and jalapeños. Cover and place in fridge for at least 30 minutes prior to serving, if possible.
2. Press the Sauté button on Instant Pot. Pat fillets dry and sprinkle evenly with seasonings. Add coconut oil to pot and let melt completely. Add tilapia to pan and sear each side 2 to 4 minutes or until fully cooked. Fish should flake easily. Press the Cancel button.
3. Chop fish into bite-sized pieces. Separate slaw into four bowls and place fish on top.
4. Cut avocado in half, remove pit, and scoop out flesh. Divide avocado among bowls. Squeeze remaining half of lime juice over dishes and sprinkle with cilantro.

Per Serving
calories: 328 | fat: 24g | protein: 20g | carbs: 9g
net carbs: 4g | fiber: 5g

Shrimp Stir-Fry

Prep time: 10 minutes | Cook time: 10 minutes
Serves 4

2 tablespoons coconut oil
1 pound (454 g) medium shrimp, shelled and deveined
2 cups broccoli florets
½ cup diced zucchini
½ cup button mushrooms
¼ cup coconut aminos
2 cloves garlic, minced
⅛ teaspoon red pepper flakes
2 cups cooked cauliflower rice

1. Set your Instant Pot to Sauté and heat the coconut oil.
2. Add shrimp and cook for 5 minutes or until pink. Remove and set aside in a bowl.
3. Add the broccoli florets, zucchini, and mushrooms, coconut aminos, garlic, and red pepper flakes to the Instant Pot. Stir-fry for 3 to 5 minutes until vegetables are softened. Return the shrimp to the pot. Stir well.
4. Divide the cauliflower rice into each bowl and top with a portion of stir-fry. Serve warm.

Per Serving
calories: 176 | fat: 7g | protein: 19g | carbs: 6g
net carbs: 3g | fiber: 3g

Lemon Butter Lobster Tail

Prep time: 5 minutes | Cook time: 4 minutes
Serves 2

1 cup chicken broth
½ cup water
1 teaspoon Old Bay seasoning
2 (12-ounce / 340-g) fresh lobster tails
Juice of ½ lemon
2 tablespoons butter, melted
¼ teaspoon salt
¼ teaspoon dried parsley
⅛ teaspoon pepper

1. Pour broth, water, and Old Bay seasoning into Instant Pot. Place trivet in bottom. Place lobster tails on trivet, shell side down. Click lid closed.
2. Press the Manual button and adjust time for 4 minutes. When timer beeps, quick-release the pressure.
3. In small bowl, combine lemon juice, butter, salt, parsley, and pepper.
4. Crack open tail and dip into butter sauce.

Per Serving
calories: 260 | fat: 17g | protein: 33g | carbs: 1g
net carbs: 1g | fiber: 0g

Easy Poke Bowl

Prep time: 5 minutes | Cook time: 3 minutes
Serves 2 to 4

1 cup coconut aminos
1 pound (454 g) wild-caught salmon
1 tablespoon lime juice
2 cups cauliflower rice, cooked

1 drop stevia, liquid
1 avocado, peeled and sliced
1 seaweed sheet
½ teaspoon ginger, finely grated

1. Pour the coconut aminos into the Instant Pot. Insert the trivet. Place the salmon on the trivet, skin-side down, and slowly pour lime juice over it.
2. Close the lid, set the pressure release to Sealing, and select Manual. Set the Instant Pot to 3 minutes on High Pressure and let cook.
3. Once cooked, perform a quick release by carefully switching the pressure valve to Venting.
4. Open the lid and remove the salmon. In a large bowl, combine the cauliflower rice, stevia, avocado, seaweed, and ginger. Then add the salmon.
5. Serve, and enjoy!

Per Serving
calories: 332 | fat: 17g | protein: 24g | carbs: 19g
net carbs: 15g | fiber: 4g

Buttered Scallops

Prep time: 5 minutes | Cook time: 5 minutes
Serves 4

2 tablespoons avocado oil
1 pound (454 g) large sea scallops

⅛ teaspoon salt
⅛ teaspoon pepper
2 tablespoons melted butter

1. Press the Sauté button and add avocado oil to Instant Pot. Allow to fully preheat.
2. Remove side muscle from scallops. Pat dry with towel and sprinkle with salt and pepper. When Instant Pot reads hot, carefully add scallops to pan and sear for 2 minutes. Carefully turn and sear opposite side for 2 to 3 minutes. They will appear opaque all the way through when finished.
3. Pour butter over scallops and serve hot.

Per Serving
calories: 190 | fat: 12g | protein: 14g | carbs: 4g
net carbs: 4g | fiber: 0g

Bang Bang Shrimp

Prep time: 10 minutes | Cook time: 6 minutes
Serves 4

1 pound (454 g) shrimp, peeled
½ cup almond flour
1 tablespoon olive oil

½ teaspoon salt
1 tablespoon mascarpone cheese

1. In the mixing bowl, mix up salt and almond flour.
2. Then dip the shrimp in the mascarpone cheese and coat in the almond flour.
3. Heat up the olive oil in the Instant Pot on Sauté mode for 2 minutes.
4. Put the coated shrimp in the Instant Pot and cook them on Sauté mode for 2 minutes from each side.

Per Serving
calories: 256 | fat: 13g | protein: 29g | carbs: 5g
net carbs: 3g | fiber: 2g

Coconut Curry Mussels

Prep time: 5 minutes | Cook time: 2 minutes
Serves 4

2 tablespoons grass-fed butter, softened
1 (14-ounce / 397-g) can full-fat coconut milk
1 pound (454 g) mussels, cleaned
¼ (4-ounce / 113-g) small onion, thinly sliced

2 teaspoons curry powder
½ teaspoon kosher salt
½ teaspoon ginger, finely grated
½ teaspoon cilantro, dried
½ teaspoon cayenne pepper, ground

1. Set the Instant Pot to Sauté mode. Add the butter, melting it gently.
2. Pour in the coconut milk, then mix in the mussels, onion, curry powder, salt, ginger, cilantro, and cayenne pepper. Close the lid, set the pressure release to Sealing, and select Manual. Set the Instant Pot to 2 minutes on High Pressure and let cook.
3. Once cooked, perform a quick release by carefully switching the pressure valve to Venting, and remove the mussels. Discard any mussels whose shells have not opened. Serve, and enjoy!

Per Serving
calories: 388 | fat: 32g | protein: 16g | carbs: 11g
net carbs: 8g | fiber: 3g

Cajun Crab Legs and Shrimp

Prep time: 10 minutes | Cook time: 5 minutes
Serves 4

2 pounds (907 g) crab legs
½ pound (227 g) large shrimp, shelled and deveined

½ pound (227 g) smoked sausage
2 cups seafood stock
1 tablespoon Cajun seasoning

1. Combine all the ingredients in the Instant Pot.
2. Lock the lid. Select the Steam mode and set the cooking time for 5 minutes at Low Pressure.
3. Once cooking is complete, do a quick pressure release. Carefully open the lid.
4. Serve warm.

Per Serving
calories: 246 | fat: 8.g | protein: 32g | carbs: 5g net carbs: 5g | fiber: 0g

Shrimp and Cauliflower Stir-Fry

Prep time: 3 minutes | Cook time: 10 minutes
Serves 2

1 pound (454 g) shrimp, peeled and deveined
½ teaspoon salt
¼ teaspoon pepper
¼ teaspoon dried parsley
¼ teaspoon garlic

powder
6 asparagus spears, cut into bite-sized pieces
1 cup water
2 tablespoons butter
1 cup uncooked cauliflower rice

1. Sprinkle seasoning on shrimp and place in a steamer basket. Add the asparagus to the basket.
2. Pour water into Instant Pot and insert the steamer basket.
3. Lock the lid. Select the Steam mode and set the cooking time for 5 minutes at Low Pressure.
4. Once cooking is complete, do a quick pressure release. Carefully open the lid.
5. Remove steamer basket and pour water out of Instant Pot.
6. Press the Sauté button on the Instant Pot and melt the butter.
7. Add the cauliflower rice and cooked shrimp and asparagus. Stir-fry for 3 to 5 minutes until cauliflower is tender.
8. Serve warm.

Per Serving
calories: 286 | fat: 12g | protein: 33g | carbs: 6g net carbs: 4g | fiber: 2g

Garlic Butter Shrimp and Asparagus

Prep time: 5 minutes | Cook time: 3 minutes
Serves 2

1 pound (454 g) uncooked peeled shrimp, deveined
1 clove garlic, finely minced
½ teaspoon salt
¼ teaspoon pepper
¼ teaspoon paprika
⅛ teaspoon red pepper

flakes
½ pound (227 g) asparagus, cut into bite-sized pieces
Juice of ½ lemon
4 tablespoons butter
2 teaspoons chopped fresh parsley
1 cup water

1. Sprinkle shrimp with garlic, salt, pepper, paprika, and red pepper flakes and place in 7-cup glass bowl. Place asparagus in bowl.
2. Squeeze lemon juice over shrimp and asparagus and gently mix. Cut butter into cubes and place around dish. Sprinkle with parsley. Cover with foil. Add water to Instant Pot and place trivet in bottom of pot. Carefully place dish on trivet and click lid closed.
3. Press the Steam button and adjust time for 3 minutes. When timer beeps, quick-release the pressure. Remove dish from pot. Serve warm.

Per Serving
calories: 381 | fat: 2g | protein: 33g | carbs: 4g net carbs: 2g | fiber: 2g

Butter Crab with Mushrooms

Prep time: 8 minutes | Cook time: 6 minutes
Serves 6

1 cup water
1½ pounds (680 g) king crab legs, halved
10 ounces (283 g) baby

bella mushrooms
½ stick butter, softened
2 garlic cloves, minced
1 lemon, sliced

1. Pour the water into the Instant Pot and insert a steamer basket. Place the crab legs in the basket.
2. Lock the lid. Select the Manual mode and set the cooking time for 3 minutes at Low Pressure.
3. When the timer beeps, perform a quick pressure release. Carefully remove the lid.
4. Wipe down the Instant Pot with a damp cloth.
5. Set your Instant Pot to Sauté and melt the butter. Cook baby Bella mushrooms with minced garlic for 2 to 3 minutes.
6. Spoon the mushrooms sauce over prepared king crab legs and serve with lemon slices.

Per Serving
calories: 179 | fat: 8g | protein: 22g | carbs: 2g net carbs: 2g | fiber: 0g

Turmeric Shrimp Scampi

Prep time: 5 minutes | Cook time: 20 minutes
Serves 4

2 tablespoons grass-fed butter, softened
1 cup grass-fed bone broth
2 cups cauliflower rice
1 pound (454 g) shrimp, deveined and deshelled
½ cup heavy whipping cream
½ cup full-fat Parmesan

cheese, grated
½ teaspoon freshly ground black pepper
½ teaspoon kosher salt
½ teaspoon garlic, minced
½ teaspoon basil, dried
½ teaspoon parsley, dried
½ teaspoon turmeric, ground

1. Set Instant Pot to Sauté and melt the butter.
2. Pour in the bone broth, then add the cauliflower rice, shrimp, whipping cream, Parmesan, black pepper, salt, garlic, basil, parsley, and turmeric. Stir together thoroughly. Press Cancel to stop the current program, then set the Instant Pot to 20 minutes cook time, on High Pressure.
3. Once cooked, perform a quick release by carefully switching the pressure valve to Venting.
4. Open the Instant Pot, serve, and enjoy!

Per Serving
calories: 356 | fat: 20g | protein: 37g | carbs: 7g
net carbs: 6g | fiber: 1g

Butter Scallops

Prep time: 10 minutes | Cook time: 10 minutes
Serves 4

1 pound (454 g) sea scallops
1 tablespoon coconut aminos
¼ cup apple cider vinegar

1 garlic clove, diced
1 teaspoon chili flakes
¼ teaspoon salt
¼ cup butter
½ cup beef broth

1. Melt the butter on Sauté mode and add scallops.
2. Cook them for 2 minutes per side.
3. Add all remaining ingredients. Close and seal the lid.
4. Cook the scallops on Manual mode at High Pressure for 3 minutes. Allow the natural pressure release for 5 minutes.

Per Serving
calories: 214 | fat: 12g | protein: 20g | carbs:4 g
net carbs: 4g | fiber: 0g

Caprese Salmon

Prep time: 10 minutes | Cook time: 15 minutes
Serves 2

10 ounces (283 g) salmon fillet (2 fillets)
4 ounces (113 g) Mozzarella, sliced
4 cherry tomatoes, sliced
1 teaspoon erythritol

1 teaspoon dried basil
½ teaspoon ground black pepper
1 tablespoon apple cider vinegar
1 tablespoon butter
1 cup water, for cooking

1. Grease the mold with butter and put the salmon inside.
2. Sprinkle the fish with erythritol, dried basil, ground black pepper, and apple cider vinegar.
3. Then top the salmon with tomatoes and Mozzarella.
4. Pour water and insert the trivet in the Instant Pot.
5. Put the fish on the trivet.
6. Close and seal the lid.
7. Cook the meal on Manual mode at High Pressure for 15 minutes. Make a quick pressure release.

Per Serving
calories: 447 | fat: 25g | protein: 46g | carbs: 15g
net carbs: 12g | fiber: 3g

Clambake

Prep time: 5 minutes | Cook time: 6 minutes
Serves 4 to 5

2 tablespoons avocado oil
1 cup grass-fed bone broth
20 clams, scrubbed

2 lobster tails, thawed if frozen
½ teaspoon kosher salt
½ teaspoon freshly ground black pepper

1. Set the Instant Pot to Sauté and heat the oil.
2. Pour in the bone broth. Working in batches (if needed), add the clams, lobster tails, salt, and pepper to the Instant Pot. Close the lid, set the pressure release to Sealing and hit Cancel to stop the current program. Select Manual, set the Instant Pot to 6 minutes on High Pressure, and let cook.
3. Immediately upon completion, carefully switch the pressure release to Venting.
4. Remove clams and lobster tails, and serve with whatever is desired!

Per Serving
calories: 137 | fat: 2g | protein: 26g | carbs: 3g
net carbs: 2g | fiber: 1g

Sour Sea Bass

Prep time: 5 minutes | Cook time: 3 minutes
Serves 2

14 ounces (397 g) sea bass steak
1 tablespoon lemon juice
1 tablespoon apple cider vinegar
¾ teaspoon salt
¾ cup coconut milk
½ teaspoon minced garlic
½ teaspoon smoked paprika

1. Mix up together the lemon juice, apple cider vinegar, salt, minced garlic, and smoked paprika.
2. Rub the sea bass steak with the spice mixture and place it in the Instant Pot.
3. Add coconut milk and lock the Instant Pot lid.
4. Set the Manual mode for 3 minutes. Make the quick-release pressure then.

Per Serving
calories: 649 | fat: 46g | protein: 47g | carbs: 6g
net carbs: 2g | fiber: 4g

Lobster Mac 'n' Cheese

Prep time: 10 minutes | Cook time: 15 minutes
Serves 4

1 large head cauliflower, chopped into bite-sized pieces
1 cup water
4 tablespoons butter
½ medium onion, diced
4 ounces (113 g) cream cheese
¼ cup heavy cream
½ cup grated Gruyère cheese
½ cup shredded sharp Cheddar cheese
1 teaspoon hot sauce
1 teaspoon salt
½ teaspoon pepper
1 pound (454 g) cooked lobster meat

1. Place cauliflower on steamer basket. Add water to Instant Pot and place steamer basket in bottom of pot. Click lid closed. Press the Steam button and adjust time for 1 minute.
2. When timer beeps, quick-release the pressure and remove steamer basket. Set cauliflower aside. Pour water out of pot and wipe dry.
3. Replace pot and press the Sauté button. Press the Adjust button to set heat to Less. Add butter and onion. Sauté for 3 to 5 minutes or until onion becomes soft and fragrant. Soften cream cheese in microwave and stir with spoon until smooth. Add cream cheese to Instant Pot. Press the Cancel button. Press the Sauté button and press the Adjust button to set heat to Normal.
4. Add heavy cream to pot and bring to simmer. Continuously stir until ingredients are fully incorporated. Press the Cancel button.

5. Add shredded cheeses and stir quickly to melt. Add cooked cauliflower into pot, stirring until fully coated with cheese. Add hot sauce and seasoning. Chop lobster into bite-sized pieces and fold into pot. Serve warm.

Per Serving
calories: 521 | fat: 34g | protein: 35g | carbs: 14g
net carbs: 9g | fiber: 5g

Easy-Peasy Seafood Paella

Prep time: 10 minutes | Cook time: 8 minutes
Serves 6

4 tablespoons extra-virgin olive oil
1 medium onion, diced
1 red bell pepper, diced
1 green bell pepper, diced
1 pound (454 g) chorizo sausages, cut into 1-inch slices
1 cup fish stock or chicken broth
2 cups cauliflower couscous
1 large pinch saffron
threads
½ teaspoon ground turmeric
½ cup chopped fresh flat leaf parsley, reserve 1 tablespoon for garnish
1 teaspoon black pepper
1 cup seafood mix (squid, meaty white fish, scallops)
2 cups mixed shellfish (clams, mussels, shrimp)

1. Turn on the Instant Pot by pressing Sauté and set to More. Insert the inner pot and wait until the panel says Hot. Heat the olive oil and sauté the onion and bell peppers for 3 minutes or until the vegetables are soft. Add the chorizo sausages and sauté for 3 minutes or until the surface is no longer pink. Add the fish stock or chicken broth, cauliflower couscous, saffron, turmeric, parsley and black pepper and mix. Add the seafood mixture, then place the shellfish on top. Do not mix.
2. Close the lid tightly and move the steam release handle to Sealing. Press Cancel, then the Manual button and set the timer for 5 minutes on High Pressure.
3. When you hear the beeping sound indicating that the time has ended, carefully turn the steam release handle to the Venting position for the steam to escape and the float valve to drop down. Press Cancel, and open the lid carefully. Serve immediately with the reserved parsley as garnish.

Per Serving
calories: 473 | fat: 39g | protein: 20g | carbs: 9g
net carbs: 7g | fiber: 2g

Shrimp and Avocado Salad

Prep time: 5 minutes | Cook time: 3 minutes
Serves 4

2 tablespoons coconut oil
1 pound (454 g) shrimp, thawed and deveined
1 cup bell peppers, chopped
½ cup spinach, chopped
½ cup kale, chopped
½ cup bok choy, chopped
1 avocado, mashed

2 tablespoons walnuts, chopped
½ teaspoon turmeric, ground
½ teaspoon parsley, dried
½ teaspoon ginger, finely grated
½ teaspoon freshly ground black pepper
½ teaspoon basil, dried

1. Set the Instant Pot to Sauté. Add the oil, melting it gently.
2. Pour 1 cup filtered water into the Instant Pot, then add the shrimp. Close the lid, set the pressure release to Sealing, and select Manual. Set the Instant Pot to 3 minutes on Low Pressure and let cook.
3. In the meantime, make a salad by tossing together the bell peppers, spinach, kale, bok choy, mashed avocado, and walnuts.
4. When the shrimp is cooked, carefully switch the pressure release to Venting.
5. Open the lid and remove the shrimp. Add it atop the tossed salad. Sprinkle the turmeric, parsley, ginger, black pepper, and basil on top, evenly. Enjoy!

Per Serving
calories: 341 | fat: 21g | protein: 28g | carbs: 10g
net carbs: 5g | fiber: 2g

Spicy Fish Balls

Prep time: 8 minutes | Cook time: 10 minutes
Serves 3

1 tablespoon butter
15 ounces (425 g) cod
¼ teaspoon dried oregano

1 teaspoon ground nutmeg
½ teaspoon dried dill

1. Grind the cod and mix it up with all spices.
2. Heat up the butter on Sauté mode.
3. Make the small balls from the cod mixture and put them in the hot butter.
4. Cook the fish balls for 3 minutes from each side on Sauté mode.

Per Serving
calories: 187 | fat: 5g | protein: 32g | carbs: 0g
net carbs: 0g | fiber: 0g

Steamed Lobster with Thyme

Prep time: 10 minutes | Cook time: 4 minutes
Serves 4

4 lobster tails
1 tablespoon butter, softened

1 teaspoon dried thyme
1 cup water

1. Pour water and insert the trivet in the Instant Pot.
2. Put the lobster tails on the trivet and close the lid.
3. Cook the meal on Manual mode at High Pressure for 4 minutes. Make a quick pressure release.
4. After this, mix up butter and dried thyme.
5. Peel the lobsters and rub them with thyme butter.

Per Serving
calories: 126 | fat: 3g | protein: 24g | carbs: 0g
net carbs: 0g | fiber: 0g

Chili Shrimp Salad

Prep time: 5 minutes | Cook time: 7 minutes
Serves 2

1 pound (454 g) shrimp, peeled and deveined
½ teaspoon Old Bay seasoning
¼ teaspoon pepper
¼ teaspoon salt

⅛ teaspoon cayenne
⅛ teaspoon garlic powder
1 cup water
¼ cup mayonnaise
2 tablespoons chili paste

1. Toss shrimp in a 7-cup glass bowl with Old Bay seasoning, salt, pepper, cayenne, and garlic powder.
2. Pour the water into Instant Pot and insert the trivet. Place the bowl with shrimp on top.
3. Lock the lid. Select the Steam mode and set the cooking time for 7 minutes at Low Pressure.
4. Once cooking is complete, do a quick pressure release. Carefully open the lid.
5. Remove the bowl from the Instant Pot and drain water.
6. In a small bowl, stir together the mayo and chili paste. Add the shrimp and toss to coat. Serve immediately.

Per Serving
calories: 403 | fat: 24g | protein: 32g | carbs: 8g
net carbs: 8g | fiber: 0g

Crab and Sundried Tomato Frittata

Prep time: 5 minutes | Cook time: 10 minutes
Serves 4

2 pounds (907 g) lump
crab meat
¼ cup sun-dried
tomatoes, chopped
¼ cup chopped fresh
flat leaf parsley, reserve
1 teaspoon for garnish
1 tablespoon dried
tarragon
8 large eggs, beaten

1 cup almond milk,
unsweetened
1 teaspoon sea salt
1 teaspoon black
pepper
½ cup shredded
Cheddar cheese,
reserve 2 tablespoons
for garnish
1 cup water

1. In a medium-sized mixing bowl, combine all of the ingredients except for 1 teaspoon of parsley, 2 tablespoons of Cheddar cheese and the water. Transfer the mixture into 4 ramekins and cover with aluminum foil. Pour the water into the inner pot of the Instant Pot and place the trivet inside. Put the prepared ramekins on the trivet, 2 on the bottom and 2 on the top, scattered.
2. Turn on the Instant Pot by pressing the Manual button and set the timer for 10 minutes on High Pressure. Close the lid tightly and move the steam release handle to Sealing.
3. When the timer ends, you will hear a beeping sound. Allow the Instant Pot to cool down naturally until the float valve drops down. Press Cancel and open the lid. Remove the ramekins, serve hot with the remaining shredded Cheddar cheese and chopped parsley as a garnish.

Per Serving
calories: 285 | fat: 16g | protein: 29g | carbs: 4g
net carbs: 3g | fiber: 1g

Lemon Turmeric Salmon

Prep time: 10 minutes | Cook time: 4 minutes
Serves 3

1 pound (454 g) salmon
fillet
1 teaspoon ground
black pepper
½ teaspoon salt

1 teaspoon ground
turmeric
1 teaspoon lemon juice
1 cup water

1. In the shallow bowl, mix up salt, ground black pepper, and ground turmeric.
2. Sprinkle the salmon fillet with lemon juice and rub with the spice mixture.
3. Then pour water in the Instant Pot and insert the trivet.

4. Wrap the salmon fillet in the foil and place it on the trivet.
5. Close and seal the lid.
6. Cook the fish on Manual mode at High Pressure for 4 minutes.
7. Make a quick pressure release and cut the fish on servings.

Per Serving
calories: 205 | fat: 9g | protein: 30g | carbs: 1g
net carbs: 1g | fiber: 0g

Peel-and-Eat Shrimp

Prep time: 5 minutes | Cook time: 3 minutes
Serves 4

2 pounds (907 g) raw
shell-on shrimp
1 cup seafood stock

1 teaspoon Old Bay
seasoning

1. Use a knife to cut slit in shell and devein shrimp while leaving rest of shell intact. Pour seafood stock and Old Bay seasoning into Instant Pot. Add shrimp. Click lid closed.
2. Press the Manual button and set time for 3 minutes. When timer beeps, quick-release the pressure. To eat, remove shell and serve warm with low-carb cocktail sauce.

Per Serving
calories: 81 | fat: 1g | protein: 16g | carbs: 1g
net carbs: 1g | fiber: 0g

Shrimp Zoodle Alfredo

Prep time: 10 minutes | Cook time: 10 minutes
Serves 4

2 zucchinis, trimmed
1 cup coconut cream
1 teaspoon butter
1 teaspoon seafood

seasoning
6 ounces (170 g)
shrimp, peeled

1. Melt the butter on Sauté mode and add shrimp.
2. Sprinkle them with seafood seasoning and sauté then for 2 minutes.
3. After this, spiralizer the zucchini with the help of the spiralizer and add in the shrimp.
4. Add coconut cream and close the lid. Cook the meal on Sauté mode for 8 minutes.

Per Serving
calories: 213 | fat: 16g | protein: 12g | carbs: 7g
net carbs: 5g | fiber: 2g

Tender Salmon Fillets

Prep time: 10 minutes | Cook time: 10 minutes
Serves 2

1 tablespoon dried dill	½ teaspoon salt
10 ounces (283 g)	1 tablespoon cream
salmon fillet (cut into 2	cheese
servings)	1 tablespoon butter

1. Gently rub the fish fillets with dill and salt.
2. Preheat the Instant Pot on the Sauté mode until it is displayed Hot.
3. Toss the butter inside and melt it.
4. Transfer the salmon fillets in the Instant Pot and cook them for 2 minutes from each side.
5. Add the cream cheese and sauté the fish for 4 minutes more.

Per Serving
calories: 260 | fat: 16g | protein: 28g | carbs: 1g
net carbs: 1g | fiber: 0g

Fish Poached in Garlic Cream Sauce

Prep time: 5 minutes | Cook time: 3 minutes
Serves 2

¼ cup heavy cream (or full-fat coconut milk for dairy-free)	¼ teaspoon ground black pepper
Cloves squeezed from 1 head roasted garlic, or 2 cloves garlic, minced	Extra-virgin olive oil, for drizzling (optional)
1 pound (454 g) walleye or cod fillets, cut into 2 by 1-inch pieces	Chopped fresh Italian parsley leaves, for garnish
1 teaspoon fine sea salt	1 lemon, thinly sliced, for garnish

1. Place the cream and garlic in a food processor or blender and purée until very smooth.
2. Set a trivet in a 6-quart Instant Pot and pour in 1½ cups of cold water.
3. Season the fish on both sides with the salt and pepper, then put the fillets in a 7-inch soufflé or casserole dish. Pour the garlic cream over the fish.
4. Set the dish on the trivet in the Instant Pot. Seal the lid, press Manual, and set the timer for 3 minutes. Once finished, let the pressure release naturally.
5. Place the fish on a serving platter and cover with the cream sauce. Drizzle with olive oil, if desired, and garnish with parsley and lemon slices.

Per Serving
calories: 314 | fat: 14g | protein: 44g | carbs: 2g
net carbs: 2g | fiber: 0g

Crustless Fish Pie

Prep time: 15 minutes | Cook time: 15 minutes
Serves 6

1 cup cauliflower, boiled, mashed	½ cup Mozzarella cheese, shredded
3 eggs, hard-boiled, peeled, chopped	½ cup heavy cream
10 ounces (283 g) salmon, chopped, boiled	¼ cup chicken broth
	1 teaspoon salt
	½ teaspoon ground paprika

1. Mix up chopped salmon and eggs and transfer them in the Instant Pot.
2. Sprinkle the mixture with salt and ground paprika.
3. After this, top it with mashed cauliflower and Mozzarella.
4. Add chicken broth and heavy cream.
5. Close and seal the lid.
6. Cook the pie for 15 minutes on Manual mode at High Pressure. Make a quick pressure release.

Per Serving
calories: 141 | fat: 9g | protein: 13g | carbs: 2g
net carbs: 2g | fiber: 0g

Tuna and Spinach Cakes

Prep time: 15 minutes | Cook time: 8 minutes
Serves 4

10 ounces (283 g) tuna, shredded	coriander
1 cup spinach	2 tablespoon coconut flakes
1 egg, beaten	1 tablespoon avocado oil
1 teaspoon ground	

1. Blend the spinach in the blender until smooth.
2. Then transfer it in the mixing bowl and add tuna, egg, and ground coriander.
3. Add coconut flakes and stir the mass with the help of the spoon.
4. Heat up avocado oil in the Instant Pot on Sauté mode for 2 minutes.
5. Then make the medium size cakes from the tuna mixture and place them in the hot oil.
6. Cook the tuna cakes on Sauté mode for 3 minutes.
7. Then flip the on another side and cook for 3 minutes more or until they are light brown.

Per Serving
calories: 163 | fat: 8g | protein:20g | carbs: 1g
net carbs: 0g | fiber: 1g

9-Minute Mahi Mahi

Prep time: 5 minutes | Cook time: 4 minutes
Serves 4

3 tablespoons grass-fed butter, softened	½ teaspoon freshly ground black pepper
1 piece ginger, grated	½ teaspoon kosher salt
½ lime, juiced	½ teaspoon garlic, minced
½ lemon, juiced	4 mahi mahi fillets
½ teaspoon basil, dried	

1. Pour ½ cup filtered water into the Instant Pot, then insert the trivet. In a large bowl, combine the butter, ginger, lime juice, lemon juice, basil, black pepper, salt, and garlic. Mix thoroughly. Coat the mahi mahi fillets with this mixture, then place the fillets into a well-greased, Instant Pot-friendly dish.
2. Place the dish onto the trivet, and cover loosely with aluminum foil. Close the lid, set the pressure release to Sealing and select Manual. Set the Instant Pot to 4 minutes on Low Pressure, and let cook.
3. Once cooked, perform a quick release by carefully switching the pressure valve to Venting. Open the Instant Pot, and remove the fillets. Serve, and enjoy!

Per Serving
calories: 310 | fat: 11g | protein: 47g | carbs: 1g
net carbs: 1g | fiber: 0g

10-Minute Salmon and Vegetables

Prep time: 5 minutes | Cook time: 5 minutes
Serves 4

½ bunch fresh parsley, plus more for garnish	1 medium lemon, thinly sliced
2 to 3 sprigs fresh tarragon	2 medium zucchinis, julienned
1½ pounds (680 g) wild salmon fillets	2 medium bell peppers (any color), seeded and julienned
1 tablespoon olive oil	2 medium carrots, julienned
Sea salt and black pepper to taste	

1. Place ¾ cup of filtered water, the parsley, and tarragon into the Instant Pot. Insert the trivet with the handles extending up.
2. Place the salmon on the trivet, skin-side down. Drizzle with the olive oil. Season generously with salt and pepper. Top with the lemon slices.
3. Close the lid, set the pressure release to Sealing, press Steam, and set the time to 3 minutes.

4. Once done, perform a quick release, being careful to avoid the released steam. Remove the lid and the trivet with the salmon. Set fillets aside and keep them warm.
5. Discard the herbs, but keep the liquid in the pot. Add the zucchinis, peppers, and carrots to the pot and close the lid.
6. Press Sauté and allow the vegetables to cook until tender, 2 to 3 minutes. When vegetables are cooked to desired tenderness, remove and season to taste with salt and pepper. Serve with the salmon and a garnish of parsley.

Per Serving
calories: 188 | fat: 9g | protein: 18g | carbs: 11g
net carbs: 8g | fiber: 3g

Basil Scallops in Port Wine

Prep time: 10 minutes | Cook time: 5 minutes
Serves 5

1 tablespoon olive oil	paprika
1 brown onion, chopped	Sea salt and ground black pepper, to taste
2 garlic cloves, minced	2 tablespoons fresh lemon juice
½ cup port wine	
½ cup fish stock	½ cup cream cheese, at room temperature
1½ pounds (680 g) scallops, peeled and deveined	2 tablespoons chopped fresh basil, for garnish
1 ripe tomato, crushed	
1 teaspoon smoked	

1. Set your Instant Pot to Sauté and heat the olive oil.
2. Cook the onion and garlic until fragrant for 2 minutes.
3. Add the wine to deglaze the bottom. Add the scallops, fish stock, tomato, salt, black pepper, and paprika.
4. Lock the lid. Select the Manual mode and set the cooking time for 1 minute at Low Pressure.
5. When the timer beeps, perform a quick pressure release. Carefully remove the lid.
6. Drizzle fresh lemon juice over the scallops and top them with cream cheese. Cover and allow to sit in the residual heat for 3 to 5 minutes. Serve warm garnished with fresh basil leaves.

Per Serving
calories: 213 | fat: 10g | protein: 19g | carbs: 9g
net carbs: 8g | fiber: 1g

Cod Lime Pieces

Prep time: 10 minutes | Cook time: 9 minutes
Serves 2

6 ounces (170 g) cod
fillet
1 teaspoon lime zest,
grated

1 tablespoon lime juice
1 tablespoon coconut
oil
1 egg, beaten

1. Cut the cod fillet into medium cubes and
   sprinkle with lime juice and lime zest.
2. Then dip the fish cubes in the egg.
3. Heat up coconut oil on Sauté mode for 3
   minutes.
4. Put the cod cubes in the hot oil in one layer
   and cook on Sauté mode for 4 minutes.
5. Then flip the on another side and cook for 2
   minutes more.

Per Serving
calories: 161 | fat: 10g | protein: 18g | carbs: 1g
net carbs: 1g | fiber: 0g

Clam Chowder with Celery

Prep time: 10 minutes | Cook time: 4 minutes
Serves 2

5 ounces (142 g) clams
1 ounce (28 g) bacon,
chopped
3 ounces (85 g) celery,

chopped
½ cup water
½ cup heavy cream

1. Cook the bacon on Sauté mode for 1 minute.
2. Then add clams, celery, water, and heavy
   cream.
3. Close and seal the lid.
4. Cook the seafood on steam mode at High
   Pressure for 3 minutes. Make a quick pressure
   release.
5. Ladle the clams with the heavy cream mixture
   in the bowls.

Per Serving
calories: 221 | fat: 17g | protein: 7g | carbs: 10g
net carbs: 9g | fiber: 1g

Cod under the Bagel Spices Crust

Prep time: 10 minutes | Cook time: 10 minutes
Serves 2

6 ounces (170 g) cod
fillet
1 tablespoon bagel

spices
1 teaspoon olive oil
1 teaspoon butter

1. Cut the cod fillet into 2 servings and sprinkle
   the bagel spices generously.

2. Then melt the butter in the Instant Pot. Add
   olive oil and stir gently.
3. Put the prepared cod fillets in the hot oil
   mixture and cook for 3.5 minutes per side on
   Sauté mode.
4. After this, close the lid and cook the fish on
   Sauté mode for 3 minutes.

Per Serving
calories: 133 | fat: 5g | protein: 17g | carbs: 6g
net carbs: 4g | fiber: 2g

Coconut Curry Shrimp

Prep time: 10 minutes | Cook time: 5 minutes
Serves 4

2 tablespoons butter
1 small onion, diced
1 teaspoon grated or
finely minced ginger
1 clove garlic, minced
or pressed
1 pound (454 g) shrimp
with shells, deveined
1 teaspoon curry
powder
½ cup water

¼ head cauliflower,
florets and stems cut
½ cup full-fat coconut
milk
½ teaspoon sea salt
1 tablespoon fresh
cilantro, chopped, for
garnish
1 tablespoon fresh
scallions, chopped, for
garnish

1. Turn on the Instant Pot by pressing Sauté
   and set to More. Insert the inner pot and wait
   until the panel says Hot. Add the butter to
   the inner pot and, when the butter melts, add
   the onion, ginger and garlic, and sauté for
   2 minutes or until the onion is soft. Add the
   shrimp, curry powder and water. Close the lid
   tightly and move the steam release handle to
   Sealing. Press the Manual button and set the
   timer for 3 minutes on High Pressure.
2. When you hear the beeping sound indicating
   that the time has ended, carefully turn the
   steam release handle to the Venting position
   to let the steam escape until the float valve
   drops down. Press Cancel, and open the lid
   carefully. Add the cauliflower, coconut milk
   and sea salt and close the lid tightly. Press
   the Manual button and set the timer to 0
   minutes. When you hear the beeping sound
   indicating that time has ended, carefully
   turn the steam release handle to the Venting
   position and let the steam escape until the
   float valve drops down. Press Cancel, and
   open the lid carefully. Garnish with the
   scallions and cilantro and serve immediately.

Per Serving
calories: 265 | fat: 15g | protein: 25g | carbs: 8g
net carbs: 6g | fiber: 2g

Tuna Hotdish

Prep time: 6 minutes | Cook time: 12 minutes
Serves 8

1 (8-ounce / 227-g)
package cream cheese
(1 cup), softened
1 cup shredded sharp
Cheddar cheese (4
ounces / 113 g), plus
more for garnish
1 cup chicken broth
1 tablespoon coconut
oil or unsalted butter
(Instant Pot only)
¼ cup diced onions

¼ cup chopped celery
4 (5-ounce / 142-g)
cans chunk tuna packed
in water, drained
2 cups halved hearts of
palm
Fine sea salt and
ground black pepper
1 cup diced mini dill
pickles
Fresh dill, for garnish

1. Place the cream cheese, Cheddar cheese, and broth in a blender and purée until smooth.
2. Place the coconut oil in a 6-quart Instant Pot and press Sauté. When hot, add the onions and celery and cook, stirring often, for 4 minutes, or until soft. Add the cheesy broth mixture, tuna, and hearts of palm and gently stir to combine. Press Cancel to stop the Sauté.
3. Seal the lid, press Manual, and set the timer for 5 minutes. Once finished, turn the valve to venting for a quick release.
4. Preheat the oven to broil.
5. Remove the lid and season the tuna mixture with salt and pepper to taste. Stir in the pickles.
6. Transfer the tuna and pickle mixture to a serving dish and top with additional Cheddar cheese. Place under the broiler for a few minutes to melt the cheese topping. Garnish with dill.

Per Serving
calories: 276 | fat: 16g | protein: 25g | carbs: 5g
net carbs: 4g | fiber: 1g

Lemon Cod Fillets

Prep time: 5 minutes | Cook time: 12 minutes
Serves 4

½ cup water
4 frozen cod fillets
(about 6 ounces / 170
g each)
1 teaspoon dried basil
Pinch of salt
Pinch of black pepper
4 lemon slices
¼ cup heavy cream
2 tablespoons butter,

softened
1 ounce (28 g) cream
cheese, softened
2 teaspoons lemon
juice
1½ teaspoons chopped
fresh basil, plus more
for garnish (optional)
Lemon wedges, for
garnish (optional)

1. Place the trivet inside the pot and add the water. Lay a piece of aluminum foil on top of the trivet and place the cod on top.
2. Sprinkle the fish with the dried basil, salt, and pepper. Set a lemon slice on top of each fillet.
3. Close the lid and seal the vent. Cook on High Pressure for 9 minutes. Quick release the steam. Press Cancel.
4. Remove the trivet and fish from the pot. Rinse the pot if needed and turn to Sauté mode.
5. Add the cream and butter and whisk as the butter melts and the cream warms up. Add the cream cheese and whisk until thickened, 2 to 3 minutes. Add the lemon juice and another pinch of salt and pepper. Once the sauce is thickened and well combined, 1 to 2 minutes, press Cancel and add the fresh basil.
6. Pour the sauce over the fish. Garnish with fresh basil or a lemon wedge, if desired.

Per Serving
calories: 221 | fat: 11g | protein: 27g | carbs: 1g
net carbs: 1g | fiber: 0g

Pesto Flounder

Prep time: 15 minutes | Cook time: 15 minutes
Serves 3

2 tablespoons pesto
sauce
½ cup butter

10 ounces (283 g)
flounder fillet
1 cup water, for cooking

1. Cut the fish into 3 servings and put in the baking pan.
2. Brush the flounder fillets with pesto sauce. Add butter.
3. Pour water and insert the trivet in the Instant Pot.
4. Put the baking pan with fish on the trivet. Close and seal the lid.
5. Cook the meal on Manual mode at High Pressure for 15 minutes. Allow the natural pressure release for 10 minutes.

Per Serving
calories: 427 | fat: 36g | protein: 24g | carbs: 1g
net carbs: 1g | fiber: 0g

Foil-Pack Haddock with Spinach

**Prep time: 15 minutes | Cook time: 15 minutes
Serves 4**

12 ounces (340 g)
haddock fillet
1 cup spinach
1 tablespoon avocado
oil

1 teaspoon minced
garlic
½ teaspoon ground
coriander
1 cup water, for cooking

1. Blend the spinach until smooth and mix
    up with avocado oil, ground coriander, and
    minced garlic.
2. Then cut the haddock into 4 fillets and place
    on the foil.
3. Top the fish fillets with spinach mixture and
    place them on the trivet.
4. Pour water and insert the trivet in the Instant
    Pot.
5. Close and seal the lid and cook the haddock
    on Manual at High Pressure for 15 minutes.
6. Do a quick pressure release.

Per Serving
calories: 103 | fat: 1g | protein: 21g | carbs: 1g
net carbs: 1g | fiber: 0g

Greek Shrimp with Tomatoes

**Prep time: 10 minutes | Cook time: 2 minutes
Serves 6**

3 tablespoons unsalted
butter
1 tablespoon garlic
½ teaspoon red pepper
flakes, or more as
needed
1½ cups chopped onion
1 (14½-ounce / 411-
g) can diced tomatoes,
undrained

1 teaspoon dried
oregano
1 teaspoon salt
1 pound (454 g) frozen
shrimp, peeled
1 cup crumbled feta
cheese
½ cup sliced black
olives
¼ cup chopped parsley

1. Preheat the Instant Pot by selecting Sauté
    and adjusting to high heat. When the inner
    cooking pot is hot, add the butter and heat
    until it foams. Add the garlic and red pepper
    flakes, and cook just until fragrant, about 1
    minute.
2. Add the onion, tomatoes, oregano, and salt,
    and stir to combine.
3. Add the frozen shrimp.
4. Lock the lid into place. Select Manual and
    adjust the pressure to Low. Cook for 1
    minute. When the cooking is complete, quick-
    release the pressure. Unlock the lid.
5. Mix the shrimp in with the lovely tomato
    broth.

6. Allow the mixture to cool slightly. Right before
    serving, sprinkle with the feta cheese, olives,
    and parsley. This dish makes a soupy broth,
    so it's great over mashed cauliflower.

Per Serving
calories: 361 | fat: 22g | protein: 30g | carbs: 13g
net carbs: 11g | fiber: 2g

Shrimp Scampi

**Prep time: 10 minutes | Cook time: 16 minutes
Serves 4**

½ cup unsalted butter
(or butter-flavored
coconut oil for dairy-
free)
2 tablespoons lemon
juice
1 tablespoon Dijon
mustard
Cloves squeezed from 1

head roasted garlic, or
2 cloves garlic, minced
4 cups very thinly sliced
cabbage, for "noodles"
1 pound (454 g)
medium shrimp, peeled
and deveined
1 tablespoon chopped
fresh flat-leaf parsley

1. Place the butter, lemon juice, mustard, and
    garlic in a 6-quart Instant Pot and press
    Sauté. Cook for 3 minutes, or until the garlic
    is fragrant.
2. Scoop out half of the garlic butter mixture
    with a measuring cup and set aside.
3. Add the cabbage to the pot and stir to coat.
    Press Cancel to stop the Sauté.
4. Seal the lid, press Manual, and set the timer
    for 8 minutes. Once finished, turn the valve
    to venting for a quick release.
5. Remove the cabbage from the pot and set
    aside on a serving platter.
6. Add the reserved garlic butter and the shrimp
    to the pot and press Sauté. Cook for 5
    minutes, or until the shrimp have just turned
    pink.
7. Add the shrimp and sauce from the pot to
    the cabbage "noodles" on the serving platter.
    Garnish with freshly ground pepper and
    parsley.

Per Serving
calories: 393 | fat: 26g | protein: 33g | carbs: 8g
net carbs: 6g | fiber: 2g

Cajun Cod

Prep time: 10 minutes | Cook time: 4 minutes
Serves 2

10 ounces (283 g) cod fillet
1 tablespoon olive oil
1 teaspoon Cajun

seasoning
2 tablespoons coconut aminos

1. Sprinkle the cod fillet with coconut aminos and Cajun seasoning.
2. Then heat up olive oil in the Instant Pot on Sauté mode.
3. Add the spiced cod fillet and cook it for 4 minutes from each side.
4. Then cut it into halves and sprinkle with the oily liquid from the Instant Pot.

Per Serving
calories: 189 | fat: 8g | protein: 25g | carbs: 3g
net carbs: 3g | fiber: 0g

Louisiana Shrimp Gumbo

Prep time: 10 minutes | Cook time: 4 minutes
Serves 6

1 pound (454 g) shrimp
¼ cup chopped celery stalk
1 chili pepper, chopped
¼ cup chopped okra

1 tablespoon coconut oil
2 cups chicken broth
1 teaspoon sugar-free tomato paste

1. Put all ingredients in the Instant Pot and stir until you get a light red color.
2. Then close and seal the lid.
3. Cook the meal on Manual mode at High Pressure for 4 minutes.
4. When the time is finished, allow the natural pressure release for 10 minutes.

Per Serving
calories: 126 | fat: 4g | protein: 19g | carbs: 2g
net carbs: 2g | fiber: 0g

Dill Salmon Fillet

Prep time: 10 minutes | Cook time: 4 minutes
Serves 4

1 pound (454 g) salmon fillet
1 tablespoon butter, melted

2 tablespoons lemon juice
1 teaspoon dried dill
1 cup water

1. Cut the salmon fillet on 4 servings.
2. Line the Instant Pot baking pan with foil and put the salmon fillets inside in one layer.

3. Then sprinkle the fish with dried dill, lemon juice, and butter.
4. Pour water in the Instant Pot and insert the trivet.
5. Place the baking pan with salmon on the trivet and close the lid.
6. Cook the meal on Manual mode at High Pressure for 4 minutes. Allow the natural pressure release for 5 minutes and remove the fish from the Instant Pot.

Per Serving
calories: 178 | fat: 10g | protein: 22g | carbs: 0g
net carbs: 0g | fiber: 0g

Chili Haddock

Prep time: 10 minutes | Cook time: 5 minutes
Serves 4

1 chili pepper, minced
1 pound (454 g) haddock, chopped
½ teaspoon ground

turmeric
½ cup fish stock
1 cup water

1. In the mixing bowl mix up chili pepper, ground turmeric, and fish stock.
2. Then add chopped haddock and transfer the mixture in the baking mold.
3. Pour water in the Instant Pot and insert the trivet.
4. Place the baking mold with fish on the trivet and close the lid.
5. Cook the meal on Manual at High Pressure for 5 minutes. Make a quick pressure release.

Per Serving
calories: 130 | fat: 1g | protein: 28g | carbs: 0g
net carbs: 0g | fiber: 0g

Alaskan Crab Legs

Prep time: 10 minutes | Cook time: 4 minutes
Serves 4

1 pound (454 g) Alaskan crab legs
1 tablespoon butter

¼ teaspoon dried cilantro
1 cup water

1. Pour water in the Instant Pot.
2. Add dried cilantro and crab legs.
3. Cook the on Manual mode at High Pressure for 4 minutes.
4. Then make a quick pressure release.
5. Peel the crab legs and sprinkle them with butter.

Per Serving
calories: 78 | fat: 3g | protein: 12g | carbs: 0g
net carbs: 0g | fiber: 0g

Cod with Olives

Prep time: 15 minutes | Cook time: 10 minutes
Serves 2

8 ounces (227 g) cod fillet
¼ cup sliced olives
1 teaspoon olive oil
¼ teaspoon salt
1 cup water, for cooking

1. Pour water and insert the trivet in the Instant Pot.
2. Then cut the cod fillet into 2 servings and sprinkle with salt and olive oil.
3. Then place the fish on the foil and top with the sliced olives. Wrap the fish and transfer it onto the trivet.
4. Close and seal the lid. Cook the fish on Manual mode at High Pressure for 10 minutes.
5. Allow the natural pressure release for 5 minutes.

Per Serving
calories: 130 | fat: 5g | protein: 20g | carbs: 1g
net carbs: 1g | fiber: 0g

Shrimp Coconut Curry

Prep time: 10 minutes | Cook time: 4 minutes
Serves 5

15 ounces (425 g) shrimp, peeled
1 teaspoon chili powder
1 teaspoon garam masala
1 cup coconut milk
1 teaspoon olive oil
½ teaspoon minced garlic

1. Heat up the Instant Pot on Sauté mode for 2 minutes.
2. Then add olive oil. Cook the ingredients for 1 minute.
3. Add shrimp and sprinkle them with chili powder, garam masala, minced garlic, and coconut milk.
4. Carefully stir the ingredients and close the lid.
5. Cook the shrimp curry on Manual mode for 1 minute. Make a quick pressure release.

Per Serving
calories: 222 | fat: 14g | protein: 21g | carbs: 4g
net carbs: 3g | fiber: 1g

Cayenne and Oregano Cod

Prep time: 10 minutes | Cook time: 10 minutes
Serves 2

2 cod fillets
¼ teaspoon chili powder
½ teaspoon cayenne pepper
½ teaspoon dried oregano
1 tablespoon lime juice
2 tablespoons avocado oil

1. Rub the cod fillets with chili powder, cayenne pepper, dried oregano, and sprinkle with lime juice.
2. Then pour the avocado oil in the Instant Pot and heat it up on Sauté mode for 2 minutes.
3. Put the cod fillets in the hot oil and cook for 5 minutes.
4. Then flip the fish on another side and cook for 5 minutes more.

Per Serving
calories: 144 | fat: 3g | protein: 20g | carbs: 2g
net carbs: 1g | fiber: 1g

Lemon Mahi Mahi

Prep time: 10 minutes | Cook time: 9 minutes
Serves 4

1 pound (454 g) mahi-mahi fillet
1 teaspoon grated lemon zest
1 tablespoon lemon juice
1 tablespoon butter, softened
½ teaspoon salt
1 cup water, for cooking

1. Cut the fish on 4 servings and sprinkle with lemon zest, lemon juice, salt, and rub with softened butter.
2. Then put the fish in the baking pan in one layer.
3. Pour water and insert the trivet in the Instant Pot.
4. Put the mold with fish on the trivet. Close and seal the lid.
5. Cook the Mahi Mahi on Manual mode at High Pressure for 9 minutes. Make a quick pressure release.

Per Serving
calories: 128 | fat: 4g | protein: 21g | carbs: 0g
net carbs: 0g | fiber: 0g

Chaptr 12 Desserts

Berries and Cream Syrup

Prep time: 2 minutes | Cook time: 4 minutes
Makes 1 cup

1 cup fresh strawberries
1 cup fresh blackberries
½ cup fresh blueberries
2 tablespoons lemon juice
1 tablespoon water

2 tablespoons heavy cream
¼ teaspoon xanthan gum
1 cup water

1. Place all berries, lemon juice, and water into 7-cup glass bowl. Insert trivet in Instant Pot and place bowl on top. Add 1 cup water to pot. Click lid closed. Press the Manual button and adjust time for 4 minutes.
2. When timer beeps, quick-release the pressure. Pour berries and juice into food processor or blender. Pulse until smooth. Use fine-mesh strainer to remove seeds and fruit skin from mixture. Whisk in heavy cream and xanthan gum. Keep in sealed container or Mason jar in fridge.

Per Serving
calories: 32 | fat: 2g | protein: 0g | carbs: 5g
net carbs: 3g | fiber: 2g

Thai Coconut Pandan Custard

Prep time: 10 minutes | Cook time: 30 minutes
Serves 4

Nonstick cooking spray
1 cup unsweetened coconut milk
3 eggs

⅓ cup Swerve
3 to 4 drops pandan extract, or use vanilla extract if you must

1. Grease a 6-inch heatproof bowl with the cooking spray.
2. In a large bowl, whisk together the coconut milk, eggs, Swerve, and pandan extract. Pour the mixture into the prepared bowl and cover it with aluminum foil.
3. Pour 2 cups of water into the inner cooking pot of the Instant Pot, then place a trivet in the pot. Place the bowl on the trivet.
4. Lock the lid into place. Select Manual and adjust the pressure to High. Cook for 30 minutes. When the cooking is complete, let the pressure release naturally. Unlock the lid.
5. Remove the bowl from the pot and remove the foil. A knife inserted into the custard should come out clean. Cool in the refrigerator for 6 to 8 hours, or until the custard is set.

Per Serving
calories: 202 | fat: 18g | protein: 6g | carbs: 4g
net carbs: 3g | fiber: 1g

Chocolate Chip Fat Bomb

Prep time: 2 minutes | Cook time: 2 minutes
Serves 12

½ cup coconut oil
½ cup no-sugar-added peanut butter
2 ounces (57 g) cream cheese, warmed

¼ cup powdered erythritol
¼ cup low-carb chocolate chips

1. Press the Sauté button and add coconut oil to Instant Pot. Allow oil to melt and press the Cancel button.
2. Stir in peanut butter, cream cheese, and erythritol. Pour mixture into silicone baking cups or 12-cup muffin tin and sprinkle chocolate chips into each. Place in freezer until firm then keep in fridge.

Per Serving
calories: 181 | fat: 17g | protein: 3g | carbs: 4g
net carbs: 4g | fiber: 1g

Ice Cream Bites

Prep time: 5 minutes | Cook time: 5 minutes
Serves 7

6 tablespoons sugar-free chocolate chips
4 ounces (113 g) full-fat cream cheese, softened
½ cup full-fat coconut milk

1 cup heavy whipping cream
½ cup Swerve, confectioners (or more, to taste)
½ teaspoon vanilla extract

1. Pour 1 cup of filtered water into the inner pot of the Instant Pot, then insert the trivet. In a large bowl, combine the chocolate chips, cream cheese, coconut milk, whipping cream, Swerve, and vanilla. Mix thoroughly and transfer into well-greased egg bites molds.
2. Place molds on top of the trivet, stacking on top of each other, if needed. Cover loosely with aluminum foil. Close the lid, set the pressure release to Sealing, and select Manual. Set the Instant Pot to 5 minutes on High Pressure, and let cook.
3. Once cooked, let the pressure release naturally, for about 10 minutes. Then, switch the pressure release to Venting. Open the Instant Pot, and remove the molds. Freeze for at least 1 hour, then serve. Keep uneaten bites stored in freezer.

Per Serving
calories: 170 | fat: 16g | protein: 2g | carbs: 6g
net carbs: 5g | fiber: 1g

Bacon and Chocolate Covered Brazil Nuts

Prep time: 5 minutes | Cook time: 5 minutes
Serves 10

2 tablespoons grass-fed butter, softened
1 cup sugar-free chocolate chips

2 slices no-sugar-added bacon, crushed up, cooked
1 cup Brazil nuts

1. Set the Instant Pot to Sauté and melt the butter.
2. Add the chocolate chips, bacon, and Brazil nuts to the Instant Pot. Mix thoroughly, until melted.
3. Pour mixture into a large bowl.
4. Refrigerate until firm. Serve, and enjoy!

Per Serving
calories: 149 | fat: 12g | protein: 3g | carbs: 13g
net carbs: 10g | fiber: 3g

Soft and Chewy Chocolate Chip Cookie Bites

Prep time: 5 minutes | Cook time: 20 minutes
Serves 7

8 tablespoons sugar-free chocolate chips
2 tablespoons grass-fed butter, softened
2 cups blanched almond flour

1 egg
½ cup Swerve, confectioners (or more, to taste)
¼ teaspoon baking soda

1. Pour 1 cup water into the Instant Pot, then insert the trivet. In a large bowl, combine the chocolate chips, butter, almond flour, egg, Swerve, and baking soda. Mix until a soft dough forms. Once mixed thoroughly, transfer into a well-greased, Instant Pot-friendly egg bites mold. Work in batches, if needed. I prefer to stack 2 egg bites molds on top of each other, separated by Mason jar lids (or similar dividers).
2. Cover loosely with aluminum foil. Close the lid, set the pressure release to Sealing, and select Manual. Set the Instant Pot to 20 minutes on High Pressure, and let cook.
3. Once cooked, let the pressure naturally disperse from the Instant Pot for about 10 minutes, then carefully switch the pressure release to Venting.
4. Open the Instant Pot, and remove the pan. Let cool, serve, and enjoy!

Per Serving
calories: 127 | fat: 11g | protein: 2g | carbs: 6g
net carbs: 5g | fiber: 1g

Coconut Whipped Cream

Prep time: 5 minutes | Cook time: 5 minutes
Serves 5 to 6

1 (14-ounce / 397-g) can full-fat coconut milk, refrigerated
½ cup heavy whipping cream

½ teaspoon vanilla extract
⅓ cup Swerve, confectioners (or more, to taste)

1. With a large spoon, carefully scoop out the cream portion of the coconut milk, discarding the remaining liquid.
2. In a small bowl, mix the coconut milk with the heavy whipping cream, vanilla, and Swerve and stir until combined.
3. Set the Instant Pot to Sauté and pour in the mixture. Melt together for one minute, stirring thoroughly.
4. Remove cream mixture from the Instant Pot and whip with an electric mixer, until reaching desired consistency. Refrigerate until ready to serve.

Per Serving
calories: 220 | fat: 23g | protein: 2g | carbs: 5g
net carbs: 3g | fiber: 2g

Chocolate Pudding

Prep time: 5 minutes | Cook time: 15 minutes
Serves 4

2 cups unsweetened vanilla almond milk, divided
½ cup heavy cream
2 egg yolks
1 teaspoon vanilla extract

⅛ teaspoon cinnamon
2 tablespoons cocoa powder
¾ teaspoon guar gum
¼ cup low-carb chocolate chips

1. Press the Sauté button and press the Adjust button to set heat to Less. Pour half of almond milk into Instant Pot. Pour in heavy cream. Bring to gentle boil.
2. In medium bowl, whisk yolks, vanilla, cinnamon, cocoa powder, and guar gum. Slowly whisk into milk mixture and continue quickly whisking until smooth. Press the Cancel button.
3. Add chocolate chips to pot and whisk very quickly until melted. Pour mixture into a large bowl and refrigerate for 2 hours.

Per Serving
calories: 224 | fat: 18g | protein: 3g | carbs: 12g
net carbs: 8g | fiber: 4g

Traditional Cheesecake

**Prep time: 5 minutes | Cook time: 25 minutes
Serves 5 to 6**

Cake:

16 ounces (454 g) full-fat cream cheese, softened
½ cup Swerve, confectioners (or more, to taste)
4 teaspoons vanilla extract
2 eggs

Toppings:

½ cup Swerve, confectioners (or more, to taste)	toasted
2 tablespoons heavy whipping cream	1 tablespoon slivered almonds (or other chopped nuts), lightly toasted
1 tablespoon coconut, shredded and lightly	2 tablespoons sugar-free chocolate chips

1. In a large bowl, combine cream cheese, Swerve, vanilla, and eggs. Mix thoroughly. Place mixture in a well-greased springform pan.
2. Pour 2 cups of filtered water into the Instant Pot, then insert the trivet. Using a sling if desired, place the springform pan on top of the trivet, and cover with aluminum foil. Close the lid, set the pressure release to Sealing, and select Manual. Set the Instant Pot to 25 minutes on High Pressure and let cook.
3. Once cooked, let pressure naturally disperse. Then remove pan, leaving foil on, and let cool for 30 minutes. For extra decadence, drizzle some extra (melted) sugar-free chocolate on top, if desired. Refrigerate for 45 minutes.
4. Take the cheesecake from the refrigerator, and remove the foil. Using a handheld mixer, in a small bowl, whip the Swerve and whipping cream until thickened, then spread evenly on top of the cake. Sprinkle with toasted coconut, slivered almonds, and chocolate chips, as desired. Enjoy!

Per Serving
calories: 337 | fat: 32g | protein: 8g | carbs: 6g
net carbs: 5g | fiber: 1g

Peppermint Chocolate Almond Butter

**Prep time: 5 minutes | Cook time: 5 minutes
Serves 6**

2 tablespoons grass-fed butter, softened	¼ cup sugar-free chocolate chips
¾ cup almond butter, smooth	⅛ teaspoon peppermint extract (or to taste)

1. Set the Instant Pot to Sauté and melt the butter.
2. Add the almond butter, chocolate chips, and peppermint to the Instant Pot. Mix thoroughly, until melted.
3. Remove mixture with a spoon, and place into a Mason jar.
4. Refrigerate until firm. Serve and enjoy! Store remaining almond butter in refrigerator, eating on its own, or using as a topping.

Per Serving
calories: 237 | fat: 22g | protein: 6g | carbs: 10g
net carbs: 6g | fiber: 4g

Holiday Ginger Cookie Bites

**Prep time: 5 minutes | Cook time: 20 minutes
Serves 4**

1 cup blanched almond flour	½ teaspoon cloves, ground
½ cup Swerve, confectioners (or more, to taste)	½ teaspoon nutmeg, ground
1 egg	½ teaspoon cinnamon, ground
1 tablespoon grass-fed butter	½ teaspoon salt
1 teaspoon ginger, finely grated	½ teaspoon vanilla extract

1. In a large bowl, mix together the flour, Swerve, egg, butter, ginger, cloves, nutmeg, cinnamon, salt, and vanilla extract. Continue stirring until a perfectly even mixture is obtained.
2. Next, pour 1 cup of filtered water into the Instant Pot and insert the trivet. Transfer the mixture from the bowl into a well-greased, Instant Pot-friendly egg bites pan. Work in batches, if need be. I prefer to stack two egg bites molds on top of each other, separated by Mason jar lids (or similar dividers).
3. Using a sling if desired, place the pan onto the trivet, and cover loosely with aluminum foil. Close the lid, set the pressure release to Sealing, and select Manual. Set the Instant Pot to 40 minutes on High Pressure, and let cook.
4. Once cooked, let the pressure naturally disperse from the Instant Pot for about 10 minutes, then carefully switch the pressure release to Venting.
5. Open the Instant Pot, and remove the pan. Once cooled, serve, and enjoy!

Per Serving
calories: 89 | fat: 8g | protein: 3g | carbs: 2g
net carbs: 1g | fiber: 1g

Coconut Cookie Bites

Prep time: 5 minutes | Cook time: 20 minutes
Serves 5 to 6

2 tablespoons grass-fed butter, softened
2 eggs
1 cup blanched almond flour
¾ cup unsweetened coconut flakes
½ cup Swerve, confectioners (or more,

to taste)
½ cup almond butter, smooth
½ teaspoon baking powder
½ teaspoon vanilla extract
½ teaspoon salt

1. In a large bowl, mix together the butter, eggs, almond flour, coconut, Swerve, almond butter, baking powder, vanilla, and salt. Combine until ingredients are fully incorporated.
2. Pour 1 cup of filtered water into the inner pot of the Instant Pot, and insert the trivet. Transfer the mixture from the bowl into a well-greased, Instant Pot-friendly egg bites pan. Work in batches, if need be. I prefer to stack 2 egg bites molds on top of each other, separated by Mason jar lids (or similar dividers).
3. Place the dish onto the trivet, and cover loosely with aluminum foil. Close the lid, set the pressure release to Sealing, and select Manual. Set the Instant Pot to 20 minutes on High Pressure, and let cook.
4. Once cooked, let the pressure naturally leave the Instant Pot, for about 10 minutes. Next, switch the pressure release to Venting.
5. Open the Instant Pot, and remove the dish. Once sufficiently cooled, serve, and enjoy!

Per Serving
calories: 129 | fat: 12g | protein: 3g | carbs: 3g
net carbs: 1g | fiber: 2g

Chocolate Almond Squares

Prep time: 5 minutes | Cook time: 40 minutes
Serves 8

1 cup almond flour
6 tablespoons sugar-free chocolate chips
¼ cup unsweetened cocoa powder
2 tablespoons coconut oil
2 eggs
2 tablespoons cacao nibs, raw

1 cup almonds, chopped
½ cup Swerve, confectioners (or more, to taste)
¼ cup full-fat coconut milk
½ teaspoon vanilla extract
½ teaspoon salt

1. In a large bowl, mix together the chocolate chips, cocoa powder, coconut oil, eggs, cacao nibs, almonds, Swerve, coconut milk, vanilla, and salt. Combine them very thoroughly.
2. Pour 1 cup of filtered water into the inner pot of the Instant Pot, and insert the trivet. Transfer the chocolate mixture from the bowl into a well-greased, Instant Pot-friendly dish.
3. Place the dish onto the trivet, and cover loosely with aluminum foil. Close the lid, set the pressure release to Sealing and select Manual. Set the Instant Pot to 40 minutes on High Pressure, and let cook.
4. Once cooked, let the pressure naturally leave the Instant Pot, for about 10 minutes. Next, switch the pressure release to Venting.
5. Open the Instant Pot, and remove the dish. Refrigerate for at least 20 minutes (or until firm). Once sufficiently firm, cut into 8 squares, serve, and enjoy!

Per Serving
calories: 213 | fat: 18g | protein: 6g | carbs: 13g
net carbs: 8g | fiber: 5g

Decadent Chocolate Mousse

Prep time: 5 minutes | Cook time: 5 minutes
Serves 5 to 6

2 tablespoons grass-fed butter, softened
¼ cup sugar-free chocolate chips
1 cup full-fat cream cheese, softened
1 tablespoon raw cacao nibs
½ teaspoon vanilla

extract
½ cup Swerve, confectioners (or more, to taste)
⅓ cup unsweetened cocoa powder
½ cup heavy whipping cream

1. Set the Instant Pot to Sauté and melt the butter. Add the chocolate chips, cream cheese, cacao nibs, vanilla, Swerve, and cocoa powder to the Instant Pot. Stir continuously for 5 minutes.
2. Once thoroughly mixed, hit Cancel to stop the current program. Remove the inner pot from the Instant Pot, and refrigerate for at least 20 minutes.
3. Whisk (or use an electric mixer) to beat the heavy whipping cream, until stiff peaks form.
4. Using a spatula, gently fold the whipped cream into the cooled chocolate mixture. Serve, and enjoy!

Per Serving
calories: 119 | fat: 11g | protein: 2g | carbs: 8g
net carbs: 5g | fiber: 3g

Tiny Pumpkin Cheesecakes

Prep time: 5 minutes | Cook time: 25 minutes
Serves 4

Cake:

8 ounces (227 g) full-fat cream cheese, softened
½ cup organic pumpkin purée
⅓ cup Swerve,

confectioners (or more, to taste)
2 teaspoons vanilla extract
1 egg

Topping:

¼ cup sugar-free chocolate chips

1. Combine the cream cheese, pumpkin, Swerve, vanilla, and egg, in a large bowl. Mix thoroughly. Place mixture into ramekins, then cover each ramekin with aluminum foil.
2. Pour 1 cup of filtered water into the inner pot of the Instant Pot, then insert the trivet, placing your covered ramekins on top. Move the valve to Sealing and close the lid.
3. Cook for 25 minutes at High Pressure. Let pressure naturally disperse. Then remove ramekins, and let cool on the countertop, uncovered, for 30 minutes. Move ramekins to the refrigerator and allow to completely chill, about 45 minutes.
4. Take the desserts from the refrigerator. Sprinkle each cheesecake with chocolate chips, serve, and enjoy.

Per Serving

calories: 285 | fat: 25g | protein: 7g | carbs: 12g
net carbs: 9g | fiber: 3g

Coconut-Almond Cake

Prep time: 10 minutes | Cook time: 40 minutes
Serves 8

Nonstick cooking spray
1 cup almond flour
½ cup unsweetened shredded coconut
⅓ cup Swerve
1 teaspoon baking powder

1 teaspoon apple pie spice
2 eggs, lightly whisked
¼ cup unsalted butter, melted
½ cup heavy (whipping) cream

1. Grease a 6-inch round cake pan with the cooking spray.
2. In a medium bowl, mix together the almond flour, coconut, Swerve, baking powder, and apple pie spice.
3. Add the eggs, then the butter, then the cream, mixing well after each addition.
4. Pour the batter into the pan and cover with aluminum foil.

5. Pour 2 cups of water into the inner cooking pot of the Instant Pot, then place a trivet in the pot. Place the pan on the trivet.
6. Lock the lid into place. Select Manual and adjust the pressure to High. Cook for 40 minutes. When the cooking is complete, let the pressure release naturally for 10 minutes, then quick-release any remaining pressure. Unlock the lid.
7. Carefully take out the pan and let it cool for 15 to 20 minutes. Invert the cake onto a plate. Sprinkle with shredded coconut, almond slices, or powdered sweetener, if desired, and serve.

Per Serving

calories: 231 | fat: 19g | protein: 3g | carbs: 12g
net carbs: 10g | fiber: 2g

Coconut Macaroons

Prep time: 5 minutes | Cook time: 20 minutes
Serves 5 to 6

Base:

2 cups blanched almond flour
1 egg white
½ cup Swerve, confectioners (or more, to taste)

¼ cup unsweetened coconut flakes
1 teaspoon vanilla extract
½ teaspoon salt
Topping:

6 tablespoons sugar-free chocolate chips

1. Pour 1 cup of filtered water into the inner pot of the Instant Pot, then insert the trivet. In a large bowl, combine almond flour, egg white, Swerve, coconut flakes, vanilla, and salt and mix well. Transfer this mixture into a well-greased, Instant Pot-friendly egg bites mold, working in batches if needed.
2. Place the dish onto the trivet, and cover loosely with aluminum foil. Close the lid, set the pressure release to Sealing, and select Manual. Set the Instant Pot to 20 minutes on High Pressure, and let cook.
3. Once cooked, let the pressure naturally disperse from the Instant Pot for about 10 minutes, then carefully switch the pressure release to Venting.
4. Open the Instant Pot, and remove the dish. Melt the chocolate chips in a medium microwave-safe bowl in the microwave for about 20 seconds. Once melted, drizzle evenly over the macaroons. Once completely cooled, serve, and enjoy!

Per Serving

calories: 106 | fat: 8g | protein: 3g | carbs: 10g
net carbs: 7g | fiber: 3g

Sugar-Free Key Lime Pie

Prep time: 5 minutes | Cook time: 40 minutes
Serves 5 to 6

Base:

1 tablespoon grass-fed butter, softened	oil
1 tablespoon coconut	1 cup blanched almond flour

Topping:

3 key limes, juiced	½ cup Swerve, confectioners (or more, to taste)
1 cup heavy whipping cream	
½ cup sour cream	

1. Pour 1 cup of filtered water into the inner pot of the Instant Pot, then insert the trivet. Using an electric mixer, thoroughly combine base ingredients. Transfer this mixture into a well-greased, Instant Pot-friendly pan, and form a crust at the bottom of the pan, with a slight coating of the mixture also on the sides. Freeze for 15 minutes. Meanwhile, thoroughly mix topping ingredients in a large bowl.
2. Remove the pan from the freezer, and pour the topping mixture evenly into the middle of the crust. Using a sling if desired, place the pan onto the trivet, and cover loosely with aluminum foil. Close the lid, set the pressure release to Sealing, and select Manual. Set the Instant Pot to 40 minutes on High Pressure, and let cook.
3. Once cooked, let the pressure naturally disperse from the Instant Pot for about 10 minutes, then carefully switch the pressure release to Venting. Remove the dish and refrigerate for at least 3 to 4 hours, before serving.

Per Serving

calories: 305 | fat: 30g | protein: 5g | carbs: 7g net carbs: 5g | fiber: 2g

10-Minute Chocolate Macadamia Butter

Prep time: 5 minutes | Cook time: 5 minutes
Serves 8

2 tablespoons coconut oil	½ cup sugar-free chocolate chips
1 cup macadamia butter	2 teaspoons coconut, shredded (optional)

1. Set the Instant Pot to Sauté and melt the oil.
2. Add macadamia butter, chocolate chips, and shredded coconut (if using) to the Instant Pot. Cook, and continue to mix until melted and smooth.

3. Remove mixture with a spoon, and place into a Mason jar.
4. Refrigerate until firm. Serve on its own, or use to top other baked goods. Store remaining macadamia butter in refrigerator.

Per Serving

calories: 111 | fat: 9g | protein: 2g | carbs: 7g net carbs: 6g | fiber: 1g

Coconut Cake

Prep time: 5 minutes | Cook time: 40 minutes
Serves 5 to 6

3 tablespoons sugar-free chocolate chips	½ cup Swerve, confectioners (or more, to taste)
2 tablespoons grass-fed butter, softened	½ cup unsweetened coconut flakes
2 eggs	½ cup heavy whipping cream
1 ⅓ cup blanched almond flour	½ teaspoon nutmeg, ground
1 tablespoon arrowroot powder	½ teaspoon cinnamon, ground
1 teaspoon baking powder	½ teaspoon vanilla extract
1 teaspoon pumpkin purée, organic	

1. In a large bowl, thoroughly mix together all ingredients, until a perfectly even mixture is obtained.
2. Next, pour 1 cup filtered water into the Instant Pot and insert the trivet.
3. Transfer the mixture from the bowl into a well-greased, Instant Pot-friendly pan (or dish).
4. Using a sling if desired, place the pan onto the trivet, and cover loosely with aluminum foil. Close the lid, set the pressure release to Sealing, and select Manual. Set the Instant Pot to 40 minutes on High Pressure, and let cook.
5. Once cooked, let the pressure naturally disperse from the Instant Pot for about 10 minutes, then carefully switch the pressure release to Venting.
6. Open the Instant Pot and remove the pan. Allow to cool completely before serving. Add any desired toppings on top of the finished dessert, serve, and enjoy!

Per Serving

calories: 227 | fat: 21g | protein: 4g | carbs: 8g net carbs: 5g | fiber: 3g

Pumpkin Pie Pudding

Prep time: 10 minutes | Cook time: 20 minutes
Serves 6

Nonstick cooking spray	1 (15-ounce / 425-g)
2 eggs	can pumpkin purée
½ cup heavy (whipping)	1 teaspoon pumpkin pie
cream or almond milk	spice
(for dairy-free)	1 teaspoon vanilla
¾ cup Swerve	extract

For Finishing:
½ cup heavy (whipping) cream

1. Grease a 6-by-3-inch pan extremely well with the cooking spray, making sure it gets into all the nooks and crannies.
2. In a medium bowl, whisk the eggs. Add the cream, Swerve, pumpkin purée, pumpkin pie spice, and vanilla, and stir to mix thoroughly.
3. Pour the mixture into the prepared pan and cover it with a silicone lid or aluminum foil.
4. Pour 2 cups of water into the inner cooking pot of the Instant Pot, then place a trivet in the pot. Place the covered pan on the trivet.
5. Lock the lid into place. Select Manual and adjust the pressure to High. Cook for 20 minutes. When the cooking is complete, let the pressure release naturally for 10 minutes, then quick-release any remaining pressure. Unlock the lid.
6. Remove the pan and place it in the refrigerator. Chill for 6 to 8 hours.
7. When ready to serve, finish by making the whipped cream. Using a hand mixer, beat the heavy cream until it forms soft peaks. Do not overbeat and turn it to butter. Serve each pudding with a dollop of whipped cream.

Per Serving
calories: 188 | fat: 17g | protein: 4g | carbs: 8g
net carbs: 6g | fiber: 2g

Lemon Ricotta Cheesecake

Prep time: 10 minutes | Cook time: 30 minutes
Serves 6

Unsalted butter, for	room temperature
greasing the pan	Zest of 1 lemon
8 ounces (227 g)	Juice of 1 lemon
cream cheese, at room	½ teaspoon lemon
temperature	extract
¼ cup Swerve, plus 1	2 eggs, at room
teaspoon, and more as	temperature
needed	2 tablespoons sour
⅓ cup full-fat or part-	cream
skim ricotta cheese, at	

1. Grease a 6-inch springform pan extremely well. I find this easiest to do with a silicone basting brush so I can get into all the nooks and crannies. Alternatively, line the sides of the pan with parchment paper.
2. In the bowl of a stand mixer, beat the cream cheese, ¼ cup of Swerve, the ricotta, lemon zest, lemon juice, and lemon extract on high speed until you get a smooth mixture with no lumps.
3. Taste to ensure the sweetness is to your liking and adjust if needed.
4. Add the eggs, reduce the speed to low and gently blend until the eggs are just incorporated. Overbeating at this stage will result in a cracked crust.
5. Pour the mixture into the prepared pan and cover with aluminum foil or a silicone lid.
6. Pour 2 cups of water into the inner cooking pot of the Instant Pot, then place a trivet in the pot. Place the covered pan on the trivet.
7. Lock the lid into place. Select Manual and adjust the pressure to High. Cook for 30 minutes. When the cooking is complete, let the pressure release naturally. Unlock the lid.
8. Carefully remove the pan from the pot, and remove the foil.
9. In a small bowl, mix together the sour cream and remaining 1 teaspoon of Swerve and spread this over the top of the warm cake.
10. Refrigerate the cheesecake for 6 to 8 hours. Do not be in a hurry! The cheesecake needs every bit of this time to be its best.

Per Serving
calories: 217 | fat: 17g | protein: 6g | carbs: 10g
net carbs: 10g | fiber: 0g

Savory Chocolate Cashews

Prep time: 5 minutes | Cook time: 5 minutes
Serves 6

2 tablespoons grass-fed	2 teaspoons coconut,
butter, softened	shredded (optional)
¼ cup sugar-free	¾ cup cashews,
chocolate chips	chopped

1. Set the Instant Pot to Sauté and melt the butter.
2. Add chocolate chips, shredded coconut (if using), and cashews to the Instant Pot, and mix thoroughly until chocolate is melted.
3. Pour mixture into a large bowl and refrigerate until firm. Break into pieces and serve.

Per Serving
calories: 203 | fat: 18g | protein: 4g | carbs: 12g
net carbs: 10g | fiber: 2g

Almond Butter Mini Cakes

Prep time: 5 minutes | Cook time: 30 minutes
Serves 6

1 egg
½ cup almond flour
¼ cup almond butter
¼ teaspoon baking
soda
⅓ cup Swerve,
confectioners

1. Mix the egg, flour, almond butter, baking soda, and Swerve in a large bowl. Use an electric mixer, until a smooth consistency is obtained. Pour this mixture evenly into ramekins.
2. Pour 1 cup of filtered water into the Instant Pot, then insert the trivet.
3. Working in batches if needed, cover the ramekins with aluminum foil, and place on top of the trivet. Close the lid, set the pressure release to Sealing, and select Manual. Set the Instant Pot to 30 minutes on High Pressure and let cook.
4. Once cooked, let the pressure naturally disperse, then remove the mini cakes, and let cool. If desired, brown cakes in the oven at 350ºF (180ºC) for 2 to 3 minutes, to finish.

Per Serving
calories: 198 | fat: 17g | protein: 6g | carbs: 8g
net carbs: 5g | fiber: 3g

Slow Cooker Peanut Butter Fudge

Prep time: 5 minutes | Cook time: 2 hours
Makes 12 squares

1 cup low-carb
chocolate chips
8 ounces (227 g) cream
cheese
¼ cup erythritol
¼ cup no-sugar-added
peanut butter
1 teaspoon vanilla
extract

1. Place all ingredients into Instant Pot and cover with slow cooker lid.
2. Allow to cook on Low for 1 hour and stir. Smooth mixture and allow to cook additional 30 minutes.
3. Pour mixture into 8 × 8-inch parchment-lined pan and chill for 2 hours. Slice.

Per Serving
calories: 159 | fat: 11g | protein: 2g | carbs: 11g
net carbs: 9g | fiber: 2g

Spiced Pudding

Prep time: 10 minutes | Cook time: 30 minutes
Serves 2

1 egg, beaten
¼ cup heavy cream
1 tablespoon erythritol
¼ teaspoon pumpkin
pie spices
1 teaspoon coconut oil
1 cup water (for Instant
Pot)

1. Whisk the egg and mix it up with the heavy cream.
2. Add erythritol and pumpkin pie spices. Stir the mixture.
3. Grease the cake pan with the coconut oil and transfer the pudding mixture inside.
4. Pour 1 cup of water in the Instant Pot.
5. Put the pudding on the trivet in the Instant Pot.
6. Cover the pudding with the foil and secure edges.
7. Select the Manual mode at High Pressure for 20 minutes.
8. Make the natural pressure release for 10 minutes.
9. Chill the pudding for 10 hours before serving.

Per Serving
calories: 101 | fat: 10g | protein: 3g | carbs: 8g
net carbs: 8g | fiber: 0g

Slow Cooker Candied Pecans

Prep time: 5 minutes | Cook time: 3 hours
Makes 2 cups

2 egg whites
2 cups whole pecans
½ cup powdered
erythritol
3 tablespoons melted
butter
3 teaspoons cinnamon
1 teaspoon vanilla
extract
1 tablespoon water
(optional)

1. Whisk egg whites and add remaining ingredients to bowl. Place in Instant Pot and press the Slow Cook button. You may use a clear slow cooker lid.
2. Place nut mixture into Instant Pot and stir every 45 minutes for 3 hours until pecans are softened. If they begin sticking to pot, add 1 tablespoon of water when stirring.

Per Serving
calories: 217 | fat: 21g | protein: 3g | carbs: 13g
net carbs: 10g | fiber: 3g

Million-Dollar Pound Cake

Prep time: 5 minutes | Cook time: 40 minutes
Serves 8

3 eggs
1 cup blanched almond flour
²/₃ cup Swerve, confectioners (or more, to taste)
¼ cup heavy cream
4 ounces (113 g) full-fat cream cheese,
softened
2 tablespoons grass-fed butter, softened
½ teaspoon baking powder
½ teaspoon vanilla extract
½ teaspoon salt

1. In a large bowl, whisk together eggs, almond flour, Swerve, and heavy cream. Stir in cream cheese, butter, baking powder, vanilla, and salt. Continue to stir for several minutes, until the mixture is well-combined and even in texture.
2. Pour 1 cup of filtered water into the inner pot of the Instant Pot, and insert the trivet. Transfer the mixture from the bowl into a well-greased, Instant Pot-friendly pan (or dish).
3. Using a sling if desired, place the pan onto the trivet, and cover loosely with aluminum foil. Close the lid, set the pressure release to Sealing, and select Manual. Set the Instant Pot to 40 minutes on High Pressure, and let cook.
4. Once cooked, let the pressure naturally leave the Instant Pot, for about 10 minutes. Next, switch the pressure release to Venting.
5. Open the Instant Pot, and remove the pan. If desired, remove aluminum foil, and finish the cake for 2 to 5 minutes in the oven at 350ºF (180ºC), to brown the top. Let cool, slice, serve, and enjoy!

Per Serving
calories: 213 | fat: 20g | protein: 6g | carbs: 2g
net carbs: 2g | fiber: 0g

Chocolate Chip Cheesecake

Prep time: 5 minutes | Cook time: 25 minutes
Serves 5 to 6

Cake:
16 ounces (454 g) full-fat cream cheese, softened
½ cup Swerve, confectioners (or more,
to taste)
2 eggs
4 teaspoons vanilla extract
Topping:
5 tablespoons sugar-free chocolate chips

1. Combine cream cheese, Swerve, eggs, and vanilla together in a large bowl, and mix thoroughly. Pour mixture in a well-greased springform pan, then cover with aluminum foil.
2. Pour 2 cups of filtered water into the Instant Pot, then insert the trivet, placing your covered pan on top. Move the valve to Sealing and close the lid.
3. Use Manual mode, to set the timer for 25 minutes, at High Pressure. Let pressure naturally disperse. Then remove pan and let cool for 30 minutes. Refrigerate until completely chilled, about 45 minutes.
4. Take the cheesecake from the refrigerator, and remove the foil. Sprinkle and evenly distribute the chocolate chips over the top of the cake, slice, serve, and enjoy!

Per Serving
calories: 339 | fat: 31g | protein: 8g | carbs: 9g
net carbs: 7g | fiber: 2g

Mint Chocolate Chip Ice Cream

Prep time: 5 minutes | Cook time: 0 minutes
Serves 5 to 6

6 egg whites
4 teaspoons vanilla extract
1 teaspoon mint extract
½ cup Swerve, confectioners (or more, to taste)
¼ cup almonds,
slivered (optional)
¼ cup coconut, shredded (optional)
2²/₃ cups heavy whipping cream
½ cup sugar-free chocolate chips

1. In a large bowl, using a handheld mixer or stand mixer, beat egg whites until stiff peaks form. Gently fold in vanilla, mint, Swerve, almond, coconut, and whipping cream. Mix thoroughly. Cover and freeze for 2 to 4 hours.
2. When ready to eat, set the Instant Pot to simmer by pressing Sauté and then pressing the Adjust button twice. Pour in the chocolate chips, stirring very frequently, until they melt together smoothly. Do not overcook. Turn off heat, and remove melted chocolate.
3. Scoop the ice cream into a bowl and drizzle the melted chocolate over it. Store leftovers in freezer.

Per Serving
calories: 351 | fat: 31g | protein: 9g | carbs: 14g
net carbs: 11g | fiber: 3g

Almond-Carrot Cake

Prep time: 10 minutes | Cook time: 40 minutes
Serves 8

Nonstick cooking spray
3 eggs
1 cup almond flour
²⁄₃ cup Swerve
1 teaspoon baking powder
1½ teaspoons apple pie

spice
¼ cup coconut oil
½ cup heavy (whipping) cream
1 cup grated carrots
½ cup walnuts, chopped

1. Grease a 6-inch cake pan with the cooking spray.
2. Put the eggs, almond flour, Swerve, baking powder, apple pie spice, oil, cream, carrots, and walnuts in a large bowl. Using a hand mixer on high speed, mix until the ingredients are well incorporated and the batter looks fluffy. This will keep the cake from being dense.
3. Pour the batter into the pan and cover with aluminum foil.
4. Pour 2 cups of water into the inner cooking pot of the Instant Pot, then place a trivet in the pot. Place the cake pan on the trivet.
5. Lock the lid into place. Select Manual, and adjust the pressure to High. Cook for 40 minutes. When the cooking is complete, let the pressure release naturally for 10 minutes, then quick-release any remaining pressure. Unlock the lid.
6. Remove the cake from the pot. Let it cool to room temperature, then invert the cake onto a plate. Ice the cake with a frosting of your choice, or serve plain.

Per Serving
calories: 198 | fat: 17g | protein: 4g | carbs: 5g
net carbs: 3g | fiber: 2g

Pecan Pie

Prep time: 20 minutes | Cook time: 25 minutes
Serves 4

2 tablespoons coconut oil
4 tablespoons almond flour
4 pecans, chopped

1 tablespoon erythritol
2 tablespoons butter
1 tablespoon coconut flour
1 cup water, for cooking

1. Make the pie crust: Mix up coconut oil and almond flour in the bowl.
2. Then knead the dough and put it in the baking pan. Flatten the dough in the shape of the pie crust.
3. Then melt erythritol, butter, and coconut flour.

4. When the mixture is liquid, add chopped pecans.
5. Pour water in the Instant Pot and insert the trivet.
6. Pour the butter-pecan mixture over the pie crust, flatten it and transfer on the trivet.
7. Cook the pecan pie on Manual mode at High Pressure for 25 minutes.
8. Allow the natural pressure release for 10 minutes and cool the cooked pie well.

Per Serving
calories: 257 | fat: 26g | protein: 3g | carbs: 8g
net carbs: 5g | fiber: 3g

Chocolate Cheesecake

Prep time: 10 minutes | Cook time: 50 minutes
Serves 12

2 cups pecans
2 tablespoons butter
16 ounces (454 g) cream cheese, softened
1 cup powdered erythritol
¼ cup sour cream
2 tablespoons cocoa powder

2 teaspoons vanilla extract
2 cups low-carb chocolate chips
1 tablespoon coconut oil
2 eggs
2 cups water

1. Preheat oven to 400ºF (205ºC). Place pecans and butter into food processor. Pulse until dough-like consistency. Press into bottom of 7-inch springform pan. Bake for 10 minutes then set aside to cool.
2. While crust bakes, mix cream cheese, erythritol, sour cream, cocoa powder, and vanilla together in large bowl using a rubber spatula. Set aside.
3. In medium bowl, combine chocolate chips and coconut oil. Microwave in 20-second increments until chocolate begins to melt and then stir until smooth. Gently fold chocolate mixture into cheesecake mixture.
4. Add eggs and gently fold in, careful not to overmix. Pour mixture over cooled pecan crust. Cover with foil.
5. Pour water into Instant Pot and place trivet in bottom. Place cheesecake on trivet and click lid closed. Press the Manual button and adjust time for 40 minutes. When timer beeps, allow a natural release. Carefully remove and let cool completely. Serve chilled.

Per Serving
calories: 468 | fat: 40g | protein: 5g | carbs: 22g
net carbs: 17g | fiber: 5g

Peanut Butter Cheesecake Bites

Prep time: 10 minutes | Cook time: 15 minutes
Serves 8

16 ounces (454 g)
cream cheese, softened
1 cup powdered
erythritol
½ cup peanut flour
¼ cup sour cream
2 teaspoons vanilla

extract
2 eggs
2 cups water
¼ cup low-carb
chocolate chips
1 tablespoon coconut
oil

1. In large bowl, beat cream cheese and erythritol until smooth. Gently fold in peanut flour, sour cream, and vanilla. Fold in eggs slowly until combined.
2. Pour batter into four 4-inch springform pans or silicone cupcake molds. Cover with foil. Pour water into Instant Pot and place trivet in pot.
3. Carefully lower pan into pot. Press the Manual button and press the Adjust button to set heat to More. Set time for 15 minutes. When timer beeps, allow a full natural release. Carefully lift cups from Instant Pot and allow to cool completely before refrigerating.
4. In small bowl, microwave chocolate chips and coconut oil for 30 seconds and whisk until smooth. Drizzle over cheesecakes. Chill in fridge.

Per Serving
calories: 263 | fat: 23g | protein: 7g | carbs: 7g
net carbs: 6g | fiber: 1g

Chocolate Cake

Prep time: 5 minutes | Cook time: 40 minutes
Serves 5 to 6

¼ cup sugar-free
chocolate chips
2 tablespoons grass-fed
butter, softened
¼ cup raw cacao nibs
3 eggs
2 tablespoons coconut
oil
1 cup blanched almond
flour
⅔ cup Swerve,

confectioners (or more,
to taste)
½ teaspoon vanilla
extract
½ cup unsweetened
cocoa powder
¼ cup sour cream, at
room temperature
¼ teaspoon baking
soda

1. In a large bowl mix together the chocolate chips, butter, cacao nibs, eggs, coconut oil, almond flour, Swerve, vanilla, cocoa powder, sour cream, and baking soda. Mix until batter is smooth.

2. Pour 1 cup of filtered water into the inner pot of the Instant Pot, and insert the trivet.
3. Transfer the mixture from the bowl into a well-greased, Instant Pot-friendly pan (or dish).
4. Place the pan onto the trivet, and cover loosely with aluminum foil. Close the lid, set the pressure release to Sealing and select Manual. Set the Instant Pot to 40 minutes on High Pressure, and let cook.
5. Once cooked, let the pressure naturally disperse from the Instant Pot for about 10 minutes, then carefully switch the pressure release to Venting.
6. Open the Instant Pot and remove the pan. Let cool, serve, and enjoy!

Per Serving
calories: 255 | fat: 22g | protein: 6g | carbs: 15g
net carbs: 8g | fiber: 7g

Chocolate Coconut Butter

Prep time: 5 minutes | Cook time: 10 minutes
Serves 16

4 tablespoons grass-fed
butter, softened
1 cup raw coconut
butter
2 tablespoons cacao
nibs, raw
½ cup sugar-free

chocolate chips
½ teaspoon vanilla
extract
½ teaspoon salt
½ cup Swerve,
confectioners (or more,
to taste)

1. In a large bowl, mix together the butter, coconut butter, cacao nibs, chocolate chips, vanilla, salt, and Swerve. Whisk or stir until the mixture reaches a smooth consistency.
2. Pour 1 cup of filtered water into the inner pot of the Instant Pot, and insert the trivet. Transfer the mixture from the bowl into a well-greased, Instant Pot-friendly dish.
3. Place the dish onto the trivet, and cover loosely with aluminum foil. Close the lid, set the pressure release to Sealing, and select Manual. Set the Instant Pot to 10 minutes on High Pressure, and let cook.
4. Once cooked, let the pressure naturally disperse from the Instant Pot for about 10 minutes, then carefully switch the pressure release to Venting.
5. Open the Instant Pot, and remove the dish. Once sufficiently cooled, cut into 16 bars, serve, and enjoy!

Per Serving
calories: 182 | fat: 19g | protein: 1g | carbs: 5g
net carbs: 3g | fiber: 2g

Coconut-Crusted Chocolate Bark

Prep time: 5 minutes | Cook time: 20 minutes
Serves 20

16 ounces (454 g) raw dark chocolate, raw
3 tablespoons raw coconut butter
2 tablespoons coconut oil
2 cups macadamia

nuts, chopped
1 tablespoon almond butter, smooth
½ teaspoon salt
⅓ cup Swerve, confectioners (or more, to taste)

1. In a large bowl, mix together the chocolate, coconut butter, coconut oil, macadamia nuts, almond butter, salt, and Swerve. Combine them very thoroughly, until a perfectly even mixture is obtained.
2. Pour 1 cup of filtered water into the Instant Pot, and insert the trivet. Transfer the mixture from the bowl into a well-greased, Instant Pot-friendly dish.
3. Place the dish onto the trivet, and cover loosely with aluminum foil. Close the lid, set the pressure release to Sealing, and select Manual. Set the Instant Pot to 20 minutes on High Pressure, and let cook.
4. Once cooked, let the pressure naturally disperse from the Instant Pot for about 10 minutes, then carefully switch the pressure release to Venting.
5. Open the Instant Pot and remove the dish. Cool in the refrigerator until set. Break into pieces, serve, and enjoy! Store remaining bark in the refrigerator or freezer.

Per Serving
calories: 258 | fat: 22g | protein: 2g | carbs: 15g
net carbs: 12g | fiber: 3g

Antioxidant-Rich Matcha Cheesecake

Prep time: 5 minutes | Cook time: 40 minutes
Serves 8

Base:
16 ounces (454 g) full-fat cream cheese, softened
3 teaspoons blanched almond flour
3 tablespoons heavy

cream
2 eggs
1 tablespoon matcha powder
½ teaspoon vanilla extract

Topping:
⅔ cup Swerve, confectioners (or more, to taste)
½ cup sour cream, at

room temperature
½ cup sugar-free chocolate chips

1. Combine the cream cheese, almond flour, heavy cream, eggs, matcha powder, and vanilla in a large bowl. Mix thoroughly. Place mixture in springform pan, then loosely cover with aluminum foil.
2. Pour 2 cups filtered water into Instant Pot, then add trivet, placing the springform pan on the trivet. Move the valve to Sealing and close the lid of the Instant Pot.
3. Set to Manual, and let cook for 40 minutes at High Pressure. Once cooked, let the pressure naturally disperse from the Instant Pot for about 10 minutes, then carefully switch the pressure release to Venting.
4. Remove pan, and let cool for 30 minutes. Then refrigerate for at least 45 minutes (a few hours is preferable).
5. Remove foil. Mix together the Swerve and sour cream in a small bowl, then spread evenly on the cake before serving and sprinkle with chocolate chips. Store any remaining cheesecake in the refrigerator.

Per Serving
calories: 325 | fat: 31g | protein: 9g | carbs: 5g
net carbs: 4g | fiber: 1g

Blackberry Crunch

Prep time: 5 minutes | Cook time: 5 minutes
Serves 1

10 blackberries
½ teaspoon vanilla extract
2 tablespoons powdered erythritol
⅛ teaspoon xanthan gum
1 tablespoon butter

¼ cup chopped pecans
3 teaspoons almond flour
½ teaspoon cinnamon
2 teaspoons powdered erythritol
1 cup water

1. Place blackberries, vanilla, erythritol, and xanthan gum in 4-inch ramekin. Stir gently to coat blackberries.
2. In small bowl, mix remaining ingredients. Sprinkle over blackberries and cover with foil. Press the Manual button and set time for 4 minutes. When timer beeps, quick-release the pressure. Serve warm. Feel free to add scoop of whipped cream on top.

Per Serving
calories: 343 | fat: 31g | protein: 3g | carbs: 13g
net carbs: 5g | fiber: 8g

Walnut Brownies

Prep time: 5 minutes | Cook time: 40 minutes
Serves 5

8 tablespoons sugar-free chocolate chips
3 tablespoons unsweetened cocoa powder
2 tablespoons grass-fed butter, softened
½ cup walnuts, chopped (optional)

1 egg
½ cup Swerve, confectioners (or more, to taste)
1 cup blanched almond flour
½ teaspoon salt
½ teaspoon vanilla extract

1. Pour 1 cup of filtered water into the inner pot of the Instant Pot, then insert the trivet. Using an electric mixer, combine chocolate chips, cocoa powder, butter, walnuts, egg, Swerve, almond flour, salt, and vanilla extract. Mix thoroughly. Transfer this mixture into a well-greased, Instant Pot-friendly dish.
2. Place the dish onto the trivet, and cover loosely with aluminum foil. Close the lid, set the pressure release to Sealing and select Manual. Set the Instant Pot to 40 minutes on High Pressure, and let cook.
3. Once cooked, let the pressure naturally disperse from the Instant Pot for about 10 minutes, then carefully switch the pressure release to Venting.
4. Open the Instant Pot, and remove the dish.
5. Let cool, slice into 10 pieces, serve, and enjoy!

Per Serving
calories: 162 | fat: 14g | protein: 5g | carbs: 9g
net carbs: 6g | fiber: 3g

Nutty Blondies

Prep time: 5 minutes | Cook time: 40 minutes
Serves 8

1 cup blanched almond flour
1 cup pecans, chopped
½ cup macadamia nuts
2 eggs
4 tablespoons heavy cream
2 tablespoons grass-fed butter, softened

1 tablespoon erythritol powder
½ teaspoon baking powder
½ teaspoon vanilla extract
½ teaspoon cinnamon, ground
½ teaspoon salt

1. In a large bowl, mix together the eggs, flour, pecans, macadamia nuts, heavy cream, butter, erythritol powder, baking powder, vanilla, cinnamon, and salt. Combine until the mixture is even and fully incorporated.

2. Pour 1 cup of filtered water into the inner pot of the Instant Pot, and insert the trivet. Transfer the mixture from the bowl into a well-greased, Instant Pot-friendly pan (or dish).
3. Using a sling if desired, place the dish onto the trivet, and cover loosely with aluminum foil. Close the lid, set the pressure release to Sealing, and select Manual. Set the Instant Pot to 40 minutes on High Pressure, and let cook.
4. Once cooked, let the pressure naturally disperse from the Instant Pot for about 10 minutes, then carefully switch the pressure release to Venting.
5. Open the Instant Pot, and remove the dish. Remove the foil and allow the blondies to cool completely on the counter. Cut into 8 bars, serve, and enjoy!

Per Serving
calories: 298 | fat: 29g | protein: 7g | carbs: 4g
net carbs: 2g | fiber: 2g

Lemon Poppy Seed Cake

Prep time: 10 minutes | Cook time: 25 minutes
Serves 6

1 cup almond flour
2 eggs
½ cup erythritol
2 teaspoons vanilla extract
1 teaspoon lemon extract
1 tablespoon poppy seeds

4 tablespoons melted butter
¼ cup heavy cream
⅛ cup sour cream
½ teaspoon baking powder
1 cup water
¼ cup powdered erythritol, for garnish

1. In large bowl, mix almond flour, eggs, erythritol, vanilla, lemon, and poppy seeds.
2. Add butter, heavy cream, sour cream, and baking powder.
3. Pour into 7-inch round cake pan. Cover with foil.
4. Pour water into Instant Pot and place trivet in bottom. Place baking pan on trivet and click lid closed. Press the Manual button and press the Adjust button to set heat to Less. Set time for 25 minutes.
5. When timer beeps, allow a 15-minute natural release, then quick-release the remaining pressure. Let cool completely. Sprinkle with powdered erythritol for serving.

Per Serving
calories: 240 | fat: 21g | protein: 3g | carbs: 3g
net carbs: 1g | fiber: 2g

Decadent Fudge

Prep time: 5 minutes | Cook time: 5 minutes
Serves 6

1 teaspoon grass-fed butter
1 teaspoon raw coconut butter
1 teaspoon vanilla extract
½ cup Swerve,

confectioners (or more, to taste)
¼ cup full-fat coconut milk
1 cup dark sugar-free chocolate chips

Flavor Add-Ins:

1 tablespoon avocado (or more, to taste)
½ cup pecans, chopped
1/3 cup almonds, chopped
¼ cup walnuts, chopped
¼ cup macadamia nuts

¼ cup hazelnuts, chopped
¼ cup pistachios, chopped
⅛ teaspoon peppermint extract

1. Set the Instant Pot to simmer by pressing Sauté and then pressing the Adjust button twice. Add all ingredients (including any desired flavors), stirring very frequently, until fudge melts together smoothly. Do not overcook.
2. Turn off Instant Pot and remove fudge. Cool briefly, then carefully pour it into a greased, deep glass dish.
3. Place into freezer for 20 minutes. Cut into 12 squares, and serve. Store leftovers in the refrigerator or freezer.

Per Serving
calories: 98 | fat: 8g | protein: 1g | carbs: 11g
net carbs: 8g | fiber: 3g

Vanilla Tea Cake

Prep time: 10 minutes | Cook time: 25 minutes
Serves 8

1 cup almond flour
2 eggs
½ cup erythritol
2 teaspoons vanilla extract
4 tablespoons melted

butter
¼ cup heavy cream
½ teaspoon baking powder
1 cup water

1. In large bowl, mix all ingredients except water. Pour into 7-inch round cake pan. Cover with foil.
2. Pour water into Instant Pot and place trivet in bottom. Place baking pan on trivet and click lid closed. Press the Manual button and press the Adjust button to set heat to Less. Set time for 25 minutes.

3. When timer beeps, allow a 15-minute natural release, then quick-release the remaining pressure. Let cool completely.

Per Serving
calories: 166 | fat: 15g | protein: 2g | carbs: 10g
net carbs: 9g | fiber: 1g

Holiday Pumpkin Pie

Prep time: 5 minutes | Cook time: 40 minutes
Serves 5 to 6

Base:

2 tablespoons grass-fed butter, softened
1 cup blanched almond

flour
½ cup pecans, chopped

Topping:

½ cup Swerve, confectioners (or more, to taste)
1/3 cup heavy whipping cream
½ teaspoon cinnamon, ground
½ teaspoon ginger, finely grated

½ teaspoon nutmeg, ground
½ teaspoon cloves, ground
1 (14-ounce / 397-g) can organic pumpkin purée
1 egg

1. Pour 1 cup of filtered water into the inner pot of the Instant Pot, then insert the trivet. Using an electric mixer, combine the butter, almond flour, and pecans. Mix thoroughly. Transfer this mixture into a well-greased, Instant Pot-friendly pan, and form a crust at the bottom of the pan, with a slight coating of the mixture also on the sides. Freeze for 15 minutes. In a large bowl, thoroughly combine the topping ingredients.
2. Take the pan from the freezer, add the topping evenly, and then place the pan onto the trivet. Cover loosely with aluminum foil. Close the lid, set the pressure release to Sealing, and select Manual. Set the Instant Pot to 40 minutes on High Pressure, and let cook.
3. Once cooked, let the pressure naturally disperse from the Instant Pot for about 10 minutes, then carefully switch the pressure release to Venting.
4. Open the Instant Pot and remove the pan. Cool in the refrigerator for 4 to 5 hours, serve, and enjoy!

Per Serving
calories: 152 | fat: 13g | protein: 3g | carbs: 6g
net carbs: 4g | fiber: 2g

Espresso Cream

Prep time: 10 minutes | Cook time: 9 minutes
Serves 4

1 cup heavy cream	powder
½ teaspoon espresso	¼ cup low-carb
powder	chocolate chips
½ teaspoon vanilla	½ cup powdered
extract	erythritol
2 teaspoons	3 egg yolks
unsweetened cocoa	1 cup water

1. Press the Sauté button and add heavy cream, espresso powder, vanilla, and cocoa powder. Bring mixture to boil and add chocolate chips. Press the Cancel button. Stir quickly until chocolate chips are completely melted.
2. In medium bowl, whisk erythritol and egg yolks. Fold mixture into Instant Pot chocolate mix. Ladle into four (4-inch) ramekins.
3. Rinse inner pot and replace. Pour in 1 cup of water and place trivet in bottom of pot. Cover ramekins with foil and carefully place on top of trivet. Click lid closed.
4. Press the Manual button and adjust time for 9 minutes. Allow a full natural release. When the pressure indicator drops, carefully remove ramekins and allow to completely cool, then refrigerate. Serve chilled with whipped topping.

Per Serving
calories: 320 | fat: 29g | protein: 3g | carbs: 8g net carbs: 7g | fiber: 1g

Pecan Cookie Bars

Prep time: 5 minutes | Cook time: 40 minutes
Serves 5 to 6

1 cup blanched almond	½ teaspoon vanilla
flour	extract
2 tablespoons butter,	½ teaspoon cinnamon,
softened	ground
½ cup Swerve,	½ teaspoon nutmeg,
confectioners (or more,	ground
to taste)	¼ teaspoon baking
½ cup pecans, chopped	soda

1. In a large bowl, mix together almond flour and butter. Add Swerve, pecans, vanilla, cinnamon, nutmeg, and baking soda, and stir until an evenly textured dough forms.
2. Add one cup filtered water into the Instant Pot, and insert the trivet.
3. Transfer the mixture from the bowl into a well-greased, Instant Pot-friendly dish or pan.

4. Place the dish onto the trivet, and cover loosely with aluminum foil. Close the lid, set the pressure release to Sealing, and select Manual. Set the Instant Pot to 40 minutes on High Pressure, and let cook.
5. Once cooked, let the pressure naturally leave the Instant Pot, for about 10 minutes. Next, switch the pressure release to Venting.
6. Open the Instant Pot, and remove the dish. Once sufficiently cooled, cut into bars, serve, and enjoy!

Per Serving
calories: 147 | fat: 16g | protein: 2g | carbs: 2g net carbs: 1g | fiber: 1g

Mini Lava Cakes

Prep time: 5 minutes | Cook time: 35 minutes
Serves 5 to 6

2 tablespoons grass-fed	almond flour
butter, softened	¼ teaspoon baking
2 eggs	soda
½ cup sugar-free	$1/_3$ cup Swerve,
chocolate chips	confectioners (or more,
½ cup unsweetened	to taste)
cocoa powder	Coconut oil (to grease)
2 ½ cups blanched	

1. Mix the butter, eggs, chocolate chips, cocoa powder, almond flour, baking soda, and Swerve in a large bowl. Stir until batter is smooth.
2. Grease smaller, Instant Pot-friendly bowls or ramekins with coconut oil. Transfer batter evenly into these bowls, working in batches if needed.
3. Pour 1 cup of filtered water into the Instant Pot, then insert the trivet. Place your bowls gently on top of the trivet.
4. Close the lid, set the pressure release to Sealing, and select Manual. Set the Instant Pot to 35 minutes on High Pressure, and let cook.
5. Once cooked, immediately switch the pressure release to Venting (do this carefully, to avoid steam).
6. Cook some additional chocolate chips in the microwave for 20 seconds (or until they melt).
7. Turn each bowl upside down, allowing cake to come out. Drizzle melted chocolate chips over each cake, and enjoy!

Per Serving
calories: 165 | fat: 13g | protein: 5g | carbs: 11g net carbs: 8g | fiber: 3g

Chocolate-Covered Pumpkin Seeds

Prep time: 5 minutes | Cook time: 5 minutes
Serves 5 to 6

2 tablespoons coconut oil
½ cup sugar-free chocolate chips

½ cup pumpkin seeds
½ teaspoon salt (optional)

1. Set the Instant Pot to Sauté and melt the oil.
2. Add chocolate chips, pumpkin seeds, and salt to the Instant Pot, and mix thoroughly, until chocolate is melted.
3. Using a spatula, scrape mixture into a large bowl or a cookie sheet in a single layer.
4. Refrigerate until firm. Serve, and enjoy! Store leftovers in the refrigerator or freezer.

Per Serving
calories: 175 | fat: 15g | protein: 4g | carbs: 13g
net carbs: 10g | fiber: 3g

Slow Cooker Mint Hot Chocolate

Prep time: 3 minutes | Cook time: 1 hour
Serves 4

4 cups unsweetened almond milk
½ cup heavy cream
3 tablespoons unsweetened cocoa powder
½ cup powdered

erythritol
¼ cup low-carb chocolate chips
1 teaspoon vanilla extract
½ teaspoon mint extract

1. Place all ingredients into Instant Pot, place slow cooker lid on pot, and press the Slow Cook button. Press the Adjust button to set heat to Low and set time for 1 hour. Stir occasionally to help chocolate chips melt and incorporate. Serve warm.

Per Serving
calories: 216 | fat: 18g | protein: 2g | carbs: 10g
net carbs: 8g | fiber: 2g

Cannoli Bites

Prep time: 5 minutes | Cook time: 20 minutes
Serves 5 to 6

3 tablespoons sugar-free chocolate chips
2 tablespoons coconut oil
1 egg
½ cup blanched almond flour
½ teaspoon vanilla

extract
½ cup Swerve, confectioners (or more, to taste)
1 (15-ounce / 425-g) container whole milk ricotta cheese

1. Pour 1 cup of filtered water into the inner pot of the Instant Pot, then insert the trivet. In a large bowl, combine the chocolate chips, coconut oil, egg, almond flour, vanilla, Swerve, and ricotta. Mix thoroughly. Once mixed, evenly pour this mixture into 6 well-greased, Instant Pot-friendly ramekins (or use an egg bites mold).
2. Place the ramekins on the trivet, and cover each loosely with aluminum foil. Close the lid, set the pressure release to Sealing, and select Manual. Set the Instant Pot to 20 minutes on High Pressure, and let cook.
3. Once cooked, let the pressure naturally disperse from the Instant Pot for about 10 minutes, then carefully switch the pressure release to Venting.
4. Open the Instant Pot, and remove the ramekins. Place in the refrigerator for at least 20 minutes. Let cool, serve, and enjoy!

Per Serving
calories: 189 | fat: 14g | protein: 10g | carbs: 8g
net carbs: 6g | fiber: 2g

Mixed Candied Nuts

Prep time: 5 minutes | Cook time: 15 minutes
Serves 8

1 cup pecan halves
1 cup walnuts, chopped
⅓ cup Swerve, confectioners (or more,

to taste)
⅓ cup grass-fed butter
1 teaspoon cinnamon, ground

1. Preheat your oven to 350ºF (180ºC), and line a baking sheet with aluminum foil.
2. While your oven is warming, pour ½ cup of filtered water into the inner pot of the Instant Pot, followed by the pecans, walnuts, Swerve, butter, and cinnamon. Stir nut mixture, close the lid, and then set the pressure valve to Sealing. Use the Manual mode to cook at High Pressure, for 5 minutes.
3. Once cooked, perform a quick release by carefully switching the pressure valve to Venting, and strain the nuts. Pour the nuts onto the baking sheet, spreading them out in an even layer. Place in the oven for 5 to 10 minutes (or until crisp, being careful not to overcook). Cool before serving. Store leftovers in the refrigerator or freezer.

Per Serving
calories: 122 | fat: 12g | protein: 4g | carbs: 3g
net carbs: 1g | fiber: 2g

Coconut Flaked Walnut Fudge

Prep time: 5 minutes | Cook time: 5 minutes
Serves 4

2 tablespoons coconut oil
1 cup sugar-free chocolate chips
½ cup full-fat coconut milk
½ cup walnuts, chopped (or more, to taste)

2 tablespoons unsweetened coconut flakes (or more, to taste)
2 tablespoons grass-fed butter, softened
1 teaspoon vanilla extract

1. Set the Instant Pot to Sauté and melt the oil.
2. Stir in the chocolate chips, coconut milk, walnuts, coconut flakes, butter, and vanilla. Mix thoroughly, until melted.
3. Remove the inner pot from the Instant Pot and carefully pour the fudge into a greased, deep glass dish. Smooth the surface with a spatula so the fudge is evenly distributed in the dish.
4. Freeze until firm, about 30 minutes. Slice into squares, serve, and enjoy!

Per Serving
calories: 152 | fat: 13g | protein: 3g | carbs: 11g
net carbs: 8g | fiber: 3g

Crème Brûlée

Prep time: 5 minutes | Cook time: 6 minutes
Serves 5

2 egg yolks
1 cup heavy whipping cream
1 teaspoon vanilla extract

½ cup Swerve, confectioners (or more, to taste)
⅛ teaspoon salt

1. Pour 1 cup of filtered water into the inner pot of the Instant Pot, then insert the trivet. In a large bowl, combine egg yolks, whipping cream, vanilla, Swerve, and salt. Mix thoroughly. Once mixed, evenly pour into 5 well-greased, Instant Pot-friendly ramekins.
2. Place the ramekins on the trivet, and cover each loosely with aluminum foil. Close the lid, set the pressure release to Sealing, and select Manual. Set the Instant Pot to 6 minutes on High Pressure, and let cook.
3. Once cooked, let the pressure naturally disperse from the Instant Pot for about 10 minutes, then carefully switch the pressure release to Venting. Open the Instant Pot, and remove the ramekins. Let cool, serve and enjoy!

Per Serving
calories: 110 | fat: 11g | protein: 3g | carbs: 1g
net carbs: 1g | fiber: 0g

Traditional Chocolate Pie

Prep time: 5 minutes | Cook time: 40 minutes
Serves 5 to 6

Crust:
1 cup blanched almond flour
1 egg
½ cup unsweetened cocoa powder

½ teaspoon salt
½ teaspoon vanilla extract
¼ teaspoon baking soda

Filling:
8 ounces (227 g) full-fat cream cheese, softened
8 tablespoons sugar-free chocolate chips
¼ cup raw cacao nibs
¼ cup heavy whipping

cream
2 tablespoons grass-fed butter, softened
⅔ cup Swerve, confectioners (or more, to taste)

1. Pour 1 cup of filtered water into the inner pot of the Instant Pot, and insert the trivet. To make the crust, mix together flour, cocoa powder, egg, salt, vanilla, and baking soda in a large bowl. Transfer the mixture from the bowl into a well-greased, Instant Pot-friendly pan (or dish), pressing down with a spatula to create a smooth crust. Coat the sides of the pan slightly, as well. Freeze for 15 minutes.
2. Mix all filling ingredients evenly in a large bowl. Remove the pan from the freezer, and pour in filling evenly. Do not overfill. Place the pan onto the trivet, and cover loosely with aluminum foil. Close the lid, set the pressure release to Sealing, and select Manual. Set the Instant Pot to 40 minutes on High Pressure, and let cook.
3. Once cooked, let the pressure naturally disperse from the Instant Pot for about 10 minutes, then carefully switch the pressure release to Venting. Remove the pan, and let cool for at least 3 to 4 hours in the refrigerator, before serving.

Per Serving
calories: 322 | fat: 21g | protein: 8g | carbs: 18g
net carbs: 10g | fiber: 8g

Cake Balls

Prep time: 5 minutes | Cook time: 5 minutes
Serves 6

4 tablespoons grass-fed butter
1/3 cup almond butter, fresh
1/4 cup blanched almond flour
1/4 cup unsweetened

cocoa powder
1/4 cup sugar-free chocolate chips
1/3 cup Swerve, confectioners (or more, to taste)

1. Spread the butter evenly inside the inner pot and then set the Instant Pot to Sauté.
2. Add the almond butter, flour, cocoa powder, chocolate chips, and Swerve to the Instant Pot. Mix thoroughly, until melted together evenly (about 5 minutes).
3. Using a spatula to help scrape the sides of the bowl, pour mixture into a silicone mini muffin (or egg bites) mold. Freeze until firm.
4. Sprinkle cake balls with additional Swerve (if desired) before serving, and enjoy! Store leftovers in the freezer.

Per Serving
calories: 130 | fat: 12g | protein: 2g | carbs: 8g
net carbs: 5g | fiber: 3g

Chocolate Cream Cheese Fudge

Prep time: 5 minutes | Cook time: 3 minutes
Makes 10 pieces

1 cup low-carb chocolate chips
8 ounces (227 g) cream cheese
1/4 cup erythritol

1/4 teaspoon cinnamon
1 teaspoon vanilla extract
1 cup water

1. Place chocolate chips, cream cheese, erythritol, cinnamon, and vanilla into 7-cup glass bowl. Cover with foil. Place on trivet inside Instant Pot. Pour water in bottom of pot.
2. Click lid closed. Press the Manual button and adjust time for 3 minutes. When timer beeps, allow a natural release. When pressure indicator drops, remove bowl carefully and stir ingredients until smooth.
3. Pour mixture into 8 × 8-inch parchment-lined pan and chill for 2 hours. Slice.

Per Serving
calories: 190 | fat: 14g | protein: 2g | carbs: 13g
net carbs: 11g | fiber: 2g

Dark Chocolate Cake

Prep time: 10 minutes | Cook time: 20 minutes
Serves 6

1 cup almond flour
2/3 cup Swerve
1/4 cup unsweetened cocoa powder
1/4 cup chopped walnuts
1 teaspoon baking

powder
3 eggs
1/3 cup heavy (whipping) cream
1/4 cup coconut oil
Nonstick cooking spray

1. Put the flour, Swerve, cocoa powder, walnuts, baking powder, eggs, cream, and coconut oil in a large bowl. Using a hand mixer on high speed, combine the ingredients until the mixture is well incorporated and looks fluffy. This will keep the cake from being too dense.
2. With the cooking spray, grease a heatproof pan, such as a 3-cup Bundt pan, that fits inside your Instant Pot. Pour the cake batter into the pan and cover with aluminum foil.
3. Pour 2 cups of water into the inner cooking pot of the Instant Pot, then place a trivet in the pot. Place the pan on the trivet.
4. Lock the lid into place. Select Manual and adjust the pressure to High. Cook for 20 minutes. When the cooking is complete, let the pressure release naturally for 10 minutes, then quick-release any remaining pressure.
5. Carefully take out the pan and let it cool for 15 to 20 minutes. Invert the cake onto a plate. It can be served hot or at room temperature. Serve with a dollop of whipped cream, if desired.

Per Serving
calories: 225 | fat: 20g | protein: 5g | carbs: 4g
net carbs: 2g | fiber: 2g

Chaptr 13 Smoothies and Drinks

Basil-Mint Green Smoothie

Prep time: 5 minutes | Cook time: 5 minutes
Serves 3

2 tablespoons grass-fed butter, softened
½ cup full-fat coconut milk
10 drops stevia liquid
2 tablespoons coconut oil
½ teaspoon turmeric, ground
½ teaspoon mint, finely chopped
½ teaspoon basil, dried
½ teaspoon parsley, dried
¼ cup heavy whipping cream
¼ avocado, mashed
¼ cup spinach, chopped
¼ cup kale, chopped
¼ cup bok choy, chopped
¼ cup broccoli, chopped
2 scoops grass-fed whey protein powder
Ice cubes, to serve

1. Pour 1½ cups of filtered water into a blender. Depending on personal taste, you can use less water to achieve a thicker consistency.
2. Set the Instant Pot to Sauté and melt the butter.
3. Pour in the coconut milk, then add the stevia, oil, turmeric, mint, basil, parsley, whipping cream, avocado, spinach, kale, bok choy, and broccoli. Stir continuously.
4. Once thoroughly mixed, hit Cancel to stop the current program. Remove the inner pot from the Instant Pot, and carefully pour this mixture into your blender.
5. Add in the protein powder, then blend until desired consistency. Serve in a tall, ice-filled glass. Store extra servings in the refrigerator, for up to two days.

Per Serving
calories: 360 | fat: 34g | protein: 10g | carbs: 6g
net carbs: 4g | fiber: 2g

Coconut Chocolate Whipped Cream Smoothie

Prep time: 5 minutes | Cook time: 5 minutes
Serves 3

2 tablespoons grass-fed butter, softened
½ cup full-fat coconut milk
10 drops liquid stevia
2 tablespoons unflavored MCT oil
2 tablespoons unsweetened coconut flakes
2 tablespoons flax seeds, soaked
2 tablespoons raw cacao nibs
2 tablespoons sugar-free chocolate chips
½ teaspoon vanilla extract
¼ cup heavy whipping cream
Ice cubes, to serve

1. Start by pouring 1½ cups of filtered water into a blender. Depending on personal taste, you can use less water, to achieve a thicker consistency.
2. Set the Instant Pot to Sauté and melt the butter.
3. Pour in the coconut milk, then add the stevia, MCT oil, coconut, flax seeds, cacao nibs, chocolate chips, vanilla, and whipping cream to the Instant Pot. Stir continuously.
4. Once thoroughly mixed, hit Cancel to stop the current program. Remove the inner pot from the Instant Pot, and carefully pour this mixture into your blender.
5. Blend until desired consistency is reached. Serve in a tall, ice-filled glass. Store extra servings in the refrigerator, for up to two days.

Per Serving
calories: 280 | fat: 31g | protein: 1g | carbs: 3g
net carbs: 2g | fiber: 1g

Golden Spice Milk

Prep time: 5 minutes | Cook time: 1 minute
Serves 4

4 cups water
1 (3-inch) piece whole turmeric, sliced
1 (2-inch) piece ginger, sliced
1 teaspoon black peppercorn
1 (1-inch) stick cinnamon
3 whole cloves
1 cup full-fat coconut milk
1 tablespoon sweetener of your choice (optional)
1 teaspoon cinnamon, ground, for garnish

1. Turn on the Instant Pot by pressing Sauté and set to More. Insert the inner pot. Add the cold filtered water, turmeric, ginger, peppercorn, cinnamon stick and cloves. Close the lid tightly and move the steam release handle to Sealing. Press the Manual button and set the timer to 0 minutes on High Pressure.
2. When you hear the beeping sound indicating that the time has ended, carefully turn the steam release handle to the Venting position for the steam to escape and the float valve to drop down. Press Cancel, and open the lid carefully. Add the coconut milk and sweetener, if using. Strain and garnish with ground cinnamon and serve immediately.

Per Serving
calories: 160 | fat: 15g | protein: 2g | carbs: 8g
net carbs: 5g | fiber: 3g

Homemade Root Beer

Prep time: 5 minutes | Cook time: 10 minutes
Serves 16

20 pieces sassafras root bark, about ½ inch in diameter
4 allspice berries
2 whole cloves
1 cinnamon stick
½ teaspoon anise seed
¼ teaspoon fine sea salt

4 cups filtered water
1 cup Swerve confectioners'-style sweetener or equivalent amount of liquid or powdered sweetener
2 quarts sparkling water, for serving

1. Rinse the sassafras root bark under cold water for 3 minutes, pat dry, and cut into ½-inch-long pieces.
2. Place the root bark, allspice berries, cloves, cinnamon stick, anise seed, salt, and water in a 6-quart Instant Pot. Seal the lid, press Manual, and set the timer for 10 minutes. Once finished, turn the valve to venting for a quick release.
3. Pour the mixture through a fine-mesh strainer into a medium-sized bowl.
4. Add the sweetener, stir well, and allow to cool. Store the root beer syrup in containers (such as large mason jars) in the fridge until ready to drink.
5. To serve, fill a glass with ice cubes. Start with a 1:2 ratio of root beer syrup to sparkling water: Pour in $^1/_3$ cup of the syrup and $^2/_3$ cup of sparkling water. Stir well and taste. If you like it stronger, add more syrup; if it's too strong, add more sparkling water.

Per Serving
calories: 3 | fat: 0g | protein: 0g | carbs: 1g
net carbs: 1g | fiber: 0g

Immune-Boosting Ginger Tea

Prep time: 5 minutes | Cook time: 1 minute
Serves 4

4 cups water
1 (3-inch) piece fresh ginger, sliced
3 whole cloves
1 (1-inch) stick cinnamon
3 jujubes (optional)

2 lemons, peels from 1 lemon, slices from 1 lemon
1 tablespoon whole stevia leaves or sweetener of your choice (optional)

1. Turn on the Instant Pot by pressing Sauté and set to More. Insert the inner pot and wait until the panel says Hot.
2. Add the cold filtered water to the inner pot. Add the ginger, cloves, cinnamon stick,

jujubes (if using), peels from one lemon and stevia leaves (if using). Close the lid tightly and move the steam release handle to Sealing. Press the Manual button and set the timer to 0 minutes on High Pressure.
3. When you hear the beeping sound indicating that the time has ended, carefully turn the steam release handle to the Venting position for the steam to escape and the float valve to drop down. Press Cancel, and open the lid carefully. Strain, add one lemon slice per cup and serve immediately.

Per Serving
calories: 29 | fat: 1g | protein: 1g | carbs: 9g
net carbs: 6g | fiber: 3g

Cashew Cream Smoothie

Prep time: 5 minutes | Cook time: 5 minutes
Serves 2

2 tablespoons grass-fed butter, softened
¼ cup full-fat coconut milk
2 tablespoons sugar-free chocolate chips
1 tablespoon unflavored MCT oil
½ teaspoon nutmeg, ground
½ teaspoon lavender,

dried
¼ cup cashew cream, refrigerated
¼ cup mixed dark berries (blueberries, strawberries, blackberries, raspberries)
1 scoop grass-fed whey protein powder (optional)

1. Pour ¾ cup of filtered water into a blender. Depending on personal taste, you can use less water, to achieve a thicker consistency.
2. Set the Instant Pot to Sauté and melt the butter.
3. Pour in the coconut milk, then add the chocolate chips, MCT oil, nutmeg, lavender, cashew cream, and dark berries to the Instant Pot. Stir continuously.
4. Once thoroughly mixed, hit Cancel to stop the current program. Remove the inner pot from the Instant Pot, and pour this mixture into your blender.
5. Add in the protein powder, then blend until desired consistency. Serve in a tall, ice-filled glass. Store extra serving in the refrigerator, for up to two days.

Per Serving
calories: 442 | fat: 38g | protein: 13g | carbs: 17g
net carbs: 15g | fiber: 2g

Cucumber-Turmeric Wellness Tonic

Prep time: 5 minutes | Cook time: 6 minutes
Serves 4

1 tablespoon grass-fed butter
1 teaspoon turmeric, ground
½ teaspoon ginger, finely grated
½ teaspoon lavender, dried
½ teaspoon cinnamon, ground
½ teaspoon vanilla extract
¼ cucumber, peeled, thinly sliced
½ cup Swerve, confectioners (or more, to taste)

1. Set the Instant Pot to Sauté mode. Add the grass-fed butter, melting it gently.
2. Mix in the turmeric, ginger, lavender, cinnamon, vanilla, and cucumber. Add 4 cups of carbonated water, then the Swerve. Stir. Close the lid, set the pressure release to Sealing, cancel the current program, and select Manual. Set the Instant Pot to 6 minutes on High Pressure and let cook.
3. When cooking is complete, let the pressure naturally disperse, for about 10 minutes. Open the lid, and remove the tonic.
4. Strain the liquid into a bowl or pitcher. Serve with lemon or lime slices (if desired), and enjoy!

Per Serving
calories: 35 | fat: 3g | protein: 0g | carbs: 1g
net carbs: 1g | fiber: 0g

Chocolate Macadamia Butter Smoothie

Prep time: 5 minutes | Cook time: 5 minutes
Serves 3

2 tablespoons grass-fed butter, softened
½ cup full-fat coconut milk
10 drops liquid stevia (or more, to taste)
2 tablespoons sugar-free chocolate chips
4 tablespoons macadamia butter
2 tablespoons coconut oil
2 tablespoons raw cacao nibs
½ cup heavy whipping cream
½ teaspoon vanilla extract
½ teaspoon cinnamon, ground
½ teaspoon nutmeg, ground
2 scoops grass-fed whey protein powder
2 tablespoons unsweetened cocoa powder
Ice cubes, to serve

1. Start by pouring 1½ cups of filtered water into a blender. Depending on personal taste, you can use less water, to achieve a thicker consistency.
2. Set the Instant Pot to Sauté and melt the grass-fed butter.

3. Pour in the coconut milk, then add the stevia, chocolate chips, macadamia butter, oil, cacao nibs, whipping cream, vanilla, cinnamon, and nutmeg to the Instant Pot. Stir continuously.
4. Once thoroughly mixed, hit Cancel to stop the current program. Remove the inner pot from the Instant Pot, and carefully pour this mixture into your blender.
5. Add the protein powder and cocoa powder, then blend until desired consistency. Serve in a tall, ice-filled glass. Store extra servings in the refrigerator, for up to two days.

Per Serving
calories: 544 | fat: 47g | protein: 22g | carbs: 12g
net carbs: 9g | fiber: 3g

Chocolate Mocha Coconut Butter Smoothie

Prep time: 5 minutes | Cook time: 5 minutes
Serves 3

2 tablespoons grass-fed butter, softened
½ cup full-fat coconut milk
10 drops liquid stevia
5 tablespoons raw coconut butter
2 tablespoons sugar-free chocolate chips
2 tablespoons unflavored MCT oil
2 tablespoons raw cacao nibs
1 teaspoon cold brew coffee
½ cup heavy whipping cream
½ teaspoon turmeric, ground
½ teaspoon cinnamon, ground
½ teaspoon erythritol, powder (or more, to taste)
2 scoops grass-fed whey protein powder
2 tablespoons unsweetened cocoa powder
Ice cubes, to serve

1. Pour 1½ cups of filtered water into a blender. Depending on personal taste, you can use less water, to achieve a thicker consistency.
2. Set the Instant Pot to Sauté and melt the grass-fed butter. Pour in the coconut milk, then add the stevia, coconut butter, chocolate chips, MCT oil, cacao nibs, coffee, whipping cream, turmeric, cinnamon, and erythritol to the Instant Pot, stirring continuously.
3. Once thoroughly mixed, hit Cancel to stop the current program. Remove the inner pot from the Instant Pot, and carefully pour this mixture into your blender.
4. Add in the protein powder and cocoa powder, then blend until desired consistency. Serve in a tall, ice-filled glass. Store extra servings in the refrigerator, for up to two days.

Per Serving
calories: 637 | fat: 62g | protein: 16g | carbs: 14g
net carbs: 9g | fiber: 5g

Coconut Milk Berry Smoothie

**Prep time: 5 minutes | Cook time: 5 minutes
Serves 3**

2 tablespoons grass-fed butter, softened
¾ cup full-fat coconut milk
10 drops liquid stevia
2 tablespoons unflavored MCT oil
2 tablespoons flax seeds, soaked
2 tablespoons sugar-free chocolate chips (optional)
½ teaspoon turmeric,

ground
½ teaspoon nutmeg, ground
¼ cup heavy whipping cream
¼ cup mixed dark berries (blueberries, strawberries, blackberries, raspberries)
2 scoops grass-fed whey protein powder
Ice cubes, to serve

1. Start by pouring 1¼ cups filtered water into a blender. Depending on personal taste, you can use less water, to achieve a thicker consistency.
2. Set the Instant Pot to Sauté and melt the butter.
3. Pour in the coconut milk, then add the stevia, MCT oil, flax seeds, chocolate chips, turmeric, nutmeg, whipping cream, and dark berries to the Instant Pot, stirring continuously.
4. Once thoroughly mixed, hit Cancel to stop the current program. Remove the inner pot from the Instant Pot, and carefully pour this mixture into your blender.
5. Add in the protein powder, then blend until desired consistency. Serve in a tall, ice-filled glass. Store extra servings in the refrigerator, for up to two days.

Per Serving
calories: 431 | fat: 40g | protein: 15g | carbs: 13g
net carbs: 9g | fiber: 4g

Approximate Chai Tea

**Prep time: 5 minutes | Cook time: 1 minute
Serves 4**

4 cups water
10 to 20 cardamom seeds in pods
4 teaspoons loose Darjeeling tea leaves
10 to 20 whole cloves
3 tablespoons fennel seeds

1 (3-inch) stick cinnamon
1 teaspoon fresh ground black pepper
1 cup full-fat coconut milk (optional)
⅓ cup sweetener of your choice (optional)

1. Turn on the Instant Pot by pressing Sauté and set to More. Insert the inner pot and wait until the panel says Hot.
2. Add the cold filtered water to the inner pot. Crush the cardamom pods and add all of the shells and seeds into the boiling water. Let the mixture boil for about 30 seconds. Then, add the rest of the spices and tea leaves. Close the lid tightly and move the steam release handle to Sealing. Press the Manual button and set the timer to 0 minutes on High Pressure.
3. When you hear the beeping sound indicating that the time has ended, carefully turn the steam release handle to the Venting position for the steam to escape and the float valve to drop down. Press Cancel, and open the lid carefully. Add the milk and sweetener, if using. Strain and serve immediately.

Per Serving
calories: 179 | fat: 15g | protein: 3g | carbs: 8g
net carbs: 5g | fiber: 3g

Gingerbread Café au Lait

**Prep time: 5 minutes | Cook time: 5 minutes
Serves 4**

4 cups unsweetened almond milk (or hemp milk for nut-free)
½ cup Swerve confectioners'-style sweetener or equivalent amount of liquid or powdered sweetener
Seeds scraped from 2 vanilla beans (about 8 inches long), or
4 teaspoons vanilla

extract
2 teaspoons ginger powder
1 teaspoon ground cinnamon
4 whole cloves, or ¼ teaspoon ground cloves
¼ teaspoon ground nutmeg, plus more for garnish
2 cups freshly brewed coffee or espresso

1. Place the milk, sweetener, vanilla seeds, ginger, cinnamon, cloves, and nutmeg in a 3-quart Instant Pot.
2. Seal the lid, press Manual, and set the timer for 5 minutes. Once finished, turn the valve to venting for a quick release.
3. Pour the mixture through a fine-mesh strainer into a 2-quart heat-safe jar or pitcher.
4. Divide the hot coffee equally among four 8-ounce (227-g) coffee cups or glass mugs.
5. Top off the coffee with the milk mixture, dividing it equally among the cups. Garnish with a sprinkle of nutmeg, if desired.

Per Serving
calories: 42 | fat: 3g | protein: 1g | carbs: 3g
net carbs: 2g | fiber: 1g

Homemade Chai

Prep time: 3 minutes | Cook time: 5 minutes
Serves 2

3 bags black tea
1 cup filtered water
1 cup unsweetened almond milk (or hemp milk for nut-free)
½ teaspoon vanilla-flavored liquid stevia
4 cinnamon sticks

4 green cardamom pods
4 thin slices fresh ginger
2 whole cloves
½ teaspoon fennel seeds

1. Place all of the ingredients in a 3-quart Instant Pot. Seal the lid, press Manual, and set the timer for 5 minutes. Once finished, turn the valve to venting for a quick release.
2. Pour the tea mixture through a fine-mesh strainer into teacups and serve.

Per Serving
calories: 28 | fat: 2g | protein: 1g | carbs: 3g net carbs: 2g | fiber: 1g

Ginger Ale

Prep time: 3 minutes | Cook time: 1 minute
Serves 4

1 pound (454 g) fresh ginger, unpeeled, cut into small dice
Peels and juice of 2 lemons
1½ cups Swerve confectioners'-style sweetener or equivalent

amount of liquid or powdered sweetener
1 quart carbonated water, plus more for serving
Lemon slices, for garnish

1. Combine the ginger and lemon juice in a food processor and process until minced, stopping the machine periodically to scrape down the sides as needed.
2. Place the ginger purée, lemon peels, sweetener, and carbonated water in a 3-quart Instant Pot. Seal the lid, press Manual, and set the timer for 1 minute. Once finished, let the pressure release naturally, about 15 minutes.
3. Stir the ginger syrup well. Pour through a strainer into a container with a lid.
4. To serve, place about 2 tablespoons of the ginger syrup in a glass full of ice. Fill the glass with carbonated water; taste and add more ginger syrup if you like. Garnish with a lime wedge, then serve.

Per Serving
calories: 19 | fat: 0g | protein: 1g | carbs: 5g net carbs: 4g | fiber: 1g

Zero Calorie Iced Tea

Prep time: 5 minutes | Cook time: 5 minutes
Serves 4

½ cup Swerve, confectioners (or more, to taste)
3 to 4 of your favorite flavor tea bags
⅛ teaspoon mint

extract
⅛ teaspoon vanilla extract
4 lemon wedges, to serve

1. Inside the inner pot, pour in 4 cups of filtered water, then add the Swerve, followed by the tea bags, mint, and vanilla.
2. Close the lid, set the pressure release to Sealing, and select Manual. Set the Instant Pot to 5 minutes on High Pressure and let cook.
3. Once cooked, let the pressure naturally disperse from the Instant Pot for about 10 minutes, then carefully switch the pressure release to Venting.
4. Open the lid, let cool, then remove tea bags with a ladle. Pour tea into a glass filled with ice, top with lemon wedges, and enjoy!

Per Serving
calories: 0 | fat: 0g | protein: 0g | carbs: 0g net carbs: 0g | fiber: 0g

Hot Chocolate

Prep time: 3 minutes | Cook time: 1 minute
Serves 2

4 cups unsweetened almond milk (or full-fat coconut milk for nut-free)
2 ounces (57 g) unsweetened baking chocolate
⅓ cup Swerve confectioners'-style sweetener or equivalent

amount of liquid or powdered sweetener
½ teaspoon fine sea salt
½ teaspoon vanilla extract
Sweetened whipped cream, for serving (optional; omit for dairy-free)

1. Place the milk, chocolate, sweetener, salt, and vanilla extract in a 3-quart Instant Pot. Seal the lid, press Manual, and set the timer for 1 minute. Once finished, let the pressure release naturally. Stir well until the chocolate is fully melted.
2. Pour the hot chocolate into two 8-ounce (227-g) glass or ceramic mugs and top with sweetened whipped cream, if desired.

Per Serving
calories: 263 | fat: 21g | protein: 6g | carbs: 9g net carbs: 4g | fiber: 5g

Appendix 1: 21-Day Meal Plan

DAYS	BREAKFAST	LUNCH	DINNER	DESSERT
1	Protein Scramble[21]	Chicken Cordon Bleu Soup[57]	Mocha Pot Roast[125]	Sugar-Free Key Lime Pie[161]
2	Denver Omelet[32]	Garlic Italian Sausages [113]	Roast Chicken[88]	Coconut-Almond Cake[160]
3	Shakshuka[34]	Pork Quiche [109]	Smoky Baby Back Ribs[111]	Chocolate Chip Cheesecake[164]
4	Pumpkin Porridge[35]	Braised Collard Greens with Ham Hocks[119]	Simple Keto Bruschetta Chicken[87]	Coconut Whipped Cream[157]
5	Chocolate Butter Pecan Fat Bombs[21]	Creamy Bacon Soup[62]	Barbacoa[129]	Coconut-Crusted Chocolate Bark[167]
6	Bacon and Spinach Quiche[21]	Tender Pork Liver[112]	Cordon Bleu[88]	Mint Chocolate Chip Ice Cream[164]
7	Chocolate Pumpkin Balls[33]	Blackberry Beef[139]	Perfect BBQ Pulled Pork[110]	Antioxidant-Rich Matcha Cheesecake[167]
8	Deconstructed Chicken Breakfast Tacos[35]	Parmesan Spaghetti Squash[84]	Greek Shrimp with Tomatoes[152]	Blackberry Crunch[167]
9	Bacon and Egg Bake[36]	Hot Chicken Caesar Sandwiches[101]	Sour Sea Bass[145]	Nutty Blondies[168]
10	Granola[31]	Hearty Hamburger Soup[62]	Lime Pulled Pork[118]	Lemon Ricotta Cheesecake[162]

11	Breakfast Burritos[30]	Dill Salmon Fillet[153]	Chicken Piccata[97]	Chocolate Cheesecake[165]
12	Zucchini Fries with Bacon and Eggs[30]	Alaskan Crab Legs[153]	Classic Lasagna[134]	Slow Cooker Mint Hot Chocolate[171]
13	Avocado Breakfast Burger[27]	Green Cabbage in Cream Sauce [82]	Indian Chicken Butter Masala[103]	Pumpkin Pie Pudding[162]
14	Hot Chocolate[27]	Chicken Broccoli Casserole[86]	Caprese Salmon[144]	Coconut-Almond Cake[160]
15	Cauliflower Egg Muffins[31]	10-Minute Pizza Soup[61]	Coconut Curry Mussels[142]	Antioxidant-Rich Matcha Cheesecake[167]
16	Greens Power Bowl[30]	BBQ Short Ribs[122]	Bruschetta and Cheese Stuffed Chicken[99]	Chocolate Chip Fat Bomb[156]
17	Crustless Kale Quiche[29]	Pork Chops in Mushroom Gravy[114]	Chili Shrimp Salad[146]	Blackberry Crunch[167]
18	Cauliflower Breakfast Pudding[27]	Mushroom Chicken Alfredo [87]	Mocha Pot Roast[125]	Peppermint Chocolate Almond Butter[158]
19	Starbucks Eggs[27]	Shrimp Scampi[152]	Spicy Brisket[124]	Chocolate Almond Squares[159]
20	Sausage and Buffalo Egg Sandwich[24]	Sour Sea Bass[145]	Parmesan Zoodles[82]	Thai Coconut Pandan Custard[156]
21	Coconut Yogurt[29]	Cheese and Mayo Turkey Breasts[86]	Pesto Flounder [151]	Nutty Blondies[168]

Appendix 2 Measurement Conversion Chart

VOLUME EQUIVALENTS(DRY)

US STANDARD	METRIC (APPROXIMATE)
1/8 teaspoon	0.5 mL
1/4 teaspoon	1 mL
1/2 teaspoon	2 mL
3/4 teaspoon	4 mL
1 teaspoon	5 mL
1 tablespoon	15 mL
1/4 cup	59 mL
1/2 cup	118 mL
3/4 cup	177 mL
1 cup	235 mL
2 cups	475 mL
3 cups	700 mL
4 cups	1 L

WEIGHT EQUIVALENTS

US STANDARD	METRIC (APPROXIMATE)
1 ounce	28 g
2 ounces	57 g
5 ounces	142 g
10 ounces	284 g
15 ounces	425 g
16 ounces (1 pound)	455 g
1.5 pounds	680 g
2 pounds	907 g

VOLUME EQUIVALENTS(LIQUID)

US STANDARD	US STANDARD (OUNCES)	METRIC (APPROXIMATE)
2 tablespoons	1 fl.oz.	30 mL
1/4 cup	2 fl.oz.	60 mL
1/2 cup	4 fl.oz.	120 mL
1 cup	8 fl.oz.	240 mL
1 1/2 cup	12 fl.oz.	355 mL
2 cups or 1 pint	16 fl.oz.	475 mL
4 cups or 1 quart	32 fl.oz.	1 L
1 gallon	128 fl.oz.	4 L

TEMPERATURES EQUIVALENTS

FAHRENHEIT(F)	CELSIUS(C) (APPROXIMATE)
225 °F	107 °C
250 °F	120 °C
275 °F	135 °C
300 °F	150 °C
325 °F	160 °C
350 °F	180 °C
375 °F	190 °C
400 °F	205 °C
425 °F	220 °C
450 °F	235 °C
475 °F	245 °C
500 °F	260 °C

Appendix 3: Instant Pot Cooking Chart

Dried Beans, Legumes and Lentils

Dried Beans and Legume	Dry (Minutes)	Soaked (Minutes)
Soy beans	25 – 30	20 – 25
Scarlet runner	20 – 25	10 – 15
Pinto beans	25 – 30	20 – 25
Peas	15 – 20	10 – 15
Navy beans	25 – 30	20 – 25
Lima beans	20 – 25	10 – 15
Lentils, split, yellow (moong dal)	15 – 18	N/A
Lentils, split, red	15 – 18	N/A
Lentils, mini, green (brown)	15 – 20	N/A
Lentils, French green	15 – 20	N/A
Kidney white beans	35 – 40	20 – 25
Kidney red beans	25 – 30	20 – 25
Great Northern beans	25 – 30	20 – 25
Pigeon peas	20 – 25	15 – 20
Chickpeas (garbanzo bean chickpeas)	35 – 40	20 – 25
Cannellini beans	35 – 40	20 – 25
Black-eyed peas	20 – 25	10 – 15
Black beans	20 – 25	10 – 15

Fish and Seafood

Fish and Seafood	Fresh (minutes)	Frozen (minutes)
Shrimp or Prawn	1 to 2	2 to 3
Seafood soup or stock	6 to 7	7 to 9
Mussels	2 to 3	4 to 6
Lobster	3 to 4	4 to 6
Fish, whole (snapper, trout, etc.)	5 to 6	7 to 10
Fish steak	3 to 4	4 to 6
Fish fillet,	2 to 3	3 to 4
Crab	3 to 4	5 to 6

Fruits

Fruits	Fresh (in Minutes)	Dried (in Minutes)
Raisins	N/A	4 to 5
Prunes	2 to 3	4 to 5
Pears, whole	3 to 4	4 to 6
Pears, slices or halves	2 to 3	4 to 5
Peaches	2 to 3	4 to 5
Apricots, whole or halves	2 to 3	3 to 4
Apples, whole	3 to 4	4 to 6
Apples, in slices or pieces	2 to 3	3 to 4

Meat

Meat and Cuts	Cooking Time (minutes)	Meat and Cuts	Cooking Time (minutes)
Veal, roast	35 to 45	Duck, with bones, cut up	10 to 12
Veal, chops	5 to 8	Cornish Hen, whole	10 to 15
Turkey, drumsticks (leg)	15 to 20	Chicken, whole	20 to 25
Turkey, breast, whole, with bones	25 to 30	Chicken, legs, drumsticks, or thighs	10 to 15
Turkey, breast, boneless	15 to 20	Chicken, with bones, cut up	10 to 15
Quail, whole	8 to 10	Chicken, breasts	8 to 10
Pork, ribs	20 to 25	Beef, stew	15 to 20
Pork, loin roast	55 to 60	Beef, shanks	25 to 30
Pork, butt roast	45 to 50	Beef, ribs	25 to 30
Pheasant	20 to 25	Beef, steak, pot roast, round, rump, brisket or blade, small chunks, chuck,	25 to 30
Lamb, stew meat	10 to 15		
Lamb, leg	35 to 45	Beef, pot roast, steak, rump, round, chuck, blade or brisket, large	35 to 40
Lamb, cubes,	10 t0 15		
Ham slice	9 to 12	Beef, ox-tail	40 to 50
Ham picnic shoulder	25 to 30	Beef, meatball	10 to 15
Duck, whole	25 to 30	Beef, dressed	20 to 25

Vegetables (fresh/frozen)

Vegetable	Fresh (minutes)	Frozen (minutes)	Vegetable	Fresh (minutes)	Frozen (minutes)
Zucchini, slices or chunks	2 to 3	3 to 4	Mixed vegetables	2 to 3	3 to 4
Yam, whole, small	10 to 12	12 to 14	Leeks	2 to 4	3 to 5
Yam, whole, large	12 to 15	15 to 19	Greens (collards, beet greens, spinach, kale, turnip greens, swiss chard) chopped	3 to 6	4 to 7
Yam, in cubes	7 to 9	9 to 11			
Turnip, chunks	2 to 4	4 to 6	Green beans, whole	2 to 3	3 to 4
Tomatoes, whole	3 to 5	5 to 7	Escarole, chopped	1 to 2	2 to 3
Tomatoes, in quarters	2 to 3	4 to 5	Endive	1 to 2	2 to 3
Sweet potato, whole, small	10 to 12	12 to 14	Eggplant, chunks or slices	2 to 3	3 to 4
Sweet potato, whole, large	12 to 15	15 to 19	Corn, on the cob	3 to 4	4 to 5
Sweet potato, in cubes	7 to 9	9 to 11	Corn, kernels	1 to 2	2 to 3
Sweet pepper, slices or chunks	1 to 3	2 to 4	Collard	4 to 5	5 to 6
Squash, butternut, slices or chunks	8 to 10	10 to 12	Celery, chunks	2 to 3	3 to 4
Squash, acorn, slices or chunks	6 to 7	8 to 9	Cauliflower flowerets	2 to 3	3 to 4
Spinach	1 to 2	3 to 4	Carrots, whole or chunked	2 to 3	3 to 4
Rutabaga, slices	3 to 5	4 to 6	Carrots, sliced or shredded	1 to 2	2 to 3
Rutabaga, chunks	4 to 6	6 to 8	Cabbage, red, purple or green, wedges	3 to 4	4 to 5
Pumpkin, small slices or chunks	4 to 5	6 to 7	Cabbage, red, purple or green, shredded	2 to 3	3 to 4
Pumpkin, large slices or chunks	8 to 10	10 to 14	Brussel sprouts, whole	3 to 4	4 to 5
Potatoes, whole, large	12 to 15	15 to 19	Broccoli, stalks	3 to 4	4 to 5
Potatoes, whole, baby	10 to 12	12 to 14	Broccoli, flowerets	2 to 3	3 to 4
Potatoes, in cubes	7 to 9	9 to 11	Beets, small roots, whole	11 to 13	13 to 15
Peas, in the pod	1 to 2	2 to 3	Beets, large roots, whole	20 to 25	25 to 30
Peas, green	1 to 2	2 to 3	Beans, green/yellow or wax, whole, trim ends and strings	1 to 2	2 to 3
Parsnips, sliced	1 to 2	2 to 3			
Parsnips, chunks	2 to 4	4 to 6	Asparagus, whole or cut	1 to 2	2 to 3
Onions, sliced	2 to 3	3 to 4	Artichoke, whole, trimmed without leaves	9 to 11	11 to 13
Okra	2 to 3	3 to 4	Artichoke, hearts	4 to 5	5 to 6

Rice and Grains

Rice & Grain	Water Quantity (Grain: Water ratios)	Cooking Time (in Minutes)	Rice & Grain	Water Quantity (Grain: Water ratios)	Cooking Time (in Minutes)
Wheat berries	1:3	25 to 30	Oats, steel-cut	1:1	10
Spelt berries	1:3	15 to 20	Oats, quick cooking	1:1	6
Sorghum	1:3	20 to 25	Millet	1:1	10 to 12
Rice, wild	1:3	25 to 30	Kamut, whole	1:3	10 to 12
Rice, white	1:1.5	8	Couscous	1:2	5 to 8
Rice, Jasmine	1:1	4 to 10	Corn, dried, half	1:3	25 to 30
Rice, Brown	1:1.3	22 to 28	Congee, thin	1:6 ~ 1:7	15 to 20
Rice, Basmati	1:1.5	4 to 8	Congee, thick	1:4 ~ 1:5	15 to 20
Quinoa, quick cooking	1:2	8	Barley, pot	1:3 ~ 1:4	25 to 30
Porridge, thin	1:6 ~ 1:7	15 to 20	Barley, pearl	1:4	25 to 30

Appendix 4: Recipe Index

Printed in Great Britain
by Amazon

80430505R00113